INTERPRETIVE SOCIAL SCIENCE

A Second Look

Edited by
Paul Rabinow
William M. Sullivan

Interpretive Social Science

A Second Look

University
of California
Press

Berkeley
Los Angeles
London

University of California Press
Berkeley and Los Angeles, California

University of California Press, Ltd.
London, England

© 1979, 1987 by
The Regents of the University of California

This volume is a substantially revised and updated
edition of *Interpretive Social Science: A Reader*, ed. Paul
Rabinow and William M. Sullivan (Berkeley and Los
Angeles: University of California Press, 1979).

LIBRARY OF CONGRESS CATALOGING-IN-
PUBLICATION DATA

Interpretive social science.

   Rev. and updated ed. of the editors' 1979 ed.
Bibliography: p.
Includes index.
   Contents: Interpretation and the sciences of
man / Charles Taylor—The problem of historical
consciousness / H. G. Gadamer—Modernity—an
incomplete project / Jürgen Habermas—[etc.]
   1. Social sciences.   I. Rabinow, Paul.
II. Sullivan, William M.
H61.I6   1988   300   86-24990
ISBN 0-520-05836-4 (alk. paper)
ISBN 0-520-05838-0 (pbk. : alk. paper)

Printed in the United States of America

3   4   5   6   7   8   9

To Robert N. Bellah

For the waking there is one world,
and it is common; but sleepers turn aside each one
into a world of his own.

HERACLITUS

Contents

PAUL RABINOW
WILLIAM M. SULLIVAN

The Interpretive Turn
A Second Look

Over the past decade interpretation has gained a certain currency, even prestige, in philosophical circles and in the social sciences. When we edited the first version of this anthology in the late 1970s, we hoped by collecting some outstanding representatives of the "interpretive turn" to inspire practitioners and students of social inquiry to violate the positivist taboo against joining evaluative concerns with descriptions of fact. With great rapidity since that time not only have the disciplinary barriers between philosophy and the social sciences been called into question but also much work has appeared which is no longer explicitly concerned with where these boundaries ought to be fixed.[1]

At the same time, the vogue of "interpretive social science" has given rise to a sustained methodological debate—an ironic develop-

1. In recent years a number of important synthetic works have appeared that provide a helpful overview of many of these issues. Among the more influential books in philosophy are Richard Rorty, *Philosophy and the Mirror of Nature* (Princeton: Princeton University Press, 1979), and Richard J. Bernstein, *Beyond Objectivism and Relativism: Science, Hermeneutics, and Praxis* (Philadelphia: University of Pennsylvania Press, 1983). An effect of the current interest in interpretation has been to recast rationality in a way that takes account of recent social thought. The first such collection was Brian Wilson, *Rationality* (New York: Harper and Row, 1970). This has been updated by Martin Hollis and Stephen Lukes, *Rationality and Relativism* (Cambridge: MIT Press, 1983). We will mention specific examples of work that integrates philosophy and the social sciences in the course of this introduction. In notes we suggest further reading for each author.

ment in that Gadamer had opposed "truth" to "method" as the core of practical wisdom. Yet, upon reflection, it is hardly surprising that hermeneutics should also fall victim to our society's obsession with technical procedures and formalistic organization of knowledge. Interpretation has too often been accepted by practitioners of the human sciences as merely one methodological option among a growing number of available investigative tools. For us, this view displaces the significance of the interpretive turn and ultimately empties it of its capacity to challenge the practices of knowing in our culture. With this in mind we have chosen a series of new readings that heighten the contrast between knowledge seen as a technical project, with all its affinities to the technological organization of life, and knowledge seen, in the human sciences, as inescapably practical and historically situated.

As long as there has been a social science, the expectation has been that it would turn from its humanistic infancy to the maturity of hard science, thereby leaving behind its dependence on value, judgment, and individual insight. The dream of modern Western man to be freed from his passions, his unconscious, his history, and his traditions through the liberating use of reason has been the deepest theme of contemporary social-scientific thought. Perhaps the deepest theme of the twentieth century, however, has been the shattering of the triumphalist view of history bequeathed to us by the nineteenth. What Comte saw as the inevitable achievement of man, positive reason, Weber saw as an iron cage.

The aim of this anthology is to present to a wide audience—historians, sociologists, anthropologists, psychologists, historians of religion, scientists, and philosophers—a carefully selected group of papers exemplary of the interpretive, or hermeneutic, approach to the study of human society.

These readings address major theoretical issues by situating the approach critically against positivist, structuralist, and neo-Marxist positions. They also provide rich and developed examples of the interpretation of symbols, cultures, and historical moments. Although our aim is not to present a school or a new dogma, we do feel that there are important unities of theme and approach present here. In this introduction the editors—an anthropologist and a philosopher—will situate in a historical and theoretical context the emergence, through the readings, of an interpretive social science.

DECONSTRUCTION

Interpreting the Crisis in the Social Sciences

Many contemporary researchers in the social sciences continue to see themselves, as did their predecessors, as the heralds of the new age of an at-last-established science. They remain, like their predecessors, disappointed.

The strength of natural science, according to Thomas Kuhn, has lain in its ability to go beyond endless methodological discussions by developing general shared paradigms which define problems and procedures. Social scientists have seized upon Kuhn's thesis in part as a way of explaining the embarrassing failure of any of the social sciences, including linguistics and economics, to develop either the agreement on method or the generally acknowledged classic examples of explanation characteristic of the natural sciences. While not denying the persistence and theoretical fruitfulness of certain explanatory schemes in the social sciences, social investigators have never reached the extraordinary degree of basic agreement that characterizes modern natural science.[2] For Kuhn, such agreements among practicing investigators constitute the stage of "paradigmatic" science, a time of secure development, of extending the explanatory capacity of an agreed-upon paradigm. Paradigms are the result of a chaotic stage that Kuhn calls "pre-paradigmatic," in which the insights and mode of discourse later to become universally accepted must fight it out with competing explanations. Most fields, throughout their history, find themselves in this situation.[3]

This much of Kuhn's argument might be construed to buttress the defenses of social sciences waiting to "take off" into a paradigm stage of science. Behaviorism, structural-functionalism, various schools of materialism, Keynesianism, structuralism, and others have all put themselves forward at some time as paradigm candidates. If none has yet succeeded in silencing its opponents with Newtonian au-

---

2. S. N. Eisenstadt has discussed the importance of these recurrent types of understanding in a recent work with M. Curelaru, *The Form of Sociology: Paradigms and Crisis* (New York: Wiley and Sons, 1976).

3. Thomas S. Kuhn, *The Structure of Scientific Revolution*, 2nd ed. (Chicago: University of Chicago Press, 1970). See esp. "Postscript—1969."

thority, perhaps after a few more studies, or theories, or methodological battles our paradigms will emerge, at last triumphant. However, even if we admit this as a possibility—and we shall show shortly that there are compelling reasons for *not* admitting it— Kuhn's account of scientific development concludes on a disquieting note. He shows that in the history of science, even after the breakthrough into the paradigm stage occurs, the stability achieved is only a relative one. The great paradigms of natural science have all, after flourishing, finally been replaced by others. The epochal case is the revolution in twentieth-century physics in which relativity theory and quantum mechanics undermined and succeeded the Newtonian system. From that point on in physics, the nineteenth century's conception of logical, cumulative progress through a purely objective science of observation and deductive explanation has been progressively undermined.

Yet the issue for the human sciences is not simply that all scientific facts depend on a context of theory, or that no logic of inquiry can be formulated to match the rigor of the procedures of scientific verification. The Kantian critical philosophy already emphasized the relations between the objects of observation and the subject of knowledge. For Kant and his followers the universal and objective validity of proven hypotheses is guaranteed precisely because the subject constituting the fields of objects is a universal and purely formal one. The explanatory power of science is the consequence of its basis in a logical, epistemic subject whose activities can be generalized and understood as context-free operations. However, for comprehending the human world Kant acknowledged the necessity of a "practical anthropology" focusing on a subject not reducible to the pure theoretical subject of the *Critique of Pure Reason*. This subject knows himself through reflection upon his own actions in the world as a subject not simply of experience but of intentional action as well. While the interpretive approach is not in any strict sense Kantian, it shares the postulate that practical understanding in context cannot be reduced to a system of categories defined only in terms of their relations to one another.

To put forward an approach to the human sciences as a paradigm candidate requires that one accept the analogy to natural science according to which human actions can be fixed in their meaning by being subsumed under the lawlike operations of the epistemic subject. Gregory Bateson's recent attempt to apply models from systems theory to the problems of the relations of mind to society and Jean Piaget's development of the structuralist project represent significant advances over what Piaget terms the atomistic empiricism of causal explanation in social science. For both, the key focus is upon holism, for which Bateson uses the metaphor of ecology.

Holistic explanation in these new forms seeks to organize a wide variety of human phenomena that cannot be comprehended through models based on linear relations among elements. The emphasis on mutually determining relationships is the powerful central insight of cybernetic and structuralist thinking. However, it is crucial that these relations are conceived as reducible to specific operations that can be defined without reference to the particular context of human action. Although this position is an advance in sophistication, it remains an effort to integrate the human sciences within a natural-scientific paradigm. Action in the historical, cultural context is again reduced to the operations of a purely epistemic subject. The Kantian criticism of this effort remains unsurpassed or at least unrefuted in that the problem of the concrete, practical subject remains unresolved.[4]

The time seems ripe, even overdue, to announce that there is not going to be an age of paradigm in the social sciences. We contend that the failure to achieve paradigm takeoff is not merely the result of methodological immaturity, but reflects something fundamental about the human world. If we are correct, the crisis of social science concerns the nature of social investigation itself. The conception of the human sciences as somehow necessarily destined to follow the path of the modern investigation of nature is at the root of this crisis. Preoccupation with that ruling expectation is chronic in social science; that *idée fixe* has often driven investigators away from a serious concern with the human world into the sterility of purely formal argument and debate. As in development theory, one can only wait so long for the takeoff. The cargo-cult view of the "about-to-arrive science" just won't do.

The interpretive turn refocuses attention on the concrete varieties

---

4. Gregory Bateson, *Steps to an Ecology of Mind* (San Francisco: Chandler, 1972); Jean Piaget, *Structuralism* (New York: Harper and Row, 1970).

of cultural meaning, in their particularity and complex texture, but without falling into the traps of historicism or cultural relativism in their classic forms. For the human sciences both the object of investigation—the web of language, symbol, and institutions that constitutes signification—and the tools by which investigation is carried out share inescapably the same pervasive context that is the human world. All this is by no means to exalt "subjective" awareness over a presumed detached scientific objectivity, in the manner of nineteenth-century Romanticism. Quite the contrary, the interpretive approach denies and overcomes the almost *de rigueur* opposition of subjectivity and objectivity. The current emergence of interpretive approaches in philosophy and the social sciences is moving in a very different direction. The interpretive approach emphatically refutes the claim that one can somehow reduce the complex world of signification to the products of a self-consciousness in the traditional philosophical sense. Rather, interpretation begins from the postulate that the web of meaning constitutes human existence to such an extent that it cannot ever be meaningfully reduced to constitutively prior speech acts, dyadic relations, or any predefined elements.[5] Intentionality and empathy are rather seen as dependent on the prior existence of the shared world of meaning within which the subjects of human discourse constitute themselves.[6] It is in this literal sense

5. Cultural meaning as intersubjective and irreducibly fundamental to understanding is the base-point of the whole interpretive project. This idea is set out powerfully by philosophers such as Paul Ricoeur and Hans-Georg Gadamer. See Hans-Georg Gadamer, "On the Scope and Function of Hermeneutical Reflection," in his *Philosophical Hermeneutics* (Berkeley and Los Angeles: University of California Press, 1976), 18–43. There Gadamer criticizes what he sees as Jürgen Habermas's grounding of meaning in a pure logic of language. Paul Ricoeur contrasts these positions lucidly in "Ethics and Culture: Habermas and Gadamer in Dialogue," *Philosophy Today* 17, no. 3 (Summer 1972): 153–65.

6. Intentionality, resident in a knowing subject, has been thought of by the phenomenological tradition stemming from Edmund Husserl as the defining human characteristic. Empathy, as intuitive access to the mind of another, is a term often associated with the interpretive tradition, especially with the early thinkers Wilhelm Dilthey and Max Weber. In fact, neither Weber nor the later Dilthey held the kind of "mystical" conception of cultural understanding often associated with the term "empathy." For a clarification of Weber's usage of "understanding" (*Verstehen*), see Max Weber, *Economy and Society: An Outline of Interpretive Sociology*, ed. Guenther Roth and Claus Wittrik (New York: Bedminster Press, 1968), vol. 1. See Wilhelm Dilthey, "The Development of Hermeneutics," in *W. Dilthey: Selected Writings*, ed. H. P. Rickman (Cambridge: Cambridge University Press, 1976), 247–63.

that interpretive social science can be called a return to the objective world, seeing that world as in the first instance the circle of meaning within which we find ourselves and that we can never fully surpass.

Charles Taylor offers us a "strong reading" of the interpretive position in his article "Interpretation and the Sciences of Man" reprinted in this volume. The baseline realities for both the observer and the observed in the human sciences are practices, socially constituted actions, "and these cannot be identified in abstraction from the languages we use to describe them."[7] These baseline practices are intersubjective and form the most general level of shared meaning. They are the basis of community, argument, and discourse. Meanings or norms "are not just in the minds of the actors but are out there in the practices themselves; practices which cannot be conceived as a set of individual actions, but which are essentially modes of social relations, or mutual action." These meanings are intersubjective; they are not reducible to individual subjective psychological states, beliefs, or propositions. They are neither subjective nor objective but what lies behind both.

A view of meaning flows from this position, and Taylor spells it out. Meaning exists for a subject in a situation; it is about something; and it constitutes a part of a field: there are no simple elements of meaning. This view in turn rests on a set of assumptions about the human situation. For Taylor, human life is characterized as an open system. It cannot be shielded from external interference and studied in a vacuum or a scientifically controlled and delimited environment. From this it follows that the exactitude that is open to the human sciences is quite different from that available to the natural sciences. Our capacity to understand is rooted in our own self-definitions, hence in what we are. We are fundamentally self-interpreting and self-defining, living always in a cultural environment, inside a "web of signification we ourselves have spun." There is no outside, detached standpoint from which we gather and present brute data. When we try to understand the cultural world, we are dealing with interpretations and interpretations of interpretations.

Culture—the shared meanings, practices, and symbols that constitute the human world—does not present itself neutrally or with one voice. It is always multivocal and overdetermined, and both the

7. See chapter 1, p. 53.

observer and the observed are always enmeshed in it; that is our situation. There is no privileged position, no absolute perspective, no final recounting.[8]

If we accept these points we must realize that as soon as we begin to conduct an inquiry we are caught in a circle. "Ultimately a good explanation is one that makes sense of behavior. But to agree on what makes sense necessitates consensus; what makes sense is a function of one's readings; and these in turn are based on the kind of sense one understands."[9] The only ways out of this circle would be to find simple, brute data which everyone could agree on, or to invent a neutral language to describe the data, or both. For Taylor neither of these exists, precisely because of the primacy of context just described.[10]

Taylor draws the most radical conclusions from these arguments, conclusions not fully shared by other practitioners of the art. He says there is "no verification procedure we can fall back on. We can only continue to offer interpretations."[11] Therefore, insight and judgment are an essential part of any inquiry. If this is the case, then some form of the claim "'if you don't understand, then your intuitions are at fault, are blind or inadequate,' will be justified; some differences will be nonarbitrable by further evidence, but each side can only make an appeal to deeper insight than the other."[12] A superior position would be one that could encompass its opponent and make its claims stick.[13]

8. See "Conclusion" to Paul Rabinow, *Reflections on Fieldwork in Morocco* (Berkeley and Los Angeles: University of California Press, 1977).

9. Ibid., 14.

10. The primacy of context is another statement of the irreducibility of cultural meaning discussed above (see note 5). This theme has extremely important implications for the understanding of the validity and use of formal models in the natural sciences, especially the field of cybernetics. Hubert Dreyfus has lucidly explored this area in *What Computers Can't Do: A Critique of Artificial Intelligence,* 2nd ed. (New York: Harper and Row, 1979).

11. See chapter 1, p. 75.

12. Ibid.

13. Such an approach to the question of how interpretations are validated and judged is quite close to the rhetorical tradition in philosophy, one which has often stood opposed to claims for strictly deductive "demonstrations" in practical matters. Philosopher Richard McKeon has ably developed the considerable resources of that tradition. See Gerard A. Hauser and Donald P. Cushman, "McKeon's Philosophy of Communication: The Architectonic and Interdisciplinary Arts," *Philosophy and Rhetoric* 6, no. 4: 211–234.

Most of the other partisans of the interpretive approach are somewhat more hesitant about this last point. Geertz and Bellah, for instance, although not explicitly confronting these issues, clearly hold to a modified notion of social science in which there is advance, contribution, and refutation of one sort or another which a community of researchers could agree on, if they agreed on starting points. Paul Ricoeur, more explicitly, directs his attention to this important point. He offers us a sketch of what he calls a "dialectic of guessing and validation."[14] He holds out hope for a new form of confirmation and refutation that would not be based on either a propositional model or falsifiability. For Ricoeur a method of mediating and judging between conflicting interpretations would look rather more like a transformed version of textual criticism in the humanities. But even he acknowledges that at present we have only the barest beginning of such a dialectic.

A formulation farther from positivist orthodoxy would be hard to find. We propose a return to the human world with all its lack of clarity, its alienation, and its depth, rather than continuing the search for a formal deductive paradigm in the social sciences. The common theme joining both Romanticist subjectivism and positivist objectivism is the search for a reality before and behind the cultural world to which that world can be reduced. For Romanticism this reality is the self or subject as present to itself as a self-evident source of meaning, whereas positivists have stressed the epistemological and ontological priority of deductive inference (and sometimes causal explanations) over the often tacit meanings guiding discourse. The idea remains to find a truth behind these elusive lived-in symbols, practices, and customs. But this has always been proposed in the face of the dependence of the constructs of both "self" and "law" upon the very context they were intended to replace. Thus the enormous attention given to strategies for demonstrating some context in which concepts would be free from cultural variation: stable, self-evident, unequivocally clear in their meanings, like the well-defined concepts of mathematics and physics.[15] For most paradigm-expectant social

14. Paul Ricoeur, "The Model of the Text: Meaningful Action Considered as a Text," *Social Research* 38, no. 3 (Autumn 1971).

15. The literature discussing the relations of logical empiricism to mathematics and physics, on the one hand, and concern with language and culture on the other, is

scientists this has meant fascination with the development of reductionist models and quantifiable techniques whose foundational concepts could be considered as securely based in logical self-evidence of one form or another.

THE DECONSTRUCTION OF THE POSITIVIST IDEA OF SCIENCE

The dominant direction in twentieth-century science and philosophy has been the thorough undermining of the Comtean ideal of science. The philosophers of interpretation have been important figures in this undermining, and it is internally consistent with their positions that they have articulated their insights through a direct concern with their society and culture in its historical context. In this they have continued the Aristotelian notion of reason as a vital aspect of human existence, a means toward awareness and self-reflection, yet thoroughly embedded in the practices of everyday life. It is important to note the impoverishment of the term that results from the equation of reason with a strictly formal scientific methodology. The aim of this innovation was not to illuminate the world of common meanings, but to explain and finally replace the contextual understandings of everyday life with context-free categories. This reductionistic ideal has come under increasing attack.

The logical empiricist ideal of a unified science embracing both the natural and the human sciences was promulgated and widely accepted in the first decades of the twentieth century. Its leading exponents, the Vienna circle centered around Rudolph Carnap, put forward the idea of an ideal logical language to stand in contrast to the "confusion" of natural languages. Russell's logical empiricism in Britain and the early Wittgenstein might be looked upon as "fellow travelers," as in a very different way could Husserl. Logical positiv-

---

vast. The work of Richard Rorty provides a useful summary and interpretations. See Richard Rorty, ed., *The Linguistic Turn: Recent Essays in Philosophical Method* (Chicago: University of Chicago Press, 1967). The single best overall discussion of the career of this ideal in social investigation is probably Gerald Radnitsky, *Contemporary Schools of Metascience* (Goteborg: Scandinavian University Books, 1970), vol. 1.

ists attempted to erect a norm for paradigmatic science. The then new discipline of metamathematics was expected to provide this norm. It offered an ideal of intelligibility according to which the meaning of any term or element in a system is unequivocally determined in a rigorous manner according to its relation to the other elements within the system. The system itself was conceived as those elements related by rules of inference whose consistency can be determined according to formalizable rules. It is important to note that while this conception of meaning is holistic in that the parts are defined in relation to the whole, the meaning derives from the self-referential and formalizable character of the system. Physics was the positivists' approximation to the formal paradigm of mathematical logic, and they issued the dictum that approximation to that approximation was the criterion of science and so of truth.[16]

The ideal of a unified science acted among social scientists to focus attention on formal models of explanation. Since it was evident from the outset that the cultural world could not meet this norm, the problem of investigation was posed as the explanation of the *ex hypothesi* confused world of "vague" meaning by means of a logically consistent system of concepts that could account for the confusion without incoherence. Since by definition only these explanatory systems could be true, strictly speaking, the role of the investigator's own prescientific understanding of these multivocal symbols was not emphasized, often ignored. At best this was conceived as a step that, once taken, could be safely forgotten until one came to replace the everyday terms with the new, formally defined concepts. So a society's world became an interlocking group of "belief systems," "institutional" systems, "personality" systems, conceptual entities the investigator put forward as the truth behind the appearance of everyday, lived experience.

Jean Piaget's synthetic conception of structuralism is one of the latest, most sophisticated restatements of this project to reduce meaning to explicit rules operationally defined. For Piaget the novelty of structuralism lies in the general conception of logic inherent in the concept of structure. Structuralism's premise is "an ideal (perhaps a

---

16. See Radnitsky, *Metascience*, 56–75.

hope) of intrinsic intelligibility supported by the postulate that structures are self-sufficient and that, to grasp them, we do not have to make reference to all sorts of extraneous elements."[17] The importance of "operational structuralism," according to Piaget, is that, thanks to the logical priority of the rules of transformation over the elements that they govern, it promises to provide mathematical models of the linguistic, personality, and symbolic systems that have resisted the older, atomistic approach of logical empiricism.[18]

From the interpretive point of view what is most striking about structuralism is not its difference from but its continuity with the older reductionism. That massive continuous theme is the priority and independence of logical structures and rules of inference from the contexts of ordinary understanding. As Lévi-Strauss puts it, one must avoid the "shop-girl's web of subjectivity" or the "swamps of experience" to arrive at structure and science. The ideal or "hope" of the intrinsic intelligibility of structures apart from "all sorts of extraneous elements" is the same animus that propelled the Vienna circle. Ricoeur, in several of his essays, has drawn the clearest implications of this position. For him, the goals of structuralism can be accomplished, in fact already have been, but at a price the structuralists ignore. The conditions which make the enterprise possible—the establishment of operations and elements, and an algebra of their combinations—assure from the beginning and by definition that one is working on a body of material which is preconstituted, stopped, closed, and in a certain sense, dead.[19] The very success of structuralism leaves behind the "understanding of action, operations and process, all of which are constitutive of meaningful discourse. Structuralism seals its formalized language off from discourse, and therefore from the human world.[20] A high price indeed for the sciences of

17. Jean Piaget, *Structuralism.*

18. Ibid., 9–10 and 141–42. The field of systems theory has developed a formal methodology very like structuralism, and subject to the same accusations and critique. A clear explication of systems theory has recently been advanced by Irvin Laszlo, *The Systems View of the World: The Natural Philosophy of the New Developments in the Sciences* (New York: George Braziller, 1972).

19. See Paul Ricoeur, "Structure, Word, Event," in *Conflict of Interpretations: Essays in Hermeneutics* (Evanston: Northwestern University Press, 1974), 79.

20. Ibid.

man, although one the structuralists are explicitly willing to pay in the name of science.[21]

For Ricoeur, discourse is about something other than itself in an absolute sense.[22] It performs the function of bringing what is said out of the immediate situation to a World which is opened up by the references in the text. Discourse being about something, one must understand the World in order to interpret it. Discourse being public and fixed, in one form or another, is therefore freed from the motivations and subjectivity of its author, it is in public, it is intersubjective and therefore open to interpretation. The concept of *Verstehen* is brought out of private minds into the cultural world.

This notion is brought to clarity by the notion of the text. The text must be treated as a whole; only then can the parts make sense. Of course, one must begin by guessing or approximating what that whole might be. This initial guess is highly fallible and is open to error and recasting, to reinterpretation. There is a dialectic of guessing and validation which Ricoeur discusses in his article.

The text is plurivocal, open to several readings and to several constructions. But it is not infinite. Human action and interpretation are subject to many but not indefinitely many constructions. Any closure of the process through an external means is violence and often occurs. But just as interpretive social science is not subjectivism, neither is it simply intuitionism.

Let us be clear. What we want to understand is not something behind the cultural object, the text, but rather something in front of it. We approach the text as a human pro-ject. To understand a text is to follow its movements from sense to reference, from what it says to what it talks about. To understand an author better than he could understand himself is to display the power of disclosure implied in his discourse beyond the limited horizon of his own existential situa-

21. An enterprise such as that of Jacques Derrida might be termed a "poststructuralism" which conceives an absolute text that refers only to itself and consists in the endless play of signifiers in a closed and again ultimately dead and meaningless system. See Jacques Derrida, "Structure, Sign and Play in the Discourse of the Human Sciences," in *The Structuralist Controversy: The Languages of Criticism and the Sciences of Man,* ed. Richard Macksey and Eugenio Donato (Baltimore: Johns Hopkins Press, 1970), 247–64.

22. Paul Ricoeur, "The Model of the Text," in ibid.

tion. Social structures, cultural objects, can be read also as attempts to cope with existential perplexities, human predicaments, and deeprooted conflict. In this sense, these structures too have a referential dimension. They point toward the *aporias* of social existence.

The thrust of this position is not to deny the role of human commitment, subjectivity, and intention in understanding human phenomena, but only to clarify it and make it accessible to public discourse. As a model of text interpretation, understanding has nothing to do with an immediate grasping of a foreign psychic life or with an emotional identification with a mental intention. Understanding is entirely mediated by the procedures that precede it and accompany it. The counterpart of this personal appropriation is not something which can be felt. It is the dynamic meaning identified earlier with the reference to the text, that is, the power of disclosing a world.[23]

In this approach understanding any action is analogous to textual interpretation. This means that the intelligibility of any action requires reference to its larger context, a cultural world. So, to take a powerfully developed example, when Clifford Geertz describes the Balinese cockfight, a text analogue, he progressively incorporates other essential Balinese symbols, institutions, and practices that are necessary to an understanding of the seemingly localized cockfight. The Balinese cultural and social world is not incorporated into the cockfight, but must be brought into the analysis in order to understand the event. This is the art of interpretation. The aim is not to uncover universals or laws but rather to explicate context and world.[24]

Interpretive social science has developed as the alternative to earlier logical empiricism as well as the later systems approaches, including structuralism, within the human sciences. It must continue to develop in opposition to and as a criticism of these tendencies. Here interpretive social science reveals itself as a response to the crisis of the human sciences that is constructive in the profound sense of es-

23. "World" is the most general term for the holistic totality of cultural meaning pointed at by the notion of "context." (See notes 6 and 11 above.) The classic discussion of this meaning of "world" is that of Martin Heidegger in *Being and Time*, trans. John Macquarrie and Edward Robinson (New York: Harper and Row, 1962), 91–148.

24. See Clifford Geertz, "Deep Play: Notes on the Balinese Cockfight," reprinted in this volume.

tablishing a connection between what is studied, the means of investigation, and the ends informing the investigators. At the same time it initiates a process of recovery and reappropriation of the richness of meaning found in the symbolic contexts of all areas of culture. But it can no longer do so naively. The incisive and convincing negative dialectic and ideology-critique as developed in the Frankfurt School has demonstrated the immense difficulty of reappropriation in the modern world. Therefore we must deal with their arguments and the directions they suggest to us.

RECONSTRUCTION

Reason as Action: Criticism for Recovery

The great strength of the Frankfurt tradition of critical theory has been continually to urge that the issue of understanding in the human sciences cannot be detached from the greater problems of living in an age of technology in which traditional understandings appear problematic, at best.[25] Beginning in the 1920s Adorno and Horkheimer elaborated a dialectical hermeneutic, a contextual reason, aimed at recuperating the cultural and political energies currently blocked by social forms of exploitation and domination.[26]

They insist that scientism, as the absorption in context-free method, is itself a distortion or "repression" of the contextual dialectic of tacit whole and articulated parts on which scientific rationality must stand. Their dialectic of criticism and recovery is based on two important presuppositions that constitute a general interpretive approach to contemporary conditions. The first presupposition is the superiority of dialectical reason over all forms of purely analytic reason.

The second presupposition of Frankfurt School interpretation situ-

---

25. For a general history of the Frankfurt School, its members, and their varied developments, see Martin Jay, *The Dialectical Imagination: A History of the Frankfurt School and the Institute of Social Research, 1923–1950* (Boston: Little, Brown, 1973).

26. The idea of a dialectical hermeneutic is well set out by Fredric Jameson in *Marxism and Form: Twentieth Century Dialectical Theories of Literature* (Princeton: Princeton University Press, 1971).

ates the internal logic of cultural discourse within the field of social practices and social relationships. When the problem of scientism is seen in this expanded context, the clarity of analytic reason is situated in the larger opacity of social relations and practices which found it in the current age. As industrial technology and functional organization have displaced traditional routines in modern life, the content of political discussion has also shifted. Instead of the older concern with the justice of certain kinds of social relationships—for example, the allocation of access to services on the basis of wealth—we have seen a tendency to speak of technical goals such as "economic growth." In fact, governmental and corporate spokesmen cannot relate their functional conception of rationality to the questions of proportional justice. Rather, justice in the sense of the good order of community life is reduced to a mere calculus of interests. The context that could make this calculus meaningful, the concrete understandings and concerns of citizens, is deemed a matter of subjective "preference" and so ruled out of any "rational" discussion of policy. Politicians and our academic experts find it easier to talk about the standard of living than about what a society might be living for. In social technocracy as in scientism, analytic reason has cut itself off from the human whole that could give some intrinsic sense to its formal operations.

The Frankfurt thinkers trace the connection between the intellectual and social forms of fragmentation and mechanical regimentation by using the Marxist theme of the dependence of consciousness on social being. Social being describes the concrete situation of thinking persons as related to their habits, practices, traditions, and social relations with other groups similarly located. This powerful facticity of the social situation is the appropriation by the Frankfurt thinkers, under the influence of their teachers Max Weber and Martin Heidegger, of Marx's materialism. For critical theory the materialist premise operates as a limiting horizon with which any interpretive formulation must come to grips if it is to avoid mystification. It is not a dogmatic assertion that culture "reflects" social relations in any simple sense, or that culture is an epiphenomenon of technology, economics, or any other "motive forces of history." The importance of the materialist presupposition is rather its insistence on the ineradicable tension between the human urges for coherent life and thought and the limitation forced on us by our involvement in bodily, social, historical existence.

From the Frankfurt School's beginning the critical theorists have concentrated on exploring the specific kinds of fragmentation and mystification that are the consequences of the increasing rationalization (in the Weberian sense) of the relations of social life. The Frankfurt thinkers have persistently made explicit the connections between the spread of ideologies of private despair or salvation and the construction of a technically managed society, bearing out Weber's doleful prophecy of systematic rationalization. The public, common world of shared symbols of morality and discourse has correspondingly shrunk and weakened. Recovery of a more fully human existence has seemed, especially to Adorno and Marcuse, to recede further from our grasp.[27] Hence their emphasis on "negative dialectics," the claim that today wholeness can be experienced only negatively as an implicit norm against which the fragmentation of late capitalist society at least appears as what it is.

This is to say that the present cultural situation is one in which the loss of community is so advanced that the unmasking of pretended totality, the "ideology-critique" of Marxism, is all that remains for intellectuals. Their task is to undermine the legitimacy of all that exists, but no longer to present a new image of integration. For Adorno and Horkheimer, if one cannot confidently identify a "subject of history," a social group whose interests can lead to a new moral community, there can be ground only for negative dialectics. In their view the failure of Marxism's identification of the proletariat with this subject of history leaves us with only a deep historical pessimism. This failure seems to question the whole conception of the *Bildungsideal,* which is the Frankfurt School's greatest legacy from German idealism. Marcuse's cultural pessimism reflects this same sense.

Without denying the gloomy prognosis for our age, later Frankfurt thinkers, especially Jürgen Habermas, have attempted to continue the tradition of "ideology-critique" without succumbing to a total pessimism. In part Habermas's ability to move beyond the posi-

27. See Theodor Adorno, *Negative Dialectics,* trans. E. B. Ashtow (New York: Seabury, 1973); Herbert Marcuse, *One-Dimensional Man: Studies in the Ideology of Advanced Industrial Society* (Boston: Beacon Press, 1964).

tion of Adorno is a result of his encounter with the interpretive tradition, particularly with the work of Hans-Georg Gadamer. Habermas's discussion of the interpretive tradition has brought it into the mainstream of debate about the social sciences. As Habermas has pointed out, cultural knowledge is possible only because, and not in spite, of the "pre-understanding, which is derived from the interpreter's initial situation. The work of traditional meaning discloses itself to the interpreter only to the extent that his own work becomes clarified at the same time. . . . The understanding of meaning is diverted in its very structure toward the attainment of possible consensus among actors in the framework of a self-understanding derived from tradition."[28]

This emphasis on discourse as the basis for the human sciences is a position common to the later Frankfurt School and the interpretive approach. It represents a reworking of and a move beyond the earlier Frankfurt search for a historical subject to reveal the final truth of history.

Behind the search for the subject of history lay the whole course of Western metaphysics, but particularly the unquestioned Enlightenment dogma that reality is a rational whole to which reason approximates. How reason approximated reality has of course been described in many ways. The tradition that brings us to Adorno runs through Hegel and Marx. For them, the cunning of reason is the unfolding of the real through history. This is the whole which makes all the parts coherent; not to see this can only lead to mystification. There are no partial truths.[29] Because of the impasse to which this tradition has come, Habermas has moved away from the Hegelian notion that the meaning of all human activity can be found in relation to the maturation of the historical subject. He attempts to reground the idealist unity of theoretical understanding, ethical norms, and social practices by returning to a position resembling a Kantian transcendentalism. Greatly simplified, this position amounts to a return to a notion of human nature in which there are universals of

28. Jürgen Habermas, *Knowledge and Human Interests* (Boston: Beacon Press, 1971), 309–10.
29. The theme of "totality" in Frankfurt dialectics is perceptively discussed by both Martin Jay and Fredric Jameson. (See notes 25 and 26 above.)

social life founded on explicit formal properties of the communication process. By doing this, while abandoning Hegel, Habermas continues the rationalist claim that the aim and basis of understanding lie in making concepts explicit, clear, and totally available to consciousness.[30]

Gadamer's appropriation of the *Bildungsideal* as the effort to "keep oneself open to what is other, to other, more universal points of view" breaks with the rationalist effort to achieve a purely theoretical understanding of human nature. For Gadamer the search for "hidden constants" of the human situation can never be fully detached from the working out of those self-formative practices which constitute culture.

This is therefore not to leave the understanding of human community in a state of opaque mystery or untranslatable "houses of being." Rather, Gadamer shows that the weaving of wider understanding, the expansion of horizons, remains particular, in a context, part of a cultural, historical world, as is the object of study. Gadamer's project reappropriates the Aristotelian dialectic of the one and the many for the human sciences. By the late twentieth century our cultural project requires such an understanding, one which neither abandons itself uncritically to romanticized particularity nor mistakes the spread of technological structures for a shortcut to a new universal culture.

The model for Gadamer is practical reason, not theoretical reason. Taylor, Ricoeur, and Gadamer all point out that cultural life is embedded in and is a reflection upon practical activity. The very possibility of coming to understand cultural life flows from that life. Theory can never replace social existence itself. "Thus it is essential that ethical sciences—while they may contribute to the clarification of the problems of ethical consciousness—never occupy the place properly belonging to concrete ethical consciousness. . . . A listener must be sufficiently mature so that he does not demand of the instruction he receives more than it can give him."[31]

Gadamer summarizes what is for us the center of the interpretive

30. See Jürgen Habermas, *Legitimation Crisis* (Boston: Beacon Press, 1975).
31. Hans-Georg Gadamer, "The Problem of Historical Consciousness," reprinted in this volume.

position, when he says that "it is indispensable that through practice and education the listener may have already formed a *habitudo* which he takes into the concrete situations of his life, a *habitudo* which will be confirmed and solidified by each new action."[32] What the Frankfurt School rightly saw as the threat to or repression of the formation of such habits remains a pervasive obstacle both to understanding and to action. This is to tie such habits intimately to the need for criticism, both theoretical *and* political, of received values, practices, and institutions. Tradition is always problematical. The only way to proceed to the future is through the appropriation, the continual reappropriation, of tradition. The goal of the interpretive approach to the human world is to cultivate such habits, to recognize that we are condemned to remain open, both to the past and to the future.

The final import of the *Bildungsideal* is that it points to the necessity for standards by which to judge the world. The immense complexity of the task should now be clearer. The necessity for it, however, remains. Meaning is *for* something: that is what meaning is. This is no utilitarian reduction but a return to an older tradition in which the end of reason, its *telos,* was the good. The aim of interpretation is not merely more interpretation; it points beyond itself to the fundamental problems—theoretical, practical, and aesthetic—of human existence.

Our purpose in this second, extensively revised reader is to clarify by example our contention that the interpretive turn is not simply a new methodology, but rather a challenge to the very idea that inquiry into the social world and the value of the understanding that results is to be determined by methodology. Charles Taylor's by now classic essay, appearing first in the readings that follow, makes this point through an unflinching critique of the methodological insufficiencies of dominant social-scientific methodology.[33] Interpretive social science seeks to replace the standing distinction between the social sciences as descriptive disciplines and the humanities as normative studies with the realization that all human inquiry is neces-

32. Ibid. This is a paraphrase of Aristotle, *Ethics,* Book I.
33. See Charles Taylor, *Human Agency and Language, Philosophical Papers, Volume 1,* and *Philosophy and the Human Sciences, Philosophical Papers, Volume 2* (Cambridge: Cambridge University Press, 1985).

sarily engaged in understanding the human world from within a specific situation. This situation is always and at once historical, moral, and political. It provides not just the starting point of inquiry but the point and purpose for the task of understanding itself. But if this is so, interpretation is not simply a dimension of science. Rather, it means that science, like all human endeavors, is rooted in a context of meaning which is itself a social reality, a particular organization of human action defining a moral and practical world.

This thesis is a challenge to the tradition of discourse in the social sciences and the humanities which denies, ironically enough, its own moral-practical, historical location. It also directly challenges the contemporary disciplinary organization of knowledge, the structuring and definition of academic inquiry. For modern disciplines reflect and enact in their practices our culture's commitment to the belief that cognitive analysis and normative judgment can be clinically severed. It follows from these dominant values that the validity of inquiry is thought to be wholly independent of the historical and practical context of research, that social truths are easily divisible from morality and power.

This tendency weakens reason understood as wisdom and reduces knowledge to contentless technique. It also constricts meaning to privileged information authorized by experts. The consequences of this two-fold transformation are momentous. Once we proceed as if reason were severed from the practices of the historical world then rationality formally considered becomes elevated into a self-sufficient norm in the form of some arbitrarily fixed canon whose meaning is presumed to be somehow self-contained. Once this canon has been established, the claims of experts become self-legitimating. We believe both of these moves to be dangerous and ultimately false. Our aim has been to argue for an interpretive position which seeks to defend critical inquiry and debate without reifying what can legitimately be called reason's claims and to open an understanding of tradition as a set of possible, but not infinite, resources for meaningful action. This interpretive position should be distinguished from three other contemporary critiques—neoconservatism, deconstructionism, and the theory of communicative rationality—which are post-positivist.

The neoconservative critique focuses on the attempt to organize modern society on the basis of supposedly neutral administrative institutions and procedures. Such neoconservatives identify the key problem as the great expansion of the modern welfare state.[34] This is not a version of Weber's critique of modern bureaucracy as a dangerous substitution of technical expertise and procedures for political debate. Rather, neoconservatives typically attack only those features of modern government which by protecting individuals from some of the negative effects of market competition are seen as undermining the moral fiber of the West and particularly the paramount importance of economic self-reliance and individual initiative. Thus, sustained criticism is reserved for governmental efforts to increase economic and social equality but not for large institutional bureaucracies serving ends such as military power. These groups have expressed alarm at what they see as foundationless criticism, confusedly tagged as secular humanism. They assert that social life must be founded on a vigilant commitment to the sources of Western greatness, including unfettered competition and the mastery of the natural environment through work and technology (which they identify as "traditional values"), not on what they see as a crippling scrutiny of the limits and consequences of these commitments. They, too, are troubled by the unrestricted extension of modern scientific rationality to all domains of life. They fear the loss of moral and political goals they have inherited and want to strengthen. However, they remain unreflectively committed to central tenets of the very project against which they are reacting. Jürgen Habermas has formulated the contradiction at the heart of neoconservative thought as its acceptance of late capitalist social and economic organization while nostalgically seeking a return to earlier cultural formations.

From our perspective the neoconservative position not only is internally inconsistent but also confuses the notion of tradition by identifying it with dogmatic certitude. We strongly object to the notion that tradition is fundamentally univocal and consequently unambiguously recuperable. By contrast, the understanding we are

---

34. For a comprehensive and insightful summary of the foremost figures who could be called neoconservative see Peter Steinfels, *The Neoconservatives: The Men Who Are Changing America's Politics* (New York: Simon and Schuster, 1979).

seeking to strengthen sees tradition and reason as inseparable, if not identical, and therefore as requiring ongoing interpretation. In his essay "The Problem of Historical Consciousness," Hans-Georg Gadamer presents a compelling case that human existence can only be adequately understood as inherently historical and inescapably embedded in tradition. However, Gadamer understands tradition to be a struggle for meaning, the possibility and necessity of a constant reappropriation of history. Social life then appears as an ongoing conversation in many voices about current reality, a process of interpretation, not a reiteration of permanently fixed truths or traditions. Thus, our essential historicity implies that the only way of preserving tradition is to treat it not as the opponent of rationality but as its necessary ground. Thus an interpretive social science sees its task as promoting this insight against reductive modernist positions.

The most novel but, for our purposes, the least consequential of these recent movements can be loosely labeled "deconstructionism." Its origins are locatable in Jacques Derrida's reflections on the Western obsession with theory as the ultimate reality. Drawing on Martin Heidegger's "deconstruction" of Western metaphysics, Derrida showed, through a powerful and novel set of readings of Plato, Rousseau and others, that all claims to truth rest on interpretation. In recent years, literature departments in American universities have turned Derrida's deconstructive forays into a method which has produced a great deal of controversial textual interpretation, the evaluation of which would take us beyond the scope of this essay. However, it seems to us that at least so far, this production of literary criticism has not been complemented by an equally sustained attention to social practice.[35]

From the interpretive perspective, the implications of the deconstructive insights are far less radical than some of their proponents have suggested. Pointing up repeated failures to discover any but historically contingent foundations for thought does not in itself

35. For an overview of deconstruction as a method in American literary criticism see Jonathan Culler, *On Deconstruction: Theory & Criticism After Structuralism* (Ithaca: Cornell University Press, 1982). One of the more successful attempts to move the insights of deconstructive criticism back to the social and political world can be found in the work of Edward Said; see *Orientalism* (New York: Pantheon Books, 1978).

have to provoke a crisis of inquiry and understanding. The failure to provide such foundations has not hindered the conduct of successful inquiry. The work of thinkers such as Ian Hacking, Richard Rorty, Alasdair MacIntyre, and Charles Taylor argues that the tradition of rational inquiry does not depend for its validity upon ontological foundations.[36] However, such insights gain their importance only when they enable us to continue longstanding interpretive traditions through confronting new historical situations.

The theory of communicative rationality, in our view the most significant of contemporary debates, continues a tradition of critical assessment of the modern project. Enlightenment philosophers exalted reason's capacity to better the conditions of human existence through a progressively more complete understanding of the world. Yet, as thinkers of the Frankfurt School have taught us, this project is fraught with potential pathology because of its identification of reason with techniques of manipulation. This critique formed the context which we sought to extend in the first edition of this book. We have chosen to include a recent essay by Jürgen Habermas as a significant clarification of this position in the face of new cultural and social changes. Although there is much to be learned from Habermas, we continue to think that his reliance on reason as our fundamental safeguard against aberrations of social life does not provide enough scope to confront these dangers. For Habermas the only finally trustworthy tradition is that of modern Western critical rationality.[37] Habermas believes that reason is the only dependable guide for shaping and criticizing the social world. This seems to presuppose, however, that reason as an intelligible guide to life can be separated out from social practice and tradition. In his essay included in this volume, Habermas explains his continuing skepticism of positions like Gadamer's which see tradition as essential to rational discourse, or thinkers like Robert Bellah who seek to guide social change by

36. Richard Rorty, J. B. Schneewind, Quentin Skinner, eds., *Philosophy in History* (Cambridge: Cambridge University Press, 1984).

37. For the full development of this position see Jürgen Habermas, *The Theory of Communicative Action: Reason and the Rationalization of Society* (Boston: Beacon Press, 1984).

identifying and strengthening remaining positive dimensions of a social practice informed by traditions such as civic humanism.

Habermas is also critical of thinkers who understand reason as itself a set of historical practices. Thus when Habermas is confronted by a thinker like Michel Foucault he sees only dangers.[38] Habermas seems, however, to remain trapped in what Foucault, in an essay in this volume, calls a tactic of "Enlightenment blackmail." Foucault applies this label to those who point to the emancipatory achievements of the Enlightenment while downplaying the development of practices of administrative rationality which have resulted from the same understanding of reality which has given us those ideals of emancipation. Not that Foucault ignores these ideals or equates them with some system of social control. Like Habermas, Foucault sees the task of modernity in light of Kant's questioning of whether and how mankind could achieve maturity. They differ profoundly on whether the key to a critical understanding of the present lies in a theory of rationality or a genealogy of rational practices.

INTERPRETATIONS

In this second edition the readings we have assembled were chosen to serve as signposts for making sense of the renewal of discussion about the interrelationships of reason and tradition. Our discussion situates these terms through specific interpretations of the interactions of various forms of rationality and traditions in a conflictual social world.

Albert Hirschman elegantly shows us the interplay between model and case. He opposes two poles, one successful and the other not. On the one hand, the model, paradigm, or theory totally overshadows both the material to be understood and the process of understanding itself. He plays off against this abuse a case where the theory is "in" the narrative itself, where the paradigm and the author's stance are kept at a low profile so that the story itself can speak. But

38. For further reading see *The Foucault Reader,* ed. Paul Rabinow (New York: Pantheon Books, 1984).

this ironically increases the power of the theory and the voice of the author. In no way is this a plea for lack of theory—quite the contrary. Hirschman emphasizes that connections must come from the material itself; that lessons and generalizations are more likely to emerge when the cognitive style which Hirschman calls "open" is present.[39]

Clifford Geertz shows that an interpretive approach does not reduce the number and diversity of means of understanding that are available, but rather increases them. If theory per se is no longer separate from the enterprise, then insights, methods, and techniques from a variety of disciplines become available to us. Theory here is seen as itself an interpretation. It is seen as being in a situation with a particular problem to work on. Therefore, it can use what is appropriate to the case. Being itself situated, both theoretically and practically, it no longer can autonomously set the terms for discussion. But a discussion of a problem is impossible without it.

Geertz shows that cultural understanding by no means entails any form of special intuition or mysterious powers of empathy. He outlines and then demonstrates how cultural understanding starts with a picture of the whole, which leads the investigator to look for symbolic forms through which and in which the conceptions of the person, the social order, and the cosmology are articulated and displayed. This is an undertaking that requires skill—and Geertz is a deft practitioner of the art—but one which is repeatable, open to correction, and comparable to other cases.

What do we learn from Geertz's elegant and revelatory essay? Taking a relatively ordinary, if exotic, sporting event, Geertz shows us that the Balinese are active interpreters of their own culture. Both anthropologist and native are busy creating and commenting on social life. As Geertz presents it, the Balinese cockfight ritualizes violent conflict and thereby orders and to an extent domesticates it. Cultural form plays a therapeutic role by organizing and thereby making comprehensible violence and inequality.[40]

39. Albert Hirschman, *The Passions and the Interests* (Princeton: Princeton University Press, 1977).
40. Clifford Geertz, *The Interpretation of Cultures* (New York: Basic Books, 1973) and *Local Knowledge: Further Essays in Interpretive Anthropology* (New York: Basic Books, 1983).

Michael Taussig, in his essay in this volume, also presents violence as comprehensible and orderly.[41] In sharp contrast to Geertz, however, Taussig shows how discourse can be a constitutive component of a very violent world. Rather than mitigating the horror of cruelty Taussig presents a case where cultural form renders this cruelty systematic and demonstrates how a particular practice can be constitutive of the whole social structure. Culture at times renders power less immediately coercive by providing a cathartic distancing through acting out the conflicting emotions the inequalities give rise to. However, things are not always so comforting. As Taussig shows us there are real human consequences and stakes involved in the ordering of human practices. Order, even elegant and intelligible order, is not always a good. The interpretive task is tied to grappling with these consequences even when we recognize that the intellectual, aesthetic, and moral standards we bring to bear are themselves matters of interpretive debate.

Michelle Rosaldo, in her "Moral/Analytic Dilemmas Posed by the Intersection of Feminism and Social Science," argues that a mature interpretation would make the categories of social science an object of scrutiny.[42] It sees that all fundamental social categories such as individual vs. collective, nature vs. nurture, and so forth, embody a way of ordering the social world. Hence, none are politically or morally neutral. Seeing this is not the end point of interpretive analysis but rather its starting point. These categories themselves are constitutive of social relations and hence elements in a system of inequalities. Rosaldo proposes that interpretation is basic to changing the social world as well understanding it.

The next two readings in the volume are concerned with technical rationality. As Donald Schön shows in "The Art of Managing: Reflection-in-Action within an Organizational Learning System," modern business administration consists of nothing more or less than practices of human interaction.[43] The belief that there is a body

41. Michael Taussig, *The Devil and Commodity Fetishism in South America* (Chapel Hill: University of North Carolina Press, 1980).

42. Michelle Z. Rosaldo, *Knowledge and Passion, Ilongot Notions of Self & Social Life* (Cambridge: Cambridge University Press, 1980).

43. This essay is taken from Donald A. Schön's *The Reflective Practitioner* (New York: Basic Books, 1983).

of theory called managerial science which can abstract from and formalize the messy, partially improvised, situation-dependent practices of successful managers into a detached body of techniques is bound to lead to problems. Far from helping the practitioner to understand the dimensions of the situation, this putative body of theory instead conceals the real skill of a successful manager. This skill consists in a kind of practical understanding which combines local-level moral and political sensitivity with insight into larger market conditions. Schön shows us the dilemma these managers face when their superiors interpret their successes as though they were the product of technical expertise alone.

These points are generalized by Hubert and Stuart Dreyfus in their essay "From Socrates to Expert Systems: The Limits of Calculative Rationality."[44] They review the successes and failures of various specific "expert system" programs and conclude that these systems are limited because they fail to recognize the real character of expert understanding. This expertise is a property of a proficient performer who, immersed in the world of his skillful activity, understands, acts, and learns from results without having to formalize these processes as discrete steps. An expert's skill has become part of his character and cannot be detached from it. This is no nostalgic call for artisan culture; it applies just as much to technicians working on advanced computer technology as to practitioners of traditional crafts. However valuable this insight into the primacy of the practical, in our view it does not achieve a full interpretive richness until it is extended into social self-reflection. Without such further reflection there is a danger that this insight could be institutionally absorbed as merely one more effective technique.

The last two readings, by Fredric Jameson and Robert N. Bellah, are the most ambitious attempts in this collection to provide the outlines of a full interpretation of contemporary civilization. Although Jameson[45] and Bellah[46] are clearly proceeding from distinct inter-

44. See also Hubert Dreyfus, *What Computers Can't Do: A Critique of Artificial Intelligence*, 2nd ed. (New York: Harper and Row, 1979).

45. Fredric Jameson, *The Political Unconscious: Narrative as a Socially Symbolic Act* (Ithaca: Cornell University Press, 1981).

46. Robert N. Bellah, Richard Madsen, William M. Sullivan, Ann Swidler, Steven M. Tipton, *Habits of the Heart: Individualism and Commitment in American Life* (Berkeley and Los Angeles: University of California Press, 1985).

pretive positions, they share certain features of what we have been calling an interpretive strategy. Their positions are extensions of two of the major political and ethical traditions which have shaped modern discourse about society. Both authors are alarmed at developments in contemporary society which lead them to turn back to their traditions for illumination and guidance. In this way, both papers exemplify the kind of engaged dialogue with the past which Gadamer sees as essential to an interpretive understanding.

These two authors differ in important ways about the available resources to make sense of and also to alter the current situation. Bellah seeks to reappropriate alternatives to radical individualism by reviving the communities that embody republican politics and biblical religion. Jameson seeks to motivate political action and inform political practice by reviving connections with critical modernism and a utopian projection offering a vision of a more coherent and less alienated social life.

Like Habermas, Jameson points to the increasing economic and administrative integration of late capitalist society. He is critical of this trend for a number of reasons. In "The Politics of Theory: Ideological Positions in the Postmodernism Debate," Jameson concentrates on the inability of contemporary cultural forms to avoid either falling into nostalgia for a supposedly more coherent past or reveling in pastiche. For Jameson pastiche occurs in cultures characterized by a type of stylistic heterogeneity that renders common understanding and discourse, if not impossible, at least extremely problematic. The Marxist concern with social totality provides Jameson with an interpretive grid to pick out these trends and to diagnose them as acute cultural alienation. By attempting his ambitious interpretation Jameson is clearly seeking to provide a means to undermine or at least understand the broadest trends at work in the world today.

In his essay "The Quest for the Self: Individualism, Morality, and Politics," Robert N. Bellah provides what could serve as a description of the inner life of a world of cultural pastiche. Bellah sees a distinctive notion of the self emerging as the central cultural form in contemporary American society. This self seeks satisfaction in endlessly improvised private solutions. What is hidden by this cultural form of life is that the self, the problems, and the solutions are all social products. Bellah relies upon elements of the tradition of civic republicanism and biblical religion, which he believes embody a richer conception of personal identity, to reveal the limitations of contemporary individualism.

The best practitioners of interpretive social science are seeking, like Jameson and Bellah, to construct a more adequate understanding of the world so as to keep open the possibility of public discussion guided by practical reason.

INTERPRETATION: REASON, TRADITION, PRACTICE

CHARLES TAYLOR

1

Interpretation and the Sciences of Man

I.i

Is there a sense in which interpretation is essential to explanation in the sciences of man? The view that it is, that there is an unavoidably "hermeneutical" component in the sciences of man, goes back to Dilthey. But recently the question has come again to the fore, for instance, in the work of Gadamer,[1] in Ricoeur's interpretation of Freud,[2] and in the writings of Habermas.[3]

Interpretation, in the sense relevant to hermeneutics, is an attempt to make clear, to make sense of an object of study. This object must, therefore, be a text, or a text-analogue, which in some way is confused, incomplete, cloudy, seemingly contradictory—in one way or another unclear. The interpretation aims to bring to light an underlying coherence or sense.

This means that any science which can be called "hermeneutical," even in an extended sense, must be dealing with one or another of

Originally published in *The Review of Metaphysics* 25, no. 1 (September 1971). Reprinted by permission.

1. See, e.g., H. G. Gadamer, *Wahrheit und Methode* (Tübingen, 1960).
2. See Paul Ricoeur, *De l'interprétation* (Paris, 1965).
3. See, e.g., J. Habermas, *Erkenntnis und Interesse* (Frankfurt, 1968).

the confusingly interrelated forms of meaning. Let us try to see a little more clearly what this involves.

We need, first, an object or a field of objects, about which we can speak in terms of coherence or its absence, of making sense or nonsense.

Second, we need to be able to make a distinction, even if only a relative one, between the sense of coherence made, and its embodiment in a particular field of carriers or signifiers. For otherwise, the task of making clear what is fragmentary or confused would be radically impossible. No sense could be given to this idea. We have to be able to make for our interpretations claims of the order: the meaning confusedly present in this text or text-analogue is clearly expressed here. The meaning, in other words, is one which admits of more than one expression, and in this sense a distinction must be possible between meaning and expression.

The point of the above qualification, that this distinction may be only relative, is that there are cases where no clear, unambiguous, nonarbitrary line can be drawn between what is said and its expression. It can be plausibly argued (I think convincingly, although there is no space to go into it here) that this is the normal and fundamental condition of meaningful expression, that exact synonymy, or equivalence of meaning, is a rare and localized achievement of specialized languages or uses of civilization. But this, if true (and I think it is), does not do away with the distinction between meaning and expression. Even if there is an important sense in which a meaning re-expressed in a new medium cannot be declared identical, this by no means entails that we can give no sense to the project of expressing a meaning in a new way. It does of course raise an interesting and difficult question about what can be meant by expressing it in a clearer way: what is the "it" which is clarified if equivalence is denied? I hope to return to this in examining interpretation in the sciences of man.

Hence the object of a science of interpretation must be describable in terms of sense and nonsense, coherence and its absence; and must admit of a distinction between meaning and its expression.

There is also a third condition it must meet. We can speak of sense or coherence, and of their different embodiments, in connection with such phenomena as gestalts, or patterns in rock formations, or snow crystals, where the notion of expression has no real warrant. What is lacking here is the notion of a subject for whom these meanings are. Without such a subject, the choice of criteria of sameness and difference, the choice among the different forms of coherence which can be identified in a given pattern, among the different conceptual fields in which it can be seen, is arbitrary.

In a text or text-analogue, on the other hand, we are trying to make explicit the meaning expressed, and this means expressed by or for a subject or subjects. The notion of expression refers us to that of a subject. The identification of the subject is by no means necessarily unproblematical, as we shall see further on; it may be one of the most difficult problems, an area in which prevailing epistemological prejudice may blind us to the nature of our object of study. I think this has been the case, as I will show below: And moreover, the identification of a subject does not assure us of a clear and absolute distinction between meaning and expression as we saw above. But any such distinction, even a relative one, is without any anchor at all, is totally arbitrary, without appeal to a subject.

The object of a science of interpretation must thus have sense, distinguishable from its expression, which is for or by a subject.

I.ii

Before going on to see in what way, if any, these conditions are realized in the sciences of man, I think it would be useful to set out more clearly what rides on this question, why it matters whether or not we think of the sciences of man as hermeneutical, what the issue is at stake here.

The issue here is at root an epistemological one. But it is inextricable from an ontological one, and hence, cannot but be relevant to our notions of science and of the proper conduct of inquiry. We might say that it is an ontological issue which has been argued ever since the seventeenth century in terms of epistemological considerations which have appeared to some to be unanswerable.

The case could be put in these terms: what are the criteria of judgment in a hermeneutical science? A successful interpretation is one which makes clear the meaning originally present in a confused, fragmentary, cloudy form. But how does one know that this interpretation is correct? Presumably because it makes sense of the original text: what is strange, mystifying, puzzling, contradictory is no longer so, is accounted for. The interpretation appeals throughout to our understanding of the "language" of expression, which understanding allows us to see that this expression is puzzling, that it is in contradiction to that other, etc., and that these difficulties are cleared up when the meaning is expressed in a new way.

But this appeal to our understanding seems to be crucially inadequate. What if someone does not "see" the adequacy of our interpretation, does not accept our reading? We try to show him how it makes sense of the original non- or partial sense. But for him to follow us he must read the original language as we do, he must recognize these expressions as puzzling in a certain way, and hence be looking for a solution to our problem. If he does not, what can we do? The answer, it would seem, can only be more of the same. We have to show him through the reading of other expressions why this expression must be read in the way we propose. But success here requires that he follow us in these other readings, and so on, it would seem, potentially forever. We cannot escape an ultimate appeal to a common understanding of the expressions, of the "language" involved. This is one way of trying to express what has been called the "hermeneutical circle." What we are trying to establish is a certain reading of text or expressions, and what we appeal to as our grounds for this reading can only be other readings. The circle can also be put in terms of part-whole relations: we are trying to establish a reading for the whole text, and for this we appeal to readings of its partial expressions; and yet because we are dealing with meaning, with making sense, where expressions only make sense or not in relation to others, the readings of partial expressions depend on those of others, and ultimately of the whole.

Put in forensic terms, as we started to do above, we can only convince an interlocutor if at some point he shares our understanding of the language concerned. If he does not, there is no further step to take in rational argument; we can try to awaken these intuitions in him or we can simply give up; argument will advance us no further. But of course the forensic predicament can be transferred into my own judging: if I am this ill-equipped to convince a stubborn interlocutor, how can I convince myself? how can I be sure? Maybe my intuitions are wrong or distorted, maybe I am locked into a circle of illusion.

Now one, and perhaps the only sane response to this would be to say that such uncertainty is an ineradicable part of our epistemological predicament. That even to characterize it as "uncertainty" is to adopt an absurdly severe criterion of "certainty," which deprives the concept of any sensible use. But this has not been the only or even the main response of our philosophical tradition. And it is another response which has had an important and far-reaching effect on the sciences of man. The demand has been for a level of certainty which can only be attained by breaking beyond the circle.

There are two ways in which this breakout has been envisaged. The first might be called the "rationalist" one and could be thought to reach a culmination in Hegel. It does not involve a negation of intuition, or of our understanding of meaning, but rather aspires to attainment of an understanding of such clarity that it would carry with it the certainty of the undeniable. In Hegel's case, for instance, our full understanding of the whole in "thought" carries with it a grasp of its inner necessity, such that we see how it could not be otherwise. No higher grade of certainty is conceivable. For this aspiration the word "breakout" is badly chosen; the aim is rather to bring understanding to an inner clarity which is absolute.

The other way, which we can call "empiricist," is a genuine attempt to go beyond the circle of our own interpretations, to get beyond subjectivity. The attempt is to reconstruct knowledge in such a way that there is no need to make final appeal to readings or judgments which cannot be checked further. That is why the basic building block of knowledge on this view is the impression, or sense datum, a unit of information which is not the deliverance of a judgment, which has by definition no element in it of reading or interpretation, which is a brute datum. The highest ambition would be to build our knowledge from such building blocks by judgments which could be anchored in a certainty beyond subjective intuition. This is what underlies the attraction of the notion of the association of ideas, or if the same procedure is viewed as a method, induction. If the original acquisition of the units of information is not the fruit of judgment or interpretation, then the constatation that two such elements occur together need not either be the fruit of interpretation, of a reading or intuition which cannot be checked. For if the occurrence of a single element is a brute datum, then so is the co-occurrence of two such elements. The path to true knowledge would then repose crucially on the correct recording of such co-occurrences.

This is what lies behind an ideal of verification which is central to an important tradition in the philosophy of science, whose main contemporary protagonists are the logical empiricists. Verification must be grounded ultimately in the acquisition of brute data. By "brute data," I mean here and throughout data whose validity cannot be questioned by offering another interpretation or reading, data whose credibility cannot be founded or undermined by further reasoning.[4] If such a difference of interpretation can arise over given data, then it must be possible to structure the argument so as to distinguish the basic, brute data from the inferences made on the basis of them.

The inferences themselves, of course, to be valid must similarly be beyond the challenge of a rival interpretation. Here the logical empiricists added to the armory of traditional empiricism which set great store by the method of induction, the whole domain of logical and mathematical inference which had been central to the rationalist position (with Leibniz at least, although not with Hegel), and which offered another brand of unquestionable certainty.

Of course, mathematical inference and empirical verification were combined in such a way that two theories or more could be verified within the same domain of facts. But this was a consequence to which logical empiricism was willing to accommodate itself. As for the surplus meaning in a theory which could not be rigorously co-ordinated with brute data, it was considered to be quite outside the logic of verification.

As a theory of perception, this epistemology gave rise to all sorts

---

4. The notion of brute data here has some relation to, but is not at all the same as, the brute facts discussed by Elizabeth Anscome, "On Brute Facts," *Analysis* 18 (1957–1958): 69–72, and John Searle, *Speech Acts: An Essay in the Philosophy of Language* (Cambridge, 1969), 50–53. For Anscombe and Searle, brute facts are contrasted to what may be called "institutional facts," to use Searle's term, i.e., facts which presuppose the existence of certain institutions. Voting would be an example. But as we shall see below, some institutional facts, such as X's have voted Liberal, can be verified as brute data in the sense used here, and thus find a place in the category of political behavior. What cannot as easily be described in terms of brute data are the institutions themselves.

of problems, not least of which was the perpetual threat of skepticism and solipsism inseparable from a conception of the basic data of knowledge as brute data, beyond investigation. As a theory of perception, however, it seems largely a thing of the past, in spite of a surprising recrudescence in the Anglo-Saxon world in the thirties and forties. But there is no doubt that it goes marching on, among other places, as a theory of how the human mind and human knowledge actually function.

In a sense, the contemporary period has seen a better, more rigorous statement of what this epistemology is about in the form of computer-influenced theories of intelligence. These try to model intelligence as consisting of operations on machine-recognizable input which could themselves be matched by programs which could be run on machines. The machine criterion provides us with our assurance against an appeal to intuition or interpretations which cannot be understood by fully explicit procedures operating on brute data—the input.[5]

The progress of natural science has lent great credibility to this epistemology, since it can be plausibly reconstructed on this model, as has been done, for instance, by the logical empiricists. And of course the temptation has been overwhelming to reconstruct the sciences of man on the same model; or rather to launch them in lines of inquiry that fit this paradigm, since they are constantly said to be in their "infancy." Psychology, where an earlier vogue of behaviorism is being replaced by a boom of computer-based models, is far from the only case.

The form this epistemological bias—one might say obsession—takes is different for different sciences. Later I should like to look at a particular case, the study of politics, where the issue can be followed out. But in general, the empiricist orientation must be hostile to a conduct of inquiry which is based on interpretation, and which encounters the hermeneutical circle as this was characterized above. This cannot meet the requirements of intersubjective, nonarbitrary verification which it considers essential to science. And along with

5. See the discussion in M. Minsky, *Computation* (Englewood Cliffs, N.J., 1967), 104–107, where Minsky explicitly argues that an effective procedure that no longer requires intuition or interpretation is one which can be realized by a machine.

the epistemological stance goes the ontological belief that reality must be susceptible to understanding and explanation by science so understood. From this follows a certain set of notions of what the sciences of man must be.

On the other hand, many, including myself, would like to argue that these notions about the sciences of man are sterile, that we cannot come to understand important dimensions of human life within the bounds set by this epistemological orientation. This dispute is of course familiar to all in at least some of its ramifications. What I want to claim is that the issue can be fruitfully posed in terms of the notion of interpretation as I began to outline it above.

I think this way of putting the question is useful because it allows us at once to bring to the surface the powerful epistemological beliefs that underlie the orthodox view of the sciences of man in our academy, and to make explicit the notion of our epistemological predicament implicit in the opposing thesis. This is in fact rather more way-out and shocking to the tradition of scientific thought than is often admitted or realized by the opponents of narrow scientism. It may not strengthen the case of the opposition to bring out fully what is involved in a hermeneutical science as far as convincing waverers is concerned, but a gain in clarity is surely worth a thinning of the ranks—at least in philosophy.

I.iii

Before going on to look at the case of political science, it might be worth asking another question: why should we even pose the question whether the sciences of man are hermeneutical? What gives us the idea in the first place that men and their actions constitute an object or a series of objects which meet the conditions outlined above?

The answer is that on the phenomenological level or that of ordinary speech (and the two converge for the purposes of this argument) a certain notion of meaning has an essential place in the characterization of human behavior. This is the sense in which we speak of a situation, an action, a demand, a prospect having a certain meaning for a person.

Now it is frequently thought that "meaning" is used here in a sense that is a kind of illegitimate extension from the notion of linguistic meaning. Whether it can be considered an extension or not is another matter; it certainly differs from linguistic meaning. But it would be very hard to argue that it is an illegitimate use of the term.

When we speak of the "meaning" of a given predicament, we are using a concept which has the following articulation. (1) Meaning is for a subject: it is not the meaning of the situation *in vacuo*, but its meaning for a subject, a specific subject, a group of subjects, or perhaps what its meaning is for the human subject as such (even though particular humans might be reproached with not admitting or realizing this). (2) Meaning is of something; that is, we can distinguish between a given element—situation, action, or whatever—and its meaning. But this is not to say that they are physically separable. Rather we are dealing with two descriptions of the element, in one of which it is characterized in terms of its meaning for the subject. But the relations between the two descriptions are not symmetrical. For, on the one hand, the description in terms of meaning cannot be unless descriptions of the other kind apply as well; or put differently, there can be no meaning without a substrate. But on the other hand, it may be that the same meaning may be borne by another substrate—e.g., a situation with the same meaning may be realized in different physical conditions. There is a necessary role for a potentially substitutable substrate; or all meanings are of something.

And (3) things only have meaning in a field, that is, in relation to the meanings of other things. This means that there is no such thing as a single, unrelated meaningful element; and it means that changes in the other meanings in the field can involve changes in the given element. Meanings cannot be identified except in relation to others, and in this way resemble words. The meaning of a word depends, for instance, on those words with which it contrasts, on those that define its place in the language (e.g., those defining "determinable" dimensions, like color, shape), on those that define the activity or "language game" it figures in (describing, invoking, establishing communion), and so on. The relations between meanings in this sense are like those between concepts in a semantic field.

Just as our color concepts are given their meaning by the field of contrast they set up together, so that the introduction of new concepts will alter the boundaries of others, so the various meanings that a subordinate's demeanor can have for us, as deferential, respectful, cringing, mildly mocking, ironical, insolent, provoking, downright rude, are established by a field of contrast; and as with finer discrimination on our part, or a more sophisticated culture, new possibilities are born, so other terms of this range are altered. And as the meaning of our terms "red," "blue," "green" is fixed by the definition of a field of contrast through the determinable term "color," so all these alternative demeanors are only available in a society which has, among other types, hierarchical relations of power and command. And corresponding to the underlying language game of designating colored objects is the set of social practices which sustain these hierarchical structures and are fulfilled in them.

Meaning in this sense—let us call it experiential meaning—thus is for a subject, of something, in a field. This distinguishes it from linguistic meaning which has a four- and not a three-dimensional structure. Linguistic meaning is for subjects and in a field, but it is the meaning of signifiers and it is about a world of referents. Once we are clear about the likenesses and differences there should be little doubt that the term "meaning" is not a misnomer, the product of an illegitimate extension into this context of experience and behavior.

There is thus a quite legitimate notion of meaning which we use when we speak of the meaning of a situation for an agent. And that this concept has a place is integral to our ordinary consciousness and hence speech about our actions. Our actions are ordinarily characterized by the purpose sought and explained by desires, feelings, emotions. But the language by which we describe our goals, feelings, desires is also a definition of the meaning things have for us. The vocabulary defining meaning—words like "terrifying," "attractive."—is linked with that describing feeling—"fear," "desire"—and that describing goals—"safety," "possession."

Moreover, our understanding of these terms moves inescapably in a hermeneutical circle. An emotion term like "shame," for instance, essentially refers us to a certain kind of situation, the "shameful," or "humiliating," and a certain mode of response, that of hiding oneself, of covering up, or else "wiping out" the blot. That is, it is essential to this feeling's identification as shame that it be related to this situation and give rise to this type of disposition. But this situation in its turn can only be identified in relation to the feelings it provokes; and the disposition is to a goal that can similarly not be understood without reference to the feelings experienced: the "hiding" in question is one which will cover up my shame; it is not the same as hiding from an armed pursuer; we can only understand what is meant by "hiding" here if we understand what kind of feeling and situation is being talked about. We have to be within the circle.

An emotion term like "shame" can only be explained by reference to other concepts which in turn cannot be understood without reference to shame. To understand these concepts we have to be in on a certain experience, we have to understand a certain language, not just of words, but also a certain language of mutual action and communication, by which we blame, exhort, admire, esteem each other. In the end we are in on this because we grow up in the ambit of certain common meanings. But we can often experience what it is like to be on the outside when we encounter the feeling, action, and experiential meaning language of another civilization. Here there is no translation, no way of explaining in other, more accessible concepts. We can only catch on by getting somehow into their way of life, if only in imagination. Thus if we look at human behavior as action done out of a background of desire, feeling, emotion, then we are looking at a reality which must be characterized in terms of meaning. But does this mean that it can be the object of a hermeneutical science as this was outlined above?

There are, to remind ourselves, three characteristics that the object of a science of interpretation has: it must have sense or coherence; this must be distinguishable from its expression; and this sense must be for a subject.

Now insofar as we are talking about behavior as action, hence in terms of meaning, the category of sense or coherence must apply to it. This is not to say that all behavior must "make sense," if we mean by this be rational, avoid contradiction, confusion of purpose, and the like. Plainly a great deal of our action falls short of this goal. But in another sense, even contradictory, irrational action is "made sense of," when we understand why it was engaged in. We make sense of action when there is a coherence between the actions of the agent and the meaning of his situation for him. We find his action puzzling until we find such a coherence. It may not be bad to repeat that this coherence in no way implies that the action is rational: the meaning of a situation for an agent may be full of confusion and contradiction, but the adequate depiction of this contradiction makes sense of it.

Making sense in this way through coherence of meaning and action, the meanings of action and situation, cannot but move in a hermeneutical circle. Our conviction that the account makes sense is contingent on our reading of action and situation. But these readings cannot be explained or justified except by reference to other such readings, and their relation to the whole. If an interlocutor does not understand this kind of reading, or will not accept it as valid, there is nowhere else the argument can go. Ultimately, a good explanation is one which makes sense of the behavior; but then to appreciate a good explanation, one has to agree on what makes good sense; what makes good sense is a function of one's readings; and these in turn are based on the kind of sense one understands.

But how about the second characteristic, that sense should be distinguishable from its embodiment? This is necessary for a science of interpretation because interpretation lays a claim to make a confused meaning clearer; hence there must be some sense in which the "same" meaning is expressed, but differently.

This immediately raises a difficulty. In talking of experiential meaning above, I mentioned that we can distinguish between a given element and its meaning, between meaning and substrate. This carried the claim that a given meaning *may* be realized in another substrate. But does this mean that we can *always* embody the same meaning in another situation? Perhaps there are some situations, standing before death, for instance, which have a meaning which cannot be embodied otherwise.

But fortunately this difficult question is irrelevant for our purposes. For here we have a case in which the analogy between text and behavior implicit in the notion of a hermeneutical science of man only applies with important modifications. The text is replaced in the interpretation by another text, one which is clearer. The text-analogue of behavior is not replaced by another such text-analogue. When this happens we have revolutionary theater, or terroristic acts designed to make propaganda of the deed, in which the hidden relations of a society are supposedly shown up in a dramatic confrontation. But this is not scientific understanding, even though it may perhaps be based on such understanding, or claim to be.

But in science the text-analogue is replaced by a text, an account.

Which might prompt the question, how we can even begin to talk of interpretation here, of expressing the same meaning more clearly, when we have two such utterly different terms of comparison, a text and a tract of behavior? Is the whole thing not just a bad pun?

This question leads us to open up another aspect of experiential meaning which we abstracted from earlier. Experiential meanings are defined in fields of contrast, as words are in semantic fields.

But what was not mentioned above is that these two kinds of definition are not independent of each other. The range of human desires, feelings, emotions, and hence meanings is bound up with the level and type of culture, which in turn is inseparable from the distinctions and categories marked by the language people speak. The field of meanings in which a given situation can find its place is bound up with the semantic field of the terms characterizing these meanings and the related feelings, desires, predicaments.

But the relationship involved here is not a simple one. There are two simple types of models of relation which could be offered here, but both are inadequate. We could think of the feeling vocabulary as simply describing preexisting feelings, as marking distinctions that would be there without them. But this is not adequate, because we often experience in ourselves or others how achieving, say, a more sophisticated vocabulary of the emotions makes our emotional life more sophisticated and not just our descriptions of it. Reading a good, powerful novel may give me the picture of an emotion which I had not previously been aware of. But we cannot draw a neat line between an increased ability to identify and an altered ability to feel emotions which this enables.

The other simple inadequate model of the relationship is to jump from the above to the conclusion that thinking makes it so. But this clearly won't do either, since not just any new definition can be forced on us, nor can we force it on ourselves; and some that we do gladly take up can be judged inauthentic, in bad faith, or just wrongheaded by others. These judgments may be wrong, but they are not in principle illicit. Rather we make an effort to be lucid about ourselves and our feelings, and admire a man who achieves this.

Thus, neither the simple correspondence view is correct, nor the view that thinking makes it so. But both have prima facie warrant. There is such a thing as self-lucidity, which points us to a correspondence view; but the achievement of such lucidity means moral change, that is, it changes the object known. At the same time, error about oneself is not just an absence of correspondence; it is also in some form inauthenticity, bad faith, self-delusion, repression of one's human feelings, or something of the kind; it is a matter of the quality of what is felt just as much as what is known about this, just as self-knowledge is.

If this is so, then we have to think of man as a self-interpreting animal. He is necessarily so, for there is no such thing as the structure of meanings for him independently of his interpretation of them; one is woven into the other. But then the text of our interpretation is not that heterogeneous from what is interpreted, for what is interpreted is itself an interpretation: a self-interpretation which is embedded in a stream of action. It is an interpretation of experiential meaning which contributes to the constitution of this meaning. Or to put it in another way, that of which we are trying to find the coherence is itself partly constituted by self-interpretation.

Our aim is to replace this confused, incomplete, partly erroneous self-interpretation by a correct one. And in doing this we look not only to the self-interpretation but to the stream of behavior in which it is set, just as in interpreting a historical document we have to place it in the stream of events which it relates to. But of course the analogy is not exact, for here we are interpreting the interpretation and the stream of behavior in which it is set together, and not just one or the other.

There is thus no utter heterogeneity of interpretation to what it is about; rather there is a slide in the notion of interpretation. Already to be a living agent is to experience one's situation in terms of certain meanings, and this in a sense can be thought of as a sort of proto-"interpretation." This is in turn interpreted and shaped by the language in which the agent lives these meanings. This whole is then at a third level interpreted by the explanation we proffer of his actions.

In this way the second condition of a hermeneutical science is met. But this account poses in a new light the question mentioned at the beginning whether the interpretation can ever express the same meaning as the interpreted. And in this case, there is clearly a way in which the two will not be congruent. For if the explanation is really clearer than the lived interpretation, then it will be such that it would alter in some way the behavior if it came to be internalized by the agent as his self-interpretation. In this way a hermeneutical science that achieves its goal, that is, attains greater clarity than the immediate understanding of agent or observer, must offer us an interpretation that is in this way crucially out of phase with the explicandum.

Thus human behavior seen as action of agents who desire and are moved, who have goals and aspirations, necessarily offers a purchase for descriptions in terms of meaning—what I have called "experiential meaning." The norm of explanation which it posits is one that "makes sense" of the behavior, that shows a coherence of meaning. This "making sense of" is the proffering of an interpretation, and we have seen that what is interpreted meets the conditions of a science of interpretation: first, that we can speak of its sense or coherence; and second, that this sense can be expressed in another form, so that we can speak of the interpretation as giving clearer expression to what is only implicit in the explicandum. The third condition, that this sense be for a subject, is obviously met in this case, although who this subject is, is by no means an unproblematical question as we shall see later on.

This should be enough to show that there is a good prima facie case to the effect that men and their actions are amenable to explanation of a hermeneutical kind. There is therefore some reason to raise the issue and challenge the epistemological orientation that would rule interpretation out of the sciences of man. A great deal more must be said to bring out what is involved in the hermeneutical sciences of man. But before getting on to this, it might help to clarify the issue with a couple of examples drawn from a specific field, that of politics.

II.i

In politics, too, the goal of a verifiable science has led to the concentration on features that can supposedly be identified in abstraction from our understanding or not understanding experiential meaning. These—let us call them brute data identifications—are what supposedly enable us to break out from the hermeneutical circle and found our science foursquare on a verification procedure which meets the requirements of the empiricist tradition.

But in politics the search for such brute data has not gone to the lengths which it has in psychology, where the object of science has been thought of by many as behavior *qua* "colorless movement," or as machine-recognizable properties. The tendency in politics has been to stop with something less basic, but—so it is thought—the identification of which cannot be challenged by the offering of another interpretation or reading of the data concerned. This is what is referred to as "behavior" in the rhetoric of political scientists, but it has not the rock-bottom quality of its psychological homonym.

Political behavior includes what we would ordinarily call actions, but ones that are supposedly brute-data-identifiable. How can this be so? Well, actions are usually described by the purpose or end state realized. But the purposes of some actions can be specified in what might be thought to be brute data terms; some actions, for instance, have physical end states, like getting the car in the garage or climbing the mountain. Others have end states which are closely tied by institutional rules to some unmistakable physical movement; thus, when I raise my hand in the meeting at the appropriate time, I am voting for the motion. The only questions we can raise about the corresponding actions, given such movements or the realization of such end states, are whether the agent was aware of what he was doing, was acting as against simply emitting reflex behavior, knew the institutional significance of his movement, and so forth. Any worries on this score generally turn out to be pretty artificial in the contexts political scientists are concerned with; and where they do arise they can be checked by relatively simple devices, for example, asking the subject: did you mean to vote for the motion?

Hence it would appear that there are actions which can be identified beyond fear of interpretative dispute; and this is what gives the foundation for the category of "political behavior." Thus, there are some acts of obvious political relevance which can be specified as such in physical terms, such as killing, sending tanks into the streets, seizing people and confining them to cells; and there is an immense range of others that can be specified from physical acts by institutional rules, such as voting, for instance. These can be the object of a science of politics which can hope to meet the stringent requirements of verification. The latter class particularly has provided matter for study in recent decades—most notably in the case of voting studies.

But of course a science of politics confined to such acts would be much too narrow. For on another level these actions also have meaning for the agents which is not exhausted in the brute data descriptions, and which is often crucial to understanding why they were done. Thus in voting for the motion I am also saving the honor of my party, or defending the value of free speech, or vindicating public morality, or saving civilization from breakdown. It is in such terms that the agents talk about the motivation of much of their political action, and it is difficult to conceive a science of politics which does not come to grips with it.

Behavioral political science comes to grips with it by taking the meanings involved in action as facts about the agent, his beliefs, his affective reactions, his "values," as the term is frequently used. For it can be thought verifiable in the brute-data sense that men will agree to subscribe or not to a certain form of words (expressing a belief, say); or express a positive or negative reaction to certain events, or symbols; or agree or not with the proposition that some act is right or wrong. We can thus get at meanings as just another form of brute data by the techniques of the opinion survey and content analysis.

An immediate objection springs to mind. If we are trying to deal with the meanings which inform political action, then surely interpretive acumen is unavoidable. Let us say we are trying to understand the goals and values of a certain group, or grasp their vision of the polity; we might try to probe this by a questionnaire asking them whether they assent or not to a number of propositions, which are meant to express different goals, evaluations, beliefs. But how did we design the questionnaire? How did we pick these propositions? Here we relied on our understanding of the goals, values, vision involved. But then this understanding can be challenged, and hence the significance of our results questioned. Perhaps the finding of our study, the compiling of proportions of assent and dissent to these propositions is irrelevant, is without significance for understanding the agents or the polity concerned. This kind of attack is frequently made by critics of mainstream political science, or for that matter social science in general.

To this the proponents of this mainstream reply with a standard move of logical empiricism: distinguishing the process of discovery from the logic of verification. Of course it is our understanding of these meanings which enables us to draw up the questionnaire which will test people's attitudes in respect to them. And of course interpretive dispute about these meanings is potentially endless; there are no brute data at this level, every affirmation can be challenged by a rival interpretation. But this has nothing to do with verifiable science. What is firmly verified is the set of correlations between, say, the assent to certain propositions and certain behavior. We discover, for instance, that people who are active politically (defined by participation in a certain set of institutions) are more likely to consent to certain sets of propositions supposedly expressing the values underlying the system.[6] This finding is a firmly verified correlation no matter what one thinks of the reasoning, or simple hunches, that went into designing the research which established it. Political science as a body of knowledge is made up of such correlations; it does not give a truth value to the background reasoning or hunch. A good interpretive nose may be useful in hitting on the right correlations to test, but science is never called on to arbitrate the disputes between interpretations.

Thus in addition to those overt acts which can be defined physically or institutionally, the category of political behavior can include assent or dissent to verbal formulae, or the occurrence or not of verbal formulae in speech, or expressions of approval or rejection of certain events or measures as observed in institutionally defined behavior (for instance, turning out for a demonstration).

Now there are a number of objections which can be made to this notion of political behavior; one might question in all sorts of ways how interpretation-free it is in fact. But I should like to question it from another angle. One of the basic characteristics of this kind of social science is that it reconstructs reality in line with certain categorical principles. These allow for an intersubjective social reality which is made up of brute data, identifiable acts and structures, certain institutions, procedures, actions. It allows for beliefs, affective reactions, evaluations as the psychological properties of individuals. And it allows for correlations, for example, between these two orders

---

6. Cf. H. McClosky, "Consensus and Ideology in American Politics," *American Political Science Review* 58 (1964): 361–82.

of reality: that certain beliefs go along with certain acts, certain values with certain institutions, and so forth.

To put it another way, what is objectively (intersubjectively) real is brute-data-identifiable. This is what social reality *is*. Social reality described in terms of its meaning for the actors, such that disputes could arise about interpretation that could not be settled by brute data (e.g., are people rioting to get a hearing, or are they rioting to redress humiliation, out of blind anger, because they recover a sense of dignity in insurrection?), is given subjective reality, that is, there are certain beliefs, affective reactions, evaluations which individuals make or have about or in relation to social reality. These beliefs or reactions can have an effect on this reality; and the fact that such a belief is held is a fact of objective social reality. But the social reality which is the object of these attitudes, beliefs, reactions can only be made up of brute data. Thus any description of reality in terms of meanings which is open to interpretive question is only allowed into this scientific discourse if it is placed, as it were, in quotes and attributed to individuals as their opinion, belief, attitude. That this opinion, belief, and so forth is held is thought of as a brute datum, since it is redefined as the respondent's giving a certain answer to the questionnaire.

This aspect of social reality which concerns its meanings for the agents has been taken up in a number of ways, but recently it has been spoken of in terms of political culture. Now the way this is defined and studied illustrates clearly the categorical principles above. For instance, political culture is referred to by Almond and Powell as the "psychological dimension of the political system."[7] Further on they state: "Political culture is the pattern of individual attitudes and orientations towards politics among the members of a political system. It is the subjective realm which underlies and gives meaning to political actions." The authors then go on to distinguish three different kinds of orientations, cognitive (knowledge and beliefs), affective (feelings), and evaluative (judgments and opinions).

From the point of view of empiricist epistemology, this set of cate-

7. Gabriel A. Almond and G. Bingham Powell, *Comparative Politics: A Developmental Approach* (Boston and Toronto, 1966), 23.

gorical principles leaves nothing out. Both reality and the meanings
it has for actors are coped with. But what it in fact cannot allow for
are intersubjective meanings, that is, it cannot allow for the validity
of descriptions of social reality in terms of meanings, hence not as
brute data, which are not in quotation marks and attributed as opinion, attitude, and so forth to individual(s). Now it is this exclusion
that I should like to challenge in the name of another set of categorical principles, inspired by a quite other epistemology.

II.ii

We spoke earlier about the brute-data identification of acts by means
of institutional rules. Thus, putting a cross beside someone's name
on a slip of paper and putting this in a box counts in the right context
as voting for that person; leaving the room, saying or writing a certain form of words, counts as breaking off the negotiations; writing
one's name on a piece of paper counts as signing the petition, and
so forth. But what is worth looking at is what underlies this set of
identifications. These identifications are the application of a language of social life, a language which marks distinctions among different possible social acts, relations, structures. But what underlies
this language?

Let us take the example of breaking off negotiations above. The
language of our society recognizes states or actions like the following: entering into negotiation, breaking off negotiations, offering to
negotiate, negotiating in good (bad) faith, concluding negotiations,
making a new offer. In other more jargon-infested language, the semantic "space" of this range of social activity is carved up in a certain way, by a certain set of distinctions which our vocabulary marks;
and the shape and nature of these distinctions is the nature of our
language in this area. These distinctions are applied in our society
with more or less formalism in different contexts.

But of course this is not true of every society. Our whole notion
of negotiation is bound up, for instance, with the distinct identity and
autonomy of the parties, with the willed nature of their relations; it is
a very contractual notion. But other societies have no such concep-

tion. It is reported about the traditional Japanese village that the foundation of its social life was a powerful form of consensus, which put a high premium on unanimous decision.[8] Such a consensus would be considered shattered if two clearly articulated parties were to separate out, pursuing opposed aims and attempting either to vote down the opposition or push it into a settlement on the most favorable possible terms for themselves. Discussion there must be, and some kind of adjustment of differences. But our idea of bargaining, with the assumption of distinct autonomous parties in willed relationship, has no place there; nor does a series of distinctions, like entering into and leaving negotiation, or bargaining in good faith (sc. with the genuine intention of seeking agreement).

Now the difference between our society and one of the kind just described could not be well expressed if we said we have a vocabulary to describe negotiation which they lack. We might say, for instance, that we have a vocabulary to describe the heavens which they lack, namely, that of Newtonian mechanics; for here we assume that they live under the same heavens as we do, only understand it differently. But it is not true that they have the same kind of bargaining as we do. The word, or whatever word of their language we translate as "bargaining," must have an entirely different gloss, which is marked by the distinctions their vocabulary allows in contrast to those marked by ours. But this different gloss is not just a difference of vocabulary, but also one of social reality.

But this still may be misleading as a way of putting the difference. For it might imply that there is a social reality which can be discovered in each society and which might exist quite independently of the vocabulary of that society, or indeed of any vocabulary, as the heavens would exist whether men theorized about them or not. And this is not the case; the realities here are practices; and these cannot be identified in abstraction from the language we use to describe them, or invoke them, or carry them out. That the practice of negotiation allows us to distinguish bargaining in good or bad faith, or entering into or breaking off negotiations, presupposes that our acts and

8. Cf. Thomas C. Smith, *The Agrarian Origins of Modern Japan* (Stanford, 1959), chap. 5. This type of consensus is also found in other traditional societies. Cf., for instance, the *desa* system of the Indonesian village.

situation have a certain description for us, for example, that we are distinct parties entering into willed relations. But they cannot have these descriptions for us unless this is somehow expressed in our vocabulary of this practice; if not in our descriptions of the practices (for we may as yet be unconscious of some of the important distinctions) in the appropriate language for carrying them on. (Thus, the language marking a distinction between public and private acts or contexts may exist even where these terms or their equivalents are not part of this language; for the distinction will be marked by the different language which is appropriate in one context and the other, be it perhaps a difference of style, or dialect, even though the distinction is not designated by specific descriptive expressions.)

The situation we have here is one in which the vocabulary of a given social dimension is grounded in the shape of social practice in this dimension; that is, the vocabulary would not make sense, could not be applied sensibly, where this range of practices did not prevail. And yet this range of practices could not exist without the prevalence of this or some related vocabulary. There is no simple one-way dependence here. We can speak of mutual dependence if we like, but really what this points up is the artificiality of the distinction between social reality and the language of description of that social reality. The language is constitutive of the reality, is essential to its being the kind of reality it is. To separate the two and distinguish them as we quite rightly distinguish the heavens from our theories about them is forever to miss the point.

This type of relation has been recently explored, for example, by John Searle, with his concept of a constitutive rule. As Searle points out,[9] we are normally induced to think of rules as applying to behavior which could be available to us whether or not the rule existed. Some rules are like this, they are regulative like commandments: don't take the goods of another. But there are other rules, for example, that governing the Queen's move in chess, which are not so separable. If one suspends these rules, or imagines a state in which they have not yet been introduced, then the whole range of behavior in question, in this case, chess playing, would not be. There would

9. Searle, *Speech Acts,* 33–42.

still, of course, be the activity of pushing a wood piece around on an eight-by-eight-inch board made of squares; but this is not chess any longer. Rules of this kind are constitutive rules. By contrast again, there are other rules of chess, such as that one say "j'adoube" when one touches a piece without intending to play it, which are clearly regulative.[10]

I am suggesting that this notion of the constitutive be extended beyond the domain of rule-governed behavior. That is why I suggest the vaguer word "practice." Even in an area where there are no clearly defined rules, there are distinctions between different sorts of behavior such that one sort is considered the appropriate form for one action or context, the other for another action or context; for example, doing or saying certain things amounts to breaking off negotiations, doing or saying other things amounts to making a new offer. But just as there are constitutive rules, that is, rules such that the behavior they govern could not exist without them, and which are in this sense inseparable from that behavior, so I am suggesting that there are constitutive distinctions, constitutive ranges of language which are similarly inseparable, in that certain practices are not without them.

We can reverse this relationship and say that all the institutions and practices by which we live are constituted by certain distinctions and hence a certain language which is thus essential to them. We can take voting, a practice which is central to large numbers of institutions in a democratic society. What is essential to the practice of voting is that some decision or verdict be delivered (a man elected, a measure passed), through some criterion of preponderance (simple majority, two-thirds majority, or whatever) out of a set of microchoices (the votes of the citizens, MPs, delegates). If there is not some such significance attached to our behavior, no amount of marking and counting pieces of paper, raising hands, walking out into lobbies amounts to voting. From this it follows that the institution of voting must be such that certain distinctions have application: for example, that between someone being elected, or a measure passed,

10. Cf. the discussion in Stanley Cavell, *Must We Mean What We Say?* (New York, 1969), 21–31.

and their failing of election, or passage; that between a valid vote and an invalid one which in turn requires a distinction between a real choice and one which is forced or counterfeited. For no matter how far we move from the Rousseauian notion that each man decide in full autonomy, the very institution of the vote requires that in some sense the enfranchised choose. For there to be voting in a sense recognizably like ours, there must be a distinction in men's self-interpretations between autonomy and forced choice.

This is to say that an activity of marking and counting papers has to bear intentional descriptions which fall within a certain range before we can agree to call it voting, just as the intercourse of two men or teams has to bear descriptions of a certain range before we will call it negotiation. Or in other words, that some practice is voting or negotiation has to do in part with the vocabulary established in a society as appropriate for engaging in it or describing it.

Hence implicit in these practices is a certain vision of the agent and his relation to others and to society. We saw in connection with negotiation in our society that it requires a picture of the parties as in some sense autonomous, and as entering into willed relations. And this picture carries with it certain implicit norms, such as that of good faith mentioned above, or a norm of rationality, that agreement correspond to one's goals as far as attainable, or the norm of continued freedom of action as far as attainable. These practices require that one's actions and relations be seen in the light of this picture and the accompanying norms, good faith, autonomy, and rationality. But men do not see themselves in this way in all societies, nor do they understand these norms in all societies. The experience of autonomy as we know it, the sense of rational action and the satisfactions thereof, are unavailable to them. The meaning of these terms is opaque to them because they have a different structure of experiential meaning open to them.

We can think of the difference between our society and the simplified version of the traditional Japanese village as consisting in this, that the range of meaning open to the members of the two societies is very different. But what we are dealing with here is not subjective meaning which can fit into the categorical grid of behavioral political science, but rather intersubjective meanings. It is not just that all or most people in our society have a given set of ideas in their heads and subscribe to a given set of goals. The meanings and norms implicit in these practices are not just in the minds of the actors but are out there in the practices themselves, practices which cannot be conceived as a set of individual actions, but which are essentially modes of social relation, of mutual action.

The actors may have all sorts of beliefs and attitudes which may be rightly thought of as their individual beliefs and attitudes, even if others share them; they may subscribe to certain policy goals or certain forms of theory about the polity, or feel resentment at certain things, and so on. They bring these with them into their negotiations, and strive to satisfy them. But what they do not bring into the negotiations is the set of ideas and norms constitutive of negotiation themselves. These must be the common property of the society before there can be any question of anyone entering into negotiation or not. Hence they are not subjective meanings, the property of one or some individuals, but rather intersubjective meanings, which are constitutive of the social matrix in which individuals find themselves and act.

The intersubjective meanings which are the background to social action are often treated by political scientists under the heading "consensus." By this is meant convergence of beliefs on certain basic matters, or of attitude. But the two are not the same. Whether there is consensus or not, the condition of there being either one or the other is a certain set of common terms of reference. A society in which this was lacking would not be a society in the normal sense of the term, but several. Perhaps some multi-racial or multi-tribal states approach this limit. Some multi-national states are bedeviled by consistent cross-purposes, for example, Canada. But consensus as a convergence of beliefs or values is not the opposite of this kind of fundamental diversity. Rather the opposite of diversity is a high degree of intersubjective meanings. And this can go along with profound cleavage. Indeed, intersubjective meanings are a condition of a certain kind of very profound cleavage, such as was visible in the Reformation, or the American Civil War, or splits in left-wing parties, where the dispute is at fever pitch just because both sides can fully understand the other.

In other words, convergence of belief or attitude or its absence presupposes a common language in which these beliefs can be formulated, and in which these formulations can be opposed. Much of this common language in any society is rooted in its institutions and practices; it is constitutive of these institutions and practices. It is part of the intersubjective meanings. To put the point another way, apart from the question of how much people's beliefs converge is the question of how much they have a common language of social and political reality in which these beliefs are expressed. This second question cannot be reduced to the first; intersubjective meaning is not a matter of converging beliefs or values. When we speak of consensus we speak of beliefs and values which could be the property of a single person, or many, or all; but intersubjective meanings could not be the property of a single person because they are rooted in social practice.

We can perhaps see this if we envisage the situation in which the ideas and norms underlying a practice are the property of single individuals. This is what happens when single individuals from one society interiorize the notions and values of another, for example, children in missionary schools. Here we have a totally different situation. We *are* really talking now about subjective beliefs and attitudes. The ideas are abstract, they are mere social "ideals." Whereas in the original society, these ideas and norms are rooted in their social relations, and are that on the basis of which they can formulate opinions and ideals.

We can see this in connection with the example we have been using all along, that of negotiations. The vision of a society based on negotiation is coming in for heavy attack by a growing segment of modern youth, as are the attendant norms of rationality and the definition of autonomy. This is a dramatic failure of "consensus." But this cleavage takes place in the ambit of this intersubjective meaning, the social practice of negotiation as it is lived in our society. The rejection would not have the bitter quality it has if what is rejected were not understood in common, because it is part of a social practice which we find hard to avoid, so pervasive is it in our society. At the same time there is a reaching out for other forms which have still the "abstract" quality of ideals which are subjective in this sense, that is, not rooted in practice; which is what makes the rebellion look so "unreal" to outsiders, and so irrational.

II.iii

Intersubjective meanings, ways of experiencing action in society which are expressed in the language and descriptions constitutive of institutions and practices, do not fit into the categorical grid of mainstream political science. This allows only for an intersubjective reality that is brute-data-identifiable. But social practices and institutions that are partly constituted by certain ways of talking about them are not so identifiable. We have to understand the language, the underlying meanings that constitute them.

We can allow, once we accept a certain set of institutions or practices as our starting point and not as objects of further questioning, that we can easily take as brute data that certain acts are judged to take place or certain states judged to hold within the semantic field of these practices—for instance, that someone has voted Liberal or signed the petition. We can then go on to correlate certain subjective meanings—beliefs, attitudes, and so forth—with this behavior or its lack. But this means that we give up trying to define further just what these practices and institutions are, what the meanings are which they require and hence sustain. For these meanings do not fit into the grid; they are not subjective beliefs or values, but are constitutive of social reality. In order to get at them we have to drop the basic premise that social reality is made up of brute data alone. For any characterization of the meanings underlying these practices is open to question by someone offering an alternative interpretation. The negation of this is what was meant as brute data. We have to admit that intersubjective social reality has to be partly defined in terms of meanings; that meanings as subjective are not just in causal interaction with a social reality made up of brute data, but that as intersubjective they are constitutive of this reality.

We have been talking here of intersubjective meanings. And earlier I was contrasting the question of intersubjective meaning with that of consensus as convergence of opinions. But there is another kind of nonsubjective meaning which is also often inadequately discussed under the head of "consensus." In a society with a strong web of intersubjective meanings, there can be a more or less powerful set of common meanings. By these I mean notions of what is significant that are not just shared in the sense that everyone has them, but are also common in the sense of being in the common reference world. Thus, almost everyone in our society may share a susceptibility to a certain kind of feminine beauty, but this may not be a common meaning. It may be known to no one, except perhaps market researchers, who play on it in their advertisements. But the survival of a national identity as francophones is a common meaning of *Québecois;* for it is not just shared, and not just known to be shared, but its being a common aspiration is one of the common reference points of all debate, communication, and all public life in the society.

We can speak of a shared belief, aspiration, and so forth when there is convergence between the subjective beliefs, aspirations, of many individuals. But it is part of the meaning of a common aspiration, belief, celebration, that it be not just shared but part of the common reference world. Or to put it another way, its being shared is a collective act, it is a consciousness which is communally sustained, whereas sharing is something we do each on his own, as it were, even if each of us is influenced by the others.

Common meanings are the basis of community. Intersubjective meaning gives a people a common language to talk about social reality and a common understanding of certain norms, but only with common meanings does this common reference world contain significant common actions, celebrations, and feelings. These are objects in the world that everybody shares. This is what makes community.

Once again, we cannot really understand this phenomenon through the usual definition of consensus as convergence of opinion and value. For what is meant here is something more than convergence. Convergence is what happens when our values are shared. But what is required for common meanings is that this shared value be part of the common world, that this sharing be shared. But we could also say that common meanings are quite other than consensus, for they can subsist with a high degree of cleavage; this is what happens when a common meaning comes to be lived and understood differently by different groups in a society. It remains a common meaning, because there is the reference point which is the common purpose, aspiration, celebration. Such is, for example, the American Way, or freedom as understood in the U.S.A. But this common meaning is differently articulated by different groups. This is the basis of the bitterest fights in a society, and this we are also seeing in the U.S. today. Perhaps one might say that a common meaning is very often the cause of the most bitter lack of consensus. It thus must not be confused with convergence of opinion, value, attitude.

Of course, common meanings and intersubjective meanings are closely interwoven. There must be a powerful net of intersubjective meanings for there to be common meanings; and the result of powerful common meanings is the development of a greater web of intersubjective meanings as people live in community.

On the other hand, when common meanings wither, which they can do through the kind of deep dissensus we described earlier, the groups tend to grow apart and develop different languages of social reality, hence to share less intersubjective meanings.

To take our above example again, there has been a powerful common meaning in our civilization around a certain vision of the free society in which bargaining has a central place. This has helped to entrench the social practice of negotiation which makes us participate in this intersubjective meaning. But there is a severe challenge to this common meaning today, as we have seen. Should those who object to it really succeed in building up an alternative society, there would develop a gap between those who remain in the present type of society and those who had founded the new one.

Common meanings, as well as intersubjective ones, fall through the net of mainstream social science. They can find no place in its categories. For they are not simply a converging set of subjective reactions, but part of the common world. What the ontology of mainstream social science lacks is the notion of meaning as not simply for an individual subject; of a subject who can be a "we" as well as an "I." The exclusion of this possibility, of the communal, comes once again from the baleful influence of the epistemological tradition for which all knowledge has to be reconstructed from the impressions imprinted on the individual subject. But if we free ourselves from the hold of these prejudices, this seems a wildly implausible view about the development of human consciousness; we are aware of the world through a "we" before we are through an "I." Hence we need the distinction between what is just shared in the sense that each of us has it in our individual worlds, and that which is in the common world. But the very idea of something that exists in the common world in contradistinction to what exists in all the individual worlds is totally opaque to empiricist epistemology, and so finds no place in mainstream social science. What this results in must now be seen.

III.i

To sum up the last pages: a social science that wishes to fulfill the requirements of the empiricist tradition naturally tries to reconstruct social reality as consisting of brute data alone. These data are the acts of people (behavior) as identified supposedly beyond interpretation either by physical descriptions or by descriptions clearly defined by institutions and practices; and secondly, they include the subjective reality of individuals' beliefs, attitudes, values, as attested by their responses to certain forms of words, or in some cases their overt nonverbal behavior.

What this excludes is a consideration of social reality as characterized by intersubjective and common meanings. It excludes, for instance, an attempt to understand our civilization, in which negotiation plays such a central part both in fact and in justificatory theory, by probing the self-definitions of agent, other, and social relatedness which it embodies. Such definitions which deal with the meaning for agents of their own and others' action, and of the social relations in which they stand, do not in any sense record brute data, in the sense that this term is being used in this argument; that is, they are in no sense beyond challenge by those who would quarrel with our interpretations of these meanings.

I tried to adumbrate above the vision implicit in the practice of negotiation by reference to certain notions of autonomy and rationality. But this reading will undoubtedly be challenged by those who have different fundamental conceptions of man, human motivation, the human condition; or even by those who judge other features of our present predicament to have greater importance. If we wish to avoid these disputes, and have a science grounded in verification as this is understood by the logical empiricists, then we have to avoid this level of study altogether and hope to make do with a correlation of behavior that is brute-data-identifiable.

A similar point goes for the distinction between common meanings and shared subjective meanings. We can hope to identify the subjective meanings of individuals if we take these in the sense in which there are adequate criteria for them in people's dissent or assent to verbal formulae or their brute-data-identifiable behavior. But once we allow the distinction between such subjective meanings which are widely shared and genuine common meanings, then we can no longer make do with brute-data identification. We are in a domain where our definitions can be challenged by those with another reading.

The profound bias of mainstream social scientists in favor of the empiricist conception of knowledge and science makes it inevitable that they should accept the verification model of political science and the categorical principles that this entails. This means in turn that a study of our civilization in terms of its intersubjective and common meanings is ruled out. Rather this whole level of study is made invisible.

On the mainstream view, therefore, the different practices and institutions of different societies are not seen as related to different clusters of intersubjective or common meanings, rather, we should be able to differentiate them by different clusters of "behavior" and/or subjective meaning. The comparison between societies requires on this view that we elaborate a universal vocabulary of behavior which will allow us to present the different forms and practices of different societies in the same conceptual web.

Now present-day political science is contemptuous of the older attempt at comparative politics through a comparison of institutions. An influential school of our day has therefore shifted comparison to certain practices, or very general classes of practices, and proposes to compare societies according to the different ways in which these practices are carried on. Such are the "functions" of the influential "developmental approach."[11] But it is epistemologically crucial that such functions be identified independently of those intersubjective meanings which are different in different societies; for otherwise, they will not be genuinely universal; or will be universal only in the

11. Cf. Almond and Powell, *Comparative Politics.*

loose and unilluminating sense that the function name can be given application in every society but with varying, and often widely varying meaning—the same term being "glossed" very differently by different sets of practices and intersubjective meanings. The danger that such universality might not hold is not even suspected by mainstream political scientists since they are unaware that there is such a level of description as that which defines intersubjective meanings and are convinced that functions and the various structures that perform them can be identified in terms of brute data behavior.

But the result of ignoring the difference in intersubjective meanings can be disastrous to a science of comparative politics, namely, that we interpret all other societies in the categories of our own. Ironically, this is what seems to have happened to American political science. Having strongly criticized the old institution-focused comparative politics for its ethnocentricity (or Western bias), it proposes to understand the politics of all society in terms of such functions, for instance, as "interest articulation" and "interest aggregation" whose definition is strongly influenced by the bargaining culture of our civilization, but which is far from being guaranteed appropriateness elsewhere. The unsurprising result is a theory of political development which places the Atlantic-type polity at the summit of human political achievement.

Much can be said in this area of comparative politics (interestingly explored by Alasdair MacIntyre in a recently published paper[12]). But I should like to illustrate the significance of these two rival approaches in connection with another common problem area of politics. This is the question of what is called "legitimacy."[13]

III.ii

It is an obvious fact, with which politics has been concerned since at least Plato, that some societies enjoy an easier, more spontaneous

---

12. "How Is a Comparative Science of Politics Possible?" in Alasdair MacIntyre, *Against the Self-Images of the Age* (London, 1971).

13. MacIntyre's article also contains an interesting discussion of legitimacy from a different, although I think related, angle.

cohesion which relies less on the use of force than others. It has been an important question of political theory to understand what underlies this difference. Among others, Aristotle, Machiavelli, Montesquieu, de Tocqueville have dealt with it.

Contemporary mainstream political scientists approach this question with the concept "legitimacy." The use of the word here can be easily understood. Those societies that are more spontaneously cohesive can be thought to enjoy a greater sense of legitimacy among their members. But the application of the term has been shifted. "Legitimacy" is a term in which we discuss the authority of the state or polity, its right to our allegiance. However we conceive of this legitimacy, it can only be attributed to a polity in the light of a number of surrounding conceptions—for example, that it provides men freedom, that it emanates from their will, that it secures them order, the rule of law, or that it is founded on tradition, or commands obedience by its superior qualities. These conceptions are all such that they rely on definitions of what is significant for men in general or in some particular society or circumstances, definitions of paradigmatic meaning which cannot be identifiable as brute data. Even where some of these terms might be given an "operational definition" in terms of brute data—a term like "freedom," for instance, can be defined in terms of the absence of legal restriction, à la Hobbes—this definition would not carry the full force of the term, and in particular that whereby it could be considered significant for men.

According to the empiricist paradigm, this latter aspect of the meaning of such a term is labeled "evaluative" and is thought to be utterly heterogeneous from the "descriptive" aspect. But this analysis is far from firmly established; no more so in fact than the empiricist paradigm of knowledge itself with which it is closely bound up. A challenge to this paradigm in the name of a hermeneutical science is also a challenge to the distinction between "descriptive" and "evaluative" and the entire conception of *Wertfreiheit* which goes with it.

In any case, whether because it is "evaluative" or can only be applied in connection with definitions of meaning, "legitimate" is not a word which can be used in the description of social reality according to the conceptions of mainstream social science. It can only be used as a description of subjective meaning. What enters into scientific consideration is thus not the legitimacy of a polity but the opinions or feelings of its member individuals concerning its legitimacy. The differences between different societies in their manner of spontaneous cohesion and sense of community are to be understood by correlations between the beliefs and feelings of their members toward them on one hand and the prevalence of certain brute data identifiable indices of stability in them on the other.

Robert Dahl in *Modern Political Analysis* speaks of the different ways in which leaders gain "compliance" for their policies.[14] The more citizens comply because of "internal rewards and deprivations," the less leaders need to use "external rewards and deprivations." But if citizens believe a government is legitimate, then their conscience will bind them to obey it; they will be internally punished if they disobey; hence government will have to use less external resources, including force.

Less crude is the discussion of Seymour Lipset in *Political Man*, but it is founded on the same basic ideas, namely, that legitimacy defined as subjective meaning is correlated with stability. "Legitimacy involves the capacity of the system to engender and maintain the belief that the existing political institutions are the most appropriate ones for the society."[15]

Lipset is engaged in a discussion of the determinants of stability in modern polities. He singles out two important ones, effectiveness and legitimacy. "Effectiveness means actual performance, the extent to which the system satisfies the basic functions of government as most of the population and such powerful groups within it as big business or the armed forces see them" (ibid.). Thus we have one factor which has to do with objective reality, what the government has actually done; and the other which has to do with subjective beliefs and "values." "While effectiveness is primarily instrumental, legitimacy is evaluative" (ibid.). Hence from the beginning the stage is set by a distinction between social reality and what men think and feel about it.

Lipset sees two types of crisis of legitimacy that modern societies have affronted more or less well. One concerns the status of major

14. Robert Dahl, *Modern Political Analysis* (Englewood Cliffs, N.J., 1963), 31–32.
15. Seymour Lipset, *Political Man* (New York, 1963), 64.

conservative institutions that may be under threat from the development of modern industrial democracies. The second concerns the degree to which all political groups have access to the political process. Under the first head, some traditional groups, such as landed aristocracy or clericals, have been roughly handled in a society like France, and have remained alienated from the democratic system for decades afterwards; whereas in England the traditional classes were more gently handled, themselves were willing to compromise and have been slowly integrated and transformed into the new order. Under the second head, some societies managed to integrate the working class or bourgeoisie into the political process at an early stage, whereas in others they have been kept out till quite recently, and consequently, have developed a deep sense of alienation from the system, have tended to adopt extremist ideologies, and have generally contributed to instability. One of the determinants of a society's performance on these two heads is whether or not it is forced to affront the different conflicts of democratic development all at once or one at a time. Another important determinant of legitimacy is effectiveness.

This approach that sees stability as partly the result of legitimacy beliefs, and these in turn as resulting partly from the way the status, welfare, access to political life of different groups fare, seems at first blush eminently sensible and well designed to help us understand the history of the last century or two. But this approach has no place for a study of the intersubjective and common meanings which are constitutive of modern civilization. And we may doubt whether we can understand the cohesion of modern societies or their present crisis if we leave these out of account.

Let us take the winning of the allegiance of the working class to the new industrial regimes in the nineteenth and the early twentieth century. This is far from being a matter simply or even perhaps most significantly of the speed with which this class was integrated into the political process and the effectiveness of the regime. Rather the consideration of the granting of access to the political process as an independent variable may be misleading.

It is not just that we often find ourselves invited by historians to account for class cohesion in particular countries in terms of other factors, such as the impact of Methodism in early nineteenth-century

England (Elie Halévy)[16] or the draw of Germany's newly successful nationalism. These factors could be assimilated to the social scientist's grid by being classed as "ideologies" or widely held "value systems" or some other such concatenations of subjective meaning.

But perhaps the most important such "ideology" in accounting for the cohesion of industrial democratic societies has been that of the society of work, the vision of society as a large-scale enterprise of production in which widely different functions are integrated into interdependence; a vision of society in which economic relations are considered as primary, as it is not only in Marxism (and in a sense not really with Marxism) but above all with the tradition of classical utilitarianism. In line with this vision there is a fundamental solidarity between all members of society that labor (to use Arendt's language),[17] for they are all engaged in producing what is indispensable to life and happiness in far-reaching interdependence.

This is the "ideology" that has frequently presided over the integration of the working class into industrial democracies, at first directed polemically against the "unproductive" classes, for example, in England with the Anti-Corn-Law League, and later with the campaigns of Joseph Chamberlain ("when Adam delved and Eve span/ who was then the gentleman"), but later as a support for social cohesion and solidarity.

Of course the reason for putting "ideology" in quotes above is that this definition of things, which has been well integrated with the conception of social life as based on negotiation, cannot be understood in the terms of mainstream social science as beliefs and "values" held by a large number of individuals. For the great interdependent matrix of labor is not just a set of ideas in people's heads but is an important aspect of the reality that we live in modern society. And at the same time these ideas are embedded in this matrix in that they are constitutive of it; that is, we would not be able to live in this type of society unless we were imbued with these ideas or some others that could call forth the discipline and voluntary coordination needed to operate this kind of economy. All industrial civilizations have required a huge wrench from the traditional peasant populations on

16. *Histoire du peuple anglais au XIX* siècle* (Paris, 1913).
17. *The Human Condition* (New York, 1959).

which they have been imposed; for they require an entirely unprecedented level of disciplined, sustained, monotonous effort, long hours unpunctuated by any meaningful rhythm, such as that of seasons or festivals. In the end this way of life can only be accepted when the idea of making a living is endowed with more significance than that of just avoiding starvation; and this it is in the civilization of labor.

Now this civilization of work is only one aspect of modern societies, along with the society based on negotiation and willed relations (in Anglo-Saxon countries), and other common and intersubjective meanings which have different importance in different countries. My point is that it is certainly not implausible to say that it has some importance in explaining the integration of the working class in modern industrial democratic society. But it can only be called a cluster of intersubjective meaning. As such it cannot come into the purview of mainstream political science; and an author like Lipset cannot take it into consideration when discussing this very problem.

But, of course, such a massive fact does not escape notice. What happens rather is that it is reinterpreted. And what has generally happened is that the interdependent productive and negotiating society has been recognized by political science, but not as one structure of intersubjective meaning among others, rather as the inescapable background of social action as such. In this guise it no longer need be an object of study. Rather it retreats to the middle distance, where its general outline takes the role of universal framework, within which (it is hoped) actions and structures will be brute-data-identifiable, and this for any society at any time. The view is then that the political actions of men in all societies can be understood as variants of the processing of "demands" which is an important part of our political life. The inability to recognize the specificity of our intersubjective meanings is thus inseparably linked with the belief in the universality of North Atlantic behavior types or "functions" which vitiates so much of contemporary comparative politics.

The notion is that what politics is about perennially is the adjustment of differences, or the production of symbolic and effective "outputs" on the basis of demand and support "inputs." The rise of the intersubjective meaning of the civilization of work is seen as the increase of correct perception of the political process at the expense of "ideology." Thus Almond and Powell introduce the concept of "political secularization" to describe "the emergence of a pragmatic, empirical orientation" to politics. A secular political culture is opposed not only to a traditional one, but also to an "ideological" culture, which is characterized by "an inflexible image of political life, closed to conflicting information" and "fails to develop the open, bargaining attitudes associated with full secularization."[18] The clear understanding here is that a secularized culture is one which essentially depends less on illusion, which sees things as they are, which is not infected with the "false consciousness" of traditional or ideological culture (to use a term which is not in the mainstream vocabulary).

III.iii

This way of looking at the civilization of work, as resulting from the retreat of illusion before the correct perception of what politics perennially and really is, is closely bound up with the epistemological premises of mainstream political science and its resultant inability to recognize the historical specificity of this civilization's intersubjective meanings. But the weakness of this approach, already visible in the attempts to explain the rise of this civilization and its relation to others, becomes even more painful when we try to account for its present malaise, even crisis.

The strains in contemporary society, the breakdown of civility, the rise of deep alienation, which is translated into even more destructive action, tend to shake the basic categories of our social science. It is not just that such a development was quite unpredicted by this science, which saw in the rise of affluence the cause rather of a further entrenching of the bargaining culture, a reduction of irrational cleavage, an increase of tolerance, in short "the end of ideology." For prediction, as we shall see below, cannot be a goal of social science as it is of natural science. It is rather that this mainstream science does not have the categories to explain this breakdown. It is forced to look on extremism either as a bargaining gambit of the desperate, deliberately raising the ante in order to force a hear-

18. *Comparative Politics*, 58, 61.

ing. Alternatively, it can recognize the novelty of the rebellion by accepting the hypothesis that heightened demands are being made on the system owing to a revolution of "expectations," or else to the eruption of new desires or aspirations which hitherto had no place in the bargaining process. But these new desires or aspirations must be in the domain of individual psychology, that is, they must be such that their arousal and satisfaction is to be understood in terms of states of individuals rather than in terms of the intersubjective meanings in which they live. For these latter have no place in the categories of the mainstream, which cannot accommodate a genuine historical psychology.

But some of the more extreme protests and acts of rebellion in our society cannot be interpreted as bargaining gambits in the name of any demands, old or new. These can only be interpreted within the accepted framework of our social science as a return to ideology, and hence as irrational. Now in the case of some of the more bizarre and bloody forms of protest, there will be little disagreement; they will be judged irrational by all but their protagonists. But within the accepted categories this irrationality can only be understood in terms of individual psychology; it is the public eruption of private pathology; it cannot be understood as a malady of society itself, a malaise which afflicts its constitutive meanings.[19]

No one can claim to begin to have an adequate explanation for these major changes which our civilization is undergoing. But in contrast to the incapacity of a science which remains within the accepted categories, a hermeneutical science of man that has a place for a study of intersubjective meaning can at least begin to explore fruitful avenues. Plainly the discipline that was integral to the civilization of work and bargaining is beginning to fail. The structures of this

19. Thus Lewis Feuer, in *The Conflict of Generations* (New York, 1969), attempts to account for the "misperception of social reality" in the Berkeley student uprising in terms of a generational conflict (466–70), which in turn is rooted in the psychology of adolescence and attaining adulthood. Yet Feuer himself in his first chapter notes the comparative recency of self-defining political generations, a phenomenon which dates from the post-Napoleonic era (33). But an adequate attempt to explain his historical shift, which after all underlies the Berkeley rising and many others, would, I believe, have taken us beyond the ambit of individual psychology to psychohistory, to a study of the intrication of psychological conflict and intersubjective meanings. A variant of this form of study has been adumbrated in the work of Erik Erikson.

civilization, interdependent work, bargaining, mutual adjustment of individual ends, are beginning to change their meaning for many, and are beginning to be felt not as normal and best suited to man, but as hateful or empty. And yet we are all caught in these intersubjective meanings insofar as we live in this society, and in a sense more and more all-pervasively as it progresses. Hence the virulence and tension of the critique of our society which is always in some real sense a self-rejection (in a way that the old socialist opposition never was).

Why has this set of meanings gone sour? Plainly, we have to accept that they are not to be understood at their face value. The free, productive, bargaining culture claimed to be sufficient for man. If it was not, then we have to assume that while it did hold our allegiance, it also had other meanings for us that commanded this allegiance and that have now gone.

This is the starting point of a set of hypotheses which attempt to redefine our past in order to make our present and future intelligible. We might think that in the past the productive, bargaining culture offered common meanings (even though there was no place for them in its philosophy), and hence a basis for community, that were essentially linked with its being in the process of building. It linked men who could see themselves as breaking with the past to build a new happiness in America, for instance. But in all essentials that future is built; the notion of a horizon to be attained by future greater production (as against social transformation) verges on the absurd in contemporary America. Suddenly the horizon that was essential to the sense of meaningful purpose has collapsed, which would show that like so many other Enlightenment-based dreams the free, productive, bargaining society can only sustain man as a goal, not as a reality.

Or we can look at this development in terms of identity. A sense of building their future through the civilization of work can sustain men as long as they see themselves as having broken with a millennial past of injustice and hardship in order to create qualitatively different conditions for their children. All the requirements of a humanly acceptable identity can be met by this predicament, a relation to the past (one soars above it but preserves it in folkloric memory), to the social world (the interdependent world of free, productive men), to the earth (the raw material which awaits shaping), to the future and one's own death (the everlasting monument in the lives of prosperous children), to the absolute (the absolute values of freedom, integrity, dignity).

But at some point the children will be unable to sustain this forward thrust into the future. This effort has placed them in a private haven of security, within which they are unable to reach and recover touch with the great realities: their parents have only a negated past, lives which have been oriented wholly to the future; the social world is distant and without shape; rather one can only insert oneself into it by taking one's place in the future-oriented productive juggernaut. But this now seems without any sense; the relation to the earth as raw material is therefore experienced as empty and alienating, but the recovery of a valid relation to the earth is the hardest thing once lost; and there is no relation to the absolute where we are caught in the web of meanings which have gone dead for us. Hence past, future, earth, world, and absolute are in some way or another occluded; and what must arise is an identity crisis of frightening proportions.

These two hypotheses are mainly focused on the crisis in American society, and they would perhaps help account for the fact that the United States is in some sense going first through this crisis of all Atlantic nations; not, that is, only because it is the most affluent, but more because it has been more fully based on the civilization of work than European countries who retained something of more traditional common meanings.

But they might also help us to understand why alienation is most severe among groups which have been but marginal in affluent bargaining societies. These have had the greatest strain in living in this civilization while their identity was in some ways antithetical to it. Such are blacks in the United States, and the community of French-speaking Canadians, each in different ways. For many immigrant groups the strain was also great, but they forced themselves to surmount the obstacles, and the new identity is sealed in the blood of the old, as it were.

But for those who would not or could not succeed in transforming themselves, but always lived a life of strain on the defensive, the breakdown of the central, powerful identity is the trigger to a deep turnover. It can be thought of as a liberation, but at the same time it is deeply unsettling, because the basic parameters of former life are being changed, and there are not yet the new images and definitions to live a new fully acceptable identity. In a sense we are in a condition where a new social compact (rather the first social compact) has to be made between these groups and those they live with, and no one knows where to start.

In the last pages, I have presented some hypotheses which may appear very speculative; and they may indeed turn out to be without foundation, even without much interest. But their aim was mainly illustrative. My principal claim is that we can only come to grips with this phenomenon of breakdown by trying to understand more clearly and profoundly the common and intersubjective meanings of the society in which we have been living. For it is these which no longer hold us, and to understand this change we have to have an adequate grasp of these meanings. But this we cannot do as long as we remain within the ambit of mainstream social science, for it will not recognize intersubjective meaning, and is forced to look at the central ones of our society as though they were the inescapable background of all political action. Breakdown is thus inexplicable in political terms; it is an outbreak of irrationality which must ultimately be explained by some form of psychological illness.

Mainstream science may thus venture into the area explored by the above hypotheses, but after its own fashion, by forcing the psychohistorical facts of identity into the grid of an individual psychology, in short, by reinterpreting all meanings as subjective. The result might be a psychological theory of emotional maladjustment, perhaps traced to certain features of family background, analogous to the theories of the authoritarian personality and the California F-scale. But this would no longer be a political or a social theory. We would be giving up the attempt to understand the change in social reality at the level of its constitutive intersubjective meanings.

IV

It can be argued, then, that mainstream social science is kept within certain limits by its categorical principles which are rooted in the traditional epistemology of empiricism; and secondly, that these restrictions are a severe handicap and prevent us from coming to grips with important problems of our day, which should be the object of political science. We need to go beyond the bounds of a science based on verification to one which would study the intersubjective and common meanings embedded in social reality.

But this science would be hermeneutical in the sense that has been developed in this paper. It would not be founded on brute data; its most primitive data would be readings of meanings, and its object would have the three properties mentioned above: the meanings are for a subject in a field or fields; they are, moreover, meanings which are partially constituted by self-definitions, which are in this sense already interpretations, and which can thus be reexpressed or made explicit by a science of politics. In our case, the subject may be a society or community; but the intersubjective meanings, as we saw, embody a certain self-definition, a vision of the agent and his society, which is that of the society or community.

But then the difficulties which the proponents of the verification model foresee will arise. If we have a science that has no brute data, that relies on readings, then it cannot but move in a hermeneutical circle. A given reading of the intersubjective meanings of a society, or of given institutions or practices, may seem well founded, because it makes sense of these practices or the development of that society. But the conviction that it does make sense of this history itself is founded on further related readings. Thus, what I said above on the identity crisis which is generated by our society makes sense and holds together only if one accepts this reading of the intersubjective meanings of our society, and if one accepts this reading of the rebellion against our society by many young people (sc. the reading in terms of identity crisis). These two readings make sense together, so that in a sense the explanation as a whole reposes on the readings, and the readings in their turn are strengthened by the explanation as a whole.

But if these readings seem implausible, or even more, if they are not understood by our interlocutor, there is no verification procedure that we can fall back on. We can only continue to offer interpretations; we are in an interpretative circle.

But the ideal of a science of verification is to find an appeal beyond differences of interpretation. Insight will always be useful in discovery, but should not have to play any part in establishing the truth of its findings. This ideal can be said to have been met by our natural sciences. But a hermeneutic science cannot but rely on insight. It requires that one have the sensibility and understanding necessary to be able to make and comprehend the readings by which we can explain the reality concerned. In physics we might argue that if someone does not accept a true theory, then either he has not been shown enough (brute data) evidence (perhaps not enough is yet available), or he cannot understand and apply some formalized language. But in the sciences of man conceived as hermeneutical, the nonacceptance of a true or illuminating theory may come from neither of these, indeed is unlikely to be due to either of these, but rather from a failure to grasp the meaning field in question, an inability to make and understand readings of this field.

In other words, in a hermeneutical science, a certain measure of insight is indispensable, and this insight cannot be communicated by the gathering of brute data, or initiation in modes of formal reasoning or some combination of these. It is unformalizable. But this is a scandalous result according to the authoritative conception of science in our tradition, which is shared even by many of those who are highly critical of the approach of mainstream psychology, or sociology, or political science. For it means that this is not a study in which anyone can engage, regardless of their level of insight; that some claims of the form "If you don't understand, then your intuitions are at fault, are blind or inadequate," some claims of this form will be justified; that some differences will be nonarbitrable by further evidence, but that each side can only make appeal to deeper insight on the part of the other. The superiority of one position over another will thus consist in this, that from the more adequate position one can understand one's own stand and that of one's opponent, but not the other way around. It goes without saying that this argument can only have weight for those in the superior position.

Thus, a hermeneutical science encounters a gap in intuitions, which is the other side, as it were, of the hermeneutical circle. But the situation is graver than this; for this gap is bound up with our divergent options in politics and life.

We speak of a gap when some cannot understand the kind of self-definition which others are proposing as underlying a certain society or set of institutions. Thus some positivistically minded thinkers will find the language of identity theory quite opaque: and some thinkers will not recognize any theory which does not fit with the categorical presuppositions of empiricism. But self-definitions are not only important to us as scientists who are trying to understand some, perhaps distant, social reality. As men we are self-defining beings, and we are partly what we are in virtue of the self-definitions which we have accepted, however we have come by them. What self-definitions we understand and what ones we do not understand are closely linked with the self-definitions that help to constitute what we are. If it is too simple to say that one only understands an "ideology" which one subscribes to, it is nevertheless hard to deny that we have great difficulty grasping definitions whose terms structure the world in ways that are utterly different from, incompatible with, our own.

Hence the gap in intuitions does not just divide different theoretical positions, it also tends to divide different fundamental options in life. The practical and the theoretical are inextricably joined here. It may not just be that to understand a certain explanation one has to sharpen one's intuitions, it may be that one has to change one's orientation—if not in adopting another orientation, at least in living one's own in a way which allows for greater comprehension of others. Thus, in the sciences of man insofar as they are hermeneutical there can be a valid response to "I don't understand" which takes the form, not only "develop your intuitions," but more radically "change yourself." This puts an end to any aspiration to a value-free or "ideology-free" science of man. A study of the science of man is inseparable from an examination of the options between which men must choose.

This means that we can speak here not only of error, but of illusion. We speak of "illusion" when we are dealing with something of greater substance than error, error that in a sense builds a counterfeit reality of its own. But errors of interpretation of meaning, which are also self-definitions of those who interpret and hence inform their lives, are more than errors in this sense: they are sustained by certain practices of which they are constitutive. It is not implausible to single out as examples two rampant illusions in our present society. One is that of the proponents of the bargaining society who can recognize nothing but either bargaining gambits or madness in those who rebel against this society. Here the error is sustained by the practices of the bargaining culture, and given a semblance of reality by the refusal to treat any protests on other terms; it hence acquires the more substantive reality of illusion. The second example is provided by much "revolutionary" activity in our society which in desperate search for an alternative mode of life purports to see its situation in that of an Andean guerilla or Chinese peasants. Lived out, this passes from the stage of laughable error to tragic illusion. One illusion cannot recognize the possibility of human variation, the other cannot see any limits to mankind's ability to transform itself. Both make a valid science of man impossible.

In face of all this, we might be so scandalized by the prospect of such a hermeneutical science, that we will want to go back to the verification model. Why can we not take our understanding of meaning as part of the logic of discovery, as the logical empiricists suggest for our unformalizable insights, and still found our science on the exactness of our predictions? Our insightful understanding of the intersubjective meanings of our society will then serve to elaborate fruitful hypotheses, but the proof of these puddings will remain in the degree to which they enable us to predict.

The answer is that if the epistemological views underlying the science of interpretation are right, such exact prediction is radically impossible. This, for three reasons of ascending order of fundamentalness.

The first is the well-known "open system" predicament, one shared by human life and meteorology, that we cannot shield a certain domain of human events, the psychological, economic, political, from external interference; it is impossible to delineate a closed system.

The second, more fundamental, is that if we are to understand men by a science of interpretation, we cannot achieve the degree of fine exactitude of a science based on brute data. The data of natural science admit of measurement to virtually any degree of exactitude. But different interpretations cannot be judged in this way. At the same time different nuances of interpretation may lead to different predictions in some circumstances, and these different outcomes may eventually create widely varying futures. Hence it is more than easy to be wide of the mark.

But the third and most fundamental reason for the impossibility of hard prediction is that man is a self-defining animal. With changes in his self-definition go changes in what man is, such that he has to be understood in different terms. But the conceptual mutations in human history can and frequently do produce conceptual webs which are incommensurable, that is, where the terms cannot be defined in relation to a common stratum of expressions. The entirely different notions of bargaining in our society and in some primitive ones provide an example. Each will be glossed in terms of practices, institutions, ideas in each society which have nothing corresponding to them in the other.

The success of prediction in the natural sciences is bound up with the fact that all states of the system, past and future, can be described in the same range of concepts, as values, say, of the same variables. Hence all future states of the solar system can be characterized, as past ones are, in the language of Newtonian mechanics. This is far from being a sufficient condition of exact prediction, but it is a necessary one in this sense, that only if past and future are brought under the same conceptual net can one understand the states of the latter as some function of the states of the former, and hence predict.

This conceptual unity is vitiated in the sciences of man by the fact of conceptual innovation, which in turn alters human reality. The very terms in which the future will have to be characterized if we are to understand it properly are not all available to us at present. Hence we have such radically unpredictable events as the culture of youth today, the Puritan rebellion of the sixteenth and seventeenth centuries, the development of Soviet society, and so forth.

And thus, it is much easier to understand after the fact than it is to predict. Human science is largely *ex post* understanding. Or often one has the sense of impending change, of some big reorganization, but is powerless to make clear what it will consist in: one lacks the vocabulary. But there is a clear asymmetry here, which there is not (or not supposed to be) in natural science, where events are said to be predicted from the theory with exactly the same ease with which one explains past events and by exactly the same process. In human science this will never be the case.

Of course, we strive *ex post* to understand the changes, and to do this we try to develop a language in which we can situate the incommensurable webs of concepts. We see the rise of Puritanism, for instance, as a shift in man's stance to the sacred; and thus, we have a language in which we can express both stances—the earlier medieval Catholic one and the Puritan rebellion—as "glosses" on this fundamental term. We thus have a language in which to talk of the transition. But think how we acquired it. This general category of the sacred is acquired not only from our experience of the shift that came in the Reformation, but from the study of human religion in general, including primitive religion, and with the detachment that came with secularization. It would be conceivable, but unthinkable, that a medieval Catholic could have this conception—or for that matter a Puritan. These two protagonists only had a language of condemnation for each other: "heretic," "idolator." The place for such a concept was preempted by a certain way of living the sacred. After a big change has happened, and the trauma has been resorbed, it is possible to try to understand it, because one now has available the new language, the transformed meaning world. But hard prediction before just makes one a laughingstock. Really to be able to predict the future would be to have explicited so clearly the human condition that one would already have preempted all cultural innovation and transformation. This is hardly in the bounds of the possible.

Sometimes men show amazing prescience: the myth of Faust, for instance, which is treated several times at the beginning of the modern era. There is a kind of prophesy here, a premonition. But what characterizes these bursts of foresight is that they see through a glass darkly, for they see in terms of the old language: Faust sells his soul to the devil. They are in no sense hard predictions. Human science looks backward. It is inescapably historical.

There are thus good grounds both in epistemological arguments and in their greater fruitfulness for opting for hermeneutical sciences of man. But we cannot hide from ourselves how greatly this option breaks with certain commonly held notions about our scientific tradition. We cannot measure such sciences against the requirements of a science of verification: we cannot judge them by their predictive capacity. We have to accept that they are founded on intuitions which all do not share, and what is worse, that these intuitions are closely bound up with our fundamental options. These sciences cannot be *wertfrei;* they are moral sciences in a more radical sense than the eighteenth century understood. Finally, their successful prosecution requires a high degree of self-knowledge, a freedom from illusion, in the sense of error which is rooted and expressed in one's way of life; for our incapacity to understand is rooted in our own self-definitions, hence in what we are. To say this is not to say anything new: Aristotle makes a similar point in Book I of the *Ethics.* But it is still radically shocking and unassimilable to the mainstream of modern science.

2

The Problem of Historical Consciousness

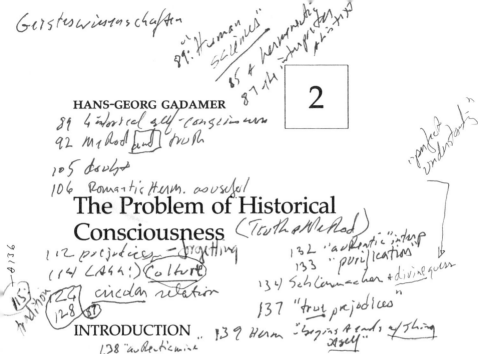

INTRODUCTION

When in 1957 I received the invitation to teach half a semester at the Cardinal Mercier Chair at the University of Louvain, I found myself in the middle of my interpretation of hermeneutic philosophy as I had conceived it from hermeneutic praxis during a quarter century of academic activity. To be called to this chair as a German and as a Protestant imposed obligations and I owe to this institution the first premature formulation of several central ideas in my work then in progress. When the French version of these lectures appeared in 1963—no German text exists—my larger book [*Wahrheit und Methode*] had already been published and hence the publication of the lectures seemed to me almost superfluous and at best a preliminary substitute in French for the larger work which is still only available

Translated by Jeff L. Close from *Le Problème de la conscience historique* (Louvain: Institut Supérieur de Philosophie, Université Catholique de Louvain, 1963). English translation published in the *Graduate Faculty Philosophy Journal* 5, no. 1 (1975). Introduction (1975) translated by Hans Fantel. Reprinted by permission. The translator gratefully acknowledges Mr. Daniel Cerezuelle's careful reading of the entire manuscript, and thanks especially Professor Gadamer for his many helpful suggestions on the translation. The translator enjoyed the tireless assistance of Mrs. Norma Newberg in the final preparation of the manuscript.

in German.[1] I have distanced myself from the ideas as I had developed them at the time, and it is now, on the occasion of their present English translation, that I reread these lectures for the first time—after a span of nearly twenty years. An Italian translation of the French original text was published in 1969, but this translation already took account of the larger book and presented the text within the problematic that had been developed since.

The present reencounter with myself does not imply the rediscovery of early stages of my later thought because *Wahrheit und Methode* had already been completed at the time I wrote my French lectures. Yet this preliminary formulation of later work does imply a new emphasis because the ideational themes confronted in the manuscript had to establish their validity independently of the larger context which later surrounded them. These lectures, like any other, contain elements marked by the occasion. The role imposed by the specific location, the Institut Supérieur de Philosophie of a university which was then still Flemish-French, is particularly evident in the attempt to introduce the hermeneutic problem from the perspective of Husserl and Heidegger, whose work then stood at the center of the Institute's concerns. Neither was the choice of the topic, the problem of historical consciousness, without a particular motivation. For although the genesis of a "historical consciousness" is a process involving all of Europe, it was only in Germany that historical consciousness played a central philosophic role, especially through Wilhelm Dilthey and his so-called *Lebensphilosophie*. The Romantic tradition of the *Geisteswissenschaften* therefore had to be especially invoked outside the German cultural sphere.

This determined the choice of the topic and posed the task to accomplishing the transition from a hermeneutic methodology, in the sense of Schleiermacher and Dilthey, to a hermeneutic philosophy in the context of the special position of the *Geisteswissenschaften* relative to the natural sciences.

It is a self-contained pattern of argument which also constitutes the central position of the latter book. It is presented here with its

1. [Now see H. G. Gadamer, *Truth and Method,* ed. Garrett Barden and John Cumming (New York: Seabury Press, 1975).]

own stringency as proof. In *Wahrheit und Methode* I have deliberately cited another instance at first, namely the experience of art and the hermeneutic dimension that certainly plays a part in the scientific approach to art, but above all, in the experience of art itself. That is generally evident in the reproductive arts in as much as reproduction is an interpretation which implies a certain *understanding* of the original text. In view of the hermeneutic experiences in the reproductive arts one is more likely to admit that there is no unequivocal objectivity and that every interpreter submits "his own" interpretation, which is nevertheless by no means arbitrary but may attain, or fail to attain, a definable degree of appropriateness. Similarly, nobody in this sphere will claim the concept of objectivity for this ideal of appropriateness. Too much of the specifically individual of the interpreter enters into the reproduction.

This reference to the reproductive arts stands in total contradiction to the theoretical orientation [*wissenschaftstheoretischen Orientierung*] under which the *Geisteswissenschaften,* particularly in Dilthey's conception, seek parity with the natural sciences. Interpretation in these two areas is certainly not similar. To be sure, the "appropriate" understanding of a text introduces into the *Geisteswissenschaften* something of the interpreter's location in time, place, and world view, but in contrast to artistic interpretation the understanding of the text as linguistically mediated in its interpretation is not independent from the original as an autonomous creation. It is not the case as in artistic interpretation that the original is "realized" only in the concrete substance of word, gesture, or tone. Reading, as distinguished from restorative "recital," does not posit itself for its own sake; it is not an autonomous realization of a thought pattern but remains subordinate to the text regenerated by the reading process. The reading is sublated in the reading of the text.

But ultimately this is also the intent guiding the interpretive process of the *Geisteswissenschaften.* Despite all the differences which separate (by circumspective linguistic expression and conceptual mediation) the interpretation from the substance of reading, there is no intention to place the realization of the text aside from the text itself. On the contrary, the ultimate ideal of appropriateness seems to be total self-effacement because the meaning [*Verständnis*] of the text has become self-evident.

All these phenomena comprise both understanding and interpretation. If Dilthey saw his task in providing an epistemic basis [*erkenntnistheoretische Grundlegung*] for the *Geisteswissenschaften,* he regarded himself not so much as a philologist understanding a text, but as a methodologist of a historical school which did not regard the "understanding of texts or other remnants of the past as its ultimate aim." These are regarded as means to the recognition of this historical reality which they make accessible. For Dilthey, as the successor of Schleiermacher, philology also remains the guiding model. His ideal is to decode the Book of History. This is the method by which Dilthey hopes to justify the self-understanding of the *verstehenden Wissenschaften* (interpretive sciences) and their scientific objectivity. Just as one understands a text because it contains "pure meaning," so history is ultimately to be understood. Hermeneutics is the universal method of the historical sciences.

My analysis of Dilthey's position attempts to show that Dilthey's theoretical self-understanding in regard to the sciences is not truly consistent with his basic position in terms of *Lebensphilosophie.* What Misch and Dilthey have termed the "free distance toward oneself" [*freie Ferne zu sich selbst*]—that is, the human possibility of reflexive thought—does not in truth coincide with the objectivation of knowledge through scientific method. The latter requires its own explication. This lies in the connection between "life," which always implies consciousness and reflexivity [*Besinnung*], and "science," which develops from life as one of its possibilities. If this is the true problem, it places the foundation of the *Geisteswissenschaften* at the center of philosophy.

This is clearly evident in Heidegger's philosophical premise. Although I bypass Heidegger's philosophic intent, the revival of the "problem of Being," it becomes nevertheless clear that only the vivid thematization of human existence as "being-in-the-world" discloses the full implications of *Verstehen* as an existential possibility and structure. The human sciences thereby attain an ontological valence which could not remain without consequences for their methodological self-understanding. If *Verstehen* is the basic moment of human *in-der-Welt-sein,* then the human sciences are nearer to human self-understanding than are the natural sciences. The objectivity of the latter is no longer an unequivocal and obligatory ideal of knowledge.

typical Gadamer BS .

Because the human sciences contribute to human self-understanding even though they do not approach the natural sciences in exactness and objectivity, they do contribute to human self-understanding because they in turn are based in human self-understanding.

Here something essentially new becomes apparent. It lies in the positive role of the determination by tradition [*Traditionsbestimmtheit*] which historical knowledge and the epistemology of the human sciences share with the basic nature of human existence. It is true that the prejudices that dominate us often impair true recognition of the historical past. But without prior self-understanding, which is prejudice in this sense, and without readiness for self-criticism—which is also grounded in our self-understanding—historical understanding would be neither possible nor meaningful. Only through others do we gain true knowledge of ourselves. Yet this implies that historical knowledge does not necessarily lead to the dissolution of the tradition in which we live; it can also enrich this tradition, confirm or alter it—in short, contribute to the discovery of our own identity. The historiography of different nations is ample proof of this.

This state of affairs necessarily leads to a gain in clarity if one dared to analyze the formation of science in modern times. In fact, this was one of the first recognitions I gained from Aristotle—to apprehend the peculiar interlacing of being and knowledge, determination through one's own becoming, *hexis*, recognition of the situational Good, and *logos*. When Aristotle, in the sixth book of the *Nicomachean Ethics*, distinguishes the manner of practical knowledge, determined in this manner, from theoretical and technical knowledge, he expresses in my opinion one of the greatest truths by which the Greeks throw light upon scientific mystification of modern society of specialization. In addition, the scientific character of practical philosophy is, as far as I can see, the only methodological model for self-understanding of the human sciences if they are to be liberated from the spurious narrowing imposed by the model of the natural sciences. It imparts a scientific justification to the practical reason which sustains all human society and which is linked through millennia to the tradition of rhetoric. Here the hermeneutic problem becomes central; only the concretization of the general imparts to it its specific content.

In a final lecture I develop the theoretical consequence resulting from these thoughts concerning a philosophic grounding of hermeneutics. In particular, the traditional theory of the hermeneutic circle gains a new aspect and fundamental significance. It is not only the formal relation between the anticipation of the whole and the construction of the particulars, as we may remember it from our Latin lesson in the admonition to "construe," and which actually constitutes the circular structure of textual understanding. The hermeneutic circle is in fact a contentually fulfilled [*inhaltlich erfüllter*] circle, which joins the interpreter and his text into a unity within a processual whole. Understanding always implies a preunderstanding which is in turn prefigured by the determinate tradition in which the interpreter lives and that shapes his prejudices. Every encounter with others therefore means the suspension of one's own prejudices, whether this involves another person through whom one learns one's own nature and limits, or an encounter with a work of art ("There is no place which does not see you. You must alter your life"), or a text: always something more is demanded than to understand the other, that is to seek and acknowledge the immanent coherence contained within the meaning claim of the other. A further invitation is always implied. Like an infinite idea, what is also implied is a transcendental demand for coherence in which the ideal of truth is located. But this requires a readiness to recognize the other as potentially right and to let him or it prevail against me.

It is a grave misunderstanding to assume that emphasis on the essential factor of tradition which enters into all understanding implies an uncritical acceptance of tradition and sociopolitical conservatism. Whoever reads the present sketch of my hermeneutic theory will recognize that such an assumption reduces hermeneutics to an idealistic and historical self-conception. In truth the confrontation of our historic tradition is always a critical challenge of this tradition. Such confrontation does not occur in the workshops of the philologist or historian or in the eagerness of bourgeois cultural institutions to impart historical education. Every experience is such a confrontation.

In *Wahrheit und Methode* I have tried to describe more accurately and in a larger context how this process of challenge mediates the new by the old and thus constitutes a communicative process built on the model of dialogue. From this I derive hermeneutics' claim to universality. It signifies nothing less than that language forms the base of everything constituting man and society. In the present lectures only the very last sentence refers to language and relatedne to language [*Sprachlichkeit, Sprachbezogenheit, Sprachfähigkeit*] as the basis of all understanding.

Every experience is a confrontation. Because every experience sets something new against something old and in every case it remains open in principle whether the new will prevail—that is, will truly become experience—or whether the old, accustomed, predictable will be confirmed in the end. We know that even in the empirical sciences, as particularly Thomas Kuhn has shown in the meantime, not every new recognition is accepted without resistance. Rather, it is set aside as long as possible by the prevailing "paradigm." So it is basically with all experience. It must either overcome tradition or fail because of tradition. The new would be nothing new if it did not have to assert itself anew against something.

In a civilization social consciousness is determined by progress in science, perfection of technology, increase in affluence and the ideal of profit—and perhaps also by intimations of the end of this dream—newness and novelty fare badly just because the old no longer offers real resistance and no longer finds an advocate. This is probably the most important aspect in the historical consciousness which today is characterized as bourgeois: not that everything old is relativized, but that the relativized new lends a possible justification to the old.

It is not true that the question concerning that which is must always be resolved in favor of the quickly obsolete new, nor in favor of that which has been. Admittedly, historical relativism has cut the ground from under the intellectual absolution [*Repristinationen*] of earlier modes of thought and all naive systemization. But the question of philosophy cannot rest. It cannot be reduced to its social function nor can it be encompassed by rejection or legitimation based in the critique of ideology. Historical consciousness has already transcended all this in order to catch up—however belatedly—with the questioning which we call philosophy.

EPISTEMOLOGICAL PROBLEMS OF THE HUMAN SCIENCES

The subject of these lectures derives from the epistemological problem currently raised by the modern *Geisteswissenschaften*.

The appearance of historical self-consciousness is very likely the most important revolution among those we have undergone since the beginning of the modern epoch. Its spiritual magnitude probably surpasses what we recognize in the applications of natural science, applications which have so visibly transformed the surface of our planet. The historical consciousness which characterizes contemporary man is a privilege, perhaps even a burden, the like of which has never been imposed on any previous generation.

Our present-day consciousness of history is fundamentally different from the manner in which the past appeared to any foregoing people or epoch. We understand historical consciousness to be the privilege of modern man to have a full awareness of the historicity of everything present and the relativity of all opinions. Inescapably, we must acknowledge the effect of historical self-consciousness on the spiritual activity of our contemporaries: we have only to think of the immense spiritual upheavals of our times. For example, the invasion of philosophical and political thought by ideas designated in German by the words *Weltanschauung* and *Kampf der Weltanschauungen* is undoubtedly at once a consequence and a symptom of historical consciousness. It is manifest again in the way various *Weltanschauungen* currently express their differences. As a matter of fact, if, as has happened more than once, disputing parties come to a reciprocal agreement that their opposing positions form a comprehensible and coherent whole (a concession which clearly presupposes that both sides no longer refuse to reflect on the relativity of their own positions), then each party must have been fully conscious of the *particular* character of its own perspective. Today no one can shield himself from this reflexivity characteristic of the modern spirit. Henceforth it would be absurd to confine oneself to the naiveté and reassuring limits of a jealous tradition while modern consciousness is ready to understand the possibility of a multiplicity of relative viewpoints. Thus we are accustomed to respond to opposing arguments by a reflection which deliberately places us in the perspective of the other.

The modern historical sciences or *Geisteswissenschaften*—let us translate the term by "human sciences," realizing that it is only a convention—are distinguished by this mode of reflection and make methodic use of it. Is not this mode of reflection what we commonly mean by "having an historical sense"? We can define "historical sense" by the historian's openness to and talent for understanding the past, sometimes even the "exotic" past, from within its own genetic context. Having an historical sense is to conquer in a consistent manner the natural naiveté which makes us judge the past by the so-called obvious scales of our current life, in the perspective of our institutions, and from our acquired values and truths. Having an historical sense signifies thinking explicitly about the historical horizon which is coextensive with the life we live and have lived.

In its spiritual motifs, the method of the human sciences dates back to Herder and German Romanticism, but it has diffused nearly everywhere and exerted its influence on the scientific progress of other countries. In obedience to this method modern life begins refusing to naively follow a tradition or complex of traditionally assumed truths. Modern consciousness—precisely as historical consciousness—takes a reflexive position concerning all that is handed down by tradition. Historical consciousness no longer listens sanctimoniously to the voice that reaches out from the past but, in reflecting on it, replaces it within the context where it took root in order to see the significance and relative value proper to it. This reflexive posture towards tradition is called *interpretation*. And if something is able to characterize the truly universal dimension of this event it is surely the role that the word *interpretation* has begun to play in the modern human sciences. This word has achieved a recognition as only happens to words which betoken the attitude of an entire epoch.

We speak of interpretation when the meaning of a text is not understood at first sight; then an interpretation is necessary. In other words, an explicit reflection is required on the conditions that enable the text to have one or another meaning. The first presupposition that implies the concept of interpretation is the "foreign" character of what is yet to be understood. Indeed, whatever is immediately evident, whatever persuades us by its simple presence, does not call for any interpretation. If we consider for a moment the art of our predecessors in textual interpretation, as applied in philology and theology, we immediately notice that it was always an occasional feature, used only when the transmitted text involved obscurities. Today, by contrast, the notion of interpretation has become a universal concept determined to encompass tradition as a whole.

Interpretation, as we understand it today, is applied not only to texts and verbal tradition, but to everything bequeathed to us by history; thus, for example, we will speak not only of the interpretation of an historical incident, but also the interpretation of spiritual and mimed expressions, the interpretation of behavior, and so forth. We always intend by this that the meaning of what is given over for our interpretation is not revealed without mediation, and that we must look beyond the immediate sense in order to discover the "true" hidden meaning. This generalized notion of interpretation dates back to a Nietzschian conception. According to Nietzsche all statements dependent upon reason are open to interpretation, since their true or real meaning only reaches us as masked and deformed by ideologies.

As a matter of fact, the modern methodology of our philosophical and historical sciences corresponds exactly to this Nietzschian conception. Indeed, it presupposes that the material upon which these sciences work (i.e., sources, vestiges of a bygone era) is such that it requires a critical interpretation. This assumption plays a decisive and fundamental role for the modern sciences of historical and, in general, social life. The dialogue we enter into with the past confronts us with a fundamentally different situation from our own—we will say a "foreign" situation—and consequently it demands an interpretative approach. The human sciences, too, use an interpretative method, thus placing them within our circle of interest. We ask ourselves: what is the meaning and import of historical consciousness in the scheme of scientific knowledge? Here again we are going to raise the same problem by examining the idea of a theory of the human sciences. Note, however, that the theory of the human sciences is not simply the methodology of a certain well-defined group of sciences, but is, as we will see, philosophy properly so called in a much more radical sense than, for instance, is the case with the methodology of natural sciences.

If we make a decided relation between the human sciences and philosophy, it is not just for a purely epistemological elucidation. The human sciences are not only a problem *for* philosophy, on the contrary, they represent a problem *of* philosophy. Indeed, anything we could say about their logical or epistemological independence vis-à-vis the natural sciences, is a very poor measure of the essence of the human sciences and their truly philosophical significance. The philosophical role played by the human sciences follows the law of nothing. They would no longer have any role at all if we took them to be imperfect realizations of the idea of a rigorous science. For it would immediately follow that so-called scientific philosophy would necessarily take the idea of mathematicized natural science for the scientific norm; as we know this would mean that philosophy would no longer be a sort of organon of the sciences. On the other hand, if we recognize an autonomous mode of knowing in the human sciences, if we accord them the impossibility of being reduced to the natural scientific idea of knowledge (implying that one backs off from the absurdity of facing them with the ideal of a perfected facsimile of the methods and degree of certainty available in the natural sciences), then philosophy itself is called into question with all of its ambitions. And so, given these parameters, it is useless to restrict the elucidation of the nature of the human sciences to a purely methodological question; it is a question not simply of defining a specific method, but rather, of recognizing an entirely different notion of knowledge and truth. Consequently, the philosophy which bears these conditions in mind will have many other ambitions than those motivated by the natural-scientific concept of truth. By an intrinsic necessity of things, to guarantee a genuine foundation for the human sciences, as Wilhelm Dilthey proposed not so long ago, is to guarantee a foundation in philosophy, that is to say, to consider the ground of nature and history, and the truth possible in each.

Let us immediately notice that, confirmed or not by the philosophic inclinations of Dilthey, the frames elaborated by the idealism of Hegel are most readily suited to this philosophic enterprise. A logic of the *Geisteswissenschaften*, we would say, is already and always a philosophy of the Spirit.

Nevertheless, what we have just suggested in alluding to Hegel seems to contradict the intimate connections that the human sciences do have with the natural sciences, precisely those connections which distinguish the human sciences from an idealistic philosophy: the human sciences, too, would be verifiable empirical sciences, free from any metaphysical intrusion, and reject all philosophical constructions of universal history. However, is it not more true to say that the filiation of the human sciences with the natural sciences, and the antiidealistic and antispeculative controversy which they inherit at the same time, have up to now hindered the human sciences from moving toward a radical self-understanding? Although the constant desire of the human sciences may be to bolster themselves with contemporary philosophy, it remains no less true that in order to achieve a scientific good conscience, they continue to be attracted to the models of the natural sciences in developing their historical-critical methods. But we must raise the question whether it is meaningful, or valid, to look by analogy with the mathematicized natural sciences for an autonomous and specific method for the human sciences which remains constant throughout the domains of its application? Why is not the Cartesian notion of method proclaimed inadequate in the domain of the human sciences: why would it not be instead the ancient Greek concept of method which is privileged in this domain?

Let us explain. According to Aristotle, for example, the idea of a single method, a method which could be determined before even having penetrated the thing, is a dangerous abstraction; *the object itself must determine the method of its own access.* Now, curiously, if we take a look at the positive research in the human sciences during the last century, it seems that concerning the effective procedures of the human sciences (I am speaking just of those procedures which acquire evidence and knowledge of new truths, and not of the reflections on those procedures), it is much more valid to characterize them by the Aristotelian concept of method than by the pseudo-Cartesian concept of the historical-critical method. We must ask if a method which justifies detaching itself from the domain in question (and we know how fruitful this method was in the case of the mathematization of the natural sciences) does not, in the human sciences, lead to a misapprehension of the natural mode of being specific to this domain? This question leads us again into the vicinity of Hegel, for whom, as we know, every method is "a method linked to the object itself."[2] Can we learn something from the Hegelian dialectic about a logic of the human sciences?

I dare say, this second allusion to Hegel can appear absurd in the light of the methodological conclusions drawn by the human sci-

2. G. W. F. Hegel, *Wissenschaft der Logik,* vol. II, ed. G. Lasson (Leipzig: Felix Meiner, 1923), 486. [*Science of Logic,* trans. A. V. Miller (New York: Humanities Press, 1969)—Tr.]

ences in the period of their real efflorescence during the nineteenth century; obviously, only the natural sciences served as a model for these conclusions. This is even betrayed by the history of the word *Geisteswissenschaften:* although admitting that the intellectual survival of idealism spurred the German translator of Mill's inductive logic to render "moral sciences" by *Geisteswissenschaften,*[3] we must, however, deny Mill the intention of having wished to attribute to the moral sciences a logic of their own. On the contrary, Mill's aim was to show that the inductive method found at the base of all empirical science is also the only valid method for the domain of the moral sciences. In this his doctrine is but the confirmation of an English secular tradition whose most powerful formulation we find in the introduction to Hume's *Treatise of Human Nature.* The moral sciences constitute no exception, Mill says, when we look for uniformities, regularities, and laws in the interest of predicting particular facts and events. Besides, the extension and applicability of the laws arrived at in the natural sciences is not always the same, but that does not impede meteorology, for example, from working on precisely the same basic principles as physics; the only difference which separates them is that in meteorology the system of data includes relatively more gaps than in physics. But this only affects the relative certainty of their respective predictions and in no way constitutes any methodological difference. Now, one will say, it is the same in the domain of moral and social phenomena, no less than in the natural sciences: in both cases the inductive method is independent of all metaphysical presuppositions. It is of no concern whatsoever to know, for example, what one thinks of the possibility of a phenomenon like human freedom; the inductive method has nothing to do with the search for any occult causes, it merely observes regularities. Thus it is possible to believe in free will and, at the same time, in the validity of predictions in the domain of social life. Drawing consequences on the basis of regularities does not imply any hypothesis about the metaphysical structure of the relations in question: one is concerned with them solely for the prediction of regularities. The actuality of free decisions is one of the moments of the universal derived

3. J. S. Mill, *System der deduktiven und induktiven Logik,* trans. Schiel (1863), 6th Book, "Von der Logik der Geisteswissenschaften oder moralischen Wissenschaften."

by induction. That is the way in which the natural-scientific ideal is adopted at the level of social phenomena.

Undoubtedly, certain researches conducted in this style, as for example in mass psychology, have been crowned with incontestable success. However, with the elementary acknowledgment that the discovery of regularities realizes actual progress in the human sciences, in the end we only conceal the genuine problem that these sciences raise. The adoption of this Humean model does not allow us to circumscribe the experience of a social-historical world; quite the contrary, we totally misunderstand the essence of this experience so long as we approach it merely by means of inductive procedures. For whatever is meant by science, neither by procuring regularities nor by their application to actual historical phenomena will one ever grasp the peculiar component of historical knowledge.

Surely we can admit that all historical knowledge involves the application of general empirical regularities to the concrete problems it faces; yet, the true intention of historical knowledge is not to explain a concrete phenomenon as a particular case of a general rule, even if this had to be subordinated to the purely practical aim of an eventual prediction. In actuality, its true goal—even in utilizing general knowledge—is to understand an historical phenomenon in its singularity, in its uniqueness. Historical consciousness is interested in knowing, not how men, people, or states develop *in general,* but, quite on the contrary, how *this* man, *this* people, or *this* state became what it is; how each of these *particulars* could come to pass and end up specifically *there.*

But what sort of knowledge do we speak of now, and what is meant by science in this case? We have just presented a type of science manifesting a character and goal radically different from the natural sciences. But doesn't this characterization come back to a purely privative definition? Must we then speak of an "inexact science"? From the perspective of this question it is desirable to examine the reflections of Hermann Helmholtz who in 1862 was already looking for a solution to the problems engaging us here.[4] Although

4. H. Helmholtz, *Vorträge und Reden,* vol. 1, 4th ed., "Über das Verhaltnis der Naturwissenschaften zur Gesamtheit der Wissenschaften," 167ff.

he insisted on the importance and human significance of the *Geistes-wissenschaften,* he was still inspired by the methodological ideal of the natural sciences when he attempted to define their logical character. Helmholtz distinguished between two species of induction: on the one side, logical induction, and on the other, instinctive induction, artistic induction, as it were. Note well that this is a psychological and not a logical distinction. For Helmholtz both sciences make use of inductive reasoning; in the human sciences, however, inductive reasoning is practiced implicitly, unconsciously, and happens as a tributary consequent of what we call in German *Taktgefühl,* a sort of tact or sympathetic sensibility. In turn, this sensitivity is supported by other mental faculties, as for example the richness of memory, acceptance of authorities, and so forth. In contrast, the explicit reasoning of the naturalist rests entirely on the use of a single function: understanding [*l'entendement*].

Although we readily admit that the great scholar has, perhaps, resisted the temptation to take his own scientific activity as the measure, nevertheless, in characterizing the procedures of the human sciences, in the end he resorted to the single logical category which he took from Mill: induction. For him as well, the model that mechanics gave to the whole of eighteenth-century science remained valid. But that this mechanics might itself be an historical phenomenon, that consequently it might be subject to historical investigation (as Pierre Duhem did so profitably much later[5]), was totally foreign to him.

Yet in the same period the problem appeared to many with a certain acuity; we have only to think of the prodigious research of the "historical school."

Would it not have been necessary to raise these investigations to the level of logical self-consciousness? As early as 1843, J. G. Droysen, the author who first drew attention to the history of Hellenism, wrote: "There is certainly no scientific discipline that is—theoretically speaking—so little justified, so little circumscribed and articulated as is history." And he appealed to a new Kant in order to disclose the living source of history in a categorical imperative, "from where springs," to use his words, "the historical life of humanity."

---

5. P. H. Duhem, *Études sur Leonard de Vinci,* 3 vols. (Paris: A. Hermann, 1906–1913); and his posthumous *Le Système du monde,* 10 vols. (Paris: A. Hermann, 1913–1959).

That Droysen called upon Kant tells us that he did not conceive of the epistemology of history to be a logical organon, but a truly philosophical task. He expected that "a deepened conception of history could make possible new progress in the human sciences and become the center of gravity stabilizing their oscillations."[6]

That it is still the natural-scientific model that matters here finds no better proof than the plural used in saying *Geisteswissenschaften* or "human sciences." However, this model does not necessarily signify an epistemological unity: on the contrary, the natural sciences constitute a model for the human sciences only insofar as the latter submit to the ideal of an autonomous and grounded scientific value. Droysen's logic of history—which he called an *Historik*—was the first sketch of an epistemology of this species.

THE IMPORTANCE AND LIMITS OF WILHELM DILTHEY'S WORK

Dilthey's philosophical work is dedicated to this same task of constructing, parallel to the critique of pure reason, a critique of historical reason. But the difference between Droysen and Dilthey is notable. Whereas Droysen remains a successor—albeit a critical one—to Hegel's philosophy (we need only recall that in his logic of history the fundamental concept of history is defined as a generic concept of man), we find in Dilthey that the Romantic and idealistic heritage is tangled with the influence Mill's logic had exerted since the middle of the century. It is true that Dilthey thought himself quite superior to English empiricism on account of his vivid intuition of the superiority of the historical school compared to all naturalistic or dogmatic thought. Indeed, he said: "Only in Germany could the practice of an authentic experience be substituted for an empiricism which was dogmatic and burgeoning with prejudices; Mill is dog-

---

6. J. G. Droysen, *Grundriss der Historik* (Halle: Max Niemeyer, republ. 1925), 97. [See *Outline of the Principles of History*, trans. E. B. Andrews (New York: Howard Fertig, 1967 reprint of 1893 ed.). This translation is from an 1867 edition of the *Historik* which does not include the final section, "Theologie der Geschichte," cited by Gadamer and which originally appeared in 1843 as an introduction to the second part of Droysen's *History of Hellenism*. For related comments on scientific and historical methods, see pp. 16, 62ff., and 107 of the Andrews translation—Tr.]

matic for lack of historical erudition."[7] These lines are found noted in Dilthey's copy of Mill's *Logic*. As a matter of fact, the difficult work accomplished by Dilthey over several decades to ground the human sciences and distinguish them from the natural sciences is a continual debate with the naturalistic methodological ideal that Mill assigned to the human sciences in his famous last chapter.[8] To a so-called explanatory psychology—in the naturalistic sense of the word—Dilthey opposed the idea of a *geisteswissenschaftliche* psychology. It is to *geisteswissenschaftliche* psychology, disencumbered from all dogmatism and every hypothetical construction, that belongs the knowledge and description of the laws of spiritual life which are to serve as the common ground for the various human sciences. Indeed, all propositions in the human sciences concern, in the end, the facts of internal experience: a domain of being which is put into relief not by the category of explanation, but by that of *understanding*.

Dilthey's effort to philosophically ground the human sciences depends upon the epistemological consequences which he drew from everything the historical school (Ranke and Droysen) had already tried to emphasize in opposition to German idealism. According to Dilthey, the greatest weakness in the reflections of the disciples of the historical school is their inconsistency: "instead of, on the one hand, exposing the epistemological presuppositions of the historical school and, on the other, examining those of idealism which made their way from Kant to Hegel, in order to discover their incompatibilities, they have uncritically confused the two, one with the other."[9] Dilthey's own intent is clear: discover on the boundary between historical experience and the idealistic heritage of the historical school a new and epistemologically solid foundation; it is this which explains his idea of completing Kant's critique of pure reason by a critique of historical reason.

Even by posing the problem in this way Dilthey already abandons speculative idealism; the analogy which conjoins the problem of historical reason with the problem of pure reason must be taken

7. W. Dilthey, *Gesammelte Schriften*, vol. V (Stuttgart: Teubner), lxxiv.
8. See ibid., vol. V, 56ff.
9. Ibid., vol. VII, 281.

literally. Historical reason is in search of justification no less than was pure reason not so long before. The critique of pure reason aimed at not only the destruction of metaphysics as a purely rational science of the world, of the soul, and of God, but also the simultaneous unveiling of a new domain within which rational science had a justifiable application. In this connection we witness, then, a double philosophical consequence. On the one side, if the critique of pure reason denounced "the dreams of visionaries," it did not, however, fail to furnish a response to the question: How is a pure science of nature possible? On the other side, by introducing the historical world into the autonomous development of reason, speculative idealism integrated historical consciousness into the domain of purely rational knowledge. History became a chapter in the Encyclopedia of the Spirit.

In this way philosophy came in effect to the following problem: how to produce for the world of historical consciousness something similar to what Kant succeeded in producing for the scientific knowledge of nature. Is there a way to justify empirical knowledge in history while totally renouncing all dogmatic constructions?

At this point Dilthey asks himself how to fit historical consciousness to the place previously held by Hegel's Absolute Knowledge of Spirit. But that raises more problems than it solves. Dilthey stressed that we can only know from within an historical perspective since, as it happens, we are ourselves historical beings. But does not the very historical mode of being of our consciousness constitute an impermeable boundary? Now Hegel solves the problem by the *Aufhebung* of history into Absolute Knowledge; but for Dilthey, who admits the possibility of unceasing variation in the interpretation of historical relations, is not the attainment of objective knowledge excluded in advance? Dilthey pondered over these problems untiringly; his reflections had precisely the goal of legitimating the scientific knowledge of the historically-conditioned as objective science. A great aid was provided him by the idea of a structure that was constituted as a unity emanating from its own center. It was a very flexible schema: the knowledge of infinitely complex historical relations became conceivable, even extending so far as to include universal historical knowledge. The notion that a structural relation could become intelligible through its own center corresponded to the old hermeneutic principle and at the same time met the exigencies of historical thought. According to these conditions every historical moment must be understood in itself and cannot be submitted to the measures of a present which may be extrinsic to it. But the application of this schema presupposes that the historian can disengage himself from his own historical situation. And, indeed, is not having an historical sense in fact claiming to be disencumbered from the hold exercised by the prejudices of the epoch in which one lives? Dilthey was convinced he had achieved a truly historical view of the world; but at bottom, what his historical reflections were able to justify was nothing other than the grandiose and epical self-effacement practiced by Ranke.

This explains in what specific sense the perspective of finitude and historicity did not cause, in Dilthey's opinion, any detriment in principle to the validity of knowledge in the human sciences. For Dilthey the task of historical consciousness is a victory gained over its own relativity, thus justifying objective knowledge in this domain. But how can one legitimate this claim to objectivity on the part of historical consciousness in spite of its conditioned and bounded mode of being—and even in opposition to all other cognitive forms known through history, forms always relative to a determinate perspective?

According to Dilthey, this legitimation can no longer be lodged in Hegel's Absolute Knowledge. This Hegelian Absolute Knowledge is an actual self-consciousness which re-totalizes the phases of the progress of Spirit. What is this if not the pretension of philosophical consciousness to contain in itself the total truth of the history of Spirit—exactly the thesis rejected by an historical vision on the world? We need, then, an historical *experience* since human consciousness is not an infinite intelligence to which everything can be simultaneously present. On principle, for a finite and historical consciousness, the absolute identity of consciousness and object is unattainable: it is always immersed in historical influences. But in what then consists its privileged capacity to transcend itself and be entitled to an objective historical knowledge?

Here is Dilthey's reply: as impenetrable as the ground of historical life may be, this life is able to historically understand its possibility of having an historical attitude. Ever since the rise and victory of historical consciousness we confront a new situation. Hereafter, this consciousness is no longer simply an unreflective expression of real life. It ceases to judge everything transmitted to it by the measures of the understanding it has of its own life and, in this way, to establish the continuity of tradition. This historical consciousness now knows how to situate itself in a reflexive relation with itself and with tradition; it understands itself by and through its own history. *Historical consciousness is a mode of self-consciousness.*

Dilthey proposes, then, that we understand the appearance and genesis of a scientific consciousness through an analysis of the essence of self-knowledge. But immediately his philosophical impasse regarding the problem he chose for himself becomes apparent.

Dilthey's point of departure is that life carries in itself reflection. We must credit Georg Misch with exposing Dilthey's orientation toward a *Lebensphilosophie*. Now this orientation has as its foundation the idea that all life as such carries within it knowledge. Even the intimate familiarity which characterizes lived experience contains a sort of reflection bound up with life, says Dilthey.[10] It is this same immanent reflexivity in life that according to Dilthey lies at the base of our lived experience of meaning. The experience of meaning in the cohesiveness of life is possible only if one is disengaged from the "pursuit of (vital) objectives"; this reflection is possible only if we take a certain retreat by placing ourselves above the connections which secure our different activities. Likewise Dilthey emphasized— and undoubtedly he had reason—that what we call the "meaning of life" takes shape well before any scientific objectivation in the natural view of life on itself. This natural view of life on itself is found objectified in the wisdom of proverbs and myths, but especially in the great works of art. Art in fact constitutes the privileged medium through which life is understood, because situated "in the confines between knowledge and action it allows life to be disclosed at a depth no longer accessible to observation, reflection and theory."[11]

10. Ibid., vol. VII, 18.
11. Ibid., vol. VII, 207. [See *Pattern and Meaning in History*, ed. H. P. Rickman (New York: Harper Torchbooks, 1961), 119; and "The Understanding of Others and Their Life Expressions," in *Theories of History*, ed. Patrick Gardner (Glencoe: Free Press, 1959)—Tr.]

Yet we must not limit the reflective meaning of life to the pure expression we find in works of art. We must say that every expression of life implies a knowledge which shapes it from within. Is not expression this plastic milieu of the spirit—Hegel's Objective Spirit—whose realm encompasses every form of human life? In his language, in his moral values and juridical forms, the individual—the isolated being—is even then and always beyond his particularity. The ethical milieu where he lives and in which he partakes constitutes something solid that allows him to orient himself despite the somewhat vague contingencies of his subjective impulses. Dedication to communal purposes, to action for the community, this is what frees man, says Dilthey, from his particularity and from his ephemeral existence.

This would still have been acceptable to Droysen, but with Dilthey it takes on a quite unique profile. "Searching for solid forms"[12]: there, according to Dilthey, is the vital tendency of our life, a tendency present in contemplation and science no less than in the reflection which practical experience always involves. Thus, we understand that for Dilthey the objectivity of scientific knowledge, no less than the inquiring reflection of philosophy, is like an unfolding of the natural tendencies of life. What guides Dilthey's reflections is not at all a pure, simple, and superficial adaptation of the method of the human sciences to the procedures of the natural sciences, rather it is the discovery of something genuinely common to both methods. It is indeed essential to the experimental method to go beyond the contingencies of subjective observation, and in this way it succeeds in discovering the laws of nature. Likewise, the underlying aspiration of the human sciences is to go beyond the contingencies of a purely subjective perspective by methodical critique and thus achieve an historical and objective knowledge. Finally, we recognize in philosophical reflection an analogous intention and sense as well, even when it gives up the pretension of pure knowledge through merely conceptual analysis: it "objectifies itself as a human and historical fact."[13]

Dilthey's position, centered entirely on the relation between life

12. Ibid., vol. VII, 347.
13. Ibid., vol. V, 339ff; see vol. VII.

and knowledge, thoroughly withstands the idealistic objection which accuses it of historical relativism. To root philosophy in the primordial fact of life amounts to abandoning the search for a simple, non-contradictory system of statements and concepts. The role occupied throughout life by *Besinnung*—self-consciousness, reflection—must also be valid, according to Dilthey, for philosophical reflection. This is a *Selbstbesinnung* which brings the reflexivity of life to its highest point; consequently, philosophy must be considered as an objectification of life itself. Thus philosophy becomes a "philosophy of philosophy," but assuredly not in the sense nor with the claims that idealism earlier attributed to itself. The program of this reflection does not start from a self-sufficient speculative principle and aim at the construction of the one and only possible philosophy, instead it intends to follow solely the path of the historical *Selbstbesinnung*. And in this sense Dilthey's philosophy is quite unscathed by the accusation of relativism.

It is true that Dilthey was not untroubled by the problem of relativism. He pondered a great deal on the question of how to assure objectivity in the midst of all these relativities, how to conceive of the relationship of the finite to the absolute. "Our task consists," he said, "in explaining how the relative values of an age can have widened out into something in some manner absolute."[14] Nevertheless, we ask Dilthey in vain for an effective answer to this problem of relativism. And this state of affairs is less because he did not find an authentic answer than because in the last analysis this problem did not touch the true center of his thought at all. In fact, throughout the unfolding of the historical *Selbstbesinnung* which carried Dilthey from relativity to relativity, he always felt sure to be on the road to the absolute. In this sense Ernst Tröltsch summarizes very well Dilthey's work by the formula "from relativity to totality." This expression corresponds perfectly to Dilthey's own formula: "To be consciously a conditioned being."[15] Obviously, this formula epigrammatizes an explicit critique of idealism for which the truth or the achievement of consciousness is real only as infinite and unconditioned consciousness, that is to say, Absolute Spirit.

14. Ibid., vol. VII, 290. [See Rickman, op. cit., 166—Tr.]
15. Ibid., vol. V, 364.

But considering his assiduous and unremitting meditations on the objection of relativism, one quickly realizes that Dilthey himself did not clearly countenance the full anti-idealistic implications of his philosophy inspired by the problem of life. Indeed, how else are we to explain the fact that Dilthey did not notice and refute the intellectualist motive in the objection of relativism, intellectualism incompatible not only with the ultimate import of his philosophy of life, but even with his chosen point of departure: the immanence of knowledge in the very heart of life.

The underlying reason for this inconsistency at the heart of Dilthey's thought undoubtedly lies in his latent Cartesianism. His historico-philosophical reflections towards grounding the human sciences cannot really be reconciled with the starting point of his *Lebensphilosophie.* He demands that his philosophy be extended to all the domains where "consciousness, by a reflexive and dubitative attitude, will be liberated from the hold of authoritarian dogmas and aspire to genuine knowledge." [16] It seems clear to us that this statement adequately reflects the spirit of modern science and philosophy in general. Also, we cannot ignore the Cartesian resonances which it conveys. And yet, curiously, Dilthey applied it in a very different sense: "Always and everywhere, life leads to reflection on that which confronts it, reflection leads to doubt, and life can only resist doubt in the pursuit of valid knowledge." [17] This citation clearly shows that in reality Dilthey, unlike the epistemologies of the Cartesian persuasion, is not aiming toward a shattering of philosophical prejudices, but rather he contends that it is real life as a whole—the moral, religious, juridical, and other traditions—that must arouse reflection and call out for a new rational order. Nevertheless, in this passage Dilthey means by "knowledge" and "reflection" something more than the simple immanence of knowing in life, a universal immanence of which we have spoken above. In fact, living traditions, like the moral, religious, and juridical traditions, are always derivatives— and without reflection—of life's spontaneous self-knowledge. We have already noted that in dedicating himself to tradition the individual is raised to the level of Objective Spirit. Thus we will agree with

16. Ibid., vol. VII, 6.
17. Ibid.

Dilthey in saying that the influence exercised by thought over life "springs from an intrinsic necessity to find, within the inconsistent variations in sense perceptions, desires and affections, something solid which makes possible a stable and harmonious behavior."[18] But this is carried out specifically through the objectifications of the spirit, such as morality, positive law, and religion, binding the particular being to the objectivity of society. Here now is something incompatible in the Diltheian *Lebensphilosophie:* at the same time he demands a "reflexive and dubitative" stance toward all these objectifications of the spirit in order to raise a work to the stature of science. Here Dilthey continues to adhere to the scientific ideal of Enlightenment philosophy. Now this Enlightenment philosophy agrees but little with the *Besinnung* immanent in life; specifically, Dilthey's *Lebensphilosophie* is in principle most radically opposed to its intellectualism and dogmatism.

Actually, the sort of certitude we acquire through doubt is fundamentally different from that other—immediate—sort that is possessed by the ends and values in life that are themselves presented to consciousness with the pretension of being absolute. There is a decisive difference between this certitude grasped in the heart of life and scientific certitude. The certitudes obtained in the sciences always possess a Cartesian resonance; they are the result of a critical method. The latter puts in doubt the accepted opinions in order to achieve, through new examination, their confirmation or rectification. Rightly we speak of methodic doubt. By the artifice of a hyperbolic doubt, through an experiment analogous to those of the laboratory, Descartes proposes to show us in his celebrated meditations the *fundamentum inconcussum:* self/consciousness. Likewise, a methodical science doubts on principle all that can be doubted in order to arrive at the certitude of its knowledge. Now it is characteristic of Dilthey's thought that he does not distinguish between this methodic doubt and the sort of doubt which assails us, so to say, without reason, without purpose, spontaneously. Dilthey treats scientific certitude as the fulfillment of this certitude which reigns at the heart

18. Ibid.

of life. On the other side, we cannot say that Dilthey, with all the weight that concrete historicity burdened him, was insensible to the uncertainty of life. Quite on the contrary, the more he was devoted to the modern sciences, the more he struggled with the tension between the tradition of his origins and the historical forces which modern life had unleashed. His search for something, as he said, "solid" is explained precisely by the sort of defensive instinct that he develops in view of the tumultuous reality of life. But it is remarkable that to conquer the uncertainty of life, he hopes to find this something "solid" in science, and not in the assurances that the experience of life itself can offer.

The personal process of secularization which made Dilthey—a theological student—a philosopher, can be paralleled to the historical process of the birth of the modern sciences. Just as the natural sciences bring to bear a limited yet sure light on the secrets of nature, now we face a scientifically developed power of understanding focused on the mysteries of life. Enlightenment philosophy is carried out in historical consciousness.

Consequently, we will understand how Dilthey is dependent on Romantic hermeneutics. In fact, Romantic hermeneutics masks the essential difference between historical experience and scientific knowledge, that is, it allows one to neglect the essential historicity of the mode of knowledge of the human sciences and to coordinate them to the methodology of the natural sciences. Thus Dilthey maintained, for example, an ideal of objectivity for the human sciences which could only serve to assure them of a rank equal to that of the natural sciences. From there also stems the frequent use Dilthey liked to make of the word "results" and his preference for methodological descriptions, a usage and preference which served the same aim. In this respect Romantic hermeneutics is useful to him, for it too misconceives the historical nature of the experience which is at the base of the human sciences. It starts off from the assumption that the proper object of understanding is the text to be deciphered and understood, but that every encounter with a text is an encounter of the spirit with itself. Every text is foreign enough to pose a problem, and yet familiar enough that, in principle, the possibility of deciphering some sense out of it is assured, even when all that one knows is the fact that it is a text, that is to say, written spirit.

As we can see with Schleiermacher, the model of hermeneutics is the reciprocal understanding attained in the relation between the I and the thou. Understanding a text carries with it the same possibility of perfect adequation as the comprehension of the thou. What the author has in view is immediately evident in his text; text and interpreter are absolutely contemporaneous. Here is the triumph of the philological method: grasp the past spirit as the present, welcome the foreign as the familiar. It is evident, then, that in spite of the diversity of methods, the differences with the natural sciences no longer exist—since in both cases we address our questions to an object already fully present, to an object that contains every answer.

From this point of view Dilthey fulfilled perfectly the task he had set for himself: he justified epistemologically the human sciences by conceiving the historical world in the manner of a text to be deciphered. This proposition epitomizes the position of the historical school. Ranke had already assigned the historian the sacred task of deciphering the hieroglyphs of history, but Dilthey goes even further. If historical reality has a sense transparent enough to be deciphered like a text, then all that is wanting is an interpreter who would reduce history to the history of Spirit. Dilthey himself draws this conclusion and recognizes in fact his kinship with Hegel's philosophy of Spirit. And whereas Schleiermacher's Romantic hermeneutics had ambitions of being a universal instrument of the spirit (but confined itself to aiding the expression of the force of salvation in the Christian faith), for Dilthey's *Grundlegung* of the human sciences, hermeneutics is the *telos* of historical consciousness. For it, there exists but one species of knowledge of the truth: that which *understands expression,* and in expression, life. In history, nothing is incomprehensible. Everything is understood since everything resembles a text. "Life and history have meaning, as letters have in a word,"[19] said Dilthey. Consequently, the study of the historical past is conceived not as an historical experience, but as deciphering. This constitutes an important difference between Dilthey's conceptions

19. Ibid., vol. VII, 281. [See Rickman, op. cit., 168—Tr.]

and the views of Romantic hermeneutics; despite his obvious attachments to these views we cannot be led astray and overlook this very real difference.

Now historical experience is defined by the historical acquirements from which it originates and by the impossibility of detaching it from this origin; never, then, will it be a pure method. There will always be certain means of deducing general rules from this experience, but the methodological meaning of this step forbids that one draw a law, properly so called, from it and forever afterwards subsume the complex of given concrete cases in an unequivocal manner. The idea of experiential rules always demands—the rules being what they are only through use—that they be tested in use. This is what remains valid, in a general and universal way, for our knowledge in the human sciences. They never attain an objectivity other than that which all experience carries with it.

Dilthey's effort to understand the human sciences through life, beginning from lived experience, is never really reconciled with the Cartesian concept of science which he did not know how to throw off. Emphasize as he might the contemplative tendencies of life itself, the attractions of something "solid" that life involves, his concept of objectivity, as he reduced it to the objectivity of results, remains attached to an origin very different from lived experience. This is why he was unable to resolve the problem he had chosen: to justify the human sciences with the express purpose of making them equal to the natural sciences.

MARTIN HEIDEGGER AND THE SIGNIFICANCE OF HIS "HERMENEUTICS OF FACTICITY" FOR THE HUMAN SCIENCES

In the meantime, however, phenomenological research, as inaugurated by Edmund Husserl, decisively broke the bonds of neo-Kantian methodologism. Husserl gave back an absolutely universal theme of research to the dimension of living experience and thus overcame the point of view limited to the purely methodological problematic of the human sciences. His analyses of the "life-world" (*Lebenswelt*) and of this anonymous constitution of all meaning and significance that forms the ground and texture of experience, showed definitively that the concept of objectivity represented by the sciences exemplifies but a special case. The opposition between nature and spirit is reexamined; the human sciences *and* the natural sciences must be understood in terms of life's universal intentionality. This understanding alone satisfies the requirements of a philosophical *Selbstbesinnung*.

To these discoveries of Husserl, and in the light of the question of being which he revived, Heidegger ascribed an even more radical meaning. He follows Husserl in that, for him as well, it is unnecessary to separate, as Dilthey had done, historical being from the being of nature in order to legitimate on the level of the theory of knowledge the methodological uniqueness of the historical sciences. On the contrary, the natural-scientific mode of knowledge is a subspecies of understanding which, as Heidegger says in *Being and Time*, "has strayed into the legitimate task of grasping the present-at-hand (the *Vorhandene*, 'substantial' being) in its essential unintelligibility."[20] For Heidegger understanding [*le comprendre*], comprehension [*la comprehension*], is no longer the ideal of knowledge to which Spirit, now grown old, must be resigned—as it was for Dilthey— but neither is it simply the methodological ideal of philosophy as with Husserl. Contrary to both, understanding is the primordial accomplishment of human *Dasein* as being-in-the-world. And prior to any differentiation of understanding into the two directions of pragmatic interest and theoretical interest, understanding is *Dasein's* mode of being which constitutes it as "potentiality-for-Being" (*Seinkönnen*) and "possibility."

On the basis of Heidegger's existential analysis of *Dasein*, with the many new perspectives that it implies for metaphysics, the function of hermeneutics in the human sciences also appears in a totally new light. While Heidegger resurrects the problem of Being in a

20. M. Heidegger, *Sein und Zeit* (1927), 153. [All quotations are from *Being and Time*, trans. John Macquarrie and Edward Robinson (New York: Harper and Row, 1962)—Tr.]

form which goes far beyond all traditional metaphysics, he secures at the same time a radically new possibility in the face of the classical a prioris of historicism: his concept of understanding carries an *ontological* weight. Moreover, understanding is no longer an operation antithetic and subsequent to the operations of the constitutive life, but a primordial mode of being of human life itself. Although Misch, in departing from Dilthey, discovers in the liberating distanciation from oneself [*la distance libre à soi*] one of the fundamental possibilities of life, the possibility upon which the phenomenon of understanding must be grounded, Heidegger—also taking his departure from Dilthey—goes further to initiate a radical ontological reflection about understanding as existential and disclose all understanding as pro-ject (*Entwurf*). Understanding is the very movement of transcendence.

For traditional hermeneutics, of course, the Heideggerian theses sound a truly provocative note. Certainly the German verb *verstehen* (to understand) has two meanings. First of all, it has the same meaning as when we say, for example: "I understand the meaning of something"; then it also signifies: "to know about or be an expert in something." Let us give an example of this last case: "er versteht nicht auf das Lesen"—translated into English: "he is incompetent when it comes to reading," that is, "he doesn't *know how* to read." In other words, the verb *verstehen* signifies beyond its theoretical sense a knowing how, an ability, a capacity to carry out a task at the practical level. But according to this last sense, it is essentially distinguished or so it seems from the understanding obtained by scientific knowledge. And yet, on closer examination, even there we find something in common. In both cases there is an act of knowing, a knowing *about* something, a knowing how to go about something. Those who understand a text—to say nothing of a law—not only project themselves in an effort of understanding toward a significance, but acquire through understanding a new liberty of the mind. This involves numerous and new possibilities, like interpreting a text, seeing the hidden relations that it conceals, drawing conclusions, and so on—precisely those things which define what we mean when we speak of the understanding or knowledge of a text. Similarly, those with mechanical know-how, or even those with a practical mastery in whatever craft, as for example the savant with hermeneutical know-how, really know "how to go about it." In sum, even if it seems perfectly evident that a simply practical understanding of a rational goal has other norms than, for instance, the understanding of a text or other expression of life, nevertheless, it is still that in the end all understandings are reducible to a common level of an "I know how to go about it," that is, a self-understanding in relation to something other.

In the same way, understanding a gesture or a pantomimed expression is more than grasping directly its immediate meaning; it is to discover what is hidden in the soul and apprehend how we ought "to go about it." In this case one rightly says that accomplishing an understanding is to form a project from one's own possibilities.

The lexicological history of the German word *verstehen* confirms this result. In fact, the primitive meaning of the word seems to be what it had in the ancient juridical language that used the expression *eine causa verstehen* (understanding a cause) in the sense of "defending the cause of a party before a tribunal." That the use of the word developed later into its current and familiar sense, may be clearly explained by the fact that the defense of a cause necessarily means that one has assumed it completely—that one has understood it—to the point of not losing any ground in the face of any possible arguments advanced by one's adversaries.

In taking account of this it is easy to see that traditional hermeneutics greatly over-restricted the horizon of problems attached to the idea of understanding. In this respect the initiative taken by Heidegger on a much vaster plane than that of Dilthey was particularly fruitful concerning our hermeneutical problem. Certainly Dilthey also rejected entirely the naturalistic methods in the human sciences, and Husserl, as we know, even deemed "absurd" the application of the naturalistic concept of objectivity to the human sciences in showing the fundamental relativity that every type of world, every type of historical knowledge, implies. But with Heidegger we witness an ontological evaluation of the problem of the structure of historical understanding, grounded on human existence which is essentially oriented toward the future.

Although having recognized the tribute that historical knowledge pays to the projective structure of *Dasein*, no one would dream of putting in doubt the immanent criteria of what we call scientific knowledge. Historical knowledge is neither a species of project, in the sense of a forecast or program, nor is it the extrapolation of deliberate ends, nor again the disposition of things according to good will, vulgar prejudices, or suggestions of a tyrant, but is a *mensuratio ad rem*. Except that the *res* is not meant in the sense of a *factum brutum:* it is not simply "substantial entity" (*bloss vorhanden*, in the Heideggerian sense), neither is it anything instrumentally determinable or measurable. To be historical is, on the contrary, itself a mode of being for human *Dasein*. But now we need to fully understand the importance of this often repeated statement. Neither does it signify that the understandable and the understood may be simply homogeneous modes of being, and that the method of the human sciences is founded on this homogeneity. That would make the historical into a psychology. The common relationship which the understandable and the understood share, this sort of affinity which ties them together, is not founded on the equivalence of their modes of being, but on what that mode of being *is*. This means that neither the knowable nor the known are "ontic" and simply "subsistant," but that they are historical; that is to say, their mode of being is historicality. As Count Yorck said, "everything depends upon the generic difference between the ontic and the historical."[21] When Yorck shows us the opposition which separates the homogeneity of being from the "affinity"—which distinguishes the *Gleichartigkeit* from the *Zugehörigkeit*—then appears the problem that Heidegger will develop in all of its radicality. For Heidegger, the fact that we can only speak of history insofar as we are ourselves historical, signifies that it is the historicity of human *Dasein*, in its incessant movement of anticipation and forgetfulness, which is the precondition for our ability to revive the past. What before appeared as prejudicial to the concept of science and method, as only a subjective approach to historical knowledge, today is placed in the foreground of fundamental inquiry. Affinity (*Zugehörigkeit*) conditions historical interest not only in the sense of the nonscientific and subjective factors which motivate the choices of a theme or question. In accepting such a hypothesis we would interpret the concept of affinity as a particular case of

21. P. Yorck in *Briefwechsel zwischen W. Dilthey und dem Grafen Paul Yorck von Wartenburg, 1877–1897* (Halle-an-der-Saale: Max Niemeyer, 1923), 191.

emotional servitude: sympathy. On the contrary, affinity with a tradition is no less primordially and essentially constitutive of the historical finitude of *Dasein* than is the fact that *Dasein* always projects itself toward its future possibilities. On this point Heidegger rightly emphasized that the two moments of "thrownness" (*Geworfenheit*) and "pro-ject" (*Entwurf*) must always be thought of together. Thus there is no understanding or interpretation whatsoever that does not bring into play the entirety of this existential structure—even if the intention does not exceed a purely literal reading of a text of stating some specific event.

These remarks still do not constitute a sufficient response to the problem raised by hermeneutics. Nevertheless, the Heideggerian interpretation of understanding as existential represents neither more nor less than its most fundamental element. If understanding is a transcendental determination of all existence, then hermeneutic understanding, too, receives a new dimension and universal importance. The phenomenon and problematic of affinity which the historical school knew not how to justify, will henceforth have a concrete significance, and the task of hermeneutics properly so called will be precisely to grasp this significance which is its own.

The existential structure of "thrownness," fundamental to understanding as the meaningful operation of *Dasein,* is a structure also found at the basis of daily-life understanding as performed in the human sciences. The concrete links that represent an ethics or a tradition, more generally the concrete historical conditions, as well as the future possibilities that they imply, define what is active at the heart of the understanding proper to the human sciences. The importance of an existential doctrine such as "thrownness"—*Geworfenheit*—is precisely to show that the *Dasein* that is projected toward its future "potentiality-for-Being" is a being which here and now *has been,* so that all of its unrestrained posturing comes up against and is halted in the face of facticity of its own being. Here, then, in opposition to the quest for a transcendental constitution in Husserlian phenomenology, is the crucial point of Heidegger's "hermeneutics of facticity." It is fully aware of the insurmountable precedence of what gives it the possibility of even having a pro-ject, a pro-ject, in fact, which by the same token can only be a finite pro-ject.

The understanding of an historical tradition will also, and necessarily, carry with it the imprint of this existential structure of *Dasein*. The problem then is how to recognize this imprint in the hermeneutics of the human sciences. For in the human sciences there can be no question of being opposed to the process of tradition which is itself historical and to which these sciences owe their access to history. Detachment or being liberated from tradition cannot be our first worry in our attitude towards the past in which we—who are ourselves historical beings—incessantly participate. Quite the contrary, the authentic attitude is that of looking at an inherited culture—in the literal sense of both inherited and culture, that is, as a development (a cultivation) and a continuation of what we recognize as being the concrete link among us all. Obviously, what is handed down by our forebears is not appreciated when it is looked at in the objectivist spirit, that is, as the object of a scientific method, as if it were something fundamentally alien or completely foreign. What we prepare to welcome is never without some resonance in ourselves; it is the mirror in which each of us recognizes himself. In fact, the reality of tradition scarcely constitutes a problem of knowledge, but a phenomenon of spontaneous and productive appropriation of the transmitted content.

This said, it is time to ask if the appearance of historical consciousness has really rent an unbridgeable abyss between our scientific attitude and our natural and spontaneous approach to history. In other words, does so-called historical consciousness not deceive itself in designating the totality of its historicity as a simple prejudice that must be overcome? The "presuppositionless science"—the *vorurteilslose Wissenschaft*—does it not itself partake, and more than it realizes, in the naive receptive and reflective attitude through which the past is presented to us as living tradition? Without other attitudes—scientific or quotidian—that it lives *only* through the solicitations which arrive to it from a tradition? Must we not admit that the meaning of the objects of investigation which it borrows from tradition is formed exclusively by a tradition? Even if a given historical object does not answer at all a current historical interest—even in this truly extreme case of historical investigation—it is still the case that there is no historical object that does not always motivate us to question it primordially as an historical phenomenon, that is to say, to grasp it as something meaningful which has nothing immutable about it except that it can never be defined once and for all.

Consequently, in order to proceed to an historical hermeneutics it is necessary to begin by clearing away the abstract opposition which lies between tradition and historical research, between history and historical knowledge. Everything that the living tradition, on the one hand, and historical research, on the other, carry with them in the end form an effective unity which can only be analyzed as a network of reciprocal actions. Thus it would be more correct to take historical consciousness, not as a radically new phenomenon, but as a relative transformation, although a revolutionary one, within which man has always constituted his attitude toward his own past. In other words, we have to recognize the role that tradition plays within the historical attitude, and inquire into its hermeneutic productivity.

THE HERMENEUTICAL PROBLEM AND ARISTOTLE'S *ETHICS*

At this point in our exposition, it would appear that the problem with which we have been occupied manifests an intimate connection to a problematic that Aristotle developed in his ethical investigations.[22] In fact, the problem hermeneutics poses can be defined by the question "What can we make of the fact that one and the same message transmitted by tradition will be grasped differently on every occasion, that it is only understood relative to the concrete historical situation of its recipient?" On the logical level, this problem of understanding is presented as the application of something general (the self-same message) to a concrete and particular situation. Now certainly Aristotelian ethics is not interested in the hermeneutical problem, much less its historical dimensions; instead its concern is precisely what role reason plays in all ethical behavior. It is the role of reason and knowledge in Aristotle's *Ethics* that manifests such striking analogies to the role of historical knowledge.

By criticizing the Socratic-Platonic intellectualism involved in the

---

22. In the following we shall refer to especially the *Nichomachean Ethics* and in particular Book VI.

question of the Good, Aristotle became the founder of ethics as a discipline independent from metaphysics. He demonstrated that the Platonic idea of the Good is a vacuous generality and contrasts to it a *human good,* that is to say, good in relation to human activity. The target of the Aristotelian critique is the identity of virtue and knowledge, of *arete* and *logos,* as it was promulgated in Socratic-Platonic ethics. In defining the fundamental element of human ethical knowledge as *orexis* (desire), and by the organization of this desire into an habitual disposition—into a *hexis*—Aristotle reduces the doctrine of his teachers to its proper scale. Remember that according to Aristotle's theory, practice and habit (*ethos*) are at the basis of *arete.* We see this significance in the very name "ethics."

Ethical being, as a specifically human undertaking, is distinguished from natural being because it is not simply a collection of capacities or innervating forces. Man, on the contrary, is a being who only becomes what he is and acquires his bearing by what he does, by the "how" of his actions. It is in this sense that Aristotle differentiates between the domain of *ethos* and that of *physics.* Although it is not devoid of all natural regularities, the ethical domain is, however, distinguished by the inconstancy of human precepts and thus stands in contrast to the natural domain where stable laws prevail.

The question raised by Aristotle at this point concerns the possibility of a philosophical knowledge of man *qua* ethical being; in this regard he must ask what function knowledge should fulfill in the constitution of ethical behavior. If, in fact, man does acquire the good—his own particular good—within an altogether concrete and practical situation, the task which befalls ethical knowledge can only be to ferret out just exactly what demands this situation places on him. We would say the same thing by affirming that the proper task of ethical consciousness is to gauge a concrete situation by the light of the most general ethical requirements. The other side of the coin is that general knowledge, by virtue of its very generality, is unmindful of concrete situations and their exigencies; in itself, general knowledge knows not how to be applied to a concrete situation and even threatens to obscure the meaning of the concrete exigencies which a factual situation could pose to it. We mean here not only that the methodological aspect of philosophical ethics is far from a simple matter, but above all that in a sense every philosophical method necessarily involves a certain ethical problem. In opposition to the Platonic doctrine of the idea of the Good, Aristotle vigorously emphasizes that in the domain of ethics there is no question of aspiring to the rarefied exactitude of mathematics; in the concrete human situations in which we find ourselves such misguided aspirations would obscure our real goal, which is always ethical being. Such a calculus could only organize the elements of an ethical problem according to their major vectors and then, through plotting their contours, furnish a sort of template [*d'appui*] to ethical consciousness. On closer examination, this immediately implies a moral problem. In fact, it is essential to the phenomenon of ethics not only that the agent knows in general how to decide and what to prefer, but also, he must know and understand how he ought to act in the given occasion, a responsibility that he can never evade. Thus it is essential that ethical sciences—while they may contribute to the clarification of the problems of ethical consciousness—never usurp the place properly belonging to concrete ethical consciousness. Indeed, for those who listen to one of Aristotle's lessons, for this audience who would find therein a template for their ethical consciousness, all of this presupposes a whole series of things. To begin with, a listener must be sufficiently mature so that he does not demand of the instruction he receives more than it can give him. In more positive terms we might say: it is indispensable that through practice and education the listener may have already formed a *habitudo* which he takes into the concrete situations of his life, a *habitudo* which will be confirmed and solidified by each new action.

As we see, conforming to his general principle, the method that Aristotle follows is defined in terms of the particular object. According to the exposition presented in Aristotle's *Ethics,* this object is determined by the relation between ethical being and ethical knowhow and we must elucidate this special relation. Aristotle remains within the Socratic-Platonic mold in the sense that for him knowledge is still an essential moment in ethical behavior. It is the balance he strikes between the Socratic-Platonic heritage and his own conception of *ethos* that will constitute the subject of our following analysis.

It is obvious from our foregoing examination that hermeneutical knowledge, too, must reject an objectivist style of knowing. More-

over, in speaking of the affinity that characterizes the relation between the interpreter and the tradition he interprets, we saw that
understanding is itself a constitutive moment in the progress of history. Now neither does Aristotle's description of ethical knowledge
put it in the objectivist camp, nor is the ethical subject or knower
found simply confronting an entity it must verify. From the first, the
subject of ethical knowledge finds itself concerned with and invested
by its object, that is, what it will have to do.

The distinction drawn by Aristotle between ethical know-how
(*phronesis*) and theoretical or scientific knowledge (*episteme*) is particularly evident when we remember that in the eyes of the Greeks,
mathematics represented the ideal of science. Science, that is, knowledge of the immutable, is grounded on demonstration, and consequently everyone is in a position to learn. It is easy to contrast ethical knowledge to this theoretical knowledge. Obviously, in terms of
this distinction, what we call the human sciences are to be considered
as moral sciences. Their object is man and what he has to know
about himself. This human self-apprehension concerns him from the
very first as an acting being; it does not in any way aim at verifying
what is always the case. Quite the opposite, it relates to what is not
necessarily what it is and what could be otherwise at some particular
moment. Only in things of this sort (i.e., in that which is not immutable) can human action intervene.

Because it is a matter of knowledge guiding activity, we could call
to mind what the Greeks called *techne,* the know-how or skill of an
artisan who knows how to produce something. Is ethical knowledge
similar to that of *techne,* as in the statement "I know perfectly well
how I ought to go about it"? Is there a similarity between the man
who makes himself what he ought to be and the artisan who acts of
his own choice in terms of a preconceived intention and plan? Is
there a similarity between the man who, as we said above, is a project of his own possibilities—let us now say of his *eidos*—and the
artisan who prepares a deliberate plan, an *eidos,* for himself and
knows how to execute it in some medium? Undeniably Socrates and
Plato uncovered something very true in applying the concept of
techne on the level of ethical activity. In fact, it is obvious that ethical
know-how and technical know-how have this in common: neither of

them is an abstract of knowledge; instead, in the definition and direction of activity, both of them imply a practical knowledge fashioned to the measure of the concrete tasks before them.

This last characterization leads us to a distinction that is very important in our perspective. It concerns the nuance which delineates the acquisitions due to a teachable technique from those acquisitions made by virtue of a thoroughly concrete experience in everyday practice. The knowledge transmitted by instruction—in a handicraft, for example—is not necessarily of a real practical value nor necessarily superior to the knowledge acquired through practice. In no way do we mean that knowledge that guides its practice (the "art") is in its turn purely theoretical; as a matter of fact, precisely in making use of this "book knowledge" in practice do we acquire the indispensable experience that is *techne.* Thus, Aristotle rightly cites the adage that "*techne* loves *tyche* and *tyche* loves *techne,*" that is to say, the chance for success is offered first to those who know their craft.

What we have said is just as applicable to ethical knowledge. It is obvious that experience by itself, rich though it may be, is an insufficient foundation for ethical know-how or a morally consistent decision; the guidance of moral consciousness by prior knowledge is always indispensable. Thus there is an obvious correspondence between ethical know-how and technical know-how. This allows us to raise the difficult and urgent problem of their difference.

No one can ignore the fact that there are radical differences between ethical know-how and technical know-how. It is evident that man does not deal with himself in the same way that an artisan deals with his material. The question, then, is to learn to distinguish the knowledge one has of oneself *qua* ethical being from the knowledge required to produce something. For Aristotle, this ethical know-how is distinguished just as much from technical knowledge as it is from theoretical knowledge. In fact, he says in a bold and original formula that ethical knowledge is a "knowledge for the sake of oneself." In this way ethical knowledge is clearly distinguished from the theoretical attitude of *episteme.* But how are we to distinguish knowledge for the sake of oneself from technical know-how?

He who knows how to make something has learned thereby a

good, and he understands this good—he knows it for its own sake—
in such a way that he can effectively proceed from the possibility of a
task to its execution. He chooses the right materials and the appropriate means. He knows how to apply what he has learned in general
to a concrete situation. The man who makes an ethical decision has
learned something, too. Through the education and training he
has received, he possesses a general knowledge of what we call right
and just behavior. The function, then, of an ethical decision is to
find what is just within the bounds of a concrete situation. In other
words, the ethical decision for the just is there in order to see all that
the concrete situation demands and to put the matter in some order.
In this sense, then, just like the artisan who is ready to initiate his
work, the putting into effect of an ethical decision deals with a "material"—the situation—and a choice of means. But this said, does
not the anticipated distinction between the two types of knowledge
vanish before our eyes?

We find a whole series of answering elements in Aristotle's analysis of *phronesis*. As Hegel once remarked, what guarantees the genius
of Aristotle is the comprehensiveness of the perspectives taken into
consideration in his descriptions. Let us call attention to just three:

1. A technique is learned and can be forgotten; we can lose a
skill. But ethical reason can neither be learned nor forgotten. Nor is it
like the professional knowledge that one can choose; one cannot put
it down, like a profession, in order to take up another one. By contrast, the subject of ethical reason, of *phronesis*, man always finds himself in an "acting situation" and he is always obliged to use ethical
knowledge and apply it according to the exigencies of his concrete
situation.

But for this very reason, it is problematic to speak of application, since we can only apply what we already possess. Now ethical
knowledge is not our property in the same way that we have something at our disposal and choose to utilize it or not. Thus if it is true
that the image that man forms of himself, that is, what he wishes and
ought to be, is constituted by governing ideas such as right and injustice, courage, fellowship, and so forth, then we readily acknowledge a difference between these ideas and those that the artisan conceives of when he prepares plans for his work. To confirm this

distinction it is sufficient to think of the way we are aware of what is just. Justice is totally relative to the ethical situation in which we find ourselves. We cannot say in a general and abstract way which actions are just and which are not; there are no just actions in themselves, independent of what the situation requires.

One might perhaps object that, nevertheless, a perfect analogy between *techne* and *phronesis* is actually confirmed by what is indexed by the phenomenon of right. Because, one might say, my rights are defined by laws, very often, moreover, by uncodified rules of behavior which are nonetheless valid for everyone. What I regard as my right, what is just, is it not simply the result of the correct application of a law to a concrete case?

However, upon reflection we will see that the idea of application used by this objection is not unequivocal. For as soon as we consider application in its negative aspect, in the form of a non-application, it becomes evident that it means something quite different on the level of an artisan's knowledge than what it does on the level of ethical knowledge. It is quite possible, in fact, that under certain conditions the artisan may be obligated to forego the exact execution of his work plans; he is subject to external conditions, he lacks a tool or material, and so forth. But the fact that he gives up and is content with an imperfect work does not imply that his knowledge of things is augmented or has become more nearly perfect through the experience of failure. On the other hand, when we apply a law the situation is entirely different. It can happen that, owing to the characteristics of a concrete situation, we may be obligated to mitigate the severity of the law—but mitigation is not exclusive of application. Mitigation does not ignore the right expressed in the law, no more than it condones an unjustifiable carelessness in its application. When we mitigate the law we do not abandon it; on the contrary, without this mitigation there would really be no justice.

Aristotle speaks very explicitly of *epieikeia* (equity) as a rectification or an accommodation of the law. He grounds his conception on the fact that every law admits of a certain internal tension with respect to the concrete possibilities of action: a law is always general and can never address itself to all the concrete complexities of a particular case. (Let us note in passing that this is the original problem of juridical hermeneutics.) A law is always insufficient, not by reason of any intrinsic fault, but because the practical world as the field of our actions is always imperfect in comparison to the ideal order envisioned by laws.

For the same reason Aristotle adopts a subtle position on the question of natural right: for him codified law does not, in itself, fulfill the conditions for finding justice. Consequently, Aristotle sees in the deliberations about the function of equity an important juridical task, namely, perfecting codified law. In marked opposition to the strict conventionalism of a juridical positivism, he distinguishes between positive law and natural law. But it would be erroneous to apply this distinction by recourse to the single criterion of the eternity and immutability of nature—by denying these characteristics to positive law while granting them to natural law. For according to Aristotle, the idea of an immutable natural law applies only to the divine world, and he declares that with us humans natural law is in the last analysis just as inconstant as positive law. This theory is confirmed by the examples we read in Aristotle. He reminds us—borrowing the idea from Plato—that, though the right hand is by nature stronger than the left, anyone can train it to become as strong as the other. Another example: measures of wine are everywhere identical; by all appearances, however, they are smaller where purchased than where sold. Aristotle, of course, does not mean that the seller always cheats the buyer, but that each concrete application of the law carries with it the implication that it is not unjust to tolerate a certain elasticity in legal exactitude.

It follows, then, according to Aristotle that the idea of natural law serves only a critical function. Nothing in the idea authorizes us to use it dogmatically by attributing the inviolability of natural law to particular and concrete juridical contents. It is legitimately useful only when the strict application of a law appears incompatible with justice. Thus, the task of a natural law is to lead us to an equitable solution more consonant with justice.

What we have just demonstrated regarding the concept of right is, in principle, valid for all the concepts man has at his disposal in order to determine what he ought to be. These concepts are not fixed in the firmament like the stars; they are what they are only in the concrete situations in which we find ourselves. Therefore, in order to define these concepts we must refer to the use and application which ethical consciousness makes of them.

2. What we have just said also entails a different conceptual relation between the end and the means in ethical knowledge on the one hand, and in technical knowledge on the other.

To begin with, let us note that contrary to what happens on the level of technique the end of ethical knowledge is not a particular thing, but that it determines the complete ethical rectitude of a lifetime. Moreover, and even more important, technical activity does not demand that the means that allow it to arrive at an end be weighed anew on each occasion and personally by the subject who is their practitioner: "He is already an expert; he already knows how to go about it." And since a similar possibility is excluded in advance from ethical knowledge, it follows that we must characterize the ethical domain as one where technical know-how gives way to deliberation and reflection. But it is better to show its positive side: in all situations ethical consciousness—without prior avail to the knowledge of all the facts—is personally responsible for its own decisions. Ethical consciousness does not keep counsel with anyone but itself. Thus the whole problem is summarized in the fact that in moral actions there is no prior knowledge of the right means which realize the end, and this is so because, above all else, the ends themselves are at stake and not perfectly fixed beforehand. This also explains why in his discussion of *phronesis* Aristotle constantly oscillates between defining it as the knowledge of the ends and the knowledge of means.

Just as there can be no dogmatic use made of natural right, still less can we make dogmatic use of ethics. When Aristotle describes the concrete forms of a balanced attitude as to the choice of valid means, he above all relies upon the ethical consciousness which is molded within the exigencies of a concrete situation. Ethical know-how oriented by these ideas is the same knowledge which must respond to the momentary contingencies of a factual situation. Thus, when it is a question of ethical ends we can never speak only of the opportunity of means; the ethical rectitude of the means is an essential component of the ethical validity of ends. To reflect on the means in moral decisions is *eo ipso* an ethical undertaking.

Now, the knowledge for the sake of oneself of which Aristotle speaks is precisely this perfect application which unfolds as personal knowledge (*savoir*) within the intimacy of a given situation. Only in the knowledge of the immediately given is ethical knowledge attained: it is, however, a knowledge that is not of the same order as sensible perceptions. For even if we must pay attention to the demands of the situation, our perception is not a brute perception of facts without meaning. Only within ethical perception does the situation appear to us as a situation for our action and in the light of what is just. Our awareness of the situation is a consciousness of an act which cuts through the situation.

Thus, justice is the opposite not of moral error or illusion but of blindness. In other words, when overwhelmed by his passions man no longer sees what is just or unjust. He is not in error but loses control of himself and, dominated by the play of his passions, is no longer oriented toward the good at all.

Thus, we call ethical knowledge that which encompasses in an entirely unique way our knowledge of ends and means; and precisely from this perspective it is opposed to a purely technical know-how. Consequently, in this field it no longer makes any sense to distinguish between knowledge and experience, since ethical knowledge is also in itself a subspecies of experience. On this score it is even an absolutely primordial form of experience, and perhaps all others constitute but secondary, nonprimordial forms by comparison.

3. The "knowledge for the sake of oneself" of ethical reflection actually implies an absolutely remarkable relation to oneself. This is what the Aristotelian analyses teach us respecting the varieties of *phronesis*.

Alongside *phronesis* there is the phenomenon of understanding in the sense of *synesis*. This is an intentional modification of ethical knowledge when it is a moral question, not for the sake of myself, but for the sake of another. This intentional modification carries with it an ethical appreciation in the sense of being placed by it in the situation of another where the other must act. Here again it is a matter not of a generalized knowledge but of its concretion motivated by the reality of the moment. However, to "live on good terms" with someone is presupposed and only manifests all of its ethical importance in the phenomenon of understanding. Understanding another as a unique phenomenon is not simply the technical knowledge of the psychologist, nor the equivalent everyday experience possessed by the wily [*malin*] or resourceful [*débrouillard*] man. It supposes that one is committed to a just cause and through this commitment one discovers a link with another. This bond is concretized in the phenomenon of moral counsel. One gives and receives, as they say, good counsel only among friends.

This emphasizes that the relationship established between two people is not that of two entities who have nothing to do with one another; instead, understanding is a question of—to employ an idea to which we are by now accustomed—"affinity." According to Aristotle understanding gives rise to the following two correlative phenomena: to a spirit of discernment of another's moral situation and to the resulting tolerance or indulgence. Now what is this discernment if not the virtue of knowing how to equitably judge the situation of another?

Clearly it is not a question here either of a technical know-how. In fact, Aristotle emphasizes the purely virtuous character of ethical know-how. And to put it in even greater relief, he gives a description of the degenerative form of *phronesis* which characterizes the *deinos:* the man who, by means of his shrewd intelligence, turns every situation to his own advantage. Its opposition to real *phronesis* is obvious: the *deinos* uses and abuses his capabilities without any reference to ethical considerations. It is not by chance that the term denoting this man, for whom every situation is an opportunity for self-aggrandizement, is faithfully translated by the word "redoubtable." Nothing is more terrifying than a genius so constituted that he takes no account of good or evil.

SKETCH OF THE FOUNDATIONS
OF A HERMENEUTIC

Let us return to the subject, properly so called, of the present lectures. If we recall the Aristotelian approach to the problem of ethics and its inherent mode of knowledge, it is evident that we have an excellent model at our disposal to guide us in the elucidation of the hermeneutical task. In hermeneutics, no less than with Aristotle, application is a constitutive moment. It can never signify a subsidiary operation appended as an afterthought to understanding: the object of our application determines from the beginning and in its totality the real and concrete content of hermeneutical understanding. Application is not a calibration of some generality given in advance in order to unravel afterwards a particular situation. In attending to a text, for example, the interpreter does not try to apply a general criterion to a particular case; on the contrary, he is interested in the fundamentally original significance of the writing under his consideration.

In order to elucidate the meaning of an authentically historical hermeneutics we started from the failure of historicism we found in Dilthey and then recalled the new ontological dimensions that we owe to the phenomenological analyses of Husserl and Heidegger. Historical knowledge cannot be described according to the model of an objectivist knowledge because it is itself a process which has all the characteristics of an historical event. Understanding must be comprehended in the sense of an existential act, and is therefore a "thrown pro-ject." Objectivism is an illusion. Even as historians, that is, as representatives of a modern and methodic science, we are members of an unbroken chain through which the past addresses us. We have seen that ethical consciousness is at the same time ethical know-how and ethical being. It is this integration of practical knowledge into the substance of morality, the "belongingness" of education or culture (in the etymological sense) to ethical consciousness and the concrete knowledge of obligations and ends, that will provide us with the model to analyze the ontological implications of historical consciousness. Just like Aristotle, though on a very different level, we will see that historical knowledge is at the same time historical know-how and historical being.

It is now a question of determining more concretely the structure of understanding found at the basis of hermeneutics; it is, we have seen, something like an essential affinity with tradition. At this point a traditional hermeneutical rule comes to our aid. It was formulated for the first time by Romantic hermeneutics, but its origin dates back to ancient rhetoric. It concerns the circular relation between the whole and its parts: the anticipated meaning of a whole is understood through the parts, but it is in light of the whole that the parts take on their illuminating function.

The study of a text in a foreign language will serve as our example. In a general way, before we understand anything in a sentence, we proceed by a certain preliminary structuration which thus constitutes the groundwork for later understanding. This process is dominated by a global meaning we have in view, and is based on the relations which an earlier context affords us. But of course this purely anticipatory global meaning awaits confirmation or amendment pending its ability to form a unified and consistent vision. Let us think of this structure in a dynamic way; the effective unity of the anticipated meaning comes out as the comprehension is enlarged and renovated by concentric circles. The perfect coherence of the global and final meaning is the criterion for *the* understanding. When coherence is wanting, we say that understanding is deficient.

The hermeneutical circle of the whole and its parts, especially in its objective and subjective aspects, was examined by Schleiermacher. On the one hand, every text belongs to the whole of the author's works and then to the literary genre from which it originates. On the other hand, if we wish to grasp the text in the authenticity of its unique meaning, then we must see it as a manifestation of a creative moment and replace it within the whole spiritual context of the author. Only from the totality formed, not only by objective facts, but in the first place by the subjectivity of the author, can understanding arise. In the extrapolation of Schleiermacher's theory we encounter Dilthey who tells us about an "orientation towards the center" to describe the understanding of the whole. In this way Dilthey applied to the complex of historical research the traditional hermeneutical principle that a text must be understood through itself. It remains to be seen, however, if the idea of the circle of understanding is grounded upon an accurate description.

To relate, as Schleiermacher and Romanticism tell us, to the subjective factors of understanding does not seem at all convincing. When we understand a text we do not put ourselves in the place of the other, and it is not a matter of penetrating the spiritual activities of the author; it is simply a question of grasping the meaning, significance, and aim of what is transmitted to us. In other words, it is a question of grasping the intrinsic worth of the arguments put forward and doing so as completely as possible. In one move we find ourselves within the dimension of the aim [*la visée*], already comprehensible in itself, and without so much as a second look at the subjectivity of the partner. The meaning of hermeneutical inquiry is to disclose the miracle of understanding texts or utterances and not the mysterious communication of souls. Understanding is a participation in the common aim.

The objective aspect of the hermeneutical circle may also be described in a different way than what we read in Schleiermacher. For it is really what we have in common with tradition that we relate to and that determines our anticipations and guides our understanding. Consequently, this circle is not at all of a purely formal nature, from neither a subjective nor an objective viewpoint. On the contrary, it comes into play solely within the space established between the text and he who understands. The purpose of the interpreter is to make himself a mediator between the text and all that the text implies. Therefore, the aim of hermeneutics is always to restore the authentic intention and reestablish the concordance, to fill in the lacunas of the argumentation. This is entirely confirmed by the history of hermeneutics when we follow closely its major contours: St. Augustine spoke to us of the Old Testament which must be seen through Christian truths; Protestantism resumed this same task during the Reformation; in the age of the Enlightenment we are persuaded that the rational meaning of a text offers the first approach to its understanding, and that only the absence of such a rational meaning demands an historical interpretation. But is it not curious: while Romanticism and Schleiermacher became the messengers of historical self-consciousness, the same Romanticism and the same Schleiermacher never even dreamed of attributing to their own tradition the value of a true foundation.

Yet, among Schleiermacher's immediate predecessors, there is one, the philologist Friedrich Ast, who had clear views of this hermeneutical task. According to him, hermeneutics plays a mediating role: that of establishing agreement between the true traditions of antiquity and Christianity. In opposition to the *Aufklärung,* this perspective creates a new situation, in the sense that it was no longer a question of reconciling the authority of tradition with natural reason but of effecting a relation between two different traditions. However, Ast resumes the old tradition to build up an intrinsic and concrete agreement of antiquity with Christianity, and thereby preserves the real task of a nonformal hermeneutics, a forgotten task by the time of Schleiermacher and his successors. If the philologist Ast avoided this forgetfulness, it is by virtue of the spiritual influence of idealistic philosophies and above all of Schelling, who inspired him.

Today, it is through Heidegger's existential analysis that we again discover the deeper meaning of the circular structure of understanding. Here is what we read in Heidegger:

> [The hermeneutic circle] is not to be reduced to the level of a vicious circle or even a circle which is merely tolerated. In the circle is hidden a positive possibility of the most primordial kind of knowing. To be sure, we genuinely take hold of this possibility only when, in our interpretation, we have understood that our first, last, and constant task is never to allow our fore-having, fore-sight, and fore-conceptions to be presented to us by fancies and popular conceptions, but rather to make the scientific theme secure by working out these fore-structures in terms of the things themselves.[23]

Just as they stand, these lines announce not only the conditions imposed on the practice of understanding; they also describe the manner in which interpretation always proceeds when it intends an understanding tempered to the "thing itself." For the very first time the positive ontological meaning of the circle that understanding implies is explicitly affirmed. Every authentic interpretation must provide itself against the happenstance arbitration of baroque ideas and against the limitations caused by unconscious habits of thought. It is evident that in order to be authentic the inquiring gaze must be focused on the thing itself, and in such a manner that it may be grasped, as it were, "in person." Likewise it is evident that an understanding faithful to the meaning of the text, for example, is not a matter of a simple, more or less vague wish nor of good and pious intentions, but rather has the same meaning as the program Heidegger designated as the "first, last, and constant task" of interpretative understanding. Now, the circular character of understanding is precisely the outcome of the effort which leads the interpreter to strictly abide by this program, despite any errors he might commit in the course of his investigations.

Let us think once more about textual interpretation. As soon as he discovers some initially understandable elements, the interpreter sketches out the meaning of the whole text. But these first meaningful elements only come to the fore provided that he sets about

23. Heidegger, op. cit., 153.

reading with a more or less definite interest. Understanding the "thing" which arises there, before him, is nothing other than elaborating a preliminary project which will be progressively corrected in the course of the interpretative reading. Let us describe this process, realizing that it is obviously only a kind of abbreviation, since the process is much more complicated. In the beginning, without the revision of the first project, there is nothing to constitute the basis for a new meaning; but at the same time, discordant projects aspire to constitute themselves as *the* unified meaning until the first interpretation is modified and replaces its initial presupposed concepts by more adequate ones. Heidegger described this perpetual oscillation of interpretative visions, that is, understanding being the formative process of a new project. One who follows this course always risks falling under the suggestion of his own rough drafts; he runs the risk that the anticipation which he has prepared may not conform to what the thing is. Therefore, the constant task of understanding lies in the elaboration of projects that are authentic and more proportionate to its object. In other words, it is a bold venture that awaits its reward in confirmation by the object. What we can term here as objectivity cannot be anything other than the confirmation of an anticipation which results even in the very course of its elaboration. For how do we judge that an anticipation is arbitrary and inadequate to its task, if not by confronting it with the only thing which can demonstrate its futility? Every textual interpretation must begin then with the interpreter's reflection on the preconceptions which result from the hermeneutical situation in which he finds himself. He must legitimate them, that is, look for their origin and adequacy.

Under these circumstances we will understand why the task of hermeneutics as described by Heidegger is not a simple matter of recommending a method. Quite the contrary, he demands nothing less than a radical account of actual understanding as everyone who understands has always accomplished it.

To give an example of the procedure that I just spoke about, let us think of the questions which arise with the analysis of an ancient text or else when we ask for a translation. It is easily seen that the enterprise must begin by our attempt to grasp the author's entirely personal manner of using words and meanings in his text: how arbitrary it would be to want to understand the text as an exclusive function of our own vocabulary and particular conceptual baggage. It is immediately evident that our understanding must be guided by the peculiar linguistic customs of the epoch or author themselves. However, we must ask how this task can be realized *in concreto,* especially with respect to semantics: how to distinguish between unconventional language in general and unconventional language specific to the text. Our reply is to bring out the fact that we get our first initiation necessarily from the text itself: the experience of an impasse—maybe the text is totally incomprehensible to us or the response it seems to offer contradicts our anticipations—discloses the possibility of an unconventional linguistic usage.

What is valuable for the implicit aims of a linguistic usage, the significant tendencies with which the words are laden, is even more valid regarding our anticipations of the content of a text, anticipations which positively determine our preconception of it. Yet this case is more complex than the one we have just seen.

It is commonly admitted that when we speak everyday language we use words in their usual sense. While presupposing this we need not presuppose that thoughts (or better, other people's opinions [*les dires d'autrui*]) which have been understood are therefore *of themselves* and from the mere fact that they have been grasped, organically integrated into my particular system of opinions and expectations. To grasp something is not yet to approve of it. It is always implied—to begin with—that I acquaint myself with other people's opinions without committing my own.

This distinction must be maintained. Nevertheless, it must be added that it practically never happens that in taking cognizance of other people's opinions I do not feel myself *ipso facto* invited to take a position on their subject matter; and furthermore, it is usually a matter of feeling invited to take a favorable position. We see in what sense we are going to be able to say that the hermeneutical intention always implies that it slips into a question of another order: that is, what is the acceptable meaning of a stated opinion, the integratable meaning of a signification? It is evident that in a concrete situation the two moments are inseparable: the latter moment, which is more than a pure and simple grasping, even determines in every case the concrete character of "grasping," and it is precisely into this nexus that the hermeneutical problem is inserted.

What in fact are the implications of this description?—But do not make me say what I have not in fact said; and I have not said that when we listen to someone or when we read we ought to forget our own opinions or shield ourselves against forming an anticipatory idea about the content of the communication. In reality, to be open to other people's opinions, to a text, and so forth, implies right off that they are *situated* in my system of opinions, or better, that I situate myself in relation to them. In other words, it is of course true—and everyone admits it—that other people's opinions can have in themselves an indefinite manifold of different meanings (in contrast to the relatively perfect concordance that dictionary words present); *in concreto*, however, when we listen to someone or read a text we discriminate, from our own standpoint, among the different possible meanings—namely, what *we* consider possible—and we reject the remainder which seem to us unquestionably absurd. On these grounds, and despite the best presumptions attached to a literal reading, we are naturally tempted to sacrifice, in the name of impossibility, everything that we totally fail to integrate into our system of anticipations.

The authentic intention of understanding, however, is this: in reading a text, in wishing to understand it, what we always expect is that it will inform us of something. A consciousness formed by the authentic hermeneutical attitude will be receptive to the origins and entirely foreign features of that which comes to it from outside its own horizons. Yet this receptivity is not acquired with an objectivist neutrality: it is neither possible, necessary, nor desirable that we put ourselves within brackets. The hermeneutical attitude supposes only that we self-consciously designate our opinions and prejudices and qualify them as such, and in so doing strip them of their extreme character. In keeping to this attitude we grant the text the opportunity to appear as an authentically different being and to manifest its own truth, over and against our own preconceived notions.

The phenomenological descriptions of Heidegger are perfectly correct when in the heart of alleged "immediate givens" he emphasizes the anticipatory structure constitutive of all understanding. But this is not all. *Being and Time* is also an example of the application to a concrete case of the universal hermeneutical task which derives from the anticipatory structure characteristic of understanding. In *Being and Time* this concrete case is the ontological problem. Still, the question posed to ontology must be posed concretely, that is, without making an abstraction of the layered density [*l' épaisseur*] of the hermeneutical situation which frames the meaning of the question. According to Heidegger, to be able to explain the hermeneutical situation of the ontological question, that is, its implicit "fore-having, fore-sight, and fore-conceptions," it is indispensable to reexamine the general ontological question in a concrete way. For this reason he systematically addresses the question to the decisive moments in the history of metaphysics. From all evidence, Heidegger's approach serves this universal task, which appears in all its exigencies only to an historical-hermeneutical consciousness.

Consequently there is a strong need to elaborate a consciousness which directs and controls the anticipations involved in our cognitive approaches. Thus we are assured of a truly valid understanding, since it is intimately linked to the immediate object of our intentions. This is what Heidegger means when he claims that we "make the scientific theme secure by working out these fore-structures in terms of the 'things themselves,'" for which they constitute the horizon.

Certainly no one will accuse us of unbridled exaggeration when we conclude by these analyses that historical consciousness is no longer an unbounded projection. It is indispensable that consciousness take account of its secular prejudices and prevailing anticipations. Without this purification, the illumination we gain by historical consciousness is but dim and ineffective. Without it our knowledge of the historically other is but a simple reduction. A cognitive procedure which involves prejudices or anticipations, but also preconceptions about method or what "must" be an historical fact, such a procedure flattens experience and inevitably leads to a betrayal of what is specifically other.

We will now examine how to develop in the hermeneutical domain what we have just established regarding an historically operative consciousness. On this point, too, the Heideggerian description marks an important turning point. The pre-Heideggerian theories confined themselves to the framework of a purely formal relation between the whole and the parts. From a subjective point of view, we can express the same thing by characterizing the hermeneutical circle as a dialectic between the divination of the meaning of the whole and its subsequent articulation in the parts. In other words, according to the Romantic theories, the circular movement is not a result, but a deficiency—however necessary—of inquiry. Having wandered through a text in all its directions and various articulations, the circular movement finally disappears in the light of a perfect understanding. For Schleiermacher this theory of hermeneutical understanding reaches its apogee in the idea of a pure, divinatory act, a purely subjective function. Obviously, such a notion of hermeneutical understanding is inclined to violate the genuinely foreign and mysterious which lies hidden in texts. In contrast, Heidegger, in his description of the interpretative circle, vigorously insists upon the fact that understanding a text never ceases to be determined by the anticipatory impulses of pre-understanding.

Let us take this one step further. I have just said that all understanding can be characterized as a system of circular relations between the whole and its parts. However, this sort of characterization must be completed by a supplementary determination: I will explain it by speaking of the anticipation of perfect coherence. To begin with, this perfect coherence can be understood in the sense of an anticipation of a purely formal nature: it is an "idea." It is, nevertheless, always at work in achieving understanding. It signifies that nothing is really understandable unless it is actually presented in the form of a coherent meaning. For example, it is implicit from the outset in our intention of reading a text that we consider the text to be coherent, unless this presupposition proves untenable, in other words, as long as the message of the text is not denounced as incomprehensible. It is at just this instant that doubt appears and we set to work with our critical instruments. We need not specify here the rules of this critical examination since in every respect their justification is inseparable from the concrete understanding of a text. Thus our understanding is guided by the anticipation of perfect coherence, and this anticipation shows that it possesses a content which is not merely formal. In fact, it is not only the unity of an *immanent* meaning which is presupposed in the concrete operations of understanding: every textual understanding presupposes that it is guided by *transcendent* expectations, expectations whose origins must be looked for in the relation between the intentional object of the text and the truth.

When we receive a letter we see what is communicated through the eyes of our correspondent, but while seeing things through his eyes, it is not his personal opinions, but, rather, the event itself that we believe we ought to know by this letter. In reading a letter, to aim at the personal thoughts of our correspondent and not at the matters about which he reports is to contradict what is meant by a letter. Likewise, the anticipations implied by our understanding of an historical document emanate from our relations to things and not the way these things are transmitted to us. Just as we give credence to the news in a letter because we assume that our correspondent personally witnessed the event or has validly learned of it, in the same way we are open to the possibility that the transmitted text may offer a more authentic picture of the thing itself than our own speculations. Only the disappointment of having let the text speak for itself and having then arrived at a bad result could prompt us to attempt understanding it by recourse to a supplementary psychological or historical point of view.

Thus, the anticipation of perfect coherence presupposes not only that the text is an adequate expression of a thought, but also that it really transmits to us the truth. This confirms that the primordial significance of the idea of understanding is that of "knowing about something" and that only in a derivative sense does it mean understanding the intentions of another as personal opinions. Thus we come back to the original conditions of every hermeneutics: it must be a shared and comprehensible reference to the things in themselves. It is this condition which determines the possibility that a unified meaning can be aimed at, and thus also the possibility that the anticipation of perfect coherence may actually be applicable.

We have emphasized the role, within our cognitive approach, played by certain absolutely fundamental anticipations, that is, anticipations common to us all. We are now in a position to determine more precisely the meaning of the phenomenon of affinity, that is to say, the factor of tradition in a historical-hermeneutical attitude. Hermeneutics must start from the fact that understanding is related to the thing itself as manifest in the tradition, and at the same time to a tradition from where the thing can speak to me. On the other hand, he who achieves hermeneutical understanding must realize that our relation to things is not a matter of course and unproblematic. We found the hermeneutical task precisely on the tension that exists between the familiar and the foreign character of the message transmitted to us by tradition. But this tension is not as it was for Schleiermacher, that is, a psychological tension. It is, on the contrary, the meaning and structure of hermeneutical historicity. It is not some psychic state, but the very thing delivered over by tradition which is the object of hermeneutical inquiry. By a relation to both the familiar and the foreign character of historical messages, hermeneutics claims a central situation. The interpreter is torn between his belongingness to a tradition and his distance from the objects which are the theme of his investigation.

This hermeneutical situation, by which hermeneutics is henceforth placed in the middle of things, serves to emphasize a phenomenon which has received scant attention thus far. It is the question of temporal distance and its meaning for understanding. Contrary to what we often imagine, time is not a chasm which we could bridge over in order to recover the past; in reality, it is the ground which supports the arrival of the past and where the present takes its roots. Temporal distance is not a distance in the sense of a distance to be bridged or overcome. This was the naive prejudice of historicism. It believed it could reach the solid terrain of historical objectivity by striving to place itself within the vantage point of a past age and think with the concepts and representations particular to that epoch. Actually, it is rather a matter of considering temporal distance as a fundament of positive and productive possibilities for understanding. It is not a distance to be overcome, but a living continuity of elements which cumulatively become a tradition, a tradition which is the light wherein all that we carry with us from our past, everything transmitted to us, makes its appearance.

It is not an exaggeration to speak of the productivity of the historical process. We all know how we make more or less arbitrary judgments when our ideas are not clarified by the passage of time. Limiting ourselves to an example, let us think of the uncertainty which characterizes our esthetic standpoint in the face of contemporary art. It is obviously a matter of uncontrollable prejudices which conceal the real content—authentic or not—of these works. Momentary relations must be erased in order to know if it is a question of masterpieces or not and if we can discover the true sense enabling contemporary art to enter an ongoing tradition. Obviously, this does not happen from one moment to another, but is developed in an indefinite process. The temporal distance which produces the filter is not of a definite magnitude, but evolves in a continuous movement of universalization. Universality purified by time is a second productive aspect of temporality. Its work develops a new set of prejudices. It is a matter of prejudices which are neither partial nor particular, but which constitute, on the contrary, the legitimate guiding for genuine understanding.

This is yet another specification of the hermeneutical task. Only by virtue of the phenomenon and clarified concept of temporal distance can the specifically *critical* task of hermeneutics be resolved, that is, of knowing how to distinguish between blind prejudices and those which illuminate, between false prejudices and true prejudices. We must raise to a conscious level the prejudices which govern understanding and in this way realize the possibility that other aims emerge in their own right from tradition—which is nothing other than realizing the possibility that we can understand something in its otherness.

To denounce something as prejudice is to suspend its presumed validity; in fact a prejudice in the strict sense of that term cannot get hold of us unless we are sufficiently unconscious of it. But we cannot successfully take a prejudice into account so long as it is simply at work; it must be somehow provoked. Now this provocation of our prejudices is precisely the fruit of a renewed encounter with a tradition which was itself, perhaps, at their origin. And, in fact, what demands our efforts at understanding is manifest before and in itself in its character of otherness. And this leads us back to a point we made above: we must realize that every understanding begins with the fact that something *calls out* to us. And since we know the precise meaning of this affirmation, we claim *ipso facto* the bracketing of prejudices. Thus we arrive at our first conclusion: bracketing our judgments in general, and naturally first of all our own prejudices, will end by imposing upon us the demands of a radical reflection on the idea of questioning as such.

The essence of questioning is to lay bare and keep alert for possibilities. We will shortly see in what sense. When one of our convictions or opinions becomes problematic as a consequence of n ' meneutical information, and though it is disclosed as prejudice, this does not imply that it is automatically replaced by a sort of definitive truth; this was the naive thesis of historical objectivism. Such a thesis forgets that the displaced conviction and the truth which denounces and replaces it are both members of an uninterrupted chain of events. The former prejudice is not simply cast aside. For in reality it has an important role to play later on, although a different one than while it was still only implicit. It must also be said that the denounced prejudice can only play its new role if it is exploited to the maximum. It is a difficult task to replace a conviction, to denounce it as a prejudice; this is precisely because whatever replaced it cannot present its credentials until the position under assault is itself unmasked and denounced as prejudice. Every new position that replaces another continues to need the former because it cannot itself be explained so long as it knows neither in what nor by what it is opposed.

We see that there are dialectical relations between the former and the new, between, on the one hand, the prejudice organically a part of my particular system of convictions or opinions, that is, the implicit prejudice, and on the other hand, the new element which denounces it, that is, the foreign element which provokes my system or one of its elements. The same can be said of the relation between my own opinion in the process of losing its implicit persuasive force by being exposed as prejudice, and the new element that, for the moment, is still external to my system of opinions, but is in the process of becoming my own though being disclosed as truly other than my own former opinion. This is to say that there are dialectical relations between the inauthentically "mine" and the authentically "mine" (the implicit prejudice in the process of being exposed as prejudice). In other words, the relation is between "my own" in the process of becoming authentic through the new hermeneutical information which provoked it, and the hermeneutical information itself, that is, the information in the process of entering into my system of opinions and convictions—in the process of becoming mine; that is to say that this new hermeneutical information gains entrance into my system by its opposition to the denounced prejudice and by this opposition it is revealed as strangely other. The universal mediator of this dialectic is that denouncing an opinion as prejudice and disclosure of the truly different in hermeneutical information transforms an implicit "mine" into an authentic "mine," makes an inadmissable other into a genuine other and thus assimilable in its otherness.

Historical objectivism is naive because it never follows its reflections to their conclusion. In its trusting blindness to the presuppositions of its method, it totally forgets the historicity which is its own. An historical consciousness which proposes the task of being truly concrete must already consider itself as an essentially historical phenomenon. However, to define consciousness as historical consciousness or to grant that it is such remains a mere verbalization so long as historical consciousness is not yet actualized: that is, we must question it and question it radically. There is a notion of the historical object which is simply the naive correlative of the thought of historical objectivism. For historical objectivism the historicity of the object is an illusion to be overcome; outside of these illusions the true object is no longer historical! Or, in other words, for historical objectivism the historical object is a mixture of the in-itself and the for-us; a mélange of the "true ahistorical object" and our historical illusions. Radical questioning denounces the notion of an historical object so characterized as a construction of objectivistic thought, motivated—I say *motivated,* an implicit motivation—by the primordial historicity of knowledge and the historical object which together have affinities. The notion of "historical illusions" as the result of a "true and ahistorical object" is the result of an objectivistic or naturalistic interpretation; furthermore, the two interpretations are interdependent: they are the mutual complements of one another.

Not only the concept, but even the expression "historical object" seems useless to me. What we mean to designate by this phrase is not an object at all, but a unity of "mine" and "other." I repeat again what I have often insisted upon: every hermeneutical understanding begins and ends with the thing itself. But it is necessary to guard against, on the one hand, a misunderstanding of the role of temporal distance that is between the beginning and the end, and, on the other hand, an idealizing objectification of the thing itself, as historical objectivism has done. The despecialization of temporal distance and the de-idealization of the thing itself allows us to understand how it is possible to know in the historical object the genuinely other despite "my own" convictions and opinions; that is to say, how it is possible to know them *both.* Thus it is more true to state that the historical object, in the authentic sense of that term, is not an object but the unity of one with the other. It is the relationship, that is, affinity, through which they both manifest themselves: the historical reality on the one hand and the reality of historical understanding on the other. It is this unity which is primordial historicity where knowledge and the historical object manifest themselves in their affiliation [*d'une manière 'affine'*]. An object which comes to us through history is not only an object which one discerns from afar, but is the "center" in which historically operative being and historically operative consciousness appear.

I will say then that the condition for hermeneutics to think about historical reality properly so called, comes to us from what I call the *principle of historical productivity*. Properly understood, this effectuates a mediation between the once and the now; it develops in itself all the continual series of perspectives through which the past presents and addresses itself to us. In this radical and universal sense, historical self-consciousness is not the abandonment of philosophy's eternal task, but is the path granted to us for reaching the truth, which is always our goal. And I see in the relation of all understanding to language, the way in which consciousness opens out to historical productivity.[24]

24. The systematic implications of an historically operative hermeneutics, such as has just been sketched here, and the centrality of the phenomenon of language, are illuminated in the third part of the author's *Wahrheit und Methode: Grundzuge einer philosophischen Hermeneutik* (Tübingen: J. C. B. Mohr, 1960, 1965), 361–465.

3

Modernity—
An Incomplete Project

In 1980, architects were admitted to the Biennial in Venice, following painters and filmmakers. The note sounded at this first Architecture Biennial was one of disappointment. I would describe it by saying that those who exhibited in Venice formed an avant-garde of reversed fronts. I mean that they sacrificed the tradition of modernity in order to make room for a new historicism. Upon this occasion, a critic of the German newspaper, *Frankfurter Allgemeine Zeitung,* advanced a thesis whose significance reaches beyond this particular event; it is a diagnosis of our times: "Postmodernity definitely presents itself as antimodernity." This statement describes an emotional current of our times which has penetrated all spheres of intellectual life. It has placed on the agenda theories of postenlightenment, postmodernity, even of posthistory.

From history we know the phrase "the ancients and the moderns." Let me begin by defining these concepts. The term "modern" has a long history, one which has been investigated by Hans Robert

This essay was originally delivered as a talk in September 1980 when Habermas was awarded the Theodor W. Adorno prize by the city of Frankfurt. It was subsequently delivered as a James Lecture of the New York Institute for the Humanities at New York University in March 1981 and published under the title "Modernity Versus Postmodernity" in *New German Critique* 22 (Winter 1981). It is reprinted here by permission of the author and the publisher.

Jauss.[1] The word "modern" in its Latin form "modernus" was used for the first time in the late fifth century in order to distinguish the present, which had become officially Christian, from the Roman and pagan past. With varying content, the term "modern" again and again expresses the consciousness of an epoch that relates itself to the past of antiquity, in order to view itself as the result of a transition from the old to the new.

Some writers restrict this concept of modernity to the Renaissance, but this is historically too narrow. People considered themselves modern during the period of Charles the Great in the twelfth century, as well as in France of the late seventeenth century at the time of the famous "Querelle des Anciens et des Modernes." That is to say, the term "modern" appeared and reappeared exactly during those periods in Europe when the consciousness of a new epoch formed itself through a renewed relationship to the ancients—whenever, moreover, antiquity was considered a model to be recovered through some kind of imitation.

The spell which the classics of the ancient world cast upon the spirit of later times was first dissolved with the ideals of the French Enlightenment. Specifically, the idea of being modern by looking back to the ancients changed with the belief, inspired by modern science, in the infinite progress of knowledge and in the infinite advance towards social and moral betterment. Another form of modernist consciousness was formed in the wake of this change. The Romantic modernist sought to oppose the antique ideals of the classicists; he looked for a new historical epoch and found it in the idealized Middle Ages. However, this new ideal age, established early in the nineteenth century, did not remain a fixed ideal. In the course of the nineteenth century, there emerged out of this Romantic spirit that radicalized consciousness of modernity which freed itself from all specific historical ties. This most recent modernism simply makes

1. Jauss is a prominent German literary historian and critic involved in "the aesthetics of reception," a type of criticism related to reader-response criticism in this country. For a discussion of "modern" see Jauss, *Ästhetische Normen und geschichtliche Reflexion in der Querelle des Anciens et des Modernes* (Munich, 1964). For a reference in English see Jauss, "History of Art and Pragmatic History," *Toward an Aesthetic of Reception*, trans. Timothy Bahti (Minneapolis: University of Minnesota Press, 1982), 46–48. [Ed.]

an abstract opposition between tradition and the present; and we are, in a way, still the contemporaries of that kind of aesthetic modernity which first appeared in the midst of the nineteenth century. Since then, the distinguishing mark of works which count as modern is "the new" which will be overcome and made obsolete through the novelty of the next style. But, while that which is merely "stylish" will soon become outmoded, that which is modern preserves a secret tie to the classical. Of course, whatever can survive time has always been considered to be a classic. But the emphatically modern document no longer borrows this power of being a classic from the authority of a past epoch; instead, a modern work becomes a classic because it has once been authentically modern. Our sense of modernity creates its own self-enclosed canons of being classic. In this sense we speak, e.g., in view of the history of modern art, of classical modernity. The relation between "modern" and "classical" has definitely lost a fixed historical reference.

THE DISCIPLINE OF AESTHETIC MODERNITY

The spirit and discipline of aesthetic modernity assumed clear contours in the work of Baudelaire. Modernity then unfolded in various avant-garde movements and finally reached its climax in the Café Voltaire of the Dadaists and in surrealism. Aesthetic modernity is characterized by attitudes that find a common focus in a changed consciousness of time. This time consciousness expresses itself through metaphors of the vanguard and the avant-garde. The avant-garde understands itself as invading unknown territory, exposing itself to the dangers of sudden, shocking encounters, conquering an as yet unoccupied future. The avant-garde must find a direction in a landscape into which no one seems to have yet ventured.

But these forward gropings, this anticipation of an undefined future and the cult of the new mean in fact the exaltation of the present. The new time consciousness, which enters philosophy in the writings of Bergson, does more than express the experience of mobility in society, of acceleration in history, of discontinuity in everyday life. The new value placed on the transitory, the elusive and the ephemeral, the very celebration of dynamism, discloses a longing for an undefiled, immaculate, and stable present.

This explains the rather abstract language in which the modernist temper has spoken of the past. Individual epochs lose their distinct forces. Historical memory is replaced by the heroic affinity of the present with the extremes of history—a sense of time wherein decadence immediately recognizes itself in the barbaric, the wild and the primitive. We observe the anarchistic intention of blowing up the continuum of history, and we can account for it in terms of the subversive force of this new aesthetic consciousness. Modernity revolts against the normalizing functions of tradition; modernity lives on the experience of rebelling against all that is normative. This revolt is one way to neutralize the standards of both morality and utility. This aesthetic consciousness continuously stages a dialectical play between secrecy and public scandal; it is addicted to a fascination with that horror which accompanies the act of profaning, and yet is always in flight from the trivial results of profanation.

On the other hand, the time consciousness articulated in avant-garde art is not simply ahistorical; it is directed against what might be called a false normativity in history. The modern, avant-garde spirit has sought to use the past in a different way; it disposes those pasts which have been made available by the objectifying scholarship of historicism, but it opposes at the same time a neutralized history which is locked up in the museum of historicism.

Drawing upon the spirit of surrealism, Walter Benjamin constructs the relationship of modernity to history in what I would call a posthistoricist attitude. He reminds us of the self-understanding of the French Revolution: "The Revolution cited ancient Rome, just as fashion cites an antiquated dress. Fashion has a scent for what is current, whenever this moves within the thicket of what was once." This is Benjamin's concept of the *Jetztzeit,* of the present as a moment of revelation; a time in which splinters of a messianic presence are enmeshed. In this sense, for Robespierre, the antique Rome was a past laden with momentary revelations.[2]

---

2. See Benjamin, "Theses on the Philosophy of History," *Illuminations,* trans. Harry Zohn (New York: Schocken, 1969), 261. [Ed.]

Now, this spirit of aesthetic modernity has recently begun to age. It has been recited once more in the 1960s; after the 1970s, however, we must admit to ourselves that this modernism arouses a much fainter response today than it did fifteen years ago. Octavio Paz, a fellow-traveller of modernity, noted already in the middle of the 1960s that "the avant-garde of 1967 repeats the deeds and gestures of those of 1917. We are experiencing the end of the idea of modern art." The work of Peter Bürger has since taught us to speak of "post-avant-garde" art; this term is chosen to indicate the failure of the sur-realist rebellion.[3] But what is the meaning of this failure? Does it signal a farewell to modernity? Thinking more generally, does the existence of a post-avant-garde mean there is a transition to that broader phenomenon called postmodernity?

This is in fact how Daniel Bell, the most brilliant of the American neoconservatives, interprets matters. In his book, *The Cultural Contradictions of Capitalism,* Bell argues that the crises of the developed societies of the West are to be traced back to a split between culture and society. Modernist culture has come to penetrate the values of everyday life; the life-world is infected by modernism. Because of the forces of modernism, the principle of unlimited self-realization, the demand for authentic self-experience and the subjectivism of a hyperstimulated sensitivity have come to be dominant. This temperament unleashes hedonistic motives irreconcilable with the discipline of professional life in society, Bell says. Moreover, modernist culture is altogether incompatible with the moral basis of a purposive, rational conduct of life. In this manner, Bell places the burden of responsibility for the dissolution of the Protestant ethic (a phenomenon which had already disturbed Max Weber) on the "adversary culture." Culture in its modern form stirs up hatred against the conventions and virtues of everyday life, which has become rationalized under the pressures of economic and administrative imperatives.

I would call your attention to a complex wrinkle in this view. The impulse of modernity, we are told on the other hand, is exhausted;

3. For Paz on the avant-garde see in particular *Children of the Mire: Modern Poetry from Romanticism to the Avant-Garde* (Cambridge: Harvard University Press, 1974), 148–64. For Burger see *Theory of the Avant-Garde* (Minneapolis: University of Minnesota Press, 1983). [Ed.]

anyone who considers himself avant-garde can read his own death warrant. Although the avant-garde is still considered to be expanding, it is supposedly no longer creative. Modernism is dominant but dead. For the neoconservative the question then arises: how can norms arise in society which will limit libertinism, reestablish the ethic of discipline and work? What new norms will put a brake on the levelling caused by the social welfare state so that the virtues of individual competition for achievement can again dominate? Bell sees a religious revival to be the only solution. Religious faith tied to a faith in tradition will provide individuals with clearly defined identities and existential security.

CULTURAL MODERNITY AND SOCIETAL MODERNIZATION

One can certainly not conjure up by magic the compelling beliefs which command authority. Analyses like Bell's, therefore, only result in an attitude which is spreading in Germany no less than in the U.S.: an intellectual and political confrontation with the carriers of cultural modernity. I cite Peter Steinfels, an observer of the new style which the neoconservatives have imposed upon the intellectual scene in the 1970s:

> The struggle takes the form of exposing every manifestation of what could be considered an oppositionist mentality and tracing its "logic" so as to link it to various forms of extremism: drawing the connection between modernism and nihilism . . . between government regulation and totalitarianism, between criticism of arms expenditures and subservience to communism, between women's liberation or homosexual rights and the destruction of the family . . . between the left generally and terrorism, anti-Semitism, and fascism . . . [4]

The *ad hominem* approach and the bitterness of these intellectual accusations have also been trumpeted loudly in Germany. They should not be explained so much in terms of the psychology of neoconser-

---

4. Peter Steinfels, *The Neoconservatives: The Men Who Are Changing America's Politics* (New York: Simon and Schuster, 1979), 65.

vative writers; rather, they are rooted in the analytical weaknesses of neoconservative doctrine itself.

Neoconservatism shifts onto cultural modernism the uncomfortable burdens of a more or less successful capitalist modernization of the economy and society. The neoconservative doctrine blurs the relationship between the welcomed process of societal modernization on the one hand, and the lamented cultural development on the other. The neoconservative does not uncover the economic and social causes for the altered attitudes toward work, consumption, achievement and leisure. Consequently, he attributes all of the following—hedonism, the lack of social identification, the lack of obedience, narcissism, the withdrawal from status and achievement competition—to the domain of culture. In fact, however, culture is intervening in the creation of all these problems in only a very indirect and mediated fashion.

In the neoconservative view, those intellectuals who still feel themselves committed to the project of modernity are then presented as taking the place of those unanalyzed causes. The mood which feeds neoconservatism today in no way originates from discontent about the antinomian consequences of a culture breaking from the museums into the stream of ordinary life. This discontent has not been called into life by modernist intellectuals. It is rooted in deep-seated reactions against the process of societal modernization. Under the pressures of the dynamics of economic growth and the organizational accomplishments of the state, this social modernization penetrates deeper and deeper into previous forms of human existence. I would describe this subordination of the life-worlds under the system's imperatives as a matter of disturbing the communicative infrastructure of everyday life.

Thus, for example, neopopulist protests only express in pointed fashion a widespread fear regarding the destruction of the urban and natural environment and of forms of human sociability. There is a certain irony about these protests in terms of neoconservatism. The tasks of passing on a cultural tradition, of social integration and of socialization require adherence to what I call communicative rationality. But the occasions for protest and discontent originate precisely when spheres of communicative action, centered on the reproduction and transmission of values and norms, are penetrated by a form of modernization guided by standards of economic and administrative rationality—in other words, by standards of rationalization quite different from those of communicative rationality on which those spheres depend. But neoconservative doctrines turn our attention precisely away from such societal processes: they project the causes, which they do not bring to light, onto the plane of a subversive culture and its advocates.

To be sure, cultural modernity generates its own aporias as well. Independently from the consequences of societal modernization and within the perspective of cultural development itself, there originate motives for doubting the project of modernity. Having dealt with a feeble kind of criticism of modernity—that of neoconservatism—let me now move our discussion of modernity and its discontents into a different domain that touches on these aporias of cultural modernity—issues that often serve only as a pretense for those positions that either call for a postmodernity, recommend a return to some form of premodernity, or throw modernity radically overboard.

THE PROJECT OF ENLIGHTENMENT

The idea of modernity is intimately tied to the development of European art, but what I call "the project of modernity" comes only into focus when we dispense with the usual concentration upon art. Let me start a different analysis by recalling an idea from Max Weber. He characterized cultural modernity as the separation of the substantive reason expressed in religion and metaphysics into three autonomous spheres. They are: science, morality, and art. These came to be differentiated because the unified worldviews of religion and metaphysics fell apart. Since the eighteenth century, the problems inherited from these older worldviews could be arranged so as to fall under specific aspects of validity: truth, normative rightness, authenticity and beauty. They could then be handled as questions of knowledge, or of justice and morality, or of taste. Scientific discourse, theories of morality, jurisprudence, and the production and criticism of art could in turn be institutionalized. Each domain of culture could be made to correspond to cultural professions in which problems could be dealt with as the concern of special experts. This professionalized treatment of the cultural tradition brings to the fore the intrinsic structures of each of the three dimensions of culture. There appear the structures of cognitive-instrumental, of moral-practical, and of aesthetic-expressive rationality, each of these under the control of specialists who seem more adept at being logical in these particular ways than other people are. As a result, the distance grows between the culture of the experts and that of the larger public. What accrues to culture through specialized treatment and reflection does not immediately and necessarily become the property of everyday praxis. With cultural rationalization of this sort, the threat increases that the life-world, whose traditional substance has already been devalued, will become more and more impoverished.

The project of modernity formulated in the eighteenth century by the philosophers of the Enlightenment consisted in their efforts to develop objective science, universal morality and law, and autonomous art according to their inner logic. At the same time, this project intended to release the cognitive potentials of each of these domains from their esoteric forms. The Enlightenment philosophers wanted to utilize this accumulation of specialized culture for the enrichment of everyday life—that is to say, for the rational organization of everyday social life.

Enlightenment thinkers of the cast of mind of Condorcet still had the extravagant expectation that the arts and sciences would promote not only the control of natural forces but also understanding of the world and of the self, moral progress, the justice of institutions and even the happiness of human beings. The twentieth century has shattered this optimism. The differentiation of science, morality, and art has come to mean the autonomy of the segments treated by the specialist and their separation from the hermeneutics of everyday communication. This splitting off is the problem that has given rise to efforts to negate the culture of expertise. But the problem won't go away: should we try to hold on to the intentions of the Enlightenment, feeble as they may be, or should we declare the entire project of modernity a lost cause? I now want to return to the problem of artistic culture, having explained why, historically, aesthetic modernity is only a part of cultural modernity in general.

THE FALSE PROGRAMS OF THE
NEGATION OF CULTURE

Greatly oversimplifying, I would say that in the history of modern art one can detect a trend towards ever greater autonomy in the definition and practice of art. The category of "beauty" and the domain of beautiful objects were first constituted in the Renaissance. In the course of the eighteenth century, literature, the fine arts, and music were institutionalized as activities independent from sacred and courtly life. Finally, around the middle of the nineteenth century an aestheticist conception of art emerged that encouraged the artist to produce his work according to the distinct consciousness of art for art's sake. The autonomy of the aesthetic sphere could then become a deliberate project: the talented artist could lend authentic expression to those experiences he had in encountering his own decentered subjectivity, detached from the constraints of routinized cognition and everyday action.

In the mid-nineteenth century, in painting and literature, a movement began which Octavio Paz finds epitomized already in the art criticism of Baudelaire. Color, lines, sounds and movement ceased to serve primarily the cause of representation; the media of expression and the techniques of production themselves became the aesthetic object. Theodor W. Adorno could therefore begin his *Aesthetic Theory* with the following sentence: "It is now taken for granted that nothing which concerns art can be taken for granted any more: neither art itself, nor art in its relationship to the whole, nor even the right of art to exist." And this is what surrealism then denied: *das Existenzrecht der Kunst als Kunst.* To be sure, surrealism would not have challenged the right of art to exist, if modern art no longer had advanced a promise of happiness concerning its own relationship to the whole of life. For Schiller, such a promise was delivered by aesthetic intuition, but not fulfilled by it. Schiller's *Letters on the Aesthetic Education of Man* speaks to us of a utopia reaching beyond art itself. But by the time of Baudelaire, who repeated this *promesse de bonheur* via art, the utopia of reconciliation with society had gone sour. A relation of opposites had come into being; art had become a critical mirror, showing the irreconcilable nature of the aesthetic and the social worlds. This modernist transformation was all the more painfully realized, the more art alienated itself from life and withdrew into the untouchableness of complete autonomy. Out of such emotional currents finally gathered those explosive energies which unloaded in the surrealist attempt to blow up the autarkical sphere of art and to force a reconciliation of art and life.

But all those attempts to level art and life, fiction and praxis, appearance and reality to one plane; the attempts to remove the distinction between artifact and object of use, between conscious staging and spontaneous excitement; the attempts to declare everything to be art and everyone to be an artist, to retract all criteria and to equate aesthetic judgment with the expression of subjective experiences— all these undertakings have proved themselves to be sort of nonsense experiments. These experiments have served to bring back to life, and to illuminate all the more glaringly, exactly those structures of art which they were meant to dissolve. They gave a new legitimacy, as ends in themselves, to appearance as the medium of fiction, to the transcendence of the artwork over society, to the concentrated and planned character of artistic production as well as to the special cognitive status of judgments of taste. The radical attempt to negate art has ended up ironically by giving due exactly to these categories through which Enlightenment aesthetics had circumscribed its object domain. The surrealists waged the most extreme warfare, but two mistakes in particular destroyed their revolt. First, when the containers of an autonomously developed cultural sphere are shattered, the contents get dispersed. Nothing remains from a desublimated meaning or a destructured form; an emancipatory effect does not follow.

Their second mistake has more important consequences. In everyday communication, cognitive meanings, moral expectations, subjective expressions and evaluations must relate to one another. Communication processes need a cultural tradition covering all spheres—cognitive, moral-practical, and expressive. A rationalized everyday life, therefore, could hardly be saved from cultural impoverishment through breaking open a single cultural sphere—art— and so providing access to just one of the specialized knowledge complexes. The surrealist revolt would have replaced only one abstraction.

In the spheres of theoretical knowledge and morality, there are

parallels to this failed attempt of what we might call the false negation of culture. Only they are less pronounced. Since the days of the
Young Hegelians, there has been talk about the negation of philosophy. Since Marx, the question of the relationship of theory and practice has been posed. However, Marxist intellectuals joined a social
movement; and only at its peripheries were there sectarian attempts
to carry out a program of the negation of philosophy similar to the
surrealist program to negate art. A parallel to the surrealist mistakes
becomes visible in these programs when one observes the consequences of dogmatism and of moral rigorism.

A reified everyday praxis can be cured only by creating uncon-
strained interaction of the cognitive with the moral-practical and the
aesthetic-expressive elements. Reification cannot be overcome by
forcing just one of those highly stylized cultural spheres to open up
and become more accessible. Instead, we see under certain circumstances a relationship emerge between terroristic activities and the
overextension of any one of these spheres into other domains: examples would be tendencies to aestheticize politics, or to replace
politics by moral rigorism or to submit it to the dogmatism of a doctrine. These phenomena should not lead us, however, into denouncing the intentions of the surviving Enlightenment tradition as intentions rooted in a "terroristic reason."[5] Those who lump together the
very project of modernity with the state of consciousness and the
spectacular action of the individual terrorist are no less short-sighted
than those who would claim that the incomparably more persistent
and extensive bureaucratic terror practiced in the dark, in the cellars
of the military and secret police, and in camps and institutions, is the
raison d'être of the modern state, only because this kind of administrative terror makes use of the coercive means of modern bureaucracies.

5. The phrase "to aestheticize politics" echoes Benjamin's famous formulation of
the false social program of the fascists in "The Work of Art in the Age of Mechanical Reproduction." Habermas's criticism here of Enlightenment critics seems directed
less at Adorno and Max Horkheimer than at the contemporary *nouveaux philosophes*
(Bernard-Henri Lévy, etc.) and their German and American counterparts. [Ed.]

ALTERNATIVES

I think that instead of giving up modernity and its project as a lost cause, we should learn from the mistakes of those extravagant programs which have tried to negate modernity. Perhaps the types of reception of art may offer an example which at least indicates the direction of a way out.

Bourgeois art had two expectations at once from its audiences. On the one hand, the layman who enjoyed art should educate himself to become an expert. On the other hand, he should also behave as a competent consumer who uses art and relates aesthetic experiences to his own life problems. This second, and seemingly harmless, manner of experiencing art has lost its radical implications exactly because it had a confused relation to the attitude of being expert and professional.

To be sure, artistic production would dry up, if it were not carried out in the form of a specialized treatment of autonomous problems and if it were to cease to be the concern of experts who do not pay so much attention to exoteric questions. Both artists and critics accept thereby the fact that such problems fall under the spell of what I earlier called the inner logic of a cultural domain. But this sharp delineation, this exclusive concentration on one aspect of validity alone and the exclusion of aspects of truth and justice, break down as soon as aesthetic experience is drawn into an individual life history and is absorbed into ordinary life. The reception of art by the layman, or by the "everyday expert," goes in a rather different direction than the reception of art by the professional critic.

Albrecht Wellmer has drawn my attention to one way that an aesthetic experience which is not framed around the experts' critical judgments of taste can have its significance altered: as soon as such an experience is used to illuminate a life-historical situation and is related to life problems, it enters into a language game which is no longer that of the aesthetic critic. The aesthetic experience then not only renews the interpretation of our needs in whose light we perceive the world. It permeates as well our cognitive significations and our normative expectations and changes the manner in which all these moments refer to one another. Let me give an example of this process.

This manner of receiving and relating to art is suggested in the first volume of the work *The Aesthetics of Resistance* by the German-Swedish writer Peter Weiss. Weiss describes the process of reappropriating art by presenting a group of politically motivated, knowledge-hungry workers in 1937 in Berlin.[6] These were young people who, through an evening high-school education, acquired the intellectual means to fathom the general and social history of European art. Out of the resilient edifice of this objective mind, embodied in works of art which they saw again and again in the museums in Berlin, they started removing their own chips of stone, which they gathered together and reassembled in the context of their own milieu. This milieu was far removed from that of traditional education as well as from the then existing regime. These young workers went back and forth between the edifice of European art and their own milieu until they were able to illuminate both.

In examples like this which illustrate the reappropriation of the expert's culture from the standpoint of the life world, we can discern an element which does justice to the intentions of the hopeless surrealist revolts, perhaps even more to Brecht's and Benjamin's interests in how art works, which having lost their aura, could yet be received in illuminating ways. In sum, the project of modernity has not yet been fulfilled. And the reception of art is only one of at least three of its aspects. The project aims at a differentiated relinking of modern culture with an everyday praxis that still depends on vital heritages, but would be impoverished through mere traditionalism. This new connection, however, can only be established under the condition that societal modernization will also be steered in a different direction. The life-world has to become able to develop institutions out of itself which set limits to the internal dynamics and imperatives of an almost autonomous economic system and its administrative complements.

If I am not mistaken, the chances for this today are not very good. More or less in the entire Western world a climate has developed

6. The reference is to the novel *Die Ästhetik des Widerstands* (1975–78) by the author perhaps best known here for his 1965 play *Marat/Sade*. The work of art "reappropriated" by the workers is the Pergamon altar, emblem of power, classicism and rationality. [Ed.]

that furthers capitalist modernization processes as well as trends critical of cultural modernism. The disillusionment with the very failures of those programs that called for the negation of art and philosophy has come to serve as a pretense for conservative positions. Let me briefly distinguish the antimodernism of the "young conservatives" from the premodernism of the "old conservatives" and from the postmodernism of the neoconservatives.

The "young conservatives" recapitulate the basic experience of aesthetic modernity. They claim as their own the revelations of a decentered subjectivity, emancipated from the imperatives of work and usefulness, and with this experience they step outside the modern world. On the basis of modernistic attitudes they justify an irreconcilable antimodernism. They remove into the sphere of the faraway and the archaic the spontaneous powers of imagination, self-experience, and emotion. To instrumental reason they juxtapose in Manichean fashion a principle only accessible through evocation, be it the will to power or sovereignty, Being or the Dionysiac force of the poetical. In France this line leads from Georges Bataille via Michel Foucault to Jacques Derrida.

The "old conservatives" do not allow themselves to be contaminated by cultural modernism. They observe the decline of substantive reason, the differentiation of science, morality, and art, the modern worldview and its merely procedural rationality, with sadness and recommend a withdrawal to a position *anterior* to modernity. Neo-Aristotelianism, in particular, enjoys a certain success today. In view of the problematic of ecology, it allows itself to call for a cosmological ethic. (As belonging to this school, which originates with Leo Strauss, one can count the interesting works of Hans Jonas and Robert Spaemann.)

Finally, the neoconservatives welcome the development of modern science, as long as this only goes beyond its sphere to carry forward technical progress, capitalist growth, and rational administration. Moreover, they recommend a politics of defusing the explosive content of cultural modernity. According to one thesis, science, when properly understood, has become irrevocably meaningless for the orientation of the life-world. A further thesis is that politics must be kept as far aloof as possible from the demands of moral-practical justification. And a third thesis asserts the pure immanence of art, disputes that it has a utopian content, and points to its illusory character in order to limit the aesthetic experience to privacy. (One could name here the early Wittgenstein, Carl Schmitt of the middle period, and Gottfried Benn of the late period.) But with the decisive confinement of science, morality, and art to autonomous spheres separated from the life-world and administered by experts, what remains from the project of cultural modernity is only what we would have if we were to give up the project of modernity altogether. As a replacement one points to traditions which, however, are held to be immune to demands of (normative) justification and validation.

This typology is like any other, of course, a simplification, but it may not prove totally useless for the analysis of contemporary intellectual and political confrontations. I fear that the ideas of antimodernity, together with an additional touch of premodernity, are becoming popular in the circles of alternative culture. When one observes the transformations of consciousness within political parties in Germany, a new ideological shift [*Tendenzwende*] becomes visible. And this is the alliance of postmodernists with premodernists. It seems to me that there is no party in particular that monopolizes the abuse of intellectuals and the position of neoconservatism. I therefore have good reason to be thankful for the liberal spirit in which the city of Frankfurt offers me a prize bearing the name of Theodor Adorno, a most significant son of this city, who as philosopher and writer has stamped the image of the intellectual in our country in incomparable fashion, who, even more, has become the very image of emulation for the intellectual.

Translated by Seyla Ben-Habib

4

What Is Enlightenment?

I

Today when a periodical asks its readers a question, it does so in order to collect opinions on some subject about which everyone has an opinion already; there is not much likelihood of learning anything new. In the eighteenth century, editors preferred to question the public on problems that did not yet have solutions. I don't know whether or not that practice was more effective; it was unquestionably more entertaining.

In any event, in line with this custom, in November 1784 a German periodical, *Berlinische Monatschrift,* published a response to the question: *Was ist Aufklärung?* And the respondent was Kant.

A minor text, perhaps. But it seems to me that it marks the discreet entrance into the history of thought of a question that modern philosophy has not been capable of answering, but that it has never managed to get rid of, either. And one that been repeated in various forms for two centuries now. From Hegel through Nietzsche or Max Weber to Horkheimer or Habermas, hardly any philosophy has failed to confront this same question, directly or indirectly. What, then, is this event that is called the *Aufklärung* and that has deter-

Originally published in *The Foucault Reader,* edited by Paul Rabinow (1984), copyright © by Pantheon Books, a division of Random House, Inc. Reprinted by permission.

mined, at least in part, what we are, what we think, and what we do today? Let us imagine that the *Berlinische Monatschrift* still exists and that it is asking its readers the question: What is modern philosophy? Perhaps we could respond with an echo: modern philosophy is the philosophy that is attempting to answer the question raised so imprudently two centuries ago: *Was ist Aufklärung?*

Let us linger a few moments over Kant's text. It merits attention for several reasons.

1. To this same question, Moses Mendelssohn had also replied in the same journal, just two months earlier. But Kant had not seen Mendelssohn's text when he wrote his. To be sure, the encounter of the German philosophical movement with the new development of Jewish culture does not date from this precise moment. Mendelssohn had been at that crossroads for thirty years or so, in company with Lessing. But up to this point it had been a matter of making a place for Jewish culture within German thought—which Lessing had tried to do in *Die Juden*—or else of identifying problems common to Jewish thought and to German philosophy; this is what Mendelssohn had done in his *Phädon; oder, Über die Unsterblichkeit der Seele.* With the two texts published in the *Berlinische Monatschrift,* the German *Aufklärung* and the Jewish *Haskala* recognize that they belong to the same history; they are seeking to identify the common processes from which they stem. And it is perhaps a way of announcing the acceptance of a common destiny—we now know to what drama that was to lead.

2. But there is more. In itself and within the Christian tradition, Kant's text poses a new problem.

It was certainly not the first time that philosophical thought had sought to reflect on its own present. But, speaking schematically, we may say that this reflection had until then taken three main forms.

• The present may be represented as belonging to a certain era of the world, distinct from the others through some inherent characteristics, or separated from the others by some dramatic event. Thus, in Plato's *The Statesman* the interlocutors recognize that they belong to one of those revolutions of the world in which the world is turning backwards, with all the negative consequences that may ensue.

• The present may be interrogated in an attempt to decipher in it the heralding signs of a forthcoming event. Here we have the principle of a kind of historical hermeneutics of which Augustine might provide an example.

• The present may also be analyzed as a point of transition toward the dawning of a new world. That is what Vico describes in the last chapter of *La Scienza Nuova;* what he sees "today" is "a complete humanity . . . spread abroad through all nations, for a few great monarchs rule over this world of peoples"; it is also "Europe . . . radiant with such humanity that it abounds in all the good things that make for the happiness of human life."[1]

Now the way Kant poses the question of *Aufklärung* is entirely different: it is neither a world era to which one belongs, nor an event whose signs are perceived, nor the dawning of an accomplishment. Kant defines *Aufklärung* in an almost entirely negative way, as an *Ausgang,* an "exit," a "way out." In his other texts on history, Kant occasionally raises questions of origin or defines the internal teleology of a historical process. In the text on *Aufklärung,* he deals with the question of contemporary reality alone. He is not seeking to understand the present on the basis of a totality or of a future achievement. He is looking for a difference: What difference does today introduce with respect to yesterday?

3. I shall not go into detail here concerning this text, which is not always very clear despite its brevity. I should simply like to point out three or four features that seem to me important if we are to understand how Kant raised the philosophical question of the present day.

Kant indicates right away that the "way out" that characterizes Enlightenment is a process that releases us from the status of "immaturity." And by immaturity, he means a certain state of our will that makes us accept someone else's authority to lead us in areas where the use of reason is called for. Kant gives three examples: we are in a state of immaturity when a book takes the place of our understanding, when a spiritual director takes the place of our conscience, when a doctor decides for us what our diet is to be. (Let us

---

1. Giambattista Vico, *The New Science of Giambattista Vico,* abridged, trans. T. G. Bergen and M. H. Fisch (Ithaca: Cornell University Press, 1970), 370, 372.

note in passing that the register of these three critiques is easy to recognize, even though the text does not make it explicit.) In any case, Enlightenment is defined by a modification of the preexisting relation linking will, authority, and the use of reason.

We must also note that this way out is presented by Kant in a rather ambiguous manner. He characterizes it as a phenomenon, an ongoing process; but he also presents it as a task and an obligation. From the very first paragraph, he notes that man himself is responsible for his immature status. Thus it has to be supposed that he will be able to escape from it only by a change that he himself will bring about in himself. Significantly, Kant says that this Enlightenment has a *Wahlspruch:* now a *Wahlspruch* is a heraldic device, that is, a distinctive feature by which one can be recognized, and it is also a motto, an instruction that one gives oneself and proposes to others. What, then, is this instruction? *Aude sapere:* "dare to know," "have the courage, the audacity, to know." Thus Enlightenment must be considered both as a process in which men participate collectively and as an act of courage to be accomplished personally. Men are at once elements and agents of a single process. They may be actors in the process to the extent that they participate in it; and the process occurs to the extent that men decide to be its voluntary actors.

A third difficulty appears here in Kant's text, in his use of the word "mankind," *Menschheit.* The importance of this word in the Kantian conception of history is well known. Are we to understand that the entire human race is caught up in the process of Enlightenment? In that case, we must imagine Enlightenment as a historical change that affects the political and social existence of all people on the face of the earth. Or are we to understand that it involves a change affecting what constitutes the humanity of human beings? But the question then arises of knowing what this change is. Here again, Kant's answer is not without a certain ambiguity. In any case, beneath its appearance of simplicity, it is rather complex.

Kant defines two essential conditions under which mankind can escape from its immaturity. And these two conditions are at once spiritual and institutional, ethical and political.

The first of these conditions is that the realm of obedience and the realm of the use of reason be clearly distinguished. Briefly characterizing the immature status, Kant invokes the familiar expression:

"Don't think, just follow orders"; such is, according to him, the form in which military discipline, political power, and religious authority are usually exercised. Humanity will reach maturity when it is no longer required to obey, but when men are told: "Obey, and you will be able to reason as much as you like." We must note that the German word used here is *räsonieren;* this word, which is also used in the *Critiques,* does not refer to just any use of reason, but to a use of reason in which reason has no other end but itself: *räsonieren* is to reason for reasoning's sake. And Kant gives examples, these too being perfectly trivial in appearance: paying one's taxes, while being able to argue as much as one likes about the system of taxation, would be characteristic of the mature state; or again, taking responsibility for parish service, if one is a pastor, while reasoning freely about religious dogmas.

We might think that there is nothing very different here from what has been meant, since the sixteenth century, by freedom of conscience: the right to think as one pleases so long as one obeys as one must. Yet it is here that Kant brings into play another distinction, and in a rather surprising way. The distinction he introduces is between the private and public uses of reason. But he adds at once that reason must be free in its public use, and must be submissive in its private use. Which is, term for term, the opposite of what is ordinarily called freedom of conscience.

But we must be somewhat more precise. What constitutes, for Kant, this private use of reason? In what area is it exercised? Man, Kant says, makes a private use of reason when he is "a cog in a machine"; that is, when he has a role to play in society and jobs to do: to be a soldier, to have taxes to pay, to be in charge of a parish, to be a civil servant, all this makes the human being a particular segment of society; he finds himself thereby placed in a circumscribed position, where he has to apply particular rules and pursue particular ends. Kant does not ask that people practice a blind and foolish obedience, but that they adapt the use they make of their reason to these determined circumstances; and reason must then be subjected to the particular ends in view. Thus there cannot be, here, any free use of reason.

On the other hand, when one is reasoning only in order to use one's reason, when one is reasoning as a reasonable being (and not as a cog in a machine), when one is reasoning as a member of reasonable humanity, then the use of reason must be free and public. Enlightenment is thus not merely the process by which individuals would see their own personal freedom of thought guaranteed. There is Enlightenment when the universal, the free, and the public uses of reason are superimposed on one another.

Now this leads us to a fourth question that must be put to Kant's text. We can readily see how the universal use of reason (apart from any private end) is the business of the subject himself as an individual; we can readily see, too, how the freedom of this use may be assured in a purely negative manner through the absence of any challenge to it; but how is a public use of that reason to be assured? Enlightenment, as we see, must not be conceived simply as a general process affecting all humanity; it must not be conceived only as an obligation prescribed to individuals: it now appears as a political problem. The question, in any event, is that of knowing how the use of reason can take the public form that it requires, how the audacity to know can be exercised in broad daylight, while individuals are obeying as scrupulously as possible. And Kant, in conclusion, proposes to Frederick II, in scarcely veiled terms, a sort of contract— what might be called the contract of rational despotism with free reason: the public and free use of autonomous reason will be the best guarantee of obedience, on condition, however, that the political principle that must be obeyed itself be in conformity with universal reason.

Let us leave Kant's text here. I do not by any means propose to consider it as capable of constituting an adequate description of Enlightenment; and no historian, I think, could be satisfied with it for an analysis of the social, political, and cultural transformations that occurred at the end of the eighteenth century.

Nevertheless, notwithstanding its circumstantial nature, and without intending to give it an exaggerated place in Kant's work, I believe that it is necessary to stress the connection that exists between this brief article and the three *Critiques*. Kant in fact describes Enlightenment as the moment when humanity is going to put its own reason to use, without subjecting itself to any authority; now it is precisely at this moment that the critique is necessary, since its role is that of defining the conditions under which the use of reason is legitimate in order to determine what can be known, what must be done, and what may be hoped. Illegitimate uses of reason are what give rise to dogmatism and heteronomy, along with illusion; on the other hand, it is when the legitimate use of reason has been clearly defined in its principles that its autonomy can be assured. The critique is, in a sense, the handbook of reason that has grown up in Enlightenment; and, conversely, the Enlightenment is the age of the critique.

It is also necessary, I think, to underline the relation between this text of Kant's and the other texts he devoted to history. These latter, for the most part, seek to define the internal teleology of time and the point toward which the history of humanity is moving. Now the analysis of Enlightenment, defining this history as humanity's passage to its adult status, situates contemporary reality with respect to the overall movement and its basic directions. But at the same time, it shows how, at this very moment, each individual is responsible in a certain way for that overall process.

The hypothesis I should like to propose is that this little text is located in a sense at the crossroads of critical reflection and reflection on history. It is a reflection by Kant on the contemporary status of his own enterprise. No doubt it is not the first time that a philosopher has given his reasons for undertaking his work at a particular moment. But it seems to me that it is the first time that a philosopher has connected in this way, closely and from the inside, the significance of his work with respect to knowledge, a reflection on history and a particular analysis of the specific moment at which he is writing and because of which he is writing. It is in the reflection on "today" as difference in history and as motive for a particular philosophical task that the novelty of this text appears to me to lie.

And, by looking at it in this way, it seems to me we may recognize a point of departure: the outline of what one might call the attitude of modernity.

II

I know that modernity is often spoken of as an epoch, or at least as a set of features characteristic of an epoch; situated on a calendar, it would be preceded by a more or less naive or archaic premodernity, and followed by an enigmatic and troubling postmodernity. And then we find ourselves asking whether modernity constitutes the sequel to the Enlightenment and its development, or whether we are to see it as a rupture or a deviation with respect to the basic principles of the eighteenth century.

Thinking back on Kant's text, I wonder whether we may not envisage modernity rather as an attitude than as a period of history. And by "attitude," I mean a mode of relating to contemporary reality; a voluntary choice made by certain people; in the end, a way of thinking and feeling; a way, too, of acting and behaving that at one and the same time marks a relation of belonging and presents itself as a task. A bit, no doubt, like what the Greeks called an *ethos*. And consequently, rather than seeking to distinguish the modern era from the premodern or postmodern, I think it would be more useful to try to find out how the attitude of modernity, ever since its formation, has found itself struggling with attitudes of "countermodernity."

To characterize briefly this attitude of modernity, I shall take an almost indispensable example, namely, Baudelaire; for his consciousness of modernity is widely recognized as one of the most acute in the nineteenth century.

1. Modernity is often characterized in terms of consciousness of the discontinuity of time: a break with tradition, a feeling of novelty, of vertigo in the face of the passing moment. And this is indeed what Baudelaire seems to be saying when he defines modernity as "the ephemeral, the fleeting, the contingent."[2] But, for him, being modern does not lie in recognizing and accepting this perpetual movement; on the contrary, it lies in adopting a certain attitude with respect to this movement; and this deliberate, difficult attitude consists in recapturing something eternal that is not beyond the present instant, nor behind it, but within it. Modernity is distinct from fashion, which does no more than call into question the course of time; modernity is the attitude that makes it possible to grasp the "heroic" aspect of the present moment. Modernity is not a phenomenon of sensitivity to the fleeting present; it is the will to heroize the present.

2. Charles Baudelaire, *The Painter of Modern Life and Other Essays*, trans. Jonathan Mayne (London: Phaidon, 1964), 13.

I shall restrict myself to what Baudelaire says about the painting of his contemporaries. Baudelaire makes fun of those painters who, finding nineteenth-century dress excessively ugly, want to depict nothing but ancient togas. But modernity in painting does not consist, for Baudelaire, in introducing black clothing onto the canvas. The modern painter is the one who can show the dark frock-coat as "the necessary costume of our time," the one who knows how to make manifest, in the fashion of the day, the essential, permanent, obsessive relation that our age entertains with death. "The dress-coat and frock-coat not only possess their political beauty, which is an expression of universal equality, but also their poetic beauty, which is an expression of the public soul—an immense cortège of undertaker's mutes (mutes in love, political mutes, bourgeois mutes . . .). We are each of us celebrating some funeral."[3] To designate this attitude of modernity, Baudelaire sometimes employs a litotes that is highly significant because it is presented in the form of a precept: "You have no right to despise the present."

2. This heroization is ironical, needless to say. The attitude of modernity does not treat the passing moment as sacred in order to try to maintain or perpetuate it. It certainly does not involve harvesting it as a fleeting and interesting curiosity. That would be what Baudelaire would call the spectator's posture. The *flâneur*, the idle, strolling spectator, is satisfied to keep his eyes open, to pay attention and to build up a storehouse of memories. In opposition to the *flâneur*, Baudelaire describes the man of modernity: "Away he goes, hurrying, searching. . . . Be very sure that this man . . . —this solitary, gifted with an active imagination, ceaselessly journeying across the great human desert—has an aim loftier than that of a mere *flâneur*, an aim more general, something other than the fugitive pleasure of circumstance. He is looking for that quality which you must allow me to call 'modernity.' . . . He makes it his business to extract from fashion whatever element it may contain of poetry within history." As an example of modernity, Baudelaire cites the artist Constantin Guys. In appearance a spectator, a collector of curiosities, he remains "the last to linger wherever there can be a glow of light, an

3. Charles Baudelaire, "On the Heroism of Modern Life," in *The Mirror of Art: Critical Studies by Charles Baudelaire*, trans. Jonathan Mayne (London: Phaidon, 1955), 127.

echo of poetry, a quiver of life or a chord of music; wherever a passion can *pose* before him, wherever natural man and conventional man display themselves in a strange beauty, wherever the sun lights up the swift joys of the *depraved animal.*"[4]

But let us make no mistake. Constantin Guys is not a *flâneur;* what makes him the modern painter *par excellence* in Baudelaire's eyes is that, just when the whole world is falling asleep, he begins to work, and he transfigures that world. His transfiguration does not entail an annulling of reality, but a difficult interplay between the truth of what is real and the exercise of freedom; "natural" things become "more than natural," "beautiful" things become "more than beautiful," and individual objects appear "endowed with an impulsive life like the soul of [their] creator."[5] For the attitude of modernity, the high value of the present is indissociable from a desperate eagerness to imagine it, to imagine it otherwise than it is, and to transform it not by destroying it but by grasping it in what it is. Baudelairean modernity is an exercise in which extreme attention to what is real is confronted with the practice of a liberty that simultaneously respects this reality and violates it.

3. However, modernity for Baudelaire is not simply a form of relationship to the present; it is also a mode of relationship that has to be established with oneself. The deliberate attitude of modernity is tied to an indispensable asceticism. To be modern is not to accept oneself as one is in the flux of the passing moments; it is to take oneself as object of a complex and difficult elaboration: what Baudelaire, in the vocabulary of his day, calls *dandysme*. Here I shall not recall in detail the well-known passages on "vulgar, earthy, vile nature"; on man's indispensable revolt against himself; on the "doctrine of elegance" which imposes "upon its ambitious and humble disciples" a discipline more despotic than the most terrible religions; the pages, finally, on the asceticism of the dandy who makes of his body, his behavior, his feelings and passions, his very existence, a work of art. Modern man, for Baudelaire, is not the man who goes off to discover himself, his secrets and his hidden truth; he is the man who tries to invent himself. This modernity does not "liberate man

4. Baudelaire, *Painter*, 12, 11.
5. Ibid., 12.

in his own being"; it compels him to face the task of producing himself.

4. Let me add just one final word. This ironic heroization of the present, this transfiguring play of freedom with reality, this ascetic elaboration of the self—Baudelaire does not imagine that these have any place in society itself, or in the body politic. They can only be produced in another, a different place, which Baudelaire calls art.

I do not pretend to be summarizing in these few lines either the complex historical event that was the Enlightenment, at the end of the eighteenth century, or the attitude of modernity in the various guises it may have taken on during the last two centuries.

I have been seeking, on the one hand, to emphasize the extent to which a type of philosophical interrogation—one that simultaneously problematizes man's relation to the present, man's historical mode of being, and the constitution of the self as an autonomous subject—is rooted in the Enlightenment. On the other hand, I have been seeking to stress that the thread that may connect us with the Enlightenment is not faithfulness to doctrinal elements, but rather the permanent reactivation of an attitude—that is, of a philosophical *ethos* that could be described as a permanent critique of our historical era. I should like to characterize this *ethos* very briefly.

A. Negatively

1. This *ethos* implies, first, the refusal of what I like to call the "blackmail" of the Enlightenment. I think that the Enlightenment, as a set of political, economic, social, institutional, and cultural events on which we still depend in large part, constitutes a privileged domain for analysis. I also think that as an enterprise for linking the progress of truth and the history of liberty in a bond of direct relation, it formulated a philosophical question that remains for us to consider. I think, finally, as I have tried to show with reference to Kant's text, that it defined a certain manner of philosophizing.

But that does not mean that one has to be for or against the Enlightenment. It even means precisely that one has to refuse everything that might present itself in the form of a simplistic and authoritarian alternative: you either accept the Enlightenment and remain within the tradition of its rationalism (this is considered a positive term by some and used by others, on the contrary, as a reproach); or else you criticize the Enlightenment and then try to escape from its principles of rationality (which may be seen once again as good or bad). And we do not break free of this blackmail by introducing "dialectical" nuances while seeking to determine what good and bad elements there may have been in the Enlightenment.

We must try to proceed with the analysis of ourselves as beings who are historically determined, to a certain extent, by the Enlightenment. Such an analysis implies a series of historical inquiries that are as precise as possible; and these inquiries will not be oriented retrospectively toward the "essential kernel of rationality" that can be found in the Enlightenment and that would have to be preserved in any event; they will be oriented toward the "contemporary limits of the necessary," that is, toward what is not or is no longer indispensable for the constitution of ourselves as autonomous subjects.

2. This permanent critique of ourselves has to avoid the always too facile confusions between humanism and Enlightenment.

We must never forget that the Enlightenment is an event, or a set of events and complex historical processes, that is located at a certain point in the development of European societies. As such, it includes elements of social transformation, types of political institution, forms of knowledge, projects of rationalization of knowledge and practices, technological mutations that are very difficult to sum up in a word, even if many of these phenomena remain important today. The one I have pointed out and that seems to me to have been at the basis of an entire form of philosophical reflection concerns only the mode of reflective relation to the present.

Humanism is something entirely different. It is a theme or, rather, a set of themes that have reappeared on several occasions, over time, in European societies; these themes, always tied to value judgments, have obviously varied greatly in their content, as well as in the values they have preserved. Furthermore, they have served as a critical principle of differentiation. In the seventeenth century, there was a humanism that presented itself as a critique of Christianity or of religion in general; there was a Christian humanism opposed to an ascetic and much more theocentric humanism. In the nineteenth century, there was a suspicious humanism, hostile and critical toward science, and another that, to the contrary, placed its hope in that same science. Marxism has been a humanism; so have existentialism and personalism; there was a time when people supported the humanistic values represented by National Socialism, and when the Stalinists themselves said they were humanists.

From this, we must not conclude that everything that has ever been linked with humanism is to be rejected, but that the humanistic thematic is in itself too supple, too diverse, too inconsistent to serve as an axis for reflection. And it is a fact that, at least since the seventeenth century, what is called humanism has always been obliged to lean on certain conceptions of man borrowed from religion, science, or politics. Humanism serves to color and to justify the conceptions of man to which it is, after all, obliged to take recourse.

Now, in this connection, I believe that this thematic, which so often recurs and which always depends on humanism, can be opposed by the principle of a critique and a permanent creation of ourselves in our autonomy: that is, a principle that is at the heart of the historical consciousness that the Enlightenment has of itself. From this standpoint, I am inclined to see Enlightenment and humanism in a state of tension rather than identity.

In any case, it seems to me dangerous to confuse them; and further, it seems historically inaccurate. If the question of man, of the human species, of the humanist, was important throughout the eighteenth century, this is very rarely, I believe, because the Enlightenment considered itself a humanism. It is worthwhile, too, to note that throughout the nineteenth century, the historiography of sixteenth-century humanism, which was so important for people like Saint-Beuve or Burckhardt, was always distinct from and sometimes explicitly opposed to the Enlightenment and the eighteenth century. The nineteenth century had a tendency to oppose the two, at least as much as to confuse them.

In any case, I think that, just as we must free ourselves from the intellectual blackmail of being for or against the Enlightenment, we must escape from the historical and moral confusionism that mixes the theme of humanism with the question of the Enlightenment. An analysis of their complex relations in the course of the last two centuries would be a worthwhile project, an important one if we are to bring some measure of clarity to the consciousness that we have of ourselves and of our past.

B. Positively

Yet while taking these precautions into account, we must obviously give a more positive content to what may be a philosophical *ethos* consisting in a critique of what we are saying, thinking, and doing, through a historical ontology of ourselves.

1. This philosophical *ethos* may be characterized as a "limit-attitude." We are not talking about a gesture of rejection. We have to move beyond the outside-inside alternative; we have to be at the frontiers. Criticism indeed consists of analyzing and reflecting upon limits. But if the Kantian question was that of knowing what limits knowledge has to renounce transgressing, it seems to me that the critical question today has to be turned back into a positive one: in what is given to us as universal, necessary, obligatory, what place is occupied by whatever is singular, contingent, and the product of arbitrary constraints? The point, in brief, is to transform the critique conducted in the form of necessary limitation into a practical critique that takes the form of a possible transgression.

This entails an obvious consequence: that criticism is no longer going to be practiced in the search for formal structures with universal value, but rather as a historical investigation into the events that have led us to constitute ourselves and to recognize ourselves as subjects of what we are doing, thinking, saying. In that sense, this criticism is not transcendental, and its goal is not that of making a metaphysics possible: it is genealogical in its design and archaeological in its method. Archaeological—and not transcendental—in the sense that it will not seek to identify the universal structures of all knowledge or of all possible moral action, but will seek to treat the instances of discourse that articulate what we think, say, and do as so many historical events. And this critique will be genealogical in the sense that it will not deduce from the form of what we are what it is impossible for us to do and to know; but it will separate out, from the contingency that has made us what we are, the possibility of no longer being, doing, or thinking what we are, do, or think. It is not seeking to make possible a metaphysics that has finally become a science; it is seeking to give new impetus, as far and wide as possible, to the undefined work of freedom.

2. But if we are not to settle for the affirmation or the empty

dream of freedom, it seems to me that this historico-critical attitude must also be an experimental one. I mean that this work done at the limits of ourselves must, on the one hand, open up a realm of historical inquiry and, on the other, put itself to the test of reality, of contemporary reality, both to grasp the points where change is possible and desirable, and to determine the precise form this change should take. This means that the historical ontology of ourselves must turn away from all projects that claim to be global or radical. In fact we know from experience that the claim to escape from the system of contemporary reality so as to produce the overall programs of another society, of another way of thinking, another culture, another vision of the world, has led only to the return of the most dangerous traditions.

I prefer the very specific transformations that have proved to be possible in the last twenty years in a certain number of areas that concern our ways of being and thinking, relations to authority, relations between the sexes, the way in which we perceive insanity or illness; I prefer even these partial transformations that have been made in the correlation of historical analysis and the practical attitude, to the programs for a new man that the worst political systems have repeated throughout the twentieth century.

I shall thus characterize the philosophical *ethos* appropriate to the critical ontology of ourselves as a historico-practical test of the limits that we may go beyond, and thus as work carried out by ourselves upon ourselves as free beings.

3. Still, the following objection would no doubt be entirely legitimate: if we limit ourselves to this type of always partial and local inquiry or test, do we not run the risk of letting ourselves be determined by more general structures of which we may well not be conscious, and over which we may have no control?

To this, two responses. It is true that we have to give up hope of ever acceding to a point of view that could give us access to any complete and definitive knowledge of what may constitute our historical limits. And from this point of view the theoretical and practical experience that we have of our limits and of the possibility of moving beyond them is always limited and determined; thus we are always in the position of beginning again.

But that does not mean that no work can be done except in disorder and contingency. The work in question has its generality, its systematicity, its homogeneity, and its stakes.

(a) Its Stakes

These are indicated by what might be called "the paradox of the relations of capacity and power." We know that the great promise or the great hope of the eighteenth century, or a part of the eighteenth century, lay in the simultaneous and proportional growth of individuals with respect to one another. And, moreover, we can see that throughout the entire history of Western societies (it is perhaps here that the root of their singular historical destiny is located—such a peculiar destiny, so different from the others in its trajectory and so universalizing, so dominant with respect to the others), the acquisition of capabilities and the struggle for freedom have constituted permanent elements. Now the relations between the growth of capabilities and the growth of autonomy are not as simple as the eighteenth century may have believed. And we have been able to see what forms of power relation were conveyed by various technologies (whether we are speaking of productions with economic aims, or institutions whose goal is social regulation, or of techniques of communication): disciplines, both collective and individual, procedures of normalization exercised in the name of the power of the state, demands of society or of population zones, are examples. What is at stake, then, is this: How can the growth of capabilities be disconnected from the intensification of power relations?

(b) Homogeneity

This leads to the study of what could be called "practical systems." Here we are taking as a homogeneous domain of reference not the representations that men give of themselves, not the conditions that determine them without their knowledge, but rather what they do and the way they do it. That is, the forms of rationality that organize their ways of doing things (this might be called the technological aspect) and the freedom with which they act within these practical systems, reacting to what others do, modifying the rules of the game, up to a certain point (this might be called the strategic side of these practices). The homogeneity of these historico-critical analyses is thus ensured by this realm of practices, with their technological side and their strategic side.

(c) Systematicity

These practical systems stem from three broad areas: relations of control over things, relations of action upon others, relations with oneself. This does not mean that each of these three areas is completely foreign to the others. It is well known that control over things is mediated by relations with others; and relations with others in turn always entail relations with oneself, and vice versa. But we have three axes whose specificity and whose interconnections have to be analyzed: the axis of knowledge, the axis of power, the axis of ethics. In other terms, the historical ontology of ourselves has to answer an open series of questions; it has to make an indefinite number of inquiries which may be multiplied and specified as much as we like, but which will all address the questions systematized as follows: How are we constituted as subjects of our own knowledge? How are we constituted as subjects who exercise or submit to power relations? How are we constituted as moral subjects of our own actions?

(d) Generality

Finally, these historico-critical investigations are quite specific in the sense that they always bear upon a material, an epoch, a body of determined practices and discourses. And yet, at least at the level of the Western societies from which we derive, they have their generality, in the sense that they have continued to recur up to our time: for example, the problem of the relationship between sanity and insanity, or sickness and health, or crime and the law; the problem of the role of sexual relations; and so on.

But by evoking this generality, I do not mean to suggest that it has to be retraced in its metahistorical continuity over time, nor that its variations have to be pursued. What must be grasped is the extent to which what we know of it, the forms of power that are exercised in it, and the experience that we have in it of ourselves constitute nothing but determined historical figures, through a certain form of problematization that defines objects, rules of action, modes of relation to oneself. The study of [modes of] problematization (that is, of what is neither an anthropological constant nor a chronological variation) is thus the way to analyze questions of general import in their historically unique form.

A brief summary, to conclude and to come back to Kant.

I do not know whether we will ever reach mature adulthood. Many things in our experience convince us that the historical event of the Enlightenment did not make us mature adults, and we have not reached that stage yet. However, it seems to me that a meaning can be attributed to that critical interrogation on the present and on ourselves which Kant formulated by reflecting on the Enlightenment. It seems to me that Kant's reflection is even a way of philosophizing that has not been without its importance or effectiveness during the last two centuries. The critical ontology of ourselves has to be considered not, certainly, as a theory, a doctrine, nor even as a permanent body of knowledge that is accumulating; it has to be conceived as an attitude, an *ethos,* a philosophical life in which the critique of what we are is at one and the same time the historical analysis of the limits that are imposed on us and an experiment with the possibility of going beyond them.

This philosophical attitude has to be translated into the labor of diverse inquiries. These inquiries have their methodological coherence in the at once archaeological and genealogical study of practices envisaged simultaneously as a technological type of rationality and as strategic games of liberties; they have their theoretical coherence in the definition of the historically unique forms in which the generalities of our relations to things, to others, to ourselves, have been problematized. They have their practical coherence in the care brought to the process of putting historico-critical reflection to the test of concrete practices. I do not know whether it must be said today that the critical task still entails faith in Enlightenment; I continue to think that this task requires work on our limits, that is, a patient labor giving form to our impatience for liberty.

Translated by Catherine Porter

INTERPRETATIONS

5

The Search for Paradigms as a Hindrance to Understanding

A recent journal article argued forcefully against the "collection of empirical materials as an end in itself and without sufficient theoretical analysis to determine appropriate criteria of selection."[1] The present essay presents a complementary critique of the opposite failing. Its target is the tendency toward compulsive and mindless theorizing—a disease at least as prevalent and debilitating, so it seems to me, as the spread of mindless number work in the social sciences.

Whereas the latter phenomenon has been caused largely by the availability of the computer, several factors are responsible for the compulsion to theorize, which is often so strong as to induce mindlessness. In the academy, the prestige of the theorist is towering. Further, extravagant use of language intimates that theorizing can rival sensuous delights: what used to be called an interesting or valuable theoretical point is commonly referred to today as a "stimulating" or even "exciting" theoretical "insight." Moreover, insofar as the social sciences in the United States are concerned, an important role has no doubt been played by the desperate need, on the part of

From "The Search for Paradigms as a Hindrance to Understanding," *World Politics* 22, no. 3 (April 1970). Copyright © by Princeton University Press. Reprinted by permission of Princeton University Press.

1. Oran R. Young, "Professor Russett: Industrious Tailor to a Naked Emperor," *World Politics* 21 (April 1969): 489–90.

the hegemonic power, for shortcuts to the understanding of multifarious reality that must be coped with and controlled and therefore be understood at once. Interestingly enough, revolutionaries experience the same compulsion: while they are fond of quoting Marx to the approximate effect that interpreting the world is not nearly as important as changing it, they are well aware of the enormous strength that is imparted to revolutionary determination by the conviction that one has indeed fully understood social reality and its "laws of change." As a result of these various factors, the quick theoretical fix has taken its place in our culture alongside the quick technical fix.

In the following pages, I do not have a central epistemological theorem to offer that would permit us to differentiate between good and bad theorizing, or between fruitful and sterile paradigmatic thinking. My accent throughout is on the kind of cognitive style that hinders, or promotes, understanding. I introduce the topic by a critical look at two books that exemplify opposite styles. Subsequently, I make an attempt to delineate various areas in which an impatience for theoretical formulation leads to serious pitfalls. Theorizing about Latin American society and economy, on the part of both Latin Americans and outside observers, receives special attention because it has been particularly marked by the cognitive style I find unfortunate.

I

John Womack's *Zapata and the Mexican Revolution*[2] and James L. Payne's *Patterns of Conflict in Colombia*[3] are the two books I shall use to open the argument. They have in common that they are both by young North American scholars; both, in fact, were originally written as doctoral dissertations; and they both reached my desk early in 1969. But this is where any possible resemblance ends. At this point I should state that both books aroused in me unusually strong feelings: I found Womack's way of telling the Zapata story extraordi-

2. New York: Knopf, 1969.
3. New Haven: Yale University Press, 1968.

narily appealing, while I was strongly repelled by Payne's book in spite of its crispness, cleverness, and occasional flashes of wit. There are of course many striking contrasts between the two books that can account for these opposite reactions, not the least perhaps being that Womack obviously fell in love with revolutionary Mexico and the Zapatistas whereas Payne's treatment exudes dislike and contempt for Colombians in general, and for Colombian politicians in particular. But the more important, and not necessarily related, difference is in the cognitive styles of the two authors. Within the first few pages of his book Payne presents us triumphantly with the key to the full and complete understanding of the Colombian political system. The rest of the book is a demonstration that the key indeed unlocks all conceivable doors of Colombian political life, past, present, and future. Womack, on the other hand, abjures any pretense at full understanding right in the preface, where he says that his book "is not an analysis but a story because the truth of the revolution in Morelos is in the feeling of it which I could not convey through defining its factors but only through telling of it." "The analysis that I could do," he continues, "and that I thought pertinent I have tried to weave into the narrative, so that it would issue at the moment right for understanding it."[4] And indeed what is remarkable about the book is the continuity of the narrative and the almost complete, one might say Flaubertian, absence from its pages of the author who could have explained, commented, moralized, or drawn conclusions. Yet whoever reads through the book will have gained immeasurably in his understanding not only of the Mexican Revolution, but of peasant revolutions everywhere, and Womack's very reticence and self-effacement stimulate the reader's curiosity and imagination. Payne's book, on the contrary, obviously explains far too much and thereby succeeds only in provoking the reader's resistance and incredulity; the only curiosity it provokes is about the kind of social science that made an obviously gifted young man go so wrong.

Here, then, is the experience behind the title of this essay: understanding as a result of one book without the shadow of a paradigm; and frustration as a result of another in which one paradigm is made to spawn thirty-four hypotheses (reproduced, for the convenience of

4. Womack, *Zapata*, x.

the reader, in the book's appendix) covering all aspects of political behavior in Colombia and, incidentally, the United States as well.

Perhaps I should explain briefly what Mr. Payne's basic "insight" or paradigm consists in: politicians in Colombia, he has found out through questionnaires, interviews, and similar devices, are motivated primarily by status considerations rather than by genuine interest in programs and policies, as is predominantly and fortunately the case in the United States. He uses the neutral-sounding terms "status incentive" and "program incentive"; the former characteristically motivates Colombian political leaders whereas the latter animates their North American counterparts. In plain language, occasionally used by the author, Colombian politicians are selfish,[5] ambitious, unscrupulous, unprincipled, exceedingly demagogic—interested exclusively in increasing their own power, always ready to betray yesterday's friends and allies, and, to top it all, incapable of having friendly personal relations with anyone because they feel comfortable only with abject supplicants.[6] On the other hand, there is the politician with a program incentive whose preferred habitat is the United States of America. *He* enjoys working on concrete policies and achieving a stated goal; hence he is principled, willing to defend unpopular causes, always ready to come to constructive agreements, hardworking, and generally lovable.

For a North American to contrast Colombian and United States politicians in terms of such invidious stereotypes is, to say the least, a distasteful spectacle. We must of course allow for the possibility that truth, as unearthed by the scholar, turns out to be distasteful. But Payne does not betray any sense of realizing the unpleasantness of his discovery. On the contrary, he evidently draws much satisfaction from the edifice he has built and takes good care to make sure that there will be no escape from it. At various points he assures us that Colombians are like that; that, as he put it in a subtitle, they are not "on the brink of anything"; that it is futile to expect any change in the pattern of Colombian politics from such incidental happenings as industrialization or urbanization or agrarian reforms: like the three characters in Sartre's *Huis Clos*, the twenty million Colombians will

5. Payne, *Patterns,* 70.
6. Ibid., 12.

just have to go on living in their self-made hell while Mr. Payne, after his seven-month diagnostic visit (from February to September 1965, as he informs us in the preface), has returned to his own, so much more fortunate section of the hemisphere.

It is easy to show that the Payne model is as wrong as it is outrageous. In the first place, it is unable to explain the very wide swings of Colombian politics; after all, during almost all of the first half of the twentieth century Colombia stood out as a "stable" democracy with peaceful transfers of power from one party to another; throughout the Great Depression of the thirties when almost all other Latin American countries experienced violent political convulsions, constitutional government continued in spite of much social unrest.

This experience is hard to explain by a theory that holds that vicious political infighting, untrammeled by any concern with programs or loyalty, holds continuous sway throughout the body politic. Moreover, such a theory ought to take a good look at—and give a special weight to—the body's head; if Payne had done that he might have noticed that his stereotype, the politician with a status incentive, simply does not apply to a number of the most outstanding leaders and recent presidents of Colombia—there is no need to mention names, but it is amusing to quote, in contrast, from a recent portrait of a contemporary president of the United States: "His preoccupation seems to have been success—in this case the achievement of power rather than its use for political purposes."[7]

Supposing even that the diagnosis is essentially correct and that politicians in Colombia are more interested in the quest for power per se than in the use of this power for the carrying out of specific programs—what does this "insight" explain? Suppose that we find, as Payne indeed does, that those self-seeking politicians frequently switched sides or voted for demagogic measures, does this finding teach us anything fundamental about the political system, its ability to accommodate change, to solve newly arising problems, to assure peace, justice, and development? It does nothing of the sort, but at best leaves us with the proposition, which incidentally is both plati-

7. Nora Beloff and Michael Davie, "Getting to Know Mr. Nixon," *The Observer*, 23 February 1969.

tudinous and wrong, that if the politicians are vicious, the ensuing politics are likely to be vicious too!

Let us pass now from the paradigms of· James Payne to John Womack, who has rigorously excluded from his universe any semblance of a paradigm. It is of course impossible to do justice to his narrative. I shall refer here only to one particular turn of the events he describes in order to show how he invites speculation and thereby contributes to the possibility of understanding.

It has perhaps not been sufficiently remarked that the book has *two* protagonists: Zapata dominates the action during the first nine chapters, but in the important last two chapters (eighty pages) the leading figure is Gildaro Magaña who became Zapata's ranking secretary after mid-1917 and, after a brief fight for the succession, the chief of the Zapatista movement following Zapata's death in April 1919. Womack honors Magaña with one of his too-rare character portraits: "From these stresses [of his youth] Gildardo Magaña somehow emerged strong and whole. What he had learned was to mediate: not to compromise, to surrender principle and to trade concessions, but to detect reason in all claims in conflict, to recognize the particular legitimacy of each, to sense where the grounds of concord were, and to bring contestants into harmony there. Instinctively he thrived on arguments, which he entered not to win but to conciliate."[8]

Womack then relates the exploits of Magaña as a resourceful negotiator of ever new alliances and contrasts him with the rigid and sectarian Palafox, Zapata's earlier principal secretary, who "seemed in retrospect the individual responsible for the Zapatistas' present plight—the man they could blame for their disastrous involvement with Villa in 1914, their alienation of worthy chiefs in the constitutionalist party, and their abiding reputation as the most intransigent group in the revolutionary movement."[9]

After the murder of Zapata, Magaña maneuvered tactfully and successfully among the various chiefs. After six months, the succession crisis was over and Magaña was recognized as commander-in-chief, with the movement virtually intact. Womack then traces the complex events through which the Zapatistas, as he puts it in the title

8. Womack, *Zapata*, 290.
9. Ibid., 306.

of his last chapter, "Inherit Morelos"—that is, how they manage, by alternately fighting and negotiating and by backing Obregón at the right moment, to pass from outlaws into social administrators and members of a national coalition. "So ended the year 1920, in peace, with populist agrarian reform instituted as a national policy, and with the Zapatista movement established in Morelos politics. In the future through thick and thin these achievements would last. This was the claim Zapata, his chiefs, and their volunteers had forced, *and Magaña had won and secured.*"[10]

Twice Womack implies that this outcome was due not only to the presence of Magaña, but perhaps also to the absence of Zapata from the scene. There is first the "extraordinary maneuver" by which Magaña offered the Carranza government the Zapatistas' support when United States intervention threatened in the Jenkins case in 1919. Womack says here flatly, "Had Zapata lived, Zapatista strategy could not have been so flexible."[11] Then again at the celebration of Obregón's victory, on 2 June 1920.

> twenty thousand Agua Prieta partisans marched in review through the Zócalo, among them the forces from Morelos. And watching with the honored new leaders from a balcony of the Palacio National . . . stood the squat, swarthy, de la O, frowning into the sun. From an angle he looked almost like Zapata, dead now for over a year. (If de la O had been killed and Zapata had lived, Zapata would probably have been there in his place, with the same uncomfortable frown, persuaded by Magaña to join the boom for Obregón but probably worrying, as Magaña was not, about when he might have to revolt again.)[12]

Out of these bits and pieces, there emerges a proposition or hypothesis that must have been on Womack's mind, but that he allows the reader to formulate: did the comparative success of the Morelos uprising within the Mexican Revolution rest on the *alternating* leadership, first of the charismatic, revolutionary Zapata and then of the skillful, though highly principled, negotiator Magaña? And what are the "lessons" of this story for other revolutions and, in particular, for revolutionary movements that are confined to a limited portion or sector of a nation-state?

10. Ibid., 369; my italics.
11. Ibid., 348.
12. Ibid., 365.

The historian is probably ambivalent about such questions. He revels in the uniqueness of the historical event, yet he constantly intimates that history holds the most precious lessons. And I believe he is right on both counts! Perhaps the rest of this essay will show why this is not a self-contradictory position.

II

First let me return briefly to the comparison of Payne and Womack. What strikes the reader of the two books most is, as I said before, the difference in cognitive style: Payne, from the first page to the last, breathes brash confidence that he has achieved complete understanding of his subject, whereas Womack draws conclusions with the utmost diffidence and circumspection. His respect for the autonomy of the actors whose deeds he recounts is what gives his book its special appeal and probably contributed to the spectacular accolade he received from Carlos Fuentes in the *New York Review of Books*.[13] For it is today a most unusual restraint. I believe that the countries of the Third World have become fair game for the model builders and paradigm molders to an intolerable degree. During the nineteenth century several "laws" were laid down for the leading industrial countries whose rapid development was disconcerting to numerous thinkers who were strongly affected by what Flaubert called "la rage de vouloir conclure."[14] Having been proven wrong by the unfolding events in almost every instance, the lawmakers then migrated to warmer climes, that is, to the less developed countries. And here they really came into their own. For the less developed, dependent countries had long been objects of history—so that to treat them as objects of iron law or rigid models from whose working there is no escape came naturally to scholars who turned their attention to them. Soon we were witnesses to a veritable deluge of paradigms and models, from the vicious circle of poverty, low-level equilibrium

13. 13 March 1969.
14. I have long looked for a good translation of this key concept into English. It now strikes me that an apt, if free, rendering of Flaubert's meaning would be "the compulsion to theorize"—which is the subject and might have been the title of the present essay.

traps, and uniform stage sequences of the economist, to the traditional or nonachievement-oriented or status-hungry personality of the sociologist, psychologist, or political scientist. A psychologist may find it interesting some day to inquire whether these theories were inspired primarily by compassion or by contempt for the underdeveloped world. The result, in any case, is that the countries of Latin America, for example, appear to any contemporary, well-read observer far more constrained than, say, the United States or France or the USSR.[15] Latin American societies seem somehow less complex and their "laws of movement" more intelligible, their medium-term future more predictable or at least formulable in terms of clearcut simple alternatives (such as "reform or revolution?"), and their average citizens more reducible to one or a very few stereotypes. Of course, all of this is so exclusively because our paradigmatic thinking makes it so. Mr. Payne is merely the latest in a long line of "law" makers, model builders, and paradigm molders who have vied with one another in getting an iron grip on Latin American reality. And it must now be said that Latin American social scientists have themselves made an important contribution to this headlong rush toward the all-revealing paradigm.

Elsewhere I have described as "the age of self-incrimination" one phase of the efforts of Latin Americans at understanding their own reality and the lag of their countries behind Europe and the United States. Incidentally, traces of this phase can be found in a few contemporary Latin American intellectuals, and they, jointly with their bygone confrères, provide Payne with some telling quotations about the despicable character of Colombian politicians and politics. By and large, the phase has fortunately passed; it has, however, been replaced by a somewhat related phase that might be called the age of the *action-arousing gloomy vision:* on the basis of some model or paradigm, the economic and social reality of Latin America is explained and the laws of movement of economy and society are formulated in such a way that current trends (of terms of trade, or of income distri-

---

15. Lévi-Strauss's structuralist anthropology has had similar effect, as it "has on the whole refrained from attempting to impose totalizing structures on the so-called higher civilizations" (Benjamin I. Schwartz, "A Brief Defense of Political and Intellectual History with Particular Reference to Non-Western Cultures," *Daedalus* 100 [Winter 1971]: 110).

bution, or of population growth) are shown to produce either stagnation, or, more usually, deterioration and disaster. The art of statistical projection has made a potent contribution to this type of forecast, which is then supposed to galvanize men into action designed to avert the threatened disaster through some fairly fundamental "structural changes."

Now I believe that this strategy for socioeconomic change has sometimes been and can on occasion again be extremely useful in just this way. But for several reasons I would caution against the exclusive reliance on it that has recently characterized Latin American social and economic thought.

There is a world of difference, by the way, between this action-arousing gloomy vision and the Marxian perspective on capitalist evolution. In the Marxian perspective, events in the absence of revolution were not at all supposed to move steadily downhill. On the contrary, capitalist development, while punctuated by crises and accompanied by increasing misery of the proletariat, was nevertheless expected to be going forward apace. It was in fact the genius of Marxism—which explains a large part of its appeal—that it was able to view both the advances and the setbacks of economic development under the capitalist system as helping toward its eventual overthrow.

My first criticism of the vision ties in directly with my dislike of paradigms laying down excessive constraints on the conceivable moves of individuals and societies. Why should all of Latin America find itself constantly impaled on the horns of some fateful and unescapable dilemma? Even if one is prepared to accept Goldenweiser's "principle of limited possibilities" in a given environment, any theory or model or paradigm propounding that there are only two possibilities—disaster or one particular road to salvation—should be prima facie suspect. After all, there *is* at least temporarily, such a place as purgatory!

The second reason for which I would advocate a de-emphasis of the action-arousing gloomy vision is that it creates more gloom than action. The spread of gloom is certain and pervasive, but the call to action may or may not be heard. And since the theory teaches that in the normal course of events things will be increasingly unsatisfactory, it is an invitation *not* to watch out for possible positive developments. On the contrary, those imbued with the gloomy vision will attempt to prove year by year that Latin America is going from bad to worse; a year like 1968—and this may hold for 1969 as well—when the economic performance of the three large and of several small countries was little short of brilliant, will come as a distinct embarrassment.

Frequently, of course, the theories I am criticizing are the result of wishful thinking: would it not be reassuring if a society that has been unable to meet some standard of social justice or if an oppressive political regime were *ipso facto* condemned to economic stagnation and deterioration? For that very reason we should be rather on our guard against any theory purporting to prove what would be so reassuring.

But the propensity to see gloom and failure everywhere is not engendered only by the desire to reprove further an oppressive regime or an unjust society. It may also be rooted in the fact that one has come to expect his country to perform poorly because of its long history of backwardness and dependence; hence any evidence that the country may possibly be doing better or may be emerging from its backwardness is going to be dissonant with previous cognitions and is therefore likely to be suppressed; on the contrary, evidence that nothing at all has changed will be picked up, underlined, and even greeted, for it does not necessitate any change in the preexisting cognitions to which one has become comfortably adjusted. This is so because people who have a low self-concept and expect failure apparently feel some discomfort when they suddenly perform well, as psychologists have shown.[16] In this manner, social psychology provides a clue to a Latin American phenomenon that has long puzzled me, yet has struck me with such force that I have invented a name for it—the "failure complex" or "fracasomania."

Finally, the paradigm-based gloomy vision can be positively harmful. When it prevails, hopeful developments either will not be perceived at all or will be considered exceptional and purely temporary. In these circumstances, they will not be taken advantage of as

16. Elliott Aronson, "Dissonance Theory: Progress and Problems," in R. P. Abelson et al., eds., *Theories of Cognitive Consistency: A Source Book* (Chicago: Rand-McNally, 1968), 24.

elements on which to build. To give an example: the rise of the fish-meal industry in Peru and the similarly spectacular growth of banana planting in Ecuador from about 1950 to the mid-sixties contradicted the doctrine that the era of export-promoted growth had ended in Latin America. As a result, economists first ignored these booms, then from year to year predicted their imminent collapse. It is quite possible that particularly the latter attitude held down the proportion of the bonanza that the two countries might otherwise have set aside for long-term economic and social capital formation; for why bother to exert oneself and, in the process, antagonize powerful interests if the payoff is expected to be so limited and short-lived? More recently, another theory of gloom has been widely propagated: it seems that now the opportunities for import-substituting industrialization have also become "exhausted" even though it can be argued that, just as earlier in the case of *desarrollo hacia afuera*, there is still much life left in *desarrollo hacia adentro*.[17] Again, if the exhaustion thesis is wholly accepted it may weaken the search for and prevent the discovery of new industrial opportunities.

In all these matters I would suggest a little more reverence for life, a little less straitjacketing of the future, a little more allowance for the unexpected—and a little less wishful thinking. This is simply a matter, once again, of cognitive style. With respect to actual socioeconomic analysis, I am of course not unaware that without models, paradigms, ideal types, and similar abstractions we cannot even start to think. But cognitive style, that is, the kind of paradigms we search out, the way we put them together, and the ambitions we nurture for their powers—all this can make a great deal of difference.

III

In trying to spell out these notions in greater detail I shall make three principal points. In the first place, I shall explain why the gloomy vision is in a sense the first stage of any reflections about a backward reality, and shall make a plea for not getting stuck in that stage. I

17. The Spanish terms *desarrollo hacia afuera* and *desarrollo hacia adentro* are convenient shorthand expressions for growth through the expansion of exports and of the domestic market, respectively.

shall then attempt to show that in evaluating the broader social and political consequences of some ongoing event we must be suspicious of paradigms that pretend to give a clearcut answer about the desirable or undesirable nature of these consequences. And finally, I shall suggest that large-scale social change typically occurs as a result of a unique constellation of highly disparate events and is therefore amenable to paradigmatic thinking only in a very special sense.

The initial effort to understand reality will almost inevitably make it appear more solidly entrenched than before. The immediate effect of social analysis is therefore to convert the real into the rational or the contingent into the necessary. Herein, rather than in any conservatism of "bourgeois" social scientists, probably lies the principal explanation of that much commented-upon phenomenon—the conservative bias of social science in general, and of functional analysis in particular. This very conservatism takes, however, a strange turn when the target of the social scientists is a society that is viewed from the outset as backward or unjust or oppressive. For analysis will then make it appear, at least to start with, that the backwardness, injustice and oppression are in reality far more deep-rooted than had been suspected. This is the origin of all the vicious circle and vicious personality theories that seem to make any change impossible in the absence of either revolution, highly competent central planning with massive injection of foreign aid, or massive abduction of the young generation so that it may be steeped elsewhere in creativity and achievement motivation.[18] Interestingly enough then, the same analytical turn of mind that leads to a conservative bias in the case of a society that we approach without a strong initial commitment to change, leads to a revolutionary or quasi-revolutionary stance in the case of societies that are viewed from the outset as unsatisfactory. In the case of the former, the analyst, like the ecologist, often becomes enamored of all the fine latent functions he uncovers, whereas in the latter case he despairs of the possibility of change (except for the

18. It is only fair to note that, in his more recent work on achievement motivation, David McClelland has changed his earlier views on these matters. Thus he writes (after having given cogent reasons for doing so): "To us it is no longer a self-evident truth that it is easier to produce long-range personality transformations in young children than it is in adults." David C. McClelland and David G. Winter, *Motivating Economic Achievement* (New York: Free Press, 1969), 356.

most massive and revolutionary varieties) because of all the inter-locking vicious circles he has come upon.

Fortunately these initial effects of social science analysis wear off after a while. In the case of the backward countries, the realization will dawn that certain so-called attributes of backwardness are not necessarily obstacles, but can be lived with and sometimes can be turned into positive assets. I have elsewhere attempted to bring together the accumulating evidence for this sort of phenomenon. This evidence, then, should make us a bit wary when new vicious circles or new development-obstructing personality types or new dead ends are being discovered. Though such discoveries are bound to occur and can be real contributions to understanding, they carry an obligation to look for ways in which they may play not a reinforcing but a neutral or debilitating role insofar as system maintenance is concerned. Perhaps social scientists could pass a rule, such as has long existed in the British Parliament, by which an M.P. proposing a new item of public expenditure must also indicate the additional revenue through which he expects the nation to finance it. Similarly it might be legislated by an assembly of social scientists that anyone who believes he has discovered a new obstacle to development is under an obligation to look for ways in which this obstacle can be overcome or can possibly be lived with or can, in certain circumstances, be transformed into a blessing in disguise.

IV

A related element of the cognitive style I am advocating derives from the recognition of one aspect of the unfolding of social events that makes prediction exceedingly difficult and contributes to that peculiar open-endedness of history that is the despair of the paradigm-obsessed social scientist. Situations in which the expertise of the social scientist is solicited frequently have the following structure: some new event or bundle of events such as industrialization, urbanization, rapid population growth, and so forth, has happened or is happening before our eyes, and we would like to know what its consequences are for a number of social and political system characteristics, such as integration of marginal or oppressed groups, loss of authority on the part of traditional elites, political stability or crisis, likely level of violence or of cultural achievement, and so on. Faced with the seemingly reasonable demand for enlightenment on the part of the layman and the policy maker, and propelled also by his own curiosity, the social scientist now opens his paradigm box to see how best to handle the job at hand. To his dismay, he then finds, provided he looks carefully, that he is faced with an embarrassment of riches: various available paradigms will produce radically different answers. The situation can be compared, in a rough way, with the quandary the forecasting economist has long experienced: the magnitudes that are of most interest to the policy makers, such as the prospective deficit or surplus in the balance of payments or the budget, or the inflationary or deflationary gap, or the rate of unemployment, are usually—and maddeningly—differences between gross magnitudes. Hence, even if the gross magnitudes are estimated with an acceptable margin of error, the estimate of the difference may be off by a very large percentage and may easily be even of the wrong sign. The hazards in forecasting qualitative social events on the basis of perfectly respectable and reliable paradigms can be rather similar. Take the question: what is the effect of industrialization and economic development on a society's propensity for civil war, or for external adventure, or for genocide, or for democracy? As with the effect, say, of accelerated growth on the balance of payments, the answer must be: it depends on the balance of the contending forces that are set in motion. Industrialization creates new tensions, but may allay old ones; it may divert the minds of the elite from external adventure while creating new capabilities for such adventure, and so forth. Thus the outcome is here also a difference whose estimate is necessarily subject to a particularly high degree of error. This ambiguous situation, incidentally, characterizes also less crucial, more "middle-range" causal relationships. An example is the effect of bigness and diversity of an organization on innovation. As James Q. Wilson has argued, bigness and diversity increase the probability that members will conceive of and propose major innovations; but they also increase the probability that any one innovation that is proposed will be turned down. Again the net effect is in doubt.[19]

19. James Q. Wilson, "Innovation in Organization: Notes Toward a Theory," in James D. Thompson, ed., *Approaches to Organizational Design* (Pittsburgh: University of Pittsburgh Press, 1966), 193–218.

Wilson's dilemma is the sort of cognitive style in paradigmatic thinking that is not often met with; ordinarily social scientists are happy enough when they have gotten hold of one paradigm or line of causation. As a result, their guesses are often farther off the mark than those of the experienced politician whose intuition is more likely to take a variety of forces into account.

V

Finally, the ability of paradigmatic thinking to illuminate the paths of change is limited in yet another, perhaps more fundamental way. In the context of most Latin American societies, many of us are concerned with the bringing about of large-scale change to be carried through in a fairly brief period of time. But ordinarily the cards are stacked so much against the accomplishment of large-scale change that when it happens, be it a result of revolution or reform or some intermediate process, it is bound to be an unpredictable and nonrepeatable event, unpredictable because it took the very actors by surprise and nonrepeatable because once the event has happened everybody is put on notice and precautions will be taken by various parties so that it will not happen again. The uniqueness and scientific opaqueness of the large-scale changes that occur when history suddenly accelerates have often been remarked upon. Womack brings this out as well as anyone in his narrative of the Mexican Revolution. I shall invoke the authority of two recent commentators belonging to rather different camps. The first is the anthropologist Max Gluckman, who addresses himself to "radical change" after having defended anthropology against the charge that it is not interested in change. He writes, "The source of radical change escapes these analyses [of other kinds of change]. Perhaps this is inevitable because social anthropology aims to be specific. Scientific method cannot deal with unique complexes of many events. The accounts of the actual course of events which produce change therefore necessarily remain historical narrative."[20]

Perhaps a more significant witness, because as a Marxist he

20. *Politics, Law and Ritual in Tribal Society* (Chicago: Aldine, 1965), 286.

should be an inveterate paradigm-lover, is Louis Althusser. In his remarkable essay, "Contradiction and Overdetermination," Althusser makes much of some striking statements of Lenin's about the unique constellation of events that made possible the Russian Revolution of 1917. The key passage from Lenin reads: "If the revolution has triumphed so rapidly it is exclusively because, as a result of a historical situation of extreme originality, a number of completely distinct currents, a number of totally heterogeneous class interests, and a number of completely opposite social and political tendencies have become fused with remarkable coherence."[21]

On the basis of Lenin's testimony Althusser then proceeds to explain that revolutions never arise purely out of the basic economic contradictions that Marx stressed, but only when these contradictions are "fused" in some unique manner with a number of other determinants. This fusion or embedding is the phenomenon he calls "overdetermination" of revolutions. Actually this is a poor term (as he himself recognizes) for it could imply that, had one of the many circumstantial factors not been present, the revolution would still have taken place. But the whole context of the essay, and certainly the quotations from Lenin, exclude this interpretation. On the contrary, it is quite clear that even with all these converging elements the revolution won by an exceedingly narrow margin. Thus, while a surprising number of heterogeneous elements almost miraculously conspired to bring the revolution about, every single one of them was still absolutely indispensable to its success. Uniqueness seems a better term for this phenomenon than overdetermination.

Incidentally, this interpretation of revolutions undermines the revolutionary's usual critique of the advocacy of reform. This critique is generally based on the high degree of improbability that a ruling group will ever tolerate or even connive at the elimination or destruction of its own privileges; the only way to achieve this end is by smashing the "system" through revolutionary assault. But with the view of revolutions as overdetermined or unique events, it turns out to be a toss-up which form of large-scale change is more unlikely—so we may as well be on the lookout for whatever rare openings in either direction appear on the horizon.

21. As quoted in Althusser, *Pour Marx* (Paris: Maspero, 1966), 98.

In sum, he who looks for large-scale social change must be possessed, with Kierkegaard, by "the passion for what is possible" rather than rely on what has been certified as probable by factor analysis.

This view of large-scale social change as a unique, nonrepeatable, and *ex ante* highly improbable complex of events is obviously damaging to the aspirations of anyone who would explain and predict these events through "laws of change." Once again, there is no denying that such "laws" or paradigms can have considerable utility. They are useful for the apprehending of many elements of the complex and often are stimuli to action before the event and indispensable devices for achieving a beginning of understanding after the event has happened. That is much, but that is all. The architect of social change can never have a reliable blueprint. Not only is each house he builds different from any other that was built before, but it also necessarily uses new construction materials and even experiments with untested principles of stress and structure. Therefore what can be most usefully conveyed by the builders of one house is an understanding of the experience that made it all possible to build under these trying circumstances. It is, I believe, in this spirit that Womack makes that, at first sight rather shocking, statement, "the truth of the revolution in Morelos is in the feeling of it." Perhaps he means not only the truth, but also the principal lesson.

CLIFFORD GEERTZ

6

Deep Play
Notes on the Balinese Cockfight

THE RAID

Early in April of 1958, my wife and I arrived, malarial and diffident, in a Balinese village we intended, as anthropologists, to study. A small place, about five hundred people, and relatively remote, it was its own world. We were intruders, professional ones, and the villagers dealt with us as Balinese seem always to deal with people not part of their life who yet press themselves upon them: as though we were not there. For them, and to a degree for ourselves, we were nonpersons, specters, invisible.

We moved into an extended family compound (that had been arranged before through the provincial government) belonging to one of the four major factions in village life. But except for our landlord and the village chief, whose cousin and brother-in-law he was, everyone ignored us in a way only a Balinese can do. As we wandered around, uncertain, wistful, eager to please, people seemed to look right through us with a gaze focused several yards behind us on some more actual stone or tree. Almost nobody greeted us; but nobody scowled or said anything unpleasant to us either, which would

Originally published in *Daedalus* 101, no. 1 (Winter 1972). Reprinted by permission of the author.

have been almost as satisfactory. If we ventured to approach some-one (something one is powerfully inhibited from doing in such an atmosphere), he moved, negligently but definitely, away. If, seated or leaning against a wall, we had him trapped, he said nothing at all, or mumbled what for the Balinese is the ultimate nonword—"yes." The indifference, of course, was studied; the villagers were watching every move we made, and they had an enormous amount of quite accurate information about who we were and what we were going to be doing. But they acted as if we simply did not exist, which, in fact, as this behavior was designed to inform us, we did not, or anyway not yet.

This is, as I say, general in Bali. Everywhere else I have been in Indonesia, and more latterly in Morocco, when I have gone into a new village, people have poured out from all sides to take a very close look at me, and often an all-too-probing feel as well. In Bal-inese villages, at least those away from the tourist circuit, nothing happens at all. People go on pounding, chatting, making offerings, staring into space, carrying baskets about while one drifts around feeling vaguely disembodied. And the same thing is true on the in-dividual level. When you first meet a Balinese, he seems virtually not to relate to you at all; he is, in the term Gregory Bateson and Margaret Mead made famous, "away."[1] Then—in a day, a week, a month (with some people the magic moment never comes)—he de-cides, for reasons I have never quite been able to fathom, that you *are* real, and then he becomes a warm, gay, sensitive, sympathetic, though, being Balinese, always precisely controlled, person. You have crossed, somehow, some moral or metaphysical shadow line. Though you are not exactly taken as a Balinese (one has to be born to that), you are at least regarded as a human being rather than a cloud or a gust of wind. The whole complexion of your relationship dramatically changes to, in the majority of cases, a gentle, almost affectionate one—a low-keyed, rather playful, rather mannered, rather bemused geniality.

My wife and I were still very much in the gust-of-wind stage, a most frustrating, and even, as you soon begin to doubt whether you

---

1. G. Bateson and M. Mead, *Balinese Character: A Photographic Analysis* (New York, 1942), 68.

are really real after all, unnerving one, when, ten days or so after our arrival, a large cockfight was held in the public square to raise money for a new school.

Now, a few special occasions aside, cockfights are illegal in Bali under the Republic (as, for not altogether unrelated reasons, they were under the Dutch), largely as a result of the pretensions to puritanism radical nationalism tends to bring with it. The elite, which is not itself so very puritan, worries about the poor, ignorant peasant gambling all his money away, about what foreigners will think, about the waste of time better devoted to building up the country. It sees cockfighting as "primitive," "backward," "unprogressive," and generally unbecoming an ambitious nation. And, as with those other embarrassments—opium smoking, begging, or uncovered breasts—it seeks, rather unsystematically, to put a stop to it.

Of course, like drinking during Prohibition or, today, smoking marihuana, cockfights, being a part of the Balinese way of life, nonetheless go on happening, and with extraordinary frequency. And as with Prohibition or marihuana, from time to time the police (who, in 1958 at least, were almost all not Balinese but Javanese) feel called upon to make a raid, confiscate the cocks and spurs, fine a few people, and even now and then expose some of them in the tropical sun for a day as object lessons which never, somehow, get learned, even though occasionally, quite occasionally, the object dies.

As a result, the fights are usually held in a secluded corner of a village in semisecrecy, a fact which tends to slow the action a little— not very much, but the Balinese do not care to have it slowed at all. In this case, however, perhaps because they were raising money for a school that the government was unable to give them, perhaps because raids had been few recently, perhaps, as I gathered from subsequent discussion, there was a notion that the necessary bribes had been paid, they thought they could take a chance on the central square and draw a larger and more enthusiastic crowd without attracting the attention of the law.

They were wrong. In the midst of the third match, with hundreds of people, including, still transparent, myself and my wife, fused into a single body around the ring, a superorganism in the literal sense, a truck full of policemen armed with machine guns roared up. Amid great screeching cries of "pulisi! pulisi!" from the crowd, the policemen jumped out, and, springing into the center of the ring, began to swing their guns around like gangsters in a motion picture, though not going so far as actually to fire them. The superorganism came instantly apart as its components scattered in all directions. People raced down the road, disappeared headfirst over walls, scrambled under platforms, folded themselves behind wicker screens, scuttled up coconut trees. Cocks armed with steel spurs sharp enough to cut off a finger or run a hole through a foot were running wildly around. Everything was dust and panic.

On the established anthropological principle of "when-in-Rome," my wife and I decided, only slightly less instantaneously than everyone else, that the thing to do was run too. We ran down the main village street, northward, away from where we were living, for we were on that side of the ring. About halfway down another fugitive ducked suddenly into a compound—his own, it turned out—and we, seeing nothing ahead of us but rice fields, open country, and a very high volcano, followed him. As the three of us came tumbling into the courtyard, his wife, who had apparently been through this sort of thing before, whipped out a table, a tablecloth, three chairs, and three cups of tea, and we all, without any explicit communication whatsoever, sat down, commenced to sip tea, and sought to compose ourselves.

A few moments later, one of the policemen marched importantly into the yard, looking for the village chief. (The chief had not only been at the fight, he had arranged it. When the truck drove up he ran to the river, stripped off his sarong, and plunged in so he could say, when at length they found him sitting there pouring water over his head, that he had been away bathing when the whole affair had occurred and was ignorant of it. They did not believe him and fined him three hundred rupiah, which the village raised collectively.) Seeing me and my wife, "white men," there in the yard, the policeman performed a classic double take. When he found his voice again he asked, approximately, what in the devil did we think we were doing there. Our host of five minutes leaped instantly to our defense, producing an impassioned description of who and what we were, so detailed and so accurate that it was my turn, having barely communicated with a living human being save my landlord and the village chief for more than a week, to be astonished. We had a perfect right to be there, he said, looking the Javanese upstart in the eye. We were American professors; the government had cleared us; we were there to study culture; we were going to write a book to tell Americans about Bali. And we had all been there drinking tea and talking about cultural matters all afternoon and did not know anything about any cockfight. Moreover, we had not seen the village chief all day; he must have gone to town. The policeman retreated in rather total disarray. And, after a decent interval, bewildered but relieved to have survived and stayed out of jail, so did we.

The next morning the village was a completely different world for us. Not only were we no longer invisible, we were suddenly the center of all attention, the object of a great outpouring of warmth, interest, and most especially, amusement. Everyone in the village knew we had fled like everyone else. They asked us about it again and again (I must have told the story, small detail by small detail, fifty times by the end of the day), gently, affectionately, but quite insistently teasing us: "Why didn't you just stand there and tell the police who you were?" "Why didn't you just say you were only watching and not betting?" "Were you really afraid of those little guns?" As always, kinesthetically minded and, even when fleeing for their lives (or, as happened eight years later, surrendering them), the world's most poised people, they gleefully mimicked, also over and over again, our graceless style of running and what they claimed were our panicstricken facial expressions. But above all, everyone was extremely pleased and even more surprised that we had not simply "pulled out our papers" (they knew about those too) and asserted our Distinguished Visitor status, but had instead demonstrated our solidarity with what were now our covillagers. (What we had actually demonstrated was our cowardice, but there is fellowship in that too.) Even the Brahmana priest, an old, grave, halfway-to-heaven type who because of its associations with the underworld would never be involved, even distantly, in a cockfight, and was difficult to approach even to other Balinese, had called us into his courtyard to ask us about what had happened, chuckling happily at the sheer extraordinariness of it all.

In Bali, to be teased is to be accepted. It was the turning point so far as our relationship to the community was concerned, and we were quite literally "in." The whole village opened up to us, probably more than it ever would have otherwise (I might actually never have gotten to that priest, and our accidental host became one of my best informants), and certainly very much faster. Getting caught, or

almost caught, in a vice raid is perhaps not a very generalizable rec-
ipe for achieving that mysterious necessity of anthropological field
work, rapport, but for me it worked very well. It led to a sudden and
unusually complete acceptance into a society extremely difficult for
outsiders to penetrate. It gave me the kind of immediate, inside-view
grasp of an aspect of "peasant mentality" that anthropologists not
fortunate enough to flee headlong with their subjects from armed
authorities normally do not get. And, perhaps most important of all,
for the other things might have come in other ways, it put me very
quickly on to a combination emotional explosion, status war, and
philosophical drama of central significance to the society whose
inner nature I desired to understand. By the time I left I had spent
about as much time looking into cockfights as into witchcraft, irrigation, caste, or marriage.

OF COCKS AND MEN

Bali, mainly because it is Bali, is a well-studied place. Its mythology,
art, ritual, social organization, patterns of child rearing, forms of law,
even styles of trance, have all been microscopically examined for
traces of that elusive substance Jane Belo called "The Balinese Temper."[2] But, aside from a few passing remarks, the cockfight has
barely been noticed, although as a popular obsession of consuming
power it is at least as important a revelation of what being a Balinese
"is really like" as these more celebrated phenomena.[3] As much of
America surfaces in a ball park, on a golf links, at a race track, or
around a poker table, much of Bali surfaces in a cock ring. For it is
only apparently cocks that are fighting there. Actually, it is men.

To anyone who has been in Bali any length of time, the deep psychological identification of Balinese men with their cocks is unmistakable. The double entendre here is deliberate. It works in
exactly the same way in Balinese as it does in English, even to pro-

2. J. Belo, "The Balinese Temper," in *Traditional Balinese Culture*, ed. J. Belo (New
York, 1970, originally published in 1935), 85–110.
3. The best discussion of cockfighting is again Bateson and Mead's *Balinese Character*, 24–25, 140; but it, too, is general and abbreviated.

ducing the same tired jokes, strained puns, and uninventive ob-
scenities. Bateson and Mead have even suggested that, in line with
the Balinese conception of the body as a set of separately animated
parts, cocks are viewed as detachable, self-operating penises, ambulant genitals with a life of their own.[4] And while I do not have the
kind of unconscious material either to confirm or disconfirm this intriguing notion, the fact that they are masculine symbols par excellence is about as indubitable, and to the Balinese about as evident, as
the fact that water runs downhill.

The language of everyday moralism is shot through, on the male
side of it, with roosterish imagery. *Sabung,* the word for cock (and
one which appears in inscriptions as early as A.D. 922), is used metaphorically to mean "hero," "warrior," "champion," "man of parts,"
"political candidate," "bachelor," "dandy," "lady-killer," or "tough
guy." A pompous man whose behavior presumes above his station is
compared to a tailless cock who struts about as though he had a
large, spectacular one. A desperate man who makes a last, irrational
effort to extricate himself from an impossible situation is likened to a
dying cock who makes one final lunge at his tormentor to drag him
along to a common destruction. A stingy man, who promises much,
gives little, and begrudges that, is compared to a cock which, held by
the tail, leaps at another without in fact engaging him. A marriage-
able young man still shy with the opposite sex or someone in a new
job anxious to make a good impression is called "a fighting cock
caged for the first time."[5] Court trials, wars, political contests, inheri-

---

4. Ibid., 25–26. The cockfight is unusual within Balinese culture in being a
single-sex public activity from which the other sex is totally and expressly excluded.
Sexual differentiation is culturally extremely played down in Bali and most activities,
formal and informal, involve the participation of men and women on equal ground,
commonly as linked couples. From religion, to politics, to economics, to kinship, to
dress, Bali is a rather "unisex" society, a fact both its customs and its symbolism
clearly express. Even in contexts where women do not in fact play much of a role—
music, painting, certain agricultural activities—their absence, which is only relative in
any case, is more a mere matter of fact than socially enforced. To this general pattern,
the cockfight, entirely of, by, and for men (women—at least Balinese women—do not
even watch), is the most striking exception.

5. C. Hooykass, *The Lay of the Jaya Prana* (London, 1958), 39. The lay has a
stanza (no. 17) comparing the reluctant bridegroom to a caged cock. Jaya Prana, the
subject of a Balinese Uriah myth, responds to the lord who has offered him the love-
liest of six hundred servant girls: "Godly King, my Lord and Master / I beg you, give

tance disputes, and street arguments are all compared to cockfights.[6] Even the very island itself is perceived from its shape as a small, proud cock, poised, neck extended, back taut, tail raised, in eternal challenge to large, feckless, shapeless Java.[7]

But the intimacy of men with their cocks is more than metaphorical. Balinese men, or anyway a large majority of Balinese men, spend an enormous amount of time with their favorites, grooming them, feeding them, discussing them, trying them out against one another, or just gazing at them with a mixture of rapt admiration and dreamy self-absorption. Whenever you see a group of Balinese men squatting idly in the council shed or along the road in their hips down, shoulders forward, knees up fashion, half or more of them will each have a rooster in his hands, holding it between his thighs, bouncing it gently up and down to strengthen its legs, ruffling its feathers with abstract sensuality, pushing it out against a neighbor's rooster to rouse its spirit, withdrawing it toward his loins to calm it again. Now and then, to get a feel for another bird, a man will fiddle this way with someone else's cock for a while, but usually by moving around to squat in place behind it, rather than just having it passed across to him as though it were merely an animal.

In the houseyard, the high-walled enclosures where the people live, fighting cocks are kept in wicker cages, moved frequently about so as to maintain the optimum balance of sun and shade. They are fed a special diet, which varies somewhat according to individual theories but which is mostly maize, sifted for impurities with far more care than it is when mere humans are going to eat it, and offered to the animal kernel by kernel. Red pepper is stuffed down their beaks and up their anuses to give them spirit. They are bathed in the same ceremonial preparation of tepid water, medicinal herbs, flowers, and onions in which infants are bathed, and for a prize cock

---

me leave to go / such things are not yet in my mind; / like a fighting cock encaged / indeed I am on my mettle / I am alone / as yet the flame has not been fanned."

6. For these, see V. E. Korn, *Het Adatrecht van Bali,* 2nd ed. (The Hague, 1932), index under *toh.*

7. There is indeed a legend to the effect that the separation of Java and Bali is due to the action of a powerful Javanese religious figure who wished to protect himself against a Balinese culture hero (the ancestor of two Ksatria castes) who was a passionate cockfighting gambler. See C. Hooykaas, *Agama Tirtha* (Amsterdam, 1964), 184.

just about as often. Their combs are cropped, their plumage dressed, their spurs trimmed, and their legs massaged, and they are inspected for flaws with the squinted concentration of a diamond merchant. A man who has a passion for cocks, an enthusiast in the literal sense of the term, can spend most of his life with them, and even those, the overwhelming majority, whose passion though intense has not entirely run away with them, can and do spend what seems not only to an outsider, but also to themselves, an inordinate amount of time with them. "I am cock crazy," my landlord, a quite ordinary *aficionado* by Balinese standards, used to moan as he went to move another cage, give another bath, or conduct another feeding. "We're all cock crazy."

The madness has some less visible dimensions, however, because although it is true that cocks are symbolic expressions or magnifications of their owner's self, the narcissistic male ego writ out in Aesopian terms, they are also expressions—and rather more immediate ones—of what the Balinese regard as the direct inversion, aesthetically, morally, and metaphysically, of human status: animality.

The Balinese revulsion against any behavior regarded as animal-like can hardly be overstressed. Babies are not allowed to crawl for that reason. Incest, though hardly approved, is a much less horrifying crime than bestiality. (The appropriate punishment for the second is death by drowning, for the first being forced to live like an animal.)[8] Most demons are represented—in sculpture, dance, ritual, myth—in some real or fantastic animal form. The main puberty rite consists in filing the child's teeth so they will not look like animal fangs. Not only defecation but eating is regarded as a disgusting, almost obscene activity, to be conducted hurriedly and privately, because of its association with animality. Even falling down or any form of clumsiness is considered to be bad for these reasons. Aside from cocks and a few domestic animals—oxen, ducks—of no emotional significance, the Balinese are aversive to animals and treat their large number of dogs not merely callously but with a phobic cruelty. In identifying with his cock, the Balinese man is identifying

---

8. An incestuous couple is forced to wear pig yokes over their necks and crawl to a pig trough and eat with their mouths there. On this, see J. Belo, "Customs Pertaining to Twins in Bali," in *Traditional Balinese Culture,* 49; on the abhorrence of animality generally, Bateson and Mead, *Balinese Character,* 22.

not just with his ideal self, or even his penis, but also, and at the same time, with what he most fears, hates, and ambivalence being what it is, is fascinated by—"the powers of darkness."

The connection of cocks and cockfighting with such powers, with the animalistic demons that threaten constantly to invade the small, cleared-off space in which the Balinese have so carefully built their lives and devour its inhabitants, is quite explicit. A cockfight, any cockfight, is in the first instance a blood sacrifice offered, with the appropriate chants and oblations, to the demons in order to pacify their ravenous, cannibal hunger. No temple festival should be conducted until one is made. (If it is omitted, someone will inevitably fall into a trance and command with the voice of an angered spirit that the oversight be immediately corrected.) Collective responses to natural evils—illness, crop failure, volcanic eruptions—almost always involve them. And that famous holiday in Bali, "the Day of Silence" (*Njepi*), when everyone sits silent and immobile all day long in order to avoid contact with a sudden influx of demons chased momentarily out of hell, is preceded the previous day by large-scale cockfights (in this case legal) in almost every village on the island.

In the cockfight, man and beast, good and evil, ego and id, the creative power of aroused masculinity and the destructive power of loosened animality fuse in a bloody drama of hatred, cruelty, violence, and death. It is little wonder that when, as is the invariable rule, the owner of the winning cock takes the carcass of the loser—often torn limb from limb by its enraged owner—home to eat, he does so with a mixture of social embarrassment, moral satisfaction, aesthetic disgust, and cannibal joy. Or that a man who has lost an important fight is sometimes driven to wreck his family shrines and curse the gods, an act of metaphysical (and social) suicide. Or that in seeking earthly analogues for heaven and hell the Balinese compare the former to the mood of a man whose cock has just won, the latter to that of a man whose cock has just lost.

THE FIGHT

Cockfights (*tetadjen; sabungan*) are held in a ring about fifty feet square. Usually they begin toward late afternoon and run three or four hours until sunset. About nine or ten separate matches (*sehet*) compose a program. Each match is precisely like the others in general pattern: there is no main match, no connection between individual matches, no variation in their format, and each is arranged on a completely ad hoc basis. After the fight has ended and the emotional debris is cleared away—the bets have been paid, the curses cursed, the carcasses possessed—seven, eight, perhaps even a dozen men slip negligently into the ring with a cock and seek to find there a logical opponent for it. This process, which rarely takes less than ten minutes, and often a good deal longer, is conducted in a very subdued, oblique, even dissembling manner. Those not immediately involved give it at best but disguised, sidelong attention; those who, embarrassedly, are, attempt to pretend somehow that the whole thing is not really happening.

A match made, the other hopefuls retire with the same deliberate indifference, and the selected cocks have their spurs (*tadji*) affixed—razor-sharp, pointed steel swords, four or five inches long. This is a delicate job which only a small proportion of men, a half-dozen or so in most villages, know how to do properly. The man who attaches the spurs also provides them, and if the rooster he assists wins, its owner awards him the spur-leg of the victim. The spurs are affixed by winding a long length of string around the foot of the spur and the leg of the cock. For reasons I shall come to presently, it is done somewhat differently from case to case, and is an obsessively deliberate affair. The lore about spurs is extensive—they are sharpened only at eclipses and the dark of the moon, should be kept out of the sight of women, and so forth. And they are handled, both in use and out, with the same curious combination of fussiness and sensuality the Balinese direct toward ritual objects generally.

The spurs affixed, the two cocks are placed by their handlers (who may or may not be their owners) facing one another in the center of the ring.[9] A coconut pierced with a small hole is placed in a pail of

9. Except for unimportant, small-bet fights (on the question of fight "importance," see below), spur affixing is usually done by someone other than the owner. Whether the owner handles his own cock or not more or less depends on how skilled he is at it, a consideration whose importance is again relative to the importance of the fight. When spur affixers and cock handlers are someone other than the owner, they

water, in which it takes about twenty-one seconds to sink, a period known as a *tjeng* and marked at the beginning and the end by the beating of a slit gong. During these twenty-one seconds the handlers (*pengangkeb*) are not permitted to touch their roosters. If, as sometimes happens, the animals have not fought during this time, they are picked up, fluffed, pulled, prodded, and otherwise insulted, and put back in the center of the ring and the process begins again. Sometimes they refuse to fight at all, or one keeps running away, in which case they are imprisoned together under a wicker cage, which usually gets them engaged.

Most of the time, in any case, the cocks fly almost immediately at one another in a wing-beating, head-thrusting, leg-kicking explosion of animal fury so pure, so absolute, and in its own way so beautiful, as to be almost abstract, a Platonic concept of hate. Within moments one or the other drives home a solid blow with his spur. The handler whose cock has delivered the blow immediately picks it up so that it will not get a return blow, for if he does not the match is likely to end in a mutually mortal tie as the two birds wildly hack each other to pieces. This is particularly true if, as often happens, the spur sticks in the victim's body, for then the aggressor is at the mercy of his wounded foe.

With the birds again in the hands of their handlers, the coconut is now sunk three times after which the cock which has landed the blow must be set down to show that he is firm, a fact he demonstrates by wandering idly around the ring for a coconut sink. The coconut is then sunk twice more and the fight must recommence.

During this interval, slightly over two minutes, the handler of the wounded cock has been working frantically over it, like a trainer patching a mauled boxer between rounds, to get it in shape for a last, desperate try for victory. He blows in its mouth, putting the whole chicken head in his mouth and sucking and blowing, fluffs it, stuffs

---

are almost always a quite close relative—a brother or a cousin—or a very intimate friend of his. They are thus almost extensions of his personality, as the fact that all three will refer to the cock as "mine," say "I" fought So-and-So, and so on, demonstrates. Also, owner-handler-affixer triads tend to be fairly fixed, though individuals may participate in several and often exchange roles within a given one.

its wounds with various sorts of medicines, and generally tries anything he can think of to arouse the last ounce of spirit which may be hidden somewhere within it. By the time he is forced to put it back down he is usually drenched in chicken blood, but, as in prize fighting, a good handler is worth his weight in gold. Some of them can virtually make the dead walk, at least long enough for the second and final round.

In the climactic battle (if there is one; sometimes the wounded cock simply expires in the handler's hands or immediately as it is placed down again), the cock who landed the first blow usually proceeds to finish off his weakened opponent. But this is far from an inevitable outcome, for if a cock can walk, he can fight, and if he can fight, he can kill, and what counts is which cock expires first. If the wounded one can get a stab in and stagger on until the other drops, he is the official winner, even if he himself topples over an instant later.

Surrounding all this melodrama—which the crowd packed tight around the ring follows in near silence, moving their bodies in kinesthetic sympathy with the movement of the animals, cheering their champions on with wordless hand motions, shiftings of the shoulders, turning of the head, falling back en masse as the cock with the murderous spurs careens toward one side of the ring (it is said that spectators sometimes lose eyes and fingers from being too attentive), surging forward again as they glance off toward another—is a vast body of extraordinarily elaborate and precisely detailed rules.

These rules, together with the developed lore of cocks and cockfighting which accompanies them, are written down in palm-leaf manuscripts (*lontar; rontal*) passed on from generation to generation as part of the general legal and cultural tradition of the villages. At a fight, the umpire (*saja komong; djuru kembar*)—the man who manages the coconut—is in charge of their application and his authority is absolute. I have never seen an umpire's judgment questioned on any subject, even by the more despondent losers, nor have I ever heard, even in private, a charge of unfairness directed against one, or, for that matter, complaints about umpires in general. Only exceptionally well trusted, solid, and, given the complexity of the code, knowledgeable citizens perform this job, and in fact men will bring their cocks only to fights presided over by such men. It is also the umpire to whom accusations of cheating, which, though rare in the extreme, occasionally arise, are referred; and it is he who in the not infrequent cases where the cocks expire virtually together decides which (if either, for though the Balinese do not care for such an outcome, there can be ties) went first. Likened to a judge, a king, a priest, and a policeman, he is all of these, and under his assured direction the animal passion of the fight proceeds within the civic certainty of the law. In the dozens of cockfights I saw in Bali, I never saw an altercation about rules. Indeed, I never saw an open altercation other than those between cocks, at all.

This crosswise doubleness of an event that, taken as a fact of nature, is rage untrammeled and, taken as a fact of culture, is form perfected, defines the cockfight as a sociological entity. A cockfight is what, searching for a name of something not vertebrate enough to be called a group and not structureless enough to be called a crowd, Erving Goffman has called a "focused gathering"—a set of persons engrossed in a common flow of activity and relating to one another in terms of that flow.[10] Such gatherings meet and disperse; the participants in them fluctuate; the activity that focuses them is discrete—a particulate process that reoccurs rather than a continuous one that endures. They take their form from the situation that evokes them, the floor on which they are placed, as Goffman puts it; but it is a form, and an articulate one, nonetheless. For the situation, the floor is itself created, in jury deliberations, surgical operations, block meetings, sit-ins, cockfights, by the cultural preoccupations—here, as we shall see, the celebration of status rivalry—which not only specify the focus but, assembling actors and arranging scenery, bring it actually into being.

In classical times (that is to say, prior to the Dutch invasion of 1908), when there were no bureaucrats around to improve popular morality, the staging of a cockfight was an explicitly societal matter. Bringing a cock to an important fight was for an adult male a compulsory duty of citizenship; taxation of fights, which were usually

10. E. Goffman, *Encounters: Two Studies in the Sociology of Interaction* (Indianapolis, 1961), 9–10.

held on market day, was a major source of public revenue; patronage of the art was a stated responsibility of princes; and the cock ring, or *wantilan,* stood in the center of the village near those other monuments of Balinese civility—the council house, the origin temple, the marketplace, the signal tower, and the banyan tree. Today, a few special occasions aside, the newer rectitude makes so open a statement of the connection between the excitements of collective life and those of blood sport impossible, but, less directly expressed, the connection itself remains intimate and intact. To expose it, however, it is necessary to turn to the aspect of cockfighting around which all the others pivot, and through which they exercise their force, an aspect I have thus far studiously ignored. I mean, of course, the gambling.

ODDS AND EVEN MONEY

The Balinese never do anything in a simple way that they can contrive to do in a complicated one, and to this generalization cockfight wagering is no exception.

In the first place, there are two sorts of bets, or *toh.*[11] There is the single axial bet in the center between the principals (*toh ketengah*), and there is the cloud of peripheral ones around the ring between members of the audience (*toh kesasi*). The first is typically large, the second typically small. The first is collective, involving coalitions of bettors clustering around the owner; the second is individual, man to man. The first is a matter of deliberate, very quiet, almost furtive arrangement by the coalition members and the umpire huddled like conspirators in the center of the ring; the second is a matter of impulsive shouting, public offers, and public acceptances by the excited

11. This word, which literally means an indelible stain or mark, as in a birthmark or a vein in a stone, is used as well for a deposit in a court case, for a pawn, for security offered in a loan, for a stand-in for someone else in a legal or ceremonial context, for an earnest advanced in a business deal, for a sign placed in a field to indicate its ownership is in dispute, and for the status of an unfaithful wife from whose lover her husband must gain satisfaction or surrender her to him. See Korn, *Het Adatrecht van Bali;* Th. Pigeaud, *Javaans-Nederlands Handwoordenboek* (Groningen, 1938); H. H. Juynboll, *Oudjavaansche-Nederlandsche Woordenlijst* (Leiden, 1923).

throng around its edges. And most curiously, and as we shall see most revealingly, where the first is always, without exception, even money, the second, equally without exception, is never such. What is a fair coin in the center is a biased one on the side.

The center bet is the official one, hedged in again with a webwork of rules, and is made between the two cock owners, with the umpire as overseer and public witness.[12] This bet, which, as I say, is always relatively and sometimes very large, is never raised simply by the owner in whose name it is made, but by him together with four or five, sometimes seven or eight, allies—kin, village mates, neighbors, close friends. He may, if he is not especially well-to-do, not even be the major contributor; though, if only to show that he is not involved in any chicanery, he must be a significant one.

Of the fifty-seven matches for which I have exact and reliable data on the center bet, the range is from fifteen ringgits to five hundred, with a mean at eighty-five and with the distribution being rather noticeably trimodal: small fights (15 ringgits either side of 35) accounting for about 45 percent of the total number; medium ones (20 ringgits either side of 70) for about 25 percent; and large (75 ringgits either side of 175) for about 20 percent, with a few very small and very large ones out at the extremes. In a society where the normal daily wage of a manual laborer—a brickmaker, an ordinary farmworker, a market porter—was about three ringgits a day, and considering the fact that fights were held on the average about every two-and-a-half days in the immediate area I studied, this is clearly serious gambling, even if the bets are pooled rather than individual efforts.

The side bets are, however, something else altogether. Rather than the solemn, legalistic pactmaking of the center, wagering takes place rather in the fashion in which the stock exchange used to work when it was out on the curb. There is a fixed and known odds para-

12. The center bet must be advanced in cash by both parties prior to the actual fight. The umpire holds the stakes until the decision is rendered and then awards them to the winner, avoiding, among other things, the intense embarrassment both winner and loser would feel if the latter had to pay off personally following his defeat. About ten percent of the winner's receipts are subtracted for the umpire's share and that of the fight sponsors.

digm which runs in a continuous series from ten-to-nine at the short end to two-to-one at the long: 10–9, 9–8, 8–7, 7–6, 6–5, 5–4, 4–3, 3–2, 2–1. The man who wishes to back the underdog cock (leaving aside how favorites, *kebut,* and underdogs, *ngai,* are established for the moment) shouts the short-side number indicating the odds he wants to be given. That is, if he shouts *gasal,* "five," he wants the underdog at five-to-four (or, for him, four-to-five); if he shouts "four," he wants it at four-to-three (again, he is putting up the "three"); if "nine," at nine-to-eight, and so on. A man backing the favorite, and thus considering giving odds if he can get them short enough, indicates the fact by crying out the color-type of that cock— "brown," "speckled," or whatever.[13]

As odds-takers (backers of the underdog) and odds-givers (backers of the favorite) sweep the crowd with their shouts, they begin to focus in on one another as potential betting pairs, often from far across the ring. The taker tries to shout the giver into longer odds,

---

13. Actually, the typing of cocks, which is extremely elaborate (I have collected more than twenty classes, certainly not a complete list), is based not on color alone but on a series of independent, interacting dimensions, which include—besides color—size, bone thickness, plumage, and temperament. (But *not* pedigree. The Balinese do not breed cocks to any significant extent, nor, so far as I have been able to discover, have they ever done so. The *asil,* or jungle cock, which is the basic fighting strain everywhere the sport is found, is native to southern Asia, and one can buy a good example in the chicken section of almost any Balinese market for anywhere from four to five ringgits up to fifty or more.) The color element is merely the one normally used as the type name, except when the two cocks of different types—as on principle they must be—have the same color, in which case a secondary indication from one of the other dimensions ("large speckled" v. "small speckled," etc.) is added. The types are coordinated with various cosmological ideas which help shape the making of matches, so that, for example, you fight a small, headstrong, speckled brown-on-white cock with flat-lying feathers and thin legs from the east side of the ring on a certain day of the complex Balinese calendar, and a large, cautious, all-black cock with tufted feathers and stubby legs from the north side on another day, and so on. All this is again recorded in palm-leaf manuscripts and endlessly discussed by the Balinese (who do not all have identical systems), and a full-scale componential-cum-symbolic analysis of cock classifications would be extremely valuable both as an adjunct to the description of the cockfight and in itself. But my data on the subject, though extensive and varied, do not seem to be complete and systematic enough to attempt such an analysis here. For Balinese cosmological ideas more generally, see Belo, ed., *Traditional Balinese Culture,* and J. L. Swellengrebel, ed., *Bali: Studies in Life, Thought, and Ritual* (The Hague, 1960).

the giver to shout the taker into shorter ones.[14] The taker, who is the wooer in this situation, will signal how large a bet he wishes to make at the odds he is shouting by holding a number of fingers up in front of his face and vigorously waving them. If the giver, the wooed, replies in kind, the bet is made; if he does not, they unlock gazes and the search goes on.

The side betting, which takes place after the center bet has been made and its size announced, consists then in a rising crescendo of shouts as backers of the underdog offer their propositions to anyone who will accept them, while those who are backing the favorite but do not like the price being offered, shout equally frenetically the color of the cock to show they too are desperate to bet but want shorter odds.

Almost always odds-calling, which tends to be very consensual in that at any one time almost all callers are calling the same thing, starts off toward the long end of the range—five-to-four or four-to-three—and then moves, also consensually, toward the short end with greater or lesser speed and to a greater or lesser degree. Men crying "five" and finding themselves answered only with cries of "brown" start crying "six," either drawing the other callers fairly quickly with them or retiring from the scene as their too-generous offers are snapped up. If the change is made and partners are still scarce, the procedure is repeated in a move to "seven," and so on, only rarely, and in the very largest fights, reaching the ultimate "nine" or "ten" levels. Occasionally, if the cocks are clearly mismatched, there may be no upward movement at all, or even a movement down the scale to four-to-three, three-to-two, very, very rarely two-to-one, a shift that is accompanied by a declining number of bets as a shift upward is accompanied by an increasing number. But the general pattern is for the betting to move a shorter or longer distance

14. For purposes of ethnographic completeness, it should be noted that it is possible for the man backing the favorite—the odds-giver—to make a bet in which he wins if his cock wins or there is a tie, a slight shortening of the odds (I do not have enough cases to be exact, but ties seem to occur about once every fifteen or twenty matches). He indicates his wish to do this by shouting *sapih* ("tie") rather than the cock-type, but such bets are in fact infrequent.

up the scale toward the, for sidebets, nonexistent pole of even money, with the overwhelming majority of bets falling in the four-to-three to eight-to-seven range.[15]

As the moment for the release of the cocks by the handlers approaches, the screaming, at least in a match where the center bet is large, reaches almost frenzied proportions as the remaining unfulfilled bettors try desperately to find a last-minute partner at a price they can live with. (Where the center bet is small, the opposite tends to occur: betting dies off, trailing into silence, as odds lengthen and people lose interest.) In a large-bet, well-made match—the kind of match the Balinese regard as "real cockfighting"—the mob scene quality, the sense that sheer chaos is about to break loose, with all those waving, shouting, pushing, clambering men is quite strong, an effect which is only heightened by the intense stillness that falls with instant suddenness, rather as if someone had turned off the current, when the slit gong sounds, the cocks are put down, and the battle begins.

When it ends, anywhere from fifteen seconds to five minutes later, all bets are immediately paid. There are absolutely no IOUs, at least to a betting opponent. One may, of course, borrow from a friend before offering or accepting a wager, but to offer or accept it you must have the money already in hand and, if you lose, you must pay it on the spot, before the next match begins. This is an iron rule, and as I have never heard of a disputed umpire's decision (though doubtless there must sometimes be some), I have also never heard of

15. The precise dynamics of the movement of the betting is one of the most intriguing, most complicated, and, given the hectic conditions under which it occurs, most difficult to study, aspects of the fight. Motion picture recording plus multiple observers would probably be necessary to deal with it effectively. Even impressionistically—the only approach open to a lone ethnographer caught in the middle of all this—it is clear that certain men lead both in determining the favorite (that is, making the opening cock-type calls which always initiate the process) and in directing the movement of the odds, these "opinion leaders" being the more accomplished cockfighters-cum-solid-citizens to be discussed below. If these men begin to change their calls, others follow; if they begin to make bets, so do others and—though there are always a large number of frustrated bettors crying for shorter or longer odds to the end—the movement more or less ceases. But a detailed understanding of the whole process awaits what, alas, it is not very likely ever to get: a decision theorist armed with precise observations of individual behavior.

a reneged bet, perhaps because in a worked-up cockfight crowd the consequences might be, as they are reported to be sometimes for cheaters, drastic and immediate.

It is, in any case, this formal asymmetry between balanced center bets and unbalanced side ones that poses the critical analytical problem for a theory which sees cockfight wagering as the link connecting the fight to the wider world of Balinese culture. It also suggests the way to go about solving it and demonstrating the link.

The first point that needs to be made in this connection is that the higher the center bet, the more likely the match will in actual fact be an even one. Simple considerations of rationality suggest that. If you are betting fifteen ringgits on a cock, you might be willing to go along with even money even if you feel your animal somewhat the less promising. But if you are betting five hundred you are very, very likely to be loathe to do so. Thus, in large-bet fights, which of course involve the better animals, tremendous care is taken to see that the cocks are about as evenly matched as to size, general condition, pugnacity, and so on as is humanly possible. The different way of adjusting the spurs of the animals are often employed to secure this. If one cock seems stronger, an agreement will be made to position his spur at a slightly less advantageous angle—a kind of handicapping, at which spur affixers are, so it is said, extremely skilled. More care will be taken, too, to employ skillful handlers and to match them exactly as to abilities.

In short, in a large-bet fight the pressure to make the match a genuinely fifty-fifty proposition is enormous, and is consciously felt as such. For medium fights the pressure is somewhat less, and for small ones less yet, though there is always an effort to make things at least approximately equal, for even at fifteen ringgits (five days' work) no one wants to make an even money bet in a clearly unfavorable situation. And, again, what statistics I have tend to bear this out. In my fifty-seven matches, the favorite won thirty-three times overall, the underdog twenty-four, a 1.4:1 ratio. But if one splits the figures at sixty ringgits center bets, the ratios turn out to be 1.1:1 (twelve favorites, eleven underdogs) for those above this line, and 1.6:1 (twenty-one and thirteen) for those below it. Or, if you take the extremes, for very large fights, those with center bets over a hundred ringgits the ratio is 1:1 (seven and seven); for very small fights, those under forty ringgits, it is 1.9:1 (nineteen and ten).[16]

Now, from this proposition—that the higher the center bet the more exactly a fifty-fifty proposition the cockfight is—two things more or less immediately follow: (1) the higher the center bet is, the greater the pull on the side betting toward the short-odds end of the wagering spectrum, and vice versa; (2) the higher the center bet is, the greater the volume of side betting, and vice versa.

The logic is similar in both cases. The closer the fight is in fact to even money, the less attractive the long end of the odds will appear and, therefore, the shorter it must be if there are to be takers. That this is the case is apparent from mere inspection, from the Balinese's own analysis of the matter, and from what more systematic observations I was able to collect. Given the difficulty of making precise and complete recordings of side betting, this argument is hard to cast in numerical form, but in all my cases the odds-giver, odds-taker consensual point, a quite pronounced mini-max saddle where the bulk (at a guess, two-thirds to three-quarters in most cases) of the bets are actually made, was three or four points further along the scale toward the shorter end for the large-center-bet fights than for the small ones, with medium ones generally in between. In detail, the fit is not, of course, exact, but the general pattern is quite consistent: the power of the center bet to pull the side bets toward its own even-money pattern is directly proportional to its size, because its size is directly proportional to the degree to which the cocks are in fact evenly matched. As for the volume question, total wagering is greater in large-center-bet fights because such fights are considered more "interesting," not only in the sense that they are less predictable, but, more crucially, that more is at stake in them—in terms of

16. Assuming only binomial variability, the departure from a fifty-fifty expectation in the sixty-ringgits-and-below case is 1.38 standard deviations, or (in a one direction test) an eight in one hundred possibility by chance alone; for the below-forty-ringgits case it is 1.65 standard deviations, or about five in one hundred. The fact that these departures though real are not extreme merely indicates, again, that even in the smaller fights the tendency to match cocks at least reasonably evenly persists. It is a matter of relative relaxation of the pressures toward equalization, not their elimination. The tendency for high-bet contests to be coin-flip propositions is, of course, even more striking, and suggests the Balinese know quite well what they are about.

money, in terms of the quality of the cocks, and consequently, as we shall see, in terms of social prestige.[17]

The paradox of fair coin in the middle, biased coin on the outside is thus a merely apparent one. The two betting systems, though formally incongruent, are not really contradictory to one another, but are part of a single larger system in which the center bet is, so to speak, the "center of gravity," drawing, the larger it is the more so, the outside bets toward the short-odds end of the scale. The center bet thus "makes the game," or perhaps better, defines it, signals what, following a notion of Jeremy Bentham's, I am going to call its "depth."

The Balinese attempt to create an interesting, if you will, "deep" match by making the center bet as large as possible so that the cocks matched will be as equal and as fine as possible, and the outcome, thus, as unpredictable as possible. They do not always succeed. Nearly half the matches are relatively trivial, relatively uninteresting—in my borrowed terminology, "shallow"—affairs. But that fact no more argues against my interpretation than the fact that most painters, poets, and playwrights are mediocre argues against the view that artistic effort is directed toward profundity and, with a certain frequency, approximates it. The image of artistic technique is indeed exact: the center bet is a means, a device, for creating "interesting," "deep" matches, *not* the reason, or at least not the main reason, *why* they are interesting, the source of their fascination, the

---

17. The reduction in wagering in smaller fights (which, of course, feeds on itself; one of the reasons people find small fights uninteresting is that there is less wagering in them, and contrariwise for large ones) takes place in three mutually reinforcing ways. First, there is a simple withdrawal of interest as people wander off to have a cup of coffee or chat with a friend. Second, the Balinese do not mathematically reduce odds, but bet directly in terms of stated odds as such. Thus, for a nine-to-eight bet, one man wagers nine ringgits, the other eight; for five-to-four, one wagers five, the other four. For any given currency unit, like the ringgit, therefore, 6.3 times as much money is involved in a ten-to-nine bet as in a two-to-one bet, for example, and, as noted, in small fights betting settles toward the longer end. Finally, the bets which are made tend to be one- rather than two-, three-, or in some of the very largest fights, four- or five-finger ones. (The fingers indicate the *multiples* of the stated bet odds at issue, not absolute figures. Two fingers in a six-to-five situation means a man wants to wager ten ringgits on the underdog against twelve, three in an eight-to-seven situation, twenty-one against twenty-four, and so on.)

substance of their depth. The question of why such matches are interesting—indeed, for the Balinese, exquisitely absorbing—takes us out of the realm of formal concerns into more broadly sociological and social-psychological ones, and to a less purely economic idea of what "depth" in gaming amounts to.[18]

PLAYING WITH FIRE

Bentham's concept of "deep play" is found in his *The Theory of Legislation*.[19] By it he means play in which the stakes are so high that it is, from his utilitarian standpoint, irrational for men to engage in it at all. If a man whose fortune is a thousand pounds (or ringgits) wagers five hundred of it on an even bet, the marginal utility of the pound he stands to win is clearly less than the marginal disutility of the one he stands to lose. In genuine deep play, this is the case for

18. Besides wagering there are other economic aspects of the cockfight, especially its very close connection with the local market system which, though secondary both to its motivation and to its function, are not without importance. Cockfights are open events to which anyone who wishes may come, sometimes from quite distant areas, but well over 90 percent, probably over 95, are very local affairs, and the locality concerned is defined not by the village, nor even by the administrative district, but by the rural market system. Bali has a three-day market week with the familiar "solar-system" type of rotation. Though the markets themselves have never been very highly developed, small morning affairs in a village square, it is the microregion such rotation rather generally marks out—ten or twenty square miles, seven or eight neighboring villages (which in contemporary Bali is usually going to mean anywhere from five to ten or eleven thousand people)—from which the core of any cockfight audience, indeed virtually all of it, will come. Most of the fights are in fact organized and sponsored by small combines of petty rural merchants under the general premise, very strongly held by them and indeed by all Balinese, that cockfights are good for the trade because "they get money out of the house, they make it circulate." Stalls selling various sorts of things as well as assorted sheer-chance gambling games are set up around the edge of the area so that this even takes on the quality of a small fair. This connection of cockfighting with markets and market sellers is very old, as, among other things, their conjunction in inscriptions [R. Goris, *Prasasti Bali*, 2 vols. (Bandung, 1954)] indicates. Trade has followed the cock for centuries in rural Bali, and the sport has been one of the main agencies of the island's monetization.

19. The phrase is found in the Hildreth translation, International Library of Psychology (1931), note to p. 106; see L. L. Fuller, *The Morality of Law* (New Haven, 1964), 6ff.

both parties. They are both in over their heads. Having come to-gether in search of pleasure they have entered into a relationship which will bring the participants, considered collectively, net pain rather than net pleasure. Bentham's conclusion was, therefore, that deep play was immoral from first principles and, a typical step for him, should be prevented legally.

But more interesting than the ethical problem, at least for our concerns here, is that despite the logical force of Bentham's analysis men do engage in such play, both passionately and often, and even in the face of law's revenge. For Bentham and those who think as he does (nowadays mainly lawyers, economists, and a few psychia-trists), the explanation is, as I have said, that such men are irra-tional—addicts, fetishists, children, fools, savages, who need only to be protected against themselves. But for the Balinese, though natu-rally they do not formulate it in so many words, the explanation lies in the fact that in such play, money is less a measure of utility, had or expected, than it is a symbol of moral import, perceived or imposed.

It is, in fact, in shallow games, ones in which smaller amounts of money are involved, that increments and decrements of cash are more nearly synonyms for utility and disutility, in the ordinary, un-expanded sense—for pleasure and pain, happiness and unhappiness. In deep ones, where the amounts of money are great, much more is at stake than material gain: namely, esteem, honor, dignity, re-spect—in a word, though in Bali a profoundly freighted word, status.[20] It is at stake symbolically, for (a few cases of ruined addict gamblers aside) no one's status is actually altered by the outcome of a cockfight; it is only, and that momentarily, affirmed or insulted. But for the Balinese, for whom nothing is more pleasurable than an af-front obliquely delivered or more painful than one obliquely re-ceived—particularly when mutual acquaintances, undeceived by surfaces, are watching—such appraisive drama is deep indeed.

This, I must stress immediately, is not to say that the money does

---

20. Of course, even in Bentham, utility is not normally confined as a concept to monetary losses and gains, and my argument here might be more carefully put in terms of a denial that for the Balinese, as for any people, utility (pleasure, happiness . . .) is merely identifiable with wealth. But such terminological problems are in any case secondary to the essential point: the cockfight is not roulette.

not matter, or that the Balinese is no more concerned about losing five hundred ringgits than fifteen. Such a conclusion would be absurd. It is because money *does,* in this hardly unmaterialistic society, matter and matter very much that the more of it one risks, the more of a lot of other things, such as one's pride, one's poise, one's dispassion, one's masculinity, one also risks, again only momentarily but again very publicly as well. In deep cockfights an owner and his collaborators, and, as we shall see, to a lesser but still quite real extent also their backers on the outside, put their money where their status is.

It is in large part *because* the marginal disutility of loss is so great at the higher levels of betting that to engage in such betting is to lay one's public self, allusively and metaphorically, through the medium of one's cock, on the line. And though to a Benthamite this might seem merely to increase the irrationality of the enterprise that much further, to the Balinese what it mainly increases is the meaningfulness of it all. And as (to follow Weber rather than Bentham) the imposition of meaning on life is the major end and primary condition of human existence, that access of significance more than compensates for the economic costs involved.[21] Actually, given the even-money quality of the larger matches, important changes in material fortune among those who regularly participate in them seem virtually non-existent, because matters more or less even out over the long run. It is, actually, in the smaller, shallow fights, where one finds the handful of more pure, addict-type gamblers involved—those who *are* in it mainly for the money—that "real" changes in social position, largely downward, are affected. Men of this sort, plungers, are highly

21. M. Weber, *The Sociology of Religion* (Boston, 1963). There is nothing specifically Balinese, of course, about deepening significance with money, as Whyte's description of corner boys in a working-class district of Boston demonstrates: "Gambling plays an important role in the lives of Cornerville people. Whatever game the corner boys play, they nearly always bet on the outcome. When there is nothing at stake, the game is not considered a real contest. This does not mean that the financial element is all-important. I have frequently heard men say that the honor of winning was much more important than the money at stake. The corner boys consider playing for money the real test of skill and, unless a man performs well when money is at stake, he is not considered a good competitor." W. F. Whyte, *Street Corner Society,* 2nd ed. (Chicago, 1955), 140.

dispraised by "true cockfighters" as fools who do not understand what the sport is all about, vulgarians who simply miss the point of it all. They are, these addicts, regarded as fair game for the genuine enthusiasts, those who do understand, to take a little money away from—something that is easy enough to do by luring them, through the force of their greed, into irrational bets on mismatched cocks. Most of them do indeed manage to ruin themselves in a remarkably short time, but there always seems to be one or two of them around, pawning their land and selling their clothes in order to bet, at any particular time.[22]

This graduated correlation of "status gambling" with deeper fights and, inversely, "money gambling" with shallower ones is in fact quite general. Bettors themselves form a sociomoral hierarchy in these terms. As noted earlier, at most cockfights there are, around the very edges of the cockfight area, a large number of mindless, sheer-chance-type gambling games (roulette, dice throw, coin-spin, pea-under-the-shell) operated by concessionaires. Only women, children, adolescents, and various other sorts of people who do not (or not yet) fight cocks—the extremely poor, the socially despised, the personally idiosyncratic—play at these games, at, of course, penny-ante levels. Cockfighting men would be ashamed to go any-where near them. Slightly above these people in standing are those who though they do not themselves fight cocks, bet on the smaller matches around the edges. Next, there are those who fight cocks in small, or occasionally medium matches, but have not the status to join the large ones, though they may bet from time to time on the

22. The extremes to which this madness is conceived on occasion to go—and the fact that it is considered madness—is demonstrated by the Balinese folk tale *I Tuhung Kuning*. A gambler becomes so deranged by his passion that, leaving on a trip, he orders his pregnant wife to take care of the prospective newborn if it is a boy but to feed it as meat to his fighting cocks if it is a girl. The mother gives birth to a girl, but rather than giving the child to the cocks she gives them a large rat and conceals the girl with her own mother. When the husband returns, the cocks, crowing a jingle, inform him of the deception and, furious, he sets out to kill the child. A goddess de-scends from heaven and takes the girl up to the skies with her. The cocks die from the food given them, the owner's sanity is restored, the goddess brings the girl back to the father, who reunites him with his wife. The story is given as "Geel Komkommertje" in J. Hooykass-van Leeuwen Boomkamp, *Sprookjes en Verhalen van Bali* (The Hague, 1956), 19–25.

side in those. And finally, there are those, the really substantial members of the community, the solid citizenry around whom local life revolves, who fight in the larger fights and bet on them around the side. The focusing element in these focused gatherings, these men generally dominate and define the sport as they dominate and define the society. When a Balinese male talks, in that almost venerative way, about "the true cockfighter," the *bebatoh* (bettor) or *djuru kurung* (cage keeper), it is this sort of person, not those who bring the mentality of the pea-and-shell game into the quite different, inappropriate context of the cockfight, the driven gambler (*potét,* a word which has the secondary meaning of thief or reprobate), and the wistful hanger-on, that they mean. For such a man, what is really going on in a match is something rather closer to an *affaire d'honneur* (though, with the Balinese talent for practical fantasy, the blood that is spilled is only figuratively human) than to the stupid, mechanical crank of a slot machine.

What makes Balinese cockfighting deep is thus not money in itself, but what, the more of it that is involved the more so, money causes to happen: the migration of the Balinese status hierarchy into the body of the cockfight. Psychologically an Aesopian representation of the ideal/demonic, rather narcissistic, male self, sociologically it is an equally Aesopian representation of the complex fields of tension set up by the controlled, muted, ceremonial, but for all that deeply felt, interaction of those selves in the context of everyday life. The cocks may be surrogates for their owners' personalities, animal mirrors of psychic form, but the cockfight is—or more exactly, deliberately is made to be—a simulation of the social matrix, the involved system of cross-cutting, overlapping, highly corporate groups—villages, kingroups, irrigation societies, temple congregations, "castes"—in which its devotees live.[23] And as prestige, the necessity to affirm it, defend it, celebrate it, justify it, and just plain bask in it (but not, given the strongly ascriptive character of Balinese stratification, to seek it), is perhaps the central driving force in the

---

23. For a fuller description of Balinese rural social structure, see C. Geertz, "Form and Variation in Balinese Village Structure," *American Anthropologist* 61 (1959): 94–108; "Tihingan, A Balinese Village," in R. M. Koentjaraningrat, *Villages in Indonesia* (Ithaca, 1967), 210–43; and, though it is a bit off the norm as Balinese villages go, V. E. Korn, *De Dorpsrepubliek tnganan Pagringsingan* (Santpoort, Netherlands, 1933).

society, so also—ambulant penises, blood sacrifices, and monetary exchanges aside—is it of the cockfight. This apparent amusement and seeming sport is, to take another phrase from Erving Goffman, "a status bloodbath."[24]

The easiest way to make this clear, and at least to some degree to demonstrate it, is to invoke the village whose cockfighting activities I observed the closest—the one in which the raid occurred and from which my statistical data are taken.

Like all Balinese villages, this one—Tihingan, in the Klungkung region of southeast Bali—is intricately organized, a labyrinth of alliances and oppositions. But, unlike many, two sorts of corporate groups, which are also status groups, particularly stand out, and we may concentrate on them, in a part-for-whole way, without undue distortion.

First, the village is dominated by four large, patrilineal, partly endogamous descent groups which are constantly vying with one another and form the major factions in the village. Sometimes they group two and two, or rather the two larger ones versus the two smaller ones plus all the unaffiliated people; sometimes they operate independently. There are also subfactions within them, subfactions within the subfactions, and so on to rather fine levels of distinction. And second, there is the village itself, almost entirely endogamous, which is opposed to all the other villages round about in its cockfight circuit (which, as was explained, is the market region), but which also forms alliances with certain of these neighbors against certain others in various supravillage political and social contexts. The exact situation is thus, as everywhere in Bali, quite distinctive, but the general pattern of a tiered hierarchy of status rivalries between highly corporate but various based groupings (and, thus, between the members of them) is entirely general.

Consider, then, as support of the general thesis that the cockfight, and especially the deep cockfight, is fundamentally a dramatization of status concerns, the following facts, which to avoid extended ethnographic description I shall simply pronounce to be facts— though the concrete evidence, examples, statements, and numbers

24. Goffman, *Encounters*, 78.

that could be brought to bear in support of them, is both extensive and unmistakable:

1. A man virtually never bets against a cock owned by a member of his own kingroup. Usually he will feel obliged to bet for it, the more so the closer the kin tie and the deeper the fight. If he is certain in his mind that it will not win, he may just not bet at all, particularly if it is only a second cousin's bird or if the fight is a shallow one. But as a rule he will feel he must support it and, in deep games, nearly always does. Thus the great majority of the people calling "five" or "speckled" so demonstratively are expressing their allegiance to their kinsman, not their evaluation of his bird, their understanding of probability theory, or even their hopes of unearned income.

2. This principle is extended logically. If your kingroup is not involved you will support an allied kingroup against an unallied one in the same way, and so on through the very involved networks of alliances which, as I say, make up this, as any other, Balinese village.

3. So, too, for the village as a whole. If an outsider cock is fighting any cock from your village, you will tend to support the local one. If, what is a rarer circumstance but occurs every now and then, a cock from outside your cockfight circuit is fighting one inside it, you will also tend to support the "home bird."

4. Cocks which come from any distance are almost always favorites, for the theory is the man would not have dared to bring it if it was not a good cock, the more so the further he has come. His followers are, of course, obliged to support him, and when the more grandscale legal cockfights are held (on holidays, and so on) the people of the village take what they regard to be the best cocks in the village, regardless of ownership, and go off to support them, although they will almost certainly have to give odds on them and to make large bets to show that they are not a cheapskate village. Actually, such "away games," though infrequent, tend to mend the ruptures between village members that the constantly occurring "home games," where village factions are opposed rather than united, exacerbate.

5. Almost all matches are sociologically relevant. You seldom get two outsider cocks fighting, or two cocks with no particular group backing, or with group backing which is mutually unrelated

in any clear way. When you do get them, the game is very shallow, betting very slow, and the whole thing very dull, with no one save the immediate principals and an addict gambler or two at all interested.

6. By the same token, you rarely get two cocks from the same group, even more rarely from the same subfaction, and virtually never from the same sub-subfaction (which would be in most cases one extended family) fighting. Similarly, in outside village fights two members of the village will rarely fight against one another, even though, as bitter rivals, they would do so with enthusiasm on their home grounds.

7. On the individual level, people involved in an institutionalized hostility relationship, called *puik*, in which they do not speak or otherwise have anything to do with each other (the causes of this formal breaking of relations are many: wife-capture, inheritance arguments, political differences) will bet very heavily, sometimes almost maniacally, against one another in what is a frank and direct attack on the very masculinity, the ultimate ground of his status, of the opponent.

8. The center-bet coalition is, in all but the shallowest games, *always* made up by structural allies—no "outside money" is involved. What is "outside" depends upon the context, of course, but given it, no outside money is mixed in with the main bet; if the principals cannot raise it, it is not made. The center bet, again especially in deeper games, is thus the most direct and open expression of social opposition, which is one of the reasons why both it and matchmaking are surrounded by such an air of unease, furtiveness, embarrassment, and so on.

9. The rule about borrowing money—that you may borrow *for* a bet but not *in* one—stems (and the Balinese are quite conscious of this) from similar considerations: you are never at the economic mercy of your enemy that way. Gambling debts, which can get quite large on a rather short-term basis, are always to friends, never to enemies, structurally speaking.

10. When two cocks are structurally irrelevant or neutral so far as you are concerned (though, as mentioned, they almost never are to each other) you do not even ask a relative or a friend whom he is

betting on, because if you know how he is betting and he knows you know, and you go the other way, it will lead to strain. This rule is explicit and rigid; fairly elaborate, even rather artificial precautions are taken to avoid breaking it. At the very least you must pretend not to notice what he is doing, and he what you are doing.

11. There is a special word for betting against the grain, which is also the word for "pardon me" (*mpura*). It is considered a bad thing to do, though if the center bet is small it is sometimes all right as long as you do not do it too often. But the larger the bet and the more frequently you do it, the more the "pardon me" tack will lead to social disruption.

12. In fact, the institutionalized hostility relation, *puik*, is often formally initiated (though its causes always lie elsewhere) by such a "pardon me" bet in a deep fight, putting the symbolic fat in the fire. Similarly, the end of such a relationship and resumption of normal social intercourse is often signalized (but, again, not actually brought about) by one or the other of the enemies supporting the other's bird.

13. In sticky, cross-loyalty situations, of which in this extraordinarily complex social system there are of course many, where a man is caught between two more or less equally balanced loyalties, he tends to wander off for a cup of coffee or something to avoid having to bet, a form of behavior reminiscent of that of American voters in similar situations.[25]

14. The people involved in the center bet are, especially in deep fights, virtually always leading members of their group—kinship, village, or whatever. Further, those who bet on the side (including these people) are, as I have already remarked, the more established members of the village—the solid citizens. Cockfighting is for those who are involved in the everyday politics of prestige as well, not for youth, women, subordinates, and so forth.

15. So far as money is concerned, the explicitly expressed attitude toward it is that it is a secondary matter. It is not, as I have said, of no importance; Balinese are no happier to lose several weeks' income than anyone else. But they mainly look on the mone-

25. B. R. Berelson, P. F. Lazersfeld, and W. N. McPhee, *Voting: A Study of Opinion Formation in a Presidential Campaign* (Chicago, 1954).

tary aspects of the cockfight as self-balancing, a matter of just moving money around, circulating it among a fairly well-defined group of serious cockfighters. The really important wins and losses are seen mostly in other terms, and the general attitude toward wagering is not any hope of cleaning up, of making a killing (addict gamblers again excepted), but that of the horse-player's prayer: "Oh, God, please let me break even." In prestige terms, however, you do not want to break even, but, in a momentary, punctuate sort of way, win utterly. The talk (which goes on all the time) is about fights against such-and-such a cock of So-and-So which your cock demolished, not on how much you won, a fact people, even for large bets rarely remember for any length of time, though they will remember the day they did in Pan Loh's finest cock for years.

16. You must bet on cocks of your own group aside from mere loyalty and considerations, for if you do not people generally will say, "What! Is he too proud for the likes of us? Does he have to go to Java or Den Pasar [the capital town] to bet, he is such an important man?" Thus there is a general pressure to bet not only to show that you are important locally, but that you are not so important that you look down on everyone else as unfit even to be rivals. Similarly, home team people must bet against outside cocks or the outsiders will accuse them—a serious charge—of just collecting entry fees and not really being interested in cockfighting, as well as again being arrogant and insulting.

17. Finally, the Balinese peasants themselves are quite aware of all this and can and, at least to an ethnographer, do state most of it in approximately the same terms as I have. Fighting cocks, almost every Balinese I have ever discussed the subject with has said, is like playing with fire only not getting burned. You activate village and kingroup rivalries and hostilities, but in "play" form, coming dangerously and entrancingly close to the expression of open and direct interpersonal and intergroup aggression (something which, again, almost never happens in the normal course of ordinary life), but not quite, because, after all, it is "only a cockfight."

More observations of this sort could be advanced, but perhaps the general point is, if not made, at least well delineated, and the whole argument thus far can be usefully summarized in a formal paradigm:

The more a match is . . .

1. between near status equals (and/or personal enemies)
2. between high status individuals

the deeper the match.

The deeper the match . . .

1. the closer the identification of cock and man (or, more properly, the deeper the match the more the man will advance his best, most closely-identified-with cock).
2. the finer the cocks involved and the more exactly they will be matched.
3. the greater the emotion that will be involved and the more general absorption in the match.
4. the higher the individual bets center and outside, the shorter the outside bet odds will tend to be, and the more betting there will be overall.
5. the less an "economic" and the more a "status" view of gaming will be involved, and the "solider" the citizens who will be gaming.[26]

Inverse arguments hold for the shallower the fight, culminating, in a reversed-signs sense, in the coin-spinning and dice-throwing amusements. For deep fights there are no absolute upper limits, though there are of course practical ones, and there are a great many legend-like tales of great duel-in-the-sun combats between lords and princes in classical times (for cockfighting has always been as much an elite concern as a popular one), far deeper than anything anyone, even aristocrats, could produce today anywhere in Bali.

Indeed, one of the great culture heroes of Bali is a prince, called after his passion for the sport the Cockfighter, who happened to be away at a very deep cockfight with a neighboring prince when the whole of his family—father, brothers, wives, sisters—were assassinated by commoner usurpers. Thus spared, he returned to dispatch

---

26. As this is a formal paradigm, it is intended to display the logical, not the causal, structure of cockfighting. Just which of these considerations leads to which, in what order, and by what mechanisms, is another matter—one I have attempted to shed some light on in the general discussion.

the upstart, regain the throne, reconstitute the Balinese high tradition, and build its most powerful, glorious, and prosperous state. Along with everything else that the Balinese see in fighting cocks—themselves, their social order, abstract hatred, masculinity, demonic power—they also see the archetype of status virtue, the arrogant, resolute, honor-mad player with real fire, the *ksatria* prince.[27]

FEATHERS, BLOOD, CROWDS, AND MONEY

"Poetry makes nothing happen," Auden says in his elegy of Yeats, "it survives in the valley of its saying . . . a way of happening, a mouth." The cockfight too, in this colloquial sense, makes nothing happen. Men go on allegorically humiliating one another and being allegorically humiliated by one another, day after day, glorying quietly in the experience if they have triumphed, crushed only slightly more openly by it if they have not. *But no one's status really changes.* You cannot ascend the status ladder by winning cockfights; you cannot, as an individual, really ascend it at all. Nor can you de-

---

27. In another of Hooykaas-van Leeuwen Boomkamp's folktales ("De Gast," *Sprookjes en Verhalen van Bali,* 172–80), a low-caste *Sudra,* a generous, pious, and carefree man who is also an accomplished cockfighter, loses, despite his accomplishment, fight after fight until he is not only out of money but down to his last cock. He does not despair, however—"I bet," he says, "upon the Unseen World."

His wife, a good and hard-working woman, knowing how much he enjoys cockfighting, gives him her last "rainy day" money to go and bet. But, filled with misgivings due to his run of ill luck, he leaves his own cock at home and bets merely on the side. He soon loses all but a coin or two and repairs to a food stand for a snack, where he meets a decrepit, odorous, and generally unappetizing old beggar leaning on a staff. The old man asks for food, and the hero spends his last coins to buy him some. The old man then asks to pass the night with the hero, which the hero gladly invites him to do. As there is no food in the house, however, the hero tells his wife to kill the last cock for dinner. When the old man discovers this fact, he tells the hero he has three cocks in his own mountain hut and says the hero may have one of them for fighting. He also asks for the hero's son to accompany him as a servant, and, after the son agrees, this is done.

The old man turns out to be Siva and, thus, to live in a great palace in the sky, though the hero does not know this. In time, the hero decides to visit his son and collect the promised cock. Lifted up into Siva's presence, he is given the choice of three cocks. The first crows: "I have beaten fifteen opponents." The second crows, "I

scend it that way.[28] All you can do is enjoy and savor, or suffer and withstand, the concocted sensation of drastic and momentary movement along an aesthetic semblance of that ladder, a kind of behind-the-mirror status jump which has the look of mobility without its actuality.

Like any art form—for that, finally, is what we are dealing with—the cockfight renders ordinary, everyday experience comprehensible by presenting it in terms of acts and objects that have had their practical consequences removed and been reduced (or, if you prefer, raised) to the level of sheer appearances, where their meaning can be more powerfully articulated and more exactly perceived. The cockfight is "really real" only to the cocks—it does not kill anyone, castrate anyone, reduce anyone to animal status, alter the hierarchical relations among people, or refashion the hierarchy; it does not even redistribute income in any significant way. What it does is what, for other peoples with other temperaments and other conventions, *Lear* and *Crime and Punishment* do; it catches up these themes—death, masculinity, rage, pride, loss, beneficence, chance—and, ordering them into an encompassing structure, presents them in such a way as

---

have beaten twenty-five opponents." The third crows, "I have beaten the king." "That one, the third, is my choice," says the hero, and returns with it to earth.

When he arrives at the cockfight, he is asked for an entry fee and replies, "I have no money; I will pay after my cock has won." As he is known never to win, he is let in because the king, who is there fighting, dislikes him and hopes to enslave him when he loses and cannot pay off. In order to insure that this happens, the king matches his finest cock against the hero's. When the cocks are placed down, the hero's flees, and the crowd, led by the arrogant king, hoots in laughter. The hero's cock then flies at the king himself, killing him with a spur stab in the throat. The hero flees. His house is encircled by the king's men. The cock changes into a Garuda, the great mythic bird of Indic legend, and carries the hero and his wife to safety in the heavens.

When the people see this, they make the hero king and his wife queen and they return as such to earth. Later their son, released by Siva, also returns and the hero-king announces his intentions to enter a hermitage. ("I will fight no more cockfights. I have bet on the Unseen and won.") He enters the hermitage and his son becomes king.

28. Addict gamblers are really less declassed (for their status is, as everyone else's, inherited) than merely impoverished and personally disgraced. The most prominent addict gambler in my cockfight circuit was actually a very high caste *satria* who sold off most of his considerable lands to support his habit. Though everyone privately regarded him as a fool and worse (some, more charitable, regarded him as sick), he was publicly treated with the elaborate deference and politeness due his rank.

to throw into relief a particular view of their essential nature. It puts a construction on them, makes them, to those historically positioned to appreciate the construction, meaningful—visible, tangible, graspable—real, in an ideational sense. An image, fiction, a model, a metaphor, the cockfight is a means of expression; its function is neither to assuage social passions nor to heighten them (though, in its playing-with-fire way it does a bit of both), but, in a medium of feathers, blood, crowds, and money, to display them.

The question of how it is that we perceive qualities in things—paintings, books, melodies, plays—that we do not feel we can assert literally to be there has come, in recent years, into the very center of aesthetic theory.[29] Neither the sentiments of the artist, which remain his, nor those of the audience, which remain theirs, can account for the agitation of one painting or the serenity of another. We attribute grandeur, wit, despair, exuberance to strings of sounds; lightness, energy, violence, fluidity to blocks of stone. Novels are said to have strength, buildings eloquence, plays momentum, ballets repose. In this realm of eccentric predicates, to say that the cockfight, in its perfected cases at least, is "disquietful" does not seem at all unnatural, merely, as I have just denied it practical consequence, somewhat puzzling.

The disquietfulness arises somehow out of a conjunction of three attributes of the fight: its immediate dramatic shape; its metaphoric content; and its social context. A cultural figure against a social ground, the fight is at once a convulsive surge of animal hatred, a mock war of symbolical selves, and a formal simulation of status tensions, and its aesthetic power derives from its capacity to force together these diverse realities. The reason it is disquietful is not that it has material effects (it has some, but they are minor); the reason that it is disquietful is that, joining pride to selfhood, selfhood to cocks, and cocks to destruction, it brings to imaginative realization a dimension of Balinese experience normally well obscured from view. The transfer of a sense of gravity into what is in itself a rather blank and

29. For four, somewhat variant, treatments, see S. Langer, *Feeling and Form* (New York, 1953); R. Wollheim, *Art and Its Objects* (New York, 1968); N. Goodman, *Languages of Art* (Indianapolis, 1968); M. Merleau-Ponty, "The Eye and the Mind," in his *The Primacy of Perception* (Evanston, Ill., 1964), 159–90.

unvarious spectacle, a commotion of beating wings and throbbing legs, is effected by interpreting it as expressive of something unsettling in the way its authors and audience live, or, even more ominously, what they are.

As a dramatic shape, the fight displays a characteristic that does not seem so remarkable until one realizes that it does not have to be there: a radically atomistical structure.[30] Each match is a world unto itself, a particulate burst of form. There is the matchmaking, there is the betting, there is the fight, there is the result—utter triumph and utter defeat—and there is the hurried, embarrassed passing of money. The loser is not consoled. People drift away from him, look around him, leave him to assimilate his momentary descent into nonbeing, reset his face, and return, scarless and intact, to the fray. Nor are winners congratulated, or events rehashed; once a match is ended the crowd's attention turns totally to the next, with no looking back. A shadow of the experience no doubt remains with the principals, perhaps even with some of the witnesses of a deep fight, as it remains with us when we leave the theater after seeing a powerful play well performed; but it quite soon fades to become at most a schematic memory—a diffuse glow or an abstract shudder—and usually not even that. Any expressive form lives only in its own present—the one it itself creates. But, here, that present is severed into a string of flashes, some more bright than others, but all of them disconnected, aesthetic quanta. Whatever the cockfight says, it says in spurts.   *penile*

But the Balinese live in spurts. Their life, as they arrange it and

---

30. British cockfights (the sport was banned there in 1840) indeed seem to have lacked it, and to have generated, therefore, a quite different family of shapes. Most British fights were "mains," in which a preagreed number of cocks were aligned into two teams and fought serially. Score was kept and wagering took place both on the individual matches and on the main as a whole. There were also "battles Royales," both in England and on the Continent, in which a large number of cocks were let loose at once with the one left standing at the end the victor. And in Wales, the so-called Welsh main followed an elimination pattern, along the lines of a present-day tennis tournament, winners proceeding to the next round. As a genre, the cock fight has perhaps less compositional flexibility than, say, Latin comedy, but it is not entirely without any. On cockfighting more generally, see A. Ruport, *The Art of Cockfighting* (New York, 1949); G. R. Scott, *History of Cockfighting* (London, 1957); and L. Fitz-Barnard, *Fighting Sports* (London, 1921).

perceive it, is less a flow, a directional movement out of the past, through the present, toward the future than an on-off pulsation of meaning and vacuity, an arrhythmic alternation of short periods when "something" (that is, something significant) is happening, and equally short ones where "nothing" (that is, nothing much) is—between what they themselves call "full" and "empty" times, or, in another idiom, "junctures" and "holes." In focusing activity down to a burning-glass dot, the cockfight is merely being Balinese in the same way in which everything from the monadic encounters of everyday life, through the clanging pointillism of *gamelan* music, to the visiting-day-of-the-gods temple celebrations are. It is not an imitation of the punctuateness of Balinese social life, nor a depiction of it, nor even an expression of it; it is an example of it, carefully prepared.[31]

If one dimension of the cockfight's structure, its lack of temporal directionality, makes it seem a typical segment of the general social life, however, the other, its flat-out, head-to-head (or spur-to-spur) aggressiveness, makes it seem a contradiction, a reversal, even a subversion of it. In the normal course of things, the Balinese are shy to the point of obsessiveness of open conflict. Oblique, cautious, subdued, controlled, masters of indirection and dissimulation—what they call *alus,* "polished," "smooth"—they rarely face what they can turn away from, rarely resist what they can evade. But here they portray themselves as wild and murderous, with manic explosions of instinctual cruelty. A powerful rendering of life as the Balinese most deeply do not want it (to adapt a phrase Frye has used of Gloucester's blinding) is set in the context of a sample of it as they do in fact have it.[32] And because the context suggests that the rendering, if less than a straightforward description, is nonetheless more than an idle fancy, it is here that the disquietfulness—the disquietfulness of the *fight,* not (or, anyway, not necessarily) its patrons, who seem in fact rather thoroughly to enjoy it—emerges. The slaughter in the cock ring is not a depiction of how things literally are among

---

31. For the necessity of distinguishing among "description," "representation," "exemplification," and "expression" (and the irrelevance of "imitation" to all of them) as modes of symbolic reference, see Goodman, *Languages of Art,* 61–110, 145–91, 225–41.

32. N. Frye, *The Educated Imagination* (Bloomington, Ind., 1964), 99.

men, but, what is almost worse, of how from a particular angle they imaginatively are.[33]

The angle, of course, is stratificatory. What, as we have already seen, the cockfight talks most forcibly about is status relationships, and what it says about them is that they are matters of life and death. That prestige is a profoundly serious business is apparent everywhere one looks in Bali—in the village, the family, the economy, the state. A peculiar fusion of Polynesian title ranks and Hindu castes, the hierarchy of pride is the moral backbone of the society. But only in the cockfight are the sentiments upon which that hierarchy rests revealed in their natural colors. Enveloped elsewhere in a haze of etiquette, a thick cloud of euphemism and ceremony, gesture and allusion, they are here expressed in only the thinnest disguise of an animal mask, a mask which in fact demonstrates them far more effectively than it conceals them. Jealousy is as much a part of Bali as poise, envy as grace, brutality as charm; but without the cockfight the Balinese would have a much less certain understanding of them, which is, presumably, why they value it so highly.

Any expressive form works (when it works) by disarranging semantic contexts in such a way that properties conventionally ascribed to certain things are unconventionally ascribed to others, which are then seen actually to possess them. To call the wind a cripple, as Stevens does, to fix tone and manipulate timbre, as Schoenberg does, or, closer to our case, to picture an art critic as a dissolute bear, as Hogarth does, is to cross conceptual wires; the established con-

---

33. There are two other Balinese values and disvalues which, connected with punctuate temporality on the one hand and unbridled aggressiveness on the other, reinforce the sense that the cockfight is at once continuous with ordinary social life and a direct negation of it: what the Balinese call *ramé*, and what they call *paling*. *Ramé* means crowded, noisy, and active, and is a highly sought-after social state: crowded markets, mass festivals, busy streets are all *ramé*, as, of course, is, in the extreme, a cockfight. *Ramé* is what happens in the "full" times (its opposite, *sepi*, "quiet," is what happens in the "empty" ones). *Paling* is social vertigo, the dizzy, disoriented, lost, turned-around feeling one gets when one's place in the coordinates of social space is not clear, and it is a tremendously disfavored, immensely anxiety-producing state. Balinese regard the exact maintenance of spatial orientation ("not to know where north is" is to be crazy), balance, decorum, status relationships, and so forth, as fundamental to ordered life (*krama*) and *paling*, the sort of whirling confusion of position the scrambling cocks exemplify as its profoundest enemy and contradiction. On *ramé*, see Bateson and Mead, *Balinese Character*, 3, 64; on *paling*, ibid., p. 11, and Belo, ed., *Traditional Balinese Culture*, 90ff.

junctions between objects and their qualities are altered, and phenomena—fall weather, melodic shape, or cultural journalism—are clothed in signifiers which normally point to other referents.[34] Similarly, to connect—and connect, and connect—the collision of roosters with the divisiveness of status is to invite a transfer of perceptions from the former to the latter, a transfer which is at once a description and a judgment. (Logically, the transfer could, of course, as well go the other way; but, like most of the rest of us, the Balinese are a great deal more interested in understanding men than they are in understanding cocks.)

What sets the cockfight apart from the ordinary course of life, lifts it from the realm of the everyday practical affairs, and surrounds it with an aura of enlarged importance is not, as functionalist sociology would have it, that it reinforces status discriminations (such reinforcement is hardly necessary in a society where every act proclaims them), but that it provides a metasocial commentary upon the whole matter of assorting human beings into fixed hierarchical ranks and then organizing the major part of collective existence around that assortment. Its function, if you want to call it that, is interpretive: it is a Balinese reading of Balinese experience, a story they tell themselves about themselves.

SAYING SOMETHING OF SOMETHING

To put the matter this way is to engage in a bit of metaphorical refocusing of one's own, for it shifts the analysis of cultural forms from

34. The Stevens reference is to his "The Motive for Metaphor" ("You like it under the trees in autumn, / Because everything is half dead. / The wind moves like a cripple among the leaves / And repeats words without meaning") [copyright © 1947 by Wallace Stevens, reprinted from *The Collected Poems of Wallace Stevens* by permission of Alfred A. Knopf, Inc., and Faber and Faber Ltd.]; the Schoenberg reference is to the third of his *Five Orchestral Pieces* (Opus 16) and is borrowed from H. H. Drager, "The Concept of 'Tonal Body,'" in *Reflections on Art*, ed. S. Langer (New York, 1961), 174. On Hogarth, and on this whole problem—there called "multiple matrix matching"—see E. H. Gombrich, "The Use of Art for the Study of Symbols," in *Psychology and the Visual Arts*, ed. J. Hogg (Baltimore, 1969), 149–70. The more usual term for this sort of semantic alchemy is "metaphorical transfer," and good technical discussions of it can be found in M. Black, *Models and Metaphors* (Ithaca, N.Y., 1962), 25ff; Goodman, *Languages of Art*, 44ff; and W. Percy, "Metaphor as Mistake," *Sewanee Review* 66 (1958): 78–99.

an endeavor in general parallel to dissecting an organism, diagnosing a symptom, deciphering a code, or ordering a system—the dominant analogies in contemporary anthropology—to one in general parallel with penetrating a literary text. If one takes the cockfight, or any other collectively sustained symbolic structure, as a means of "saying something of something" (to invoke a famous Aristotelian tag), then one is faced with a problem not in social mechanics but social semantics.[35] For the anthropologist, whose concern is with formulating sociological principles, not with promoting or appreciating cockfights, the question is, what does one learn about such principles from examining culture as an assemblage of texts?

Such an extension of the notion of a text beyond written material, and even beyond verbal, is, though metaphorical, not, of course, all that novel. The *interpretatio naturae* tradition of the Middle Ages, that, culminating in Spinoza, attempted to read nature as Scripture, the Nietzschean effort to treat value systems as glosses on the will to power (or the Marxian one to treat them as glosses on property relations), and the Freudian replacement of the enigmatic text of the manifest dream with the plain one of the latent, all offer precedents, if not equally recommendable ones.[36] But the idea remains theoretically undeveloped; and the more profound corollary, so far as anthropology is concerned, that cultural forms can be treated as texts, as imaginative works built out of social materials, has yet to be systematically exploited.[37]

In the case at hand, to treat the cockfight as a text is to bring out a feature of it (in my opinion, the central feature of it) that treating it as a rite or a pastime, the two most obvious alternatives, would tend

Aristotle

Spinoza
Nietzsche
Marx
Freud

35. The tag is from the second book of the *Organon, On Interpretation.* For a discussion of it, and for the whole argument for freeing "the notion of text . . . from the notion of scripture or writing" and constructing, thus, a general hermeneutics, see P. Ricoeur, *Freud and Philosophy* (New Haven, 1970), 20ff.

36. Ibid.

37. Lévi-Strauss's structuralism might seem an exception. But it is only an apparent one, for, rather than taking myths, totem rites, marriage rules, or whatever as texts to interpret, Lévi-Strauss takes them as ciphers to solve, which is very much not the same thing. He does not seek to understand symbolic forms in terms of how they function in concrete situations to organize perceptions (meanings, emotions, concepts, attitudes); he seeks to understand them entirely in terms of their internal structure, *indépendent de tout sujet, de tout objet, et de toute contexte.*

to obscure: its use of emotion for cognitive ends. What the cockfight says it says in a vocabulary of sentiment—the thrill of risk, the despair of loss, the pleasure of triumph. Yet what it says is not merely that risk is exciting, loss depressing, or triumph gratifying, banal tautologies of affect, but that it is of these emotions, thus exampled, that society is built and individuals are put together. Attending cockfights and participating in them is for the Balinese a kind of sentimental education. What he learns there is what his culture's *ethos* and his private sensibility (or, anyway, certain aspects of them) look like when spelled out externally in a collective text; that the two are near enough alike to be articulated in the symbolics of a single such text; and—the disquieting part—that the text in which this revelation is accomplished consists of a chicken hacking another mindlessly to bits.

Every people, the proverb has it, loves its own form of violence. The cockfight is the Balinese reflection on theirs: on its look, its uses, its force, its fascination. Drawing on almost every level of Balinese experience, it brings together themes—animal savagery, male narcissism, opponent gambling, status rivalry, mass excitement, blood sacrifice—whose main connection is their involvement with rage and the fear of rage, and, binding them into a set of rules which at once contains them and allows them play, builds a symbolic structure in which, over and over again, the reality of their inner affiliation can be intelligibly felt. If, to quote Northrop Frye again, we go to see *Macbeth* to learn what a man feels like after he has gained a kingdom and lost his soul, Balinese go to cockfights to find out what a man, usually composed, aloof, almost obsessively self-absorbed, a kind of moral autocosm, feels like when, attacked, tormented, challenged, insulted, and driven in result to the extremes of fury, he has totally triumphed or been brought totally low. The whole passage, as it takes us back to Aristotle (though to the *Poetics* rather than the *Hermeneutics*), is worth quotation:

> But the poet [as opposed to the historian], Aristotle says, never makes any real statements at all, certainly no particular or specific ones. The poet's job is not to tell you what happened, but what happens: not what did take place, but the kind of thing that always does take place. He gives you the typical, recurring, or what Aristotle calls universal event. You wouldn't go to *Macbeth* to learn about the history of Scotland—you go to it to learn what a man feels like after he's gained a kingdom and lost his soul. When you meet such a character as Micawber in Dickens, you

don't feel that there must have been a man Dickens knew who was exactly like this: you feel that there's a bit of Micawber in almost everybody you know, including yourself. Our impressions of human life are picked up one by one, and remain for most of us loose and disorganized. But we constantly find things in literature that suddenly coordinate and bring into focus a great many such impressions, and this is part of what Aristotle means by the typical or universal human event.[38]

It is this kind of bringing of assorted experiences of everyday life to focus that the cockfight, set aside from that life as "only a game" and reconnected to it as "more than a game," accomplishes, and so creates what, better than typical or universal, could be called a paradigmatic human event—that is, one that tells us less what happens than the kind of thing that would happen if, as is not the case, life were art and could be as freely shaped by styles of feeling as *Macbeth* and *David Copperfield* are.

Enacted and reenacted, so far without end, the cockfight enables the Balinese, as, read and reread, *Macbeth* enables us, to see a dimension of his own subjectivity. As he watches fight after fight, with the active watching of an owner and a bettor (for cockfighting has no more interest as a pure spectator sport than does croquet or dog racing), he grows familiar with it and what it has to say to him, much as the attentive listener to string quartets or the absorbed viewer of still life grows slowly more familiar with them in a way which opens his subjectivity to himself.[39]

Yet, because—in another of those paradoxes, along with painted feelings and unconsequenced acts, that haunt aesthetics—that subjectivity does not properly exist until it is thus organized, art forms generate and regenerate the very subjectivity they pretend only to display. Quartets, still lifes, and cockfights are not merely reflections

38. Frye, *The Educated Imagination,* 63–64.

39. The use of the, to Europeans, "natural" visual idiom for perception—"see," "watches," and so forth—is more than usually misleading here, for the fact that, as mentioned earlier, Balinese follow the progress of the fight as much (perhaps, as fighting cocks are actually rather hard to see except as blurs of motion, more) with their bodies as with their eyes, moving their limbs, heads, and trunks in gestural mimicry of the cocks' maneuvers, means that much of the individual's experience of the fight is kinesthetic rather than visual. If ever there was an example of Kenneth Burke's definition of a symbolic act as "the dancing of an attitude" (*The Philosophy of Literary Form,* rev. ed. [New York, 1957], 9) the cockfight is it. On the enormous role of kinesthetic

of a preexisting sensibility analogically represented; they are positive
agents in the creation and maintenance of such a sensibility. If we
see ourselves as a pack of Micawbers, it is from reading too much
Dickens (if we see ourselves as unillusioned realists, it is from reading too little); and similarly for Balinese, cocks, and cockfights. It is
in such a way, coloring experience with the light they cast it in,
rather than through whatever material effects they may have, that
the arts play their role, as arts, in social life.[40]

In the cockfight, then, the Balinese forms and discovers his temperament and his society's temper at the same time. Or, more exactly, he forms and discovers a particular facet of them. Not only are
there a great many other cultural texts providing commentaries on
status hierarchy and self-regard in Bali, but there are a great many
other critical sectors of Balinese life besides the stratificatory and the
agonistic that receive such commentary. The ceremony consecrating
a Brahmana priest, a matter of breath control, postural immobility,
and vacant concentration upon the depths of being, displays a radically different, but to the Balinese equally real, property of social hierarchy—its reach toward the numinous transcendent. Set not in the
matrix of the kinetic emotionality of animals, but in that of the static
passionlessness of divine mentality, it expresses tranquility not disquiet. The mass festivals at the village temples, which mobilize the
whole local population in elaborate hostings of visiting gods—
songs, dances, compliments, gifts—assert the spiritual unity of village mates against their status inequality and project a mood of

---

perception in Balinese life, Bateson and Mead, *Balinese Character,* 84–88; on the active
nature of aesthetic perception in general, Goodman, *Languages of Art,* 241–44.

40. All this coupling of the Occidental great with the Oriental lowly will doubtless disturb certain sorts of aestheticians as the earlier efforts of anthropologists to
speak of Christianity and totemism in the same breath disturbed certain sorts of theo-
logians. But as ontological questions are (or should be) bracketed in the sociology of
religion, judgmental ones are (or should be) bracketed in the sociology of art. In any
case, the attempt to deprovincialize the concept of art is but part of the general anthropological conspiracy to deprovincialize all important social concepts—marriage, religion, law, rationality—and though this is a threat to aesthetic theories which regard
certain works of art as beyond the reach of sociological analysis, it is no threat to the
conviction, for which Robert Graves claims to have been reprimanded at his Cambridge tripos, that some poems are better than others.

amity and trust.[41] The cockfight is not the master key to Balinese life, any more than bullfighting is to Spanish. What it says about that life is not unqualified nor even unchallenged by what other equally eloquent cultural statements say about it. But there is nothing more surprising in this than in the fact that Racine and Molière were contemporaries, or that the same people who arrange chrysanthemums cast swords.[42]

The culture of a people is an ensemble of texts, themselves ensembles, that the anthropologist strains to read over the shoulders of those to whom they properly belong. There are enormous difficulties in such an enterprise, methodological pitfalls to make a Freudian quake, and some moral perplexities as well. Nor is it the only way that symbolic forms can be sociologically handled. Functionalism lives, and so does psychologism. But to regard such forms as "saying something of something," and saying it to somebody, is at least to open up the possibility of an analysis which attends to their substance rather than to reductive formulas professing to account for them.

As in more familiar exercises in close reading, one can start anywhere in a culture's repertoire of forms and end up anywhere else.

41. For the consecration ceremony, see V. E. Korn, "The Consecration of the Priest," in Swellengrebel, ed., *Bali: Studies*, 131–54; for (somewhat exaggerated) village communion, R. Goris, "The Religious Character of the Balinese Village," ibid., 79–100.

42. That what the cockfight has to say about Bali is not altogether without perception, and the disquiet it expresses about the general pattern of Balinese life is not wholly without reason, is attested by the fact that in two weeks of December 1965, during the upheavals following the unsuccessful coup in Djakarta, between forty and eighty thousand Balinese (in a population of about two million) were killed, largely by one another—the worst outburst in the country. [J. Hughes, *Indonesian Upheaval* (New York, 1967), 173–83. Hughes's figures are, of course, rather casual estimates, but they are not the most extreme.] This is not to say, of course, that the killings were caused by the cockfight, could have been predicted on the basis of it, or were some sort of enlarged version of it with real people in the place of the cocks—all of which is nonsense. It is merely to say that if one looks at Bali not just through the medium of its dances, its shadow-plays, its sculpture, and its girls, but—as the Balinese themselves do—also through the medium of its cockfight, the fact that the massacre occurred seems, if no less appalling, less like a contradiction to the laws of nature. As more than one real Gloucester has discovered, sometimes people actually get life precisely as they most deeply do not want it.

One can stay, as I have here, within a single, more or less bounded form, and circle steadily within it. One can move between forms in search of broader unities or informing contrasts. One can even compare forms from different cultures to define their character in reciprocal relief. But whatever the level at which one operates, and however intricately, the guiding principle is the same: societies, like lives, contain their own interpretations. One has only to learn how to gain access to them.

MICHAEL TAUSSIG

7

Culture of Terror—Space of Death

Roger Casement's Putumayo Report and the Explanation of Torture

This essay is about torture and the culture of terror, which for most of us, including myself, are known only through the words of others. Thus my concern is with the mediation of the culture of terror through narration—and with the problems of writing effectively against terror.

Jacobo Timerman ends his recent book, *Prisoner without a Name, Cell without a Number,* with the imprint of the gaze of hope in the space of death.

> Have any of you looked into the eyes of another person, on the floor of a cell, who knows that he's about to die though no one has told him so? He knows that he's about to die but clings to his biological desire to live, as a single hope, since no one has told him he's to be executed.
>
> I have many such gazes imprinted upon me. . . .
>
> Those gazes which I encountered in the clandestine prisons of Argentina and which I've retained one by one, were the culminating point, the purest moment of my tragedy.
>
> They are here with me today. And although I might wish to do so, I could not and would not know how to share them with you.[1]

From "Culture of Terror, Space of Death: Roger Casement's Putumayo Report and the Explanation of Torture," *Comparative Studies in Society and History* 26, no. 3 (July 1984). Reprinted by permission of Cambridge University Press and the author.

1. Jacobo Timerman, *Prisoner without a Name, Cell without a Number* (New York: Vintage Books, 1982), 164.

The space of death is crucial to the creation of meaning and consciousness, nowhere more so than in societies where torture is endemic and where the culture of terror flourishes. We may think of the space of death as a threshold, yet it is a wide space whose breadth offers positions of advance as well as of extinction. Sometimes a person goes through it and returns to us to tell the tale, like Timerman, who entered it, he says, because he believed the battle against military dictatorship had to be fought.[2]

Timerman fought with words, with his newspaper *La Opinion,* in and against the silence imposed by the arbiters of discourse who beat out a new reality in the prison cells where the torturers and the tortured came together. "We victims and victimizers, we're part of the same humanity, colleagues in the same endeavor to prove the existence of ideologies, feelings, heroic deeds, religions, obsessions. And the rest of humanity, what are they engaged in?"[3]

The construction of colonial reality that occurred in the New World has been and will remain a topic of immense curiosity and study—the New World where the Indian and the African became subject to an initially far smaller number of Christians. Whatever conclusions we draw as to how that hegemony was so speedily effected, we would be most unwise to overlook or underestimate the role of terror. And by this I mean us to think through terror, which as well as being a physiological state is also a social fact and a cultural construction whose baroque dimensions allow it to serve as the mediator par excellence of colonial hegemony. The space of death is one of the crucial spaces where Indian, African, and white gave birth to the New World.

This space of death has a long and rich culture. It is where the social imagination has populated its metamorphosing images of evil and the underworld: in the Western tradition, Homer, Virgil, the Bible, Dante, Bosch, the Inquisition, Baudelaire, Rimbaud, *Heart of Darkness;* in Northwest Amazonian tradition, zones of visions, communication between terrestrial and supernatural beings, putrefaction, death, rebirth, and genesis, perhaps in the rivers and land of

---

2. Timerman, *Prisoner,* 28.
3. Ibid., 111.

maternal milk bathed eternally in subtle green light of coca leaves.[4] With European conquest and colonization, these spaces of death blend as a common pool of key signifiers or caption points binding the culture of the conqueror with that of the conquered. The space of death is preeminently a space of transformation: through the experience of death, life; through fear, loss of self and conformity to a new reality; or through evil, good. Lost in the dark woods, then journeying through the underworld with his guide, Dante achieves paradise only after he has mounted Satan's back. Timerman can be a guide for us, analogous to the ways Putumayo shamans I know are guides to those lost in the space of death.

An old Ingano Indian from the Putumayo once told me of this space:

> With the fever I was aware of everything. But after eight days I became unconscious. I knew not where I was. Like a madman I wandered, consumed by fever. They had to cover me up where I fell, mouth down. Thus after eight days I was aware of nothing. I was unconscious. Of what people were saying, I remembered nothing. Of the pain of the fever, I remembered nothing; only the space of death—walking in the space of death. Thus, after the noises that spoke, I remained unconscious. Now the world remained behind. Now the world was removed. Well, then I understood. Now the pains were speaking. I knew that I would live no longer. Now I was dead. My sight had gone. Of the world I knew nothing, nor the sound of my ears. Of speech, nothing. Silence. And one knows the space of death, there. . . . And this is death—the space that I saw. I was in its center, standing. Then I went to the heights. From the heights a star-point seemed my due. I was standing. Then I came down. There I was searching for the five continents of the world, to remain, to find me a place in the five continents of the world—in the space in which I was wandering. But I was not able.

We might ask, What place in the five continents of the world will the wanderer in the space of death find himself? And by extension, Where will a whole society find itself? The old man fears the evil of sorcery, the struggle for his soul. Between himself, the sorcerer, and the curing shaman, the five continents are sought and fought for. Yet here there is laughter too, puncturing the fear of the mystery, re-

---

4. Gerardo Reichel-Dolmatoff, *Amazonian Cosmos: The Sexual and Religious Symbolism of the Tukano Indians* (Chicago: University of Chicago Press, 1971).

minding us of Walter Benjamin's comment on the way in which Romanticism may perniciously misunderstand the nature of intoxication. "Any serious exploration of occult, surrealistic, phantasmagoric gifts and phenomena," he writes,

> presupposes a dialectical intertwinement to which a romantic turn of mind is impervious. For histrionic or fanatical stress on the mysterious side of the mysterious takes us no further; we penetrate the mystery only to the degree that we recognize it in the everyday world, by virtue of a dialectical optic that perceives the everyday as impenetrable, the impenetrable as everyday.[5]

From Timerman's chronicle and texts like Miguel Angel Asturias's *El señor presidente* it is abundantly clear that cultures of terror are based on and nourished by silence and myth in which the fanatical stress on the mysterious side of the mysterious flourishes by means of rumor and fantasy woven in a dense web of magical realism. It is also clear that the victimizer needs the victim for the purpose of making truth, objectifying the victimizer's fantasies in the discourse of the other. To be sure, the torturer's desire is also prosaic: to acquire information, to act in concert with large-scale economic strategies elaborated by the masters and exigencies of production. Yet equally if not more important is the need to control massive populations through the cultural elaboration of fear.

That is why silence is imposed, why Timerman, the publisher, was so important, why he knew when to be silent and close off reality in the torture chamber. "Such silence," he tells us,

> begins in the channels of communication. Certain political leaders, institutions, and priests attempt to denounce what is happening, but are unable to establish contact with the population. The silence begins with a strong odor. People sniff the suicides, but it eludes them. Then silence finds another ally: solitude. People fear suicides as they fear madmen. And the person who wants to fight senses his solitude and is frightened.[6]

Hence, there is the need for us to fight that solitude, fear, and silence, to examine these conditions of truth-making and culture-

---

5. Walter Benjamin, "Surrealism: The Last Snapshot of the European Intelligentsia," in the collection of his essays entitled *Reflections,* trans. Edmund Jephcott (New York and London: Harcourt Brace Jovanovich, 1978), 189–90.

6. Timerman, *Prisoner,* 52.

making, to follow Michel Foucault in "seeing historically how effects of truth are produced within discourses which are in themselves neither true nor false."[7] At the same time we not only have to see, we also have to see anew through the creation of counterdiscourses.

If effects of truth are power, then the question is raised not only concerning the power to speak and write, but as to what form shall that counterdiscourse take. This issue of form has lately been of much concern to those involved in writing histories and ethnographies. But faced with the endemicity of torture, terror, and the growth of armies, we in the New World are today assailed with a new urgency. There is the effort to understand terror, in order to make *others* understand. Yet the reality at stake here makes a mockery of understanding and derides rationality, as when the young boy Jacobo Timerman asks his mother, "Why do they hate us?" And she replies, "Because they do not understand." And after his ordeal, the old Timerman writes of the need for a hated object and the simultaneous fear of that object—the almost magical inevitability of hatred. "No," he concludes, "there can be no doubt my mother was the one who was mistaken. It is not the anti-Semites who must be made to understand. It is we Jews."[8]

Hated and feared, objects to be despised, yet also of awe, the reified essence of evil in the very being of their bodies, these figures of the Jew, the black, the Indian, and woman herself, are clearly objects of cultural construction, the leaden keel of evil and of mystery stabilizing the ship and course that is Western history. With the cold war we add the communist. With the time bomb ticking inside the nuclear family, we add the feminists and the gays. The military and the New Right, like the conquerors of old, discover the evil they have imputed to these aliens, and mimic the savagery they have imputed.

What sort of understanding—what sort of speech, writing, and construction of meaning by any mode—can deal with and subvert that?

On one thing Timerman is clear. To counterpose the eroticization and romanticization of violence by the same means or by forms

7. Michel Foucault, "Truth and Power," in *Power/Knowledge,* Colin Gordon, ed. (New York: Pantheon, 1980), 118.
8. Timerman, *Prisoner,* 62, 66.

equally mystical is a dead end. Yet to offer one or all of the standard rational explanations of the culture of terror is similarly pointless. For behind the search for profits, the need to control labor, the need to assuage frustration, and so on, lie intricately construed long-standing cultural logics of meaning—structures of feeling—whose basis lies in a symbolic world and not in one of rationalism. Ultimately there are two features: the crudest of empirical facts such as the electrodes and the mutilated human body, and the experience of going through torture. In his text Timerman does create a powerful counterdiscourse, precisely because, like torture itself, it moves us through that space of death where reality is up for grabs, to confront the hallucination of the military. His text of madness and evil establishes a revolutionary and, to my mind, sound poetics because it finds its counterweight and sanity in what I take to be the most difficult of political positions marked out by a contradictory space between socialism and anarchism. He is to Victor Serge as V. S. Naipaul is to Arthur Koestler and Joseph Conrad.

Conrad's way of dealing with the terror of the rubber boom in the Congo was *Heart of Darkness*. There were three realities there, comments Frederick Karl: King Leopold's, made out of intricate disguises and deceptions; Roger Casement's studied realism; and Conrad's, which, to quote Karl, "fell midway between the other two, as he attempted to penetrate the veil and yet was anxious to retain its hallucinatory quality."[9]

This formulation is sharp and important: *to penetrate the veil while retaining its hallucinatory quality.* It evokes Paul Ricoeur's two hermeneutics in his major discussion of Freud: that of suspicion (or reduction) and that of revelation.[10] As to the political effect of *Heart of Darkness,* while Ian Watt regards it as the enduring and most powerful literary indictment of imperialism,[11] I am not so sure that its strikingly literary quality and hallucinatory filmness do not finally blind and stun the reader into a trance, drowning in a sea-storm of imag-

9. Frederick R. Karl, *Joseph Conrad: The Three Lives* (New York: Farrar, Straus and Giroux, 1979), 286.

10. Paul Ricoeur, *Freud and Philosophy: An Essay on Interpretation* (New Haven: Yale University Press, 1970).

11. Ian Watt, *Conrad: In the Nineteenth Century* (Berkeley and Los Angeles: University of California Press, 1979), 161.

ery. The danger here lies with aestheticizing horror, and while Conrad manages to stop short of doing that, we must realize that just to the side lurks the seductive poetics of fascism and the imaginative source of terror and torture embedded deep within us all. The political and artistic problem is to engage with that, to maintain that hallucinatory quality, while effectively turning it against itself. That would be the true catharsis, the great counterdiscourse whose poetics we must ponder in the political terrain now urgently exposed today; the form wherein all that appeals and seduces in the iconography and sensuality of the underworld becomes its own force for self-subversion. Foucault's concept of discourse eludes this aspiration and concept of dialectically engaged subversion. But it is with this poetics that we must develop the cultural politics appropriate to our times.

Casement offers a useful and startling contrast to Conrad, all the more vivid because of the ways their paths crossed in the Congo in 1890, because of the features common to their political backgrounds as exiles or quasi-exiles from imperialized European societies, Poland and Ireland, and because of an indefinable if only superficial similarity in their temperaments and love of literature. Yet it was Casement who resorted to militant action on behalf of his native land, organizing gun running from Germany to the rebels at Dublin for Easter Sunday 1916, and was hung for treason, while Conrad resolutely stuck to his task as an artist, bathed in nostalgia and guilt for Poland, lending his name but otherwise refusing to assist Casement in the Congo Reform Society, claiming he was but a "wretched novelist." The key text for our purposes is Conrad's letter to his beloved friend and socialist, the aristocrat don Roberto, otherwise known as R. B. Cunninghame Graham (whom Jorge Borges regards together with that other great English romantic, W. H. Hudson, as providing the most accurate sketches and literary works of nineteenth-century pampa society). In this letter, dated 26 December 1903, Conrad salutes don Roberto on the excellence of his book on the great Spanish conquistador, Hernando de Soto, and especially for the sympathetic insight into the souls of the *conquistadores*—the glamour, the pathos, and romance of those times—which functions as an anodyne inducing one to forget the modern *conquistadores* such as Leopold and the lack of romance and vision in nineteenth- and early twentieth-century bourgeois imperialism. Conrad then goes on to inform don Roberto about "a man called Casement" and his plans for a Congo reform society to stop the terror associated with the rubber industry there, the same terror which inspired Conrad's novella. Conrad likens Casement to a *conquistador,* and indulges in a hopelessly romanticized image of him—curtly corrected by Brian Inglis, one of Casement's biographers, seventy years later.[12] What is so galling and instructive about this sort of indulgence, which stems from and informs Conrad's theory of poetics as formulated in the introduction to *The Nigger of the Narcissus,* is that at the time of Casement's trial for treason and villification as a homosexual in 1916, Conrad displayed a permutation of the romanticism which had led him almost to deify the Casement he first met in the Congo in 1890. Writing to John Quinn, Conrad re-images his first acquaintance with Casement, now pigeonholing him not as in the *Congo Diary* as a man who "thinks, speaks well, [is] most intelligent and very sympathetic," but as a labor recruiter. He goes on to disparage Casement as a romantic opportunist and adds:

> He was a good companion, but already in Africa I judged that he was a man, properly speaking, of no mind at all. I don't mean stupid. I mean he was all emotion. By emotional force (Congo report, Putumayo—etc) he made his way, and sheer emotionalism has undone him. A creature of sheer temperament—a truly tragic personality: all but the greatness of which he had not a trace. Only vanity. But in the Congo it was not visible yet.[13]

12. Brian Inglis, *Roger Casement* (London: Hodder Paperbacks, 1974), 32. The text of Conrad's letter to Cunninghame Graham reads: "I can assure you that he [Casement] is a limpid personality. There is a touch of the conquistador in him too; for I've seen him start off into an unspeakable wilderness swinging a crook-handled stick for all weapons, with two bulldogs, Paddy (white) and Biddy (brindle) at his heels, and a Loanda boy carrying a bundle for all company. A few months afterwards it so happened that I saw him come out again, a little leaner, a little browner, with his stick, dogs and Loanda boy, and quietly serene as though he had been for a stroll in a park." Inglis comments: "Time had embroidered Conrad's recollection. Casement himself described what the construction work entailed, in a letter to his young cousin [and] the countryside through which the railway was being constructed, he told her, consisted of grassy plains covered with scrub—inhospitable, but hardly unspeakable." The Jorge Borges reference is "About the Purple Land" in *Borges: A Reader,* Emir Rodriguez Monegal and A. Reid, eds. (New York: Dutton, 1981), 136–39.

13. Karl, *Joseph Conrad,* 289n. The full text of Conrad's letter to Cunninghame Graham may be found in C. T. Watts, *Joseph Conrad's Letters to R. B. Cunninghame*

Yet it remains a fact that Casement's reports on the Congo and the Putumayo did much to stop the pervasive brutality there and, in Edmund Morel's opinion, "innoculated the diplomacy of this country [Britain] with a moral toxin" such that "historians will cherish these occasions as the only two in which British diplomacy rose above the commonplace."[14]

In addition to the coincidences of imperialist history, what brings Casement and Conrad together is the problem they jointly create concerning the rhetorical power and political effect of social realism and mythic realism. Between the emotional consul-general who wrote effectively on the side of the colonized as a realist and a rationalist, and the great artist who did not, lie many of the crucial problems concerning the domination of culture and cultures of domination.

THE PUTUMAYO REPORT

At this point it is instructive to analyze briefly Casement's Putumayo report, which was submitted to Sir Edward Grey, head of the British Foreign Service, and published by the House of Commons on 13 July 1913 when Casement was forty-nine years old.

At the outset it should be noted that Casement's attachment to the cause of Irish home rule and his anger at British imperialism made his almost life-long work as a British consul extremely fraught with contradiction; in addition, he felt his experiences in Africa and South America increased his understanding of the effects of the colonialism in Ireland, which in turn stimulated his ethnographic and political sensibilities regarding conditions south of the equator. He claimed, for example, that it was his knowledge of Irish history which allowed him to understand the Congo atrocities, whereas the Foreign Office could not because the empirical evidence made no sense to them. In a letter to his close friend Alice Green he noted:

> I knew the Foreign Office would not understand the thing, for I realized that I was looking at this tragedy with the eyes of another race of people

---

Graham (Cambridge: The University Press, 1969), 148–52. Also see *Joseph Conrad: Congo Diary and Other Uncollected Pieces*, Zdzislaw Najder, ed. (Garden City, N.Y.: Doubleday, 1978), 7.

14. Inglis, *Roger Casement*, 46.

once hunted themselves, whose hearts were based on affection as the root principle of contact with their fellow men, and whose estimate of life was not something eternally to be appraised at its market price.[15]

In the article he wrote for the respected *Contemporary Review* in 1912, he argued that the Putumayo Indians were more highly developed, morally speaking, than their white oppressors. The Indian lacked a competitive streak; he was "a socialist by temperament, habit, and possibly, age-long memory of Inca and pre-Inca precept." In conclusion, Casement asked, "Is it too late to hope that by means of the same humane and brotherly agency, something of the good-will and kindness of Christian life may be imparted to the remote, friendless, and lost children of the forest?"[16] He later referred to the peasants of Connemara in Ireland as "white Indians."[17]

The essence of his 136-page Putumayo report, based on seven weeks of travel in 1910 through the rubber-gathering areas of the jungles of the Caraparaná and Igaraparaná affluents of the middle reaches of the Putumayo river, and on some six months in the Amazon basin, lay in its detail of the terror and tortures together with Casement's explanation of causes and his estimate of the toll in human life. Putumayo rubber would be unprofitable were it not for the forced labor of local Indians, principally those called Huitotos. For the twelve years from 1900, the Putumayo output of some 4,000 tons of rubber cost thousands of Indians their lives. Deaths from torture, disease, and possibly flight had decreased the population of the area by around 30,000 during that time.[18]

15. Ibid., 131.
16. Ibid., 214.
17. Ibid., 234.
18. Some authorities glean Casement's report and state the figure of 30,000 deaths from 1900 to 1912 as a fact, while others, who had some knowledge of the area and its history, either present different figures (a wide range) or state that it is impossible to give any figure because census-taking was impossibly difficult. Furthermore, how much of the population decrease was due to disease (especially smallpox), and how much to torture or flight, is a very vexed question. Similarly, the number of Huitotos living in the Igaraparaná and Caraparaná region in the late nineteenth century is variously stated as around 50,000 all the way up to a quarter of a million(!), the latter estimate being that of Joaquin Rocha, *Memorandum de un viaje* (Bogotá: Editorial El Mercurio, 1905), 138. In any event, the number of Indians in the area seems to have been extremely large by Upper Amazon standards and an important cause for the es-

The British government felt obliged to send Casement as its consular representative to the Putumayo because of the public outcry aroused in 1909 by a series of articles in the London magazine, *Truth;* the series depicted the brutality of the rubber company, which since 1907 had been a consortium of Peruvian and British interests in the region. Entitled "The Devil's Paradise: A British Owned Congo," these articles were the work of a young "engineer" and adventurer from the United States named Walter Hardenburg, who had with a companion entered the remote corner of the Amazon basin from the Colombian Andes in 1907 and had been taken prisoner by the Peruvian Rubber Company founded by Julio César Arana in 1903. Hardenburg's chronicle is to an important extent an elaboration on a text basic to the Putumayo saga, an article published in the Iquitos newspaper *La Sanción* shortly before its publication was suspended by the Peruvian government and Arana.

Asserting that the rubber trees are in rapid decline and will be exhausted in four years' time because of the rapacity of the production system, the article continues by declaring that the peaceful Indians work night and day collecting rubber without the slightest remuneration. They are given nothing to eat or wear. Their crops, together with the women and children, are taken for the pleasure of the whites. They are inhumanly flogged until their bones are visible. Given no medical treatment, they are left to die after torture, eaten by the company's dogs. They are castrated, and their ears, fingers, arms, and legs are cut off. They are also tortured by means of fire, water, and crucifixion tied head-down. The whites cut them to pieces with machetes and dash out the brains of small children by hurling them against trees and walls. The elderly are killed when they can no longer work. To amuse themselves, company officials practice shooting, using Indians as targets, and on special occasions such as Easter

---

tablishment of rubber trading there. It is worth noting that Casement in his report was extremely cautious in presenting figures on population and population decrease. He gives details of the problem in his evidence presented to the British Parliamentary Select Committee on Putumayo (*House of Commons Sessional Papers,* 1913, vol. 14, 30, #707). Father Gaspar de Pinell, *Un viaje por el Putumayo el Amazonas* (Bogotá: Imprenta Nacional, 1924), 38–39, presents an excellent discussion, as does his *Excursión apostólica por los ríos Putumayo, San Miguel de Sucumbios, Cuyabueno, Carquetá, y Caguán* (Bogotá: Imprenta Nacional, 1929 [also dated 1928]), 227–35.

Saturday—Saturday of Glory—shoot them down in groups or, in preference, douse them in kerosene and set them on fire to enjoy their agony.[19]

In a letter written to Hardenburg by an employee of the company we read how a "commission" was sent out by a rubber-station manager to exterminate a group of Indians for not bringing in sufficient rubber. The commission returned in four days with fingers, ears, and several heads of Indians to prove the orders had been carried out.[20] On another occasion, the manager called in hundreds of Indians to assemble at the station:

> He grasped his carbine and machete and began the slaughter of these defenseless Indians, leaving the ground covered with over 150 corpses, among them men, women, and children. Bathed in blood and appealing for mercy, the survivors were heaped with the dead and burned to death, while the manager shouted, "I want to exterminate all the Indians who do not obey my orders about the rubber that I require them to bring in."

"When they get drunk," adds the correspondent, "the upper-level employees of the company toast with champagne the man who can boast of the greatest number of murders."[21]

The drama perhaps most central to the Putumayo terror, quoted from an Iquitos newspaper article in 1908, and affirmed as fact by both Casement and Hardenburg, concerns the weighing-in of rubber brought by the Indians from the forest:

> The Indian is so humble that as soon as he sees that the needle of the scale does not mark the ten kilos, he himself stretches out his hands and throws himself on the ground to receive the punishment. Then the chief [of the rubber station] or a subordinate advances, bends down, takes the Indian by the hair, strikes him, raises his head, drops it face downwards on the ground, and after the face is beaten and kicked and covered with blood, the Indian is scourged. This is when they are treated best, for often they cut them to pieces with machetes.[22]

---

19. Walter Hardenburg, *The Putumayo: The Devil's Paradise. Travels in the Peruvian Amazon Region and an Account of the Atrocities Committed upon the Indians Therein* (London: T. Fisher Unwin, 1912), 214. The first publication of Hardenburg's revelations, in the magazine *Truth* in 1909, began with this article from the Iquitos newspaper, *La Sanción*. These articles, and probably the later book, were possibly ghostwritten by Sidney Paternoster, assistant editor of *Truth*.

20. Hardenburg, *Putumayo*, 258.

21. Ibid., 260, 259.

22. Ibid., 236. Also cited by Casement in his Putumayo report to Sir Edward Grey. There Casement declares that his description was repeated to him "again and

In the rubber station of Matanzas, continues the writer, "I have seen Indians tied to a tree, their feet about half a yard above the ground. Fuel is then placed below, and they are burnt alive. This is done to pass the time."

Casement's report to the House of Commons is staid and sober, somewhat like a lawyer arguing a case and in marked contrast to his diary covering the same experience. He piles fact on brutal fact, suggests an over-all analysis, and makes his recommendations. His material comes from three sources: what he personally witnessed; testimony of 30 Barbados blacks who, with 166 others, were contracted by the company during 1903–1904 to serve as overseers, and whose statements occupy 85 published foolscap pages; and, interspersed with Casement's direct observations, numerous stories from local residents and company employees.

Early on in the report, in a vivid throwaway line, he evokes the banality of the cruelty. "The employees at all the stations passed the time when not hunting Indians, either lying in their hammocks or in gambling."[23] The unreal atmosphere of ordinariness, of the ordinariness of the extraordinary, can be startling. "At some of the stations the principal flogger was the station cook—two such men were directly named to me, and I ate the food they prepared, while many of their victims carried my baggage from station to station, and showed often terrible scars on their limbs inflicted at the hands of these men."[24]

From the evidence of scarring, Casement found that the "great majority" (perhaps up to 90 percent) of the more than 1,600 Indians he saw had been badly beaten.[25] Some of the worst affected were small boys, and deaths due to flogging were frequent, either under the lash, or more frequently, a few days later when the wounds be-

---

again . . . by men who had been employed in this work." Roger Casement, "Correspondence respecting the Treatment of British Colonial Subjects and Native Indians employed in the Collection of Rubber in the Putumayo District," *House of Commons Sessional Papers,* 14 February 1912 to 7 March 1913, vol. 68 (hereafter cited as Casement, *Putumayo Report*), 35.

23. Casement, *Putumayo Report,* 17.

24. Ibid., 34.

25. Ibid., 33, 34.

came maggot-infested.[26] Floggings occurred when an Indian brought in insufficient rubber and were most sadistic for those who dared to flee. Flogging was mixed with other tortures such as near drowning, "designed," as Casement points out, "to just stop short of taking life while inspiring the acute mental fear and inflicting much of the physical agony of death."[27] Casement was informed by a man who had himself often flogged Indians that he had seen mothers flogged because their little sons had not brought in enough rubber. While the boy stood terrified and crying at the sight, his mother would be beaten "just a few strokes" to make him a better worker.[28]

Deliberate starvation was resorted to repeatedly, sometimes to frighten, more often to kill. Men and women were kept in the stocks until they died of hunger. One Barbadian related how he had seen Indians in this situation "scraping up the dirt with their fingers and eating it." Another declared he had seen them eating the maggots in their wounds.[29]

The stocks were sometimes placed on the upper verandah or residential part of the main dwelling house of the rubber stations, in direct view of the manager and his employees. Children, men, and women might be confined in them for months, and some of the Barbados men said they had seen women raped while in the stocks.[30]

Much of the surveillance and punishment was carried out by the corps of Indian guards known as the *muchachos*. Members of this armed corps had been trained by the company from an early age, and were used to control *salvajes* other than those to whom they were kin. Casement thought them to be generally every bit as evil as their white masters.[31] When Barbados men were present, they were fre-

---

26. Ibid., 37.
27. Ibid., 39.
28. Ibid., 37.
29. Ibid., 39.
30. Ibid., 42.

31. Ibid., 31. From various estimates it appears that the ratio of armed supervisors to wild Indians gathering rubber was somewhere between 1:16 and 1:50. Of these armed supervisors, the *muchachos* outnumbered the whites by around 2:1. See Howard Wolf and Ralph Wolf, *Rubber: A Story of Glory and Greed* (New York: Covici, Friede, 1936), 88; U.S. Consul Charles C. Eberhardt, *Slavery in Peru*, 7 February 1913, report prepared for U.S. House of Representatives, 62d Cong., 3d Sess., 1912, H. Doc. 1366, p. 112; Roger Casement, British Parliamentary Select Committee on Putumayo, *House of Commons Sessional Papers*, 1913, vol. 14, xi; Casement, *Putumayo Report*, 33.

quently assigned the task of flogging, but, Casement emphasizes, "no monopoly of flogging was enjoyed by any employee as a right. The chief of the section frequently himself took the lash, which, in turn, might be wielded by every member of the civilized or 'rational staff.'"[32]

"Such men," reports Casement, "had lost all sight or sense of rubber-gathering—they were simply beasts of prey who lived upon the Indians and delighted in shedding their blood." Moreover, the station managers from the areas where Casement got his most precise information were in debt (despite their handsome rates of commission), running their operations at a loss to the company which in some sections ran to many thousands of pounds sterling.[33]

It is necessary at this point to note that although the Indians received the brunt of the terror, whites and blacks were also targets. Whether as competitors for Indian rubber gatherers, like the independent Colombian rubber traders who first conquered the Putumayo and were then dislodged by Arana's company in 1908, or as employees of the company, extremely few escaped the ever-present threat of degradation and torture. Asked by Casement if he did not know it to be wrong to torture Indians, one of the Barbados men replied that he was unable to refuse orders, "that a man might be a man down in Iquitos, but 'you couldn't be a man up there.'"[34] In addition, most of the company's white and black employees were themselves trapped in a debt-peonage system, but one quite different from the one the company used in controlling its Indians.

From the testimony of the Barbados men it is clear that dissension, hatred, and mistrust ran riot among all members of the company—to the degree that one has to consider seriously the hypothesis that only in their group ritualization of torturing Indians could such anomie and mistrust be held in check, thus guaranteeing to the company the solidarity required to sustain it as an effective social unit.

To read Casement's secondhand and Hardenburg's eyewitness accounts of the company attacks against independent white Colom-

---

32. Casement, *Putumayo Report*, 33.
33. Ibid., 44–45.
34. Ibid., 55.

bian traders is to become further aware of the ritualistic features which assured the violence of the Putumayo rubber boom of its success as a culture of terror.

CASEMENT'S ANALYSIS

Casement's main line of analysis lies with his argument that it was not rubber but labor that was scarce in the Putumayo, and that this scarcity was the basic cause of the use of terror. Putumayo rubber was of the lowest quality, the remoteness of its source made its transport expensive relative to rubber from other zones, and wages for free labor were very high. Hence, he reasons, the company resorted to the use of forced labor under a debt-peonage system, and used torture to maintain labor discipline.

The problem with this argument, which assumes the purported rationality of business and the capital-logic of commodities (such as labor), is that it encounters certain contradictions and, while not exactly wrong, strikes me as giving insufficient weight to two fundamental considerations. The first consideration concerns the forms of labor and economic organization that local history and Indian society made available, or potentially available, to world capitalism in the jungles of the Putumayo. The second, put crudely, is that terror and torture do not derive only from market pressure (which we can regard here as a trigger) but also from the process of cultural construction of evil as well. "Market pressure" assumes the paradigm of scarcity essential to capitalist economism and capitalist socioeconomic theory. Leaving aside the question of how accurate a depiction of capitalist society results from this paradigm, it is highly dubious that it reveals much of the reality of the Putumayo rubber boom where the problem facing capitalist enterprise was precisely that there were no capitalist social institutions and no market for abstract labor into which capital could be fed and multiplied. Indeed, one could go further to develop an argument that begins with the premise that it was just this lack of commoditized social relationships, in interaction with commodity forces emanating from the world rubber market, that accounts for the production of torture and terror. We can say that the culture of terror was functional to the needs of the labor system, but that tells us little about the most significant contradictions to emerge from Casement's report, namely, that the slaughter of this precious labor was on a scale vast beyond belief, and that, as Casement himself states, not only were the station managers costing the company large sums of money but that "such men had lost all sight or sense of rubber-gathering—they were simply beasts of prey who lived upon the Indians and delighted in shedding their blood." To claim the rationality of business for this is to claim and sustain an illusory rationality, obscuring our understanding of the way business can transform the use of terror from the means to an end in itself.

The consideration of local history and economic organization requires far fuller treatment than can be attempted here. But it should be noted in passing that "scarcity" of labor cannot refer to a scarcity of Indians, of whom there seems to have been an abundance, but rather to the fact that the Indians would not work in the regular and dependable manner necessary to a large-scale capitalist enterprise. Casement downplayed this phenomenon, now often referred to as "the backward sloping supply curve of labor," and did so even though in the Congo he had himself complained that the problem was that the natives would not work;[35] he felt sure that if paid with more goods, the Indians would work to the level required by the company without force. Many people with far longer experience in the Putumayo denied this naïve assertion and pointed out, with logic as impeccable as Casement's, that the scarcity of labor and the ease with which the Indians could live off the forest obliged employers elsewhere in the Putumayo to treat them with consideration.[36] In ei-

35. Inglis, *Roger Casement,* 29.
36. Rocha, *Memorandum de un viaje,* 123–24, asserts that because the Indians are "naturally loafers" they postpone paying off their advances from the rubber traders, thus compelling the traders to use physical violence. Eberhardt, *Slavery in Peru,* 110, writes that "the Indian enters the employ of some rubber gatherer, often willingly, though not infrequently by force, and immediately becomes indebted to him for food etc. . . . However, the scarcity of labor and the ease with which the Indians can usually escape and live on the natural products of the forest oblige the owners to treat them with some consideration. The Indians realize this and their work is not at all satisfactory, judging from our standards. This was particularly noticeable during a recent visit I made to a mill where 'cachassa' or aguardiente is extracted from cane. The men seemed to work when and how they chose, requiring a liberal amount of the liquor each day (of which they are all particularly fond), and if this is not forthcoming or they are treated harshly in any way they run to the forests. The employer has the

ther case, however, with or without the use of coercion, the labor productivity obtained fell far short of what employers desired.

The contradictions mount further on close examination of the debt-peonage system, which Casement regards as slavery. It was a pretext, he says, that the Indian in such a relation was in debt, for the Indian was bound by physical force to work for the company and could not escape.[37] One then must ask why the company persisted in this pretense, especially given the means of coercion at its disposal.

Accounts of advances paid in goods (such as machetes, cloth, shotguns) were supposedly kept for each rubber gatherer; the advances were roughly equal to fivepence per pound weight of rubber, which was fetching three shillings tenpence on the London market in 1910. (In West Africa, natives were paid an equivalent of between two shillings and two shillings sixpence per pound of "Ibi Red niggers" rubber, equal in quality to the Putumayan.)[38] A station manager told Casement that the Indians never asked the price or value of rubber. Sometimes a single coin was given, and Casement met numbers of Indian women wearing necklaces made of coins.[39] Joaquin Rocha writes that the Indians of the Tres Esquinas rubber station valued money not as a means of exchange but as a precious object; they would beat coins into smooth and shining triangular shapes to use as nose rings or ear pendants.[40] Yet, it would be naïve to suppose that the Indians lacked interest or understanding of the terms of trade and of what the whites got for rubber in the outside world. "You buy these with the rubber we produce," said an Indian chief as one entranced, looking through Casement's binoculars.[41] Casement

---

law on his side, and if he can find the runaway he is at liberty to bring him back; but the time lost and the almost useless task of trying to track the Indian through the dense forests and small streams makes it far more practical that the servant be treated with consideration in the first place."

37. Casement, British Parliamentary Select Committee on Putumayo, *House of Commons Sessional Papers,* 1913, vol. 14, p. 113, #2809.

38. E. D. Morel, British Parliamentary Select Committee on Putumayo, *House of Commons Sessional Papers,* 1913, vol. 14, pp. 553, 556. Also see the evidence of the British accountant, H. Parr, of the Peruvian Amazon Company, in 1909–10, at the La Chorrera station (pp. 336–48).

39. Casement, *Putumayo Report,* 50.

40. Rocha, *Memorandum de un viaje,* 75.

41. Peter Singleton-Gates and Maurice Girodias, *The Black Diaries* (New York: Grove Press, 1959), 261.

was told that the station managers would fix the quantity of rubber due from each individual according to the goods that had been advanced, and in this connection Father Gridilla relates an episode of interest from when he travelled up the Caraparaná in 1912.

It was at a time when thousands of Indians came to the rubber station of La Occidente to deliver rubber. First there was a great dance lasting five days—the sort of event Joaquin Rocha a decade earlier likened to a harvest festival. Then the rubber was handed over and goods were advanced, Father Gridilla commenting "the savages don't know money, their needs are very limited, and they ask only for shotguns, ammunition, axes, machetes, mirrors, and occasionally hammocks." An Indian he described as a corpulent and ugly savage declined to accept anything and, on being pressed, replied, "I don't want anything. I've got everything." The whites insisted again and again that he must ask for something. Finally he retorted, "I want a black dog!" "And where am I going to find a black dog or even a white one if there aren't any in all of Putumayo?" responded the station manager. "You ask me for rubber," replied the savage, "and I bring you rubber. If I ask for a black dog, you have to give me one!"[42]

Relying on stories told him, Hardenburg wrote that the Indians received their advances with great pleasure, because if they did not, they were flogged to death.[43]

Pretext as it was, the debt which ensured peonage was nonetheless real, and as a pretense its magical realism was as essential to the labor organization of the Putumayo rubber boom as is the "commodity fiction" Karl Polanyi describes for a mature capitalist economy.[44] To analyze the construction of these fictional realities we need now to turn to some of their more obviously mythic features, enclosed as they are in the synergistic relation of savagery and business, cannibalism and capitalism. Interrogated by the British Parliamentary Select Committee on Putumayo in 1913, Julio César Arana,

42. P. Alberto Gridilla, *Un año en el Putumayo* (Lima: Colección Descalzos, 1943), 29. Rocha's description is of a Colombian rubber trading post, and not one of Arana's; Rocha, *Memorandum de un viaje*, 119–20.

43. Hardenburg, *Putumayo*, 218.

44. Karl Polanyi, *The Great Transformation* (Boston: Beacon Press, 1957), 72. Cf. Michael Taussig, *The Devil and Commodity Fetishism in South America* (Chapel Hill: University of North Carolina Press, 1980).

the driving force of the rubber company, was asked to clarify what he meant when he stated that the Indians had resisted the establishment of civilization in their districts, that they had been resisting for many years, and had practiced cannibalism. "What I mean by that," he replied, "is that they did not admit of exchange, or anybody to do business with them—Whites, for example."[45]

JUNGLE AND SAVAGERY

There is a problem that I have only hinted at in all of the accounts of the atrocities of the Putumayo rubber boom. While the immensity of the cruelty is beyond question, most of the evidence comes through stories. The meticulous historian would seize upon this fact as a challenge to winnow out truth from exaggeration or understatement. But the more basic implication, it seems to me, is that the narratives are *in themselves evidence* of the process whereby a culture of terror was created and sustained.

Two interlacing motifs stand out: the horrors of the jungle, and the horrors of savagery. All the facts are bent through the prism formed by these motifs, which, in keeping with Conrad's theory of art, mediate effective truth not so much through the dissemination of information as through the appeal of temperaments through sensory impressions. Here the European and colonist image of the primeval jungle with its vines and rubber trees and domination of man's domination stands forth as the colonially apt metaphor of the great space of terror and deep cruelties (late-nineteenth-century Europeans penetrating the ancient forests of the tropics). Carlos Fuentes asserts that Latin American literature is woven between the poles formed by nature and the dictator, in which the destructiveness of the former serves to reflect even more destructive social relations. A Colombian author, José Eustacio Rivera writes in the 1920s as a debt-entrapped peon in the Putumayo:

> I have been a *cauchero* [rubber gatherer] and I will always be a *cauchero*. I live in the slimy mire in the solitude of the forests with my gang of ma-

45. Julio César Arana, Evidence to the British Parliamentary Select Committee on Putumayo, *House of Commons Sessional Papers*, 1913, vol. 14, p. 488, #12,222.

larial men, piercing the bark of trees whose blood runs white, like that of gods. . . . I have been and always will be a *cauchero*. And what my hand inflicts on the trees, it can also inflict on men.[46]

In *Heart of Darkness,* the narrator Marlow sits back, like a Buddha, introducing his yarn, prefiguring the late-nineteenth-century colonial exploitation of the Congo by evoking a soldier of imperial Rome moving through the marshes of the Thames:

> Land in a swamp, march through the woods, and in some inland post feel the savagery, the utter savagery had closed around him,—all that mysterious life of the wilderness that stirs in the forest, in the jungles, in the hearts of wild men. There's no initiation either into such mysteries. He has to live in the midst of the incomprehensible, which is also detestable. And it has a fascination, too, that goes to work upon him. The fascination of the abomination—you know, imagine the growing regrets, the longing to escape, the powerless disgust, the surrender, the hate.

The Capuchin father, Gaspar de Pinell, who made a legendary *excursión apostólica* to the Huitotos and other savage tribes in the Putumayo forests in the late 1920s, records how his white guide, a man of much experience, sickened and sought cure from a Huitoto shaman (whom the padre calls a witch) rather than from the pharmacy of the whites. He died shortly thereafter, providing Father Pinell with the moral dilemma of the colonist: "This shows," he wrote, "that it is more likely that the civilized man will become a savage on mixing with Indians, than the Indians are likely to become civilized through the actions of the civilized."[47] And with a torrent of phenomenological virtuosity, his colleague, Father Francisco de Vilanova, addresses the same vexing problem, only here it is the Putumayo jungle which constitutes the great figure of savagery. In a book describing Capuchin endeavors among the Huitotos from the 1920s, we read:

> It is almost something unbelievable to those who do not know the jungle. It is an irrational fact that enslaves those who go there. It is a whirlwind of savage passions that dominates the civilized person who

46. See Carlos Fuentes, *La nueva novela hispanoamericana* (Mexico, D.F.: Editorial Joaquin Mortiz, 1969), 10–11. Jose Eustasio Rivera, *La vorágine* (Bogota: Editorial Pax, 1974), 277, 279.

47. Pinell, *Excursión apostólica,* 156.

has too much confidence in himself. It is a degeneration of the spirit in a drunkenness of improbable but real circumstances. The rational and civilized man loses respect for himself and his domestic place. He throws his heritage into the mire from where who knows when it will be retrieved. One's heart fills with morbidity and the sentiment of savagery. It becomes insensible to the most pure and great things of humanity. Even cultivated spirits, finely formed and well educated, have succumbed.[48]

But of course it is not the jungle but the sentiments men project into it that is decisive in filling their hearts with savagery. And what the jungle can accomplish, so much more can its native inhabitants, the wild Indians, like those tortured into gathering rubber. It must not be overlooked that the colonially constructed image of the wild Indian here at stake was a powerfully ambiguous image, a seesawing, bifocalized, and hazy composite of the animal and the human. In their human or humanlike form, the wild Indians could all the better reflect back to the colonists the vast and baroque projections of human wildness that the colonists needed to establish their reality as civilized (not to mention businesslike) people. And it was only because the wild Indians were human that they were able to serve as labor—and as subjects of torture. For it is not the victim as animal that gratifies the torturer, but the fact that the victim is human, thus enabling the torturer to become the savage.

HOW SAVAGE WERE THE HUITOTOS?

The savagery of the wild Indians occupied a key role in the propaganda of the rubber company. Hardenburg writes that the Huitotos "are hospitable to a marked degree," and that while the Church improves their morals, in the company's domain, priests have been carefully excluded. "Indeed," he continues, "in order to frighten people and thus prevent them from entering the region, the company has circulated the most blood curdling reports of the ferocity and cannibalism of these helpless Indians, whom travellers such as myself

48. P. Francisco de Vilanova, introduction to P. Francisco de Igualada, *Indios Amazonicas: Colección Misiones Capuchinas*, vol. VI (Barcelona: Imprenta Myria, 1948).

have found to be timid, peaceful, mild, industrious and humble."[49] Father Pinell has published a document from Peru describing a film commissioned by Arana's company in 1917. Shown in the cinemas of Lima, it portrayed the civilizing effect of the company on "these savage regions that as recently as 25 years ago were peopled entirely by cannibals. Owing to the energy of this tireless struggler [Arana] they have been converted into useful elements of labor."[50]

Propaganda usually flowers only where the soil has been long and well prepared, and it seems to me that Arana's was no exception since the mythology of savagery dates from times long before his. Yet, the passions unleashed by the rubber boom invigorated this mythology with a seductive power. Before probing further into the ways the rubber company acquired the savagery it imputed to the Indians, it is necessary to pause and examine the colonists' mythology and folklore concerning the Upper Amazon forest people.

Time and again Casement tells us that the Huitotos and all Upper Amazon Indians were gentle and docile. He downplays their cannibalism, says that they were thoughtless rather than cruel, and regards their docility as a *natural* and remarkable characteristic. This helps him to explain the ease with which they were conquered and forced to gather rubber.

> An Indian would promise anything for a gun, or for some of the other tempting things offered as inducements to him to work rubber. Many Indians submitted to the alluring offer only to find that once in the "conquistadores'" books they had lost all liberty, and were reduced to unending demands for more rubber and varied tasks. A cacique or "capitán" might be bought over to dispose of the labor of his clan, and as the cacique's influence was very great and the natural docility of the Indian a remarkable characteristic of Upper Amazon tribes, the work of conquering a primitive people and reducing them to a continual strain of rubber-finding was less difficult than might at first be supposed.[51]

Yet, on the other hand, such docility makes the violence of the whites even harder to understand.

49. Hardenburg, *Putumayo*, 163.
50. Pinell, *Excursión apostólica*, 196.
51. Casement, *Putumayo Report*, 27–28.

Many points can be contested in Casement's rendering here, such as his assertion of the degree of chiefly power and the deceptive simplicity he evokes with regard to the issue of toughness and tenderness in a society so foreign to his own. It should also not be forgotten that the story he wanted to tell was one of innocent and gentle childlike Indians brutalized by the rubber company, and this controlling image gives his report considerable rhetorical power. In addition there was his tendency to equate the sufferings of the Irish with those of the Indians and see in both of their preimperialist histories a culture more humane than that of their civilizing overlords. (Conrad never indulged in that kind of transference.) Still another factor blended with the foregoing, and that was the innate tenderness of Casement's character and his ability to draw that quality out of others, as testified by numerous people. It is this aspect of his homosexuality, and not sexual lust, which should be dwelt on here, as shown, for example, in this note in his Putumayo diary:

> . . . floggings and putting in guns and floggings with machetes across the back. . . . I bathed in the river, delightful, and Andokes [Indians] came down and caught butterflies for Barnes and I. Then a captain [Indian chief] embraced us laying his head down against our breasts. I never saw so touching a thing, poor soul, he felt we were their friends.[52]

Alfred Simson, an Englishman who travelled the Putumayo and Napo rivers in the 1880s and spent far more time there than Casement, conveys a picture quite different from Casement's. An example is his description of the Zaparos, who, like the Huitotos, were considered by the whites to be wild Indians. Noting that they raided other groups and abducted their children for sale to white traders, Simson goes on to state:

> When unprovoked they are, like really wild Indians, very shy and retiring, but are perfectly fearless, and will suffer no one, either whites or others, to employ force with them. They can only be managed by tact, good treatment, and sometimes simple reasoning: otherwise resenting ill-treatment or an attempt to resort to blows, [they react] with the worst of violence. . . . At all times they are changeable and unreliable, betray-

---

52. Singleton-Gates and Girodias, *Black Diaries,* 251.

ing under different circumstances, and often apparently under the same, in common with so many of their class, all the most opposite traits of character, excepting perhaps servility—a true characteristic of the old world—and stinginess, which I have never observed in them. The absence of servility is typical of all the independent Indians of Ecuador.[53]

And he observes that "they also gain great enjoyment from the destruction of life. They are always ready to kill animals or people, and they delight in it."[54]

Simson was employed on the first steam launch to ascend the Putumayo, that of Rafael Reyes, later a president of Colombia. Hence he witnessed the opening of the region to modern commerce, and was in a special position to observe the institutionalization of ideologies concerning race and class. Not only does he present a contrary and more complex estimate of Indian toughness than does Casement: he also provides the clue and ethnographic motif necessary to understand why such contrary images coexist and flourish, how Indian images of wildness come halfway, as it were, to meet and merge with white colonial images of savagery, and, finally, how such imagery functions in the creation of terror.

It is first necessary to observe that the inhabitants of the Putumayo were, according to Joaquin Rocha at the turn of the century, divided into two great classes of social types: whites and savage Indians. The category whites (also referred to as "rationals," Christians, and "civilized") included not only people phenotypically white, but also mestizos, negros, mulattos, Zambos, and Indians "of those groups incorporated into civilization since the time of the Spanish conquest."[55] Simson takes us further into this classification, and although his remarks here pertain to the *montaña* region at the headwaters of the rivers, they seem to me generally applicable to the middle reaches of the Putumayo as well, and are certainly relevant to the understanding of colonist culture.

Simson notes that what he calls the "pure Indians of the forest"

53. Alfred Simson, *Travels in the Wilds of Ecuador and the Exploration of the Putumayo River* (London: Samson Low, 1886), 170.

54. Simson, *Travels,* 170–71.

55. Rocha, *Memorandum de un viaje,* 64.

are divided, by whites and Spanish-speaking Indians, into two classes; Indians (*Indios*) and heathens (*infieles*). The *Indios* are Quichua-speaking, salt-eating semi-Christians, while the heathens, also known as *aucas,* speak distinct languages, eat salt rarely, and know nothing of baptism or of the Catholic Church.[56] In passing it should be observed that today, if not in times long past, the term *auca* also connotes cannibals who roam the forest naked, are without marriage rules, and practice incest.

Simson also states that the term *auca* as commonly understood bears "the full meaning it did anciently in Peru under the Incas. It includes the sense of infidel, traitor, barbarian, and is often applied in a malignant sense." In Peru it was used, he says, "to designate those who rebelled against their king and incarnation of their deity, the Inca."[57] Whether or not this assertion is historically accurate (as it certainly seems to be) is somewhat beside the point, for its importance lies in its character as a myth informing everyday life at the time of the rubber boom.

Simson's second major point about *aucas* concerns their animal-like qualities, so pronounced, he says, that they partake of the occult and spiritual. With reference to the Zaparos, for example, he writes that their perceptions of eye and ear are perfectly marvellous, and surpass those of the non-*auca* Indians considerably. Their knowledge of the forest is so perfect that they often travel at night in unknown parts. They are great fighters, and can detect sounds and

56. Simson, *Travels,* 58. It is worth noting that during the seventeenth or eighteenth century missionaries worked among at least some of the Indian groups Simson designates as *auca,* and thus it is not true that they (to quote Simson), "know nothing of the Catholic Church." See P. José Chantre y Herrera, *Historia de las misiones de la Companía de Jesus en el Marañon español, 1637–1767* (Madrid: Imprenta de A. Avrial, 1901), 283, 321–28, 365–69.

57. Simson, *Travels,* 58. This meaning of rebel against the Inca is sustained, referring to the Auracanians of Chile, in John M. Cooper, "The Auracanians," in Vol. II of *The Handbook of South American Indians,* Julian H. Steward, ed. (New York: Cooper Square, 1963), 690. For the eastern montaña of the northern Andes, the term *auca* means pagan as against Christian Indians, according to Steward and Alfred Metraux, "Tribes of the Ecuadorian and Peruvian Montaña," in Vol. III of the *Handbook,* 535–656, esp. 629 (Zaparos), 637 (Canelos/Napos), 653 (Quijos). Unlike Simson, the mere traveller, these anthropologists of the *Handbook* fail dismally to indicate the magical and mythic connotations of the term *auca.*

footmarks where white men perceive nothing. On the trail of an animal, they suddenly swerve, then change again as if following the scent of their prey. Their motions are catlike and they move unscathed through the entangled underwood and thorns. To communicate with each other, they generally imitate the whistle of the toucan or partridge—and all this is in marked contrast to non-*aucas* or civilized Indians, "who stand in fear and respect of them, but despise or affect to despise them as infidels behind their backs."[58]

I should add that the highland Indian shaman with whom I work in the Colombian Andes which overlook the Putumayo jungles regards the jungle shamans below as *aucas*, as animal/spirit hybrids possessing great magic. He singles out the Huitotos as a spiritual force with whom he makes a mystical pact in incantations and songs, with or without hallucinogens, to assure the success of his own magical battles with evil.

It is crucial to grasp the dialectic of sentiments involved here by the appellation *auca*, a dialectic enshrouded in magic and composed of both fear and contempt—identical to the mysticism, hatred, and awe projected onto the Zionist socialist Timerman in the torture chambers of the military. In the case of the *aucas*, this projection is inseparable from the imputation of their resistance to sacred imperial authority and the further imputation of magical power possessed by lowland forest dwellers as a class and by their oracles, seers, and healers—their shamans—in particular. Moreover, this indigenous, and what may well be a pre-Colombian, construction blends with the medieval European mythology of the Wild Man brought to the Andes and the Amazon by the Spaniards and Portuguese. Today, in the upper reaches of the Putumayo with which I am acquainted, the mythology of *auca* and Wild Man underlies the resort to Indian shamans by white and black colonists who seek cure from sorcery and hard times, while these very same colonists despise Indians as savages.[59] In the rubber boom, with its desperate need for Indian labor, the same mythology nourished incalculable cruelty and para-

58. Simson, *Travels*, 166, 168.

59. Michael Taussig, "Folk Healing and the Structure of Conquest," *Journal of Latin American Lore*, 6, no. 2 (1980), 217–78.

noia on the part of the whites. It is to this mythic endowment inherited by world capitalism in the jungles of the Putumayo that we need to pay attention if we are to understand the irrational "excesses" of the terror and torture depicted by Casement.

FEAR OF INDIAN REBELLION

Casement mentions the possibility that, in addition to their drive for profit, the whites' fear of Indian rebellion impelled them toward viciousness. But in keeping with his stress on Indian docility, he gives four reasons why Indian rebellion was unlikely. Indian communities were disunited long before the advent of the rubber boom, while the whites were armed and well organized. The Indians were poorly armed and their blowpipes, bows, and lances had been confiscated. Most important in his opinion was the fact that the elders had been systematically murdered by the company for the crime of giving "bad advice."[60]

Rocha, who was in the area some seven years before Casement, thought differently. He claims that the whites feared the consequences of the Indians' hatred and that this fear was central to their policies and thought. "Life for the Whites in the land of the Huitotos," he declares, "hangs by a thread." Small uprisings were common, and he provides an account of one of these.

In 1903 the Colombian Emilio Gutiérrez navigated up the Caquetá from Brazil searching for Indians to use to establish a rubber station. Reaching the area whose conquest he desired, he sent the bulk of his men back to carry in merchandise, and he and three others remained. While asleep, Gutiérrez and the companions were killed by wild Indians. Hearing the news, other whites prepared to retaliate when news reached them that thirty of Gutiérrez's civilized Indian work force had also been killed, all at the same time yet in different parts of the jungle. Indians working for whites were set in pursuit of the rebels; some were caught and killed outright, some

60. Casement, *Putumayo Report*, 45.

were taken as prisoners for the whites, and the majority escaped. A few more were captured and eaten by the Indian mercenaries—so the tale goes.[61]

In 1910 Casement heard the same episode from a Peruvian, who introduced his story by saying that the methods used by Colombian conquerors were very bad. In this version, the rebel Indians decapitated Gutiérrez together with an unstated number of other whites and exposed their skulls on the walls of their "drum house," keeping the limbless bodies in water for as long as possible to show them off to other Indians. Casement's informant said he had found the bodies of twelve others tied to stakes, assuring Casement that the reason they had not been eaten was that Indians "had a repugnance to eating white men, whom they hated too much." Terrible reprisals subsequently fell upon the Indians, notes Casement.[62]

Considered separately, and especially in relation to Rocha's version, this account of Casement's establishes the point that the white fear of Indian rebellion was not unjustified, but that, in addition, such rebellion was perceived in a mythic and colonially paranoid vision in which the image of dismemberment and cannibalism glowed vividly.

FEAR OF CANNIBALISM

Cannibalism acquired great ideological potency for the colonists from the beginning of the European conquest of the New World. The figure of the cannibal was elaborated and used for many sorts of ends, responding as it did to some of the most powerful symbolic forces known to humankind. It could be used to justify enslavement and as such was apparently important in the early economy of Brazil,[63] thereby affecting even the headwaters of the Amazon such as

---

61. Rocha, *Memorandum de un viaje,* 125–26.

62. Casement, *Putumayo Report,* 30. Father Pinell was told of a large uprising by rubber-working and other Indians along the Igaraparaná in 1917; the use of Peruvian troops was required to put it down. Pinell, *Un viaje,* 39–40.

63. An excellent discussion of this is to be found in David Sweet, "A Rich Realm of Nature Destroyed: The Middle Amazon Valley, 1640–1750" (Ph.D. diss., University of Wisconsin, 1975), I, 113–14, 116, 120, 126, 130–31, 141, 347.

the Putumayo where cannibalism was kept luridly alive in the imagination of the whites down to the era of the rubber boom.

Rocha provides many examples. He signals his arrival at Huitoto territory writing of "this singular land of the cannibals, the land of the Huitotos conquered by a dozen valiant Colombians repeating the heroism of their Spanish ancestors."[64] The rubber traders, he emphatically asserts, have tried to stamp out cannibalism with severe punishments. Yet cannibalism is an addiction. The Huitotos think they can deceive the whites about this, but "they succumb to the satisfaction of their beastly appetites."[65] The most notorious of the modern *conquistadores,* the Colombian Crisóstomo Hernandez (a Colombian highlands mulatto who had fled the police and sought refuge in the jungle), had, so Rocha was told, killed all the children, women, and men of an Indian long house because they practiced cannibalism—a surprising story given the need for labor, yet typical of white folktales in the Putumayo.[66]

Don Crisóstomo was the hero of another legendary story as well, one which makes the point that although Indian customs could conflict with those of whites, as, for example, in their "misunderstandings" over the value of money and of work, there were nevertheless ritual features of Indian culture which whites could harness to the needs of the rubber company. The practice of sometimes delivering rubber in conjunction with a great dance as a prelude to a sort of gift-giving exchange, as reported by Gridilla and Rocha, has been mentioned. Even more interesting is the rite the whites called *chupe del tabaco,* or tobacco-sucking, by adult Indian men during most if not all ritual occasions, a rite which perhaps fascinated the whites even more than it did the Indians.

Seated in a circle, usually at night, with the women and children set back in their hammocks but within earshot, the men took turns to place a finger in a thick concoction of cooked tobacco juice and then sucked it. Hardenburg reports that this ceremony was indispensable to any fiesta or to solemnize any agreement or contract. These were times when the men in general and the chief in particular held forth

64. Rocha, *Memorandum de un viaje,* 92–93.
65. Ibid., 118.
66. Ibid., 106–7.

with great oratory lasting perhaps the entire night. "This is the Huitoto's solemn oath," writes Hardenburg, "and is never said to be
broken. Whenever the whites wish to enter into any important
agreement with the Indians, they always insist upon this ceremony
being performed."[67] Casement says the same, yet goes on to quote
from a French explorer, Eugenio Robuchon, under whose name it
was written that this rite was one "in which the Indians recall their
lost liberty and their actual sufferings, and formulate terrible vows of
vengeance against the whites."[68]

Rocha was told that Crisóstomo Hernandez was a marvellously
skilled orator, taking his place as a *capitán* or *capitán general* among
the circle of Indian men. Gathering with a large assembly of chiefs
around the tobacco pot, don Cristóstomo would orate in Huitoto
language and style from eight in the evening till four in the morning,
with such power of seduction that the chiefs unanimously adopted
his proposals. This, says Rocha, was before he reigned through ter-

---

67. Hardenburg, *Putumayo*, 155. For use of coca in the *chupe del tabaco*, see Joseph
F. Woodroffe, *The Upper Reaches of the Amazon* (London: Methuen, 1914), 151–55.
With regard to the reliability and sources of Hardenburg's statements, it is perhaps of
use to cite some of the evidence he gave to the British Parliamentary Select Committee on Putumayo, *House of Commons Sessional Papers*, 1913, vol. 14. Asked what he saw
himself of actual cruelties to the Indians, Hardenburg replied, "Of actual crimes being
committed I did not see anything, practically; all I saw was that the Indians in [the rubber station of] El Encanto were nearly naked and very thin and cadaverous-looking; I
saw several scores of them, and I saw what they were being fed on" (p. 510, #12848).
His information came through accounts from other people: "In fact, I think I might
say that most of the people came through others. They would say, 'I know another
man who could state this and that,' and they would bring them" (p. 511, #12881).
Asked if he questioned these people in detail about their statements, Hardenburg replied: "I cannot say I did much of that" (p. 511, #12882). It was, said Hardenburg,
general knowledge that the atrocities were occurring. This "general knowledge" is
precisely what I have been at pains to track down, not because I believe that the atrocities were less than described by the several authors upon whom I draw, but because it
is this general knowledge in the shape of mythic narratives that acts as a screen and as
a network of signifiers without which "the facts" would not exist. More specifically,
the function of this screen of signifiers is to heighten dread and hence the controlling
function of the culture of terror. Casement's evidence is altogether of another category, being more carefully gathered, cross-checked, etc., and as a result of it we can
affirm reports, such as Hardenburg's, which are less well substantiated. Nevertheless,
Casement's evidence serves not to puncture the mythic character so much as indicate
its terrific reality.

68. Casement, *Putumayo Report*, 48. Robuchon's text appeared as a book ("Official
Edition"), printed in Lima in 1907 and entitled *En el Putumayo y sus afluentes*. It was

ror and military might; his dominion came to rest on force of arms, yet it was through oratory that he initiated his conquest, "because for the Huitotos, he was their king and god."[69]

The story which most impressed Rocha was the one about the Huitoto rite of judicial murder, or capital punishment. One can easily imagine the chords of exotic terror it provoked among the colonists and employees of the rubber company listening to it in the chit-chat of a jungle night.

> All the individuals of the nation that has captured the prisoner retire to an area of the bush to which women are absolutely prohibited, except for one who acts a special role. Children are rigorously excluded also. In the center, a pot of cooked tobacco juice is placed for the pleasure of the men, and in a corner seated on a little bench and firmly bound is the captive.
>
> Clasping each other's arms, the savages form a long line, and to the sound of drum beats advance dancing very close to the victim. They retreat and advance many times, with individuals separating to drink from the pot of tobacco. Then the drum stops for the dancing cannibals, and so that the unfortunate victim can see how much he is going to lose by dying, the most beautiful girl of the tribe enters, regally attired with the most varied and brilliant feathers of the birds of these woods. The drum starts again, and the beautiful girl dances alone in front of and almost touching him. She twists and advances, showering him with passionate looks and gestures of love, turning around and repeating this three or four times. She then leaves, terminating the second act of this solemn occasion. The third follows with the same men's dance as before, except that each time the line of dancers approaches the prisoner, one of the men detaches himself and declaims something like this: "Remember when your people killed Jatijiko, man of our nation whom you couldn't take prisoner because he knew how to die before allowing himself to be

---

edited by Carlos Rey de Castro, a lackey of Julio César Arana's and one-time Peruvian consul in Brazil, from Robuchon's papers after his mysterious death in the Putumayo rain forest. Judging from Rey de Castro's book on the Putumayo, *Los pobladores del Putumayo* (Barcelona: Imp. Vda de Luis Tasso, 1917), and his relation to Arana, one can surmise that it would be unwise to read the Robuchon text as though it were really Robuchon's unadulterated work. The chances are that it was edited with a view to presenting a case favorable to Arana. The importance of prehistory, ethnohistory, and Indian history in the ideological war for world opinion is well brought out by Rey de Castro's bold stroke in his *Los pobladores del Putumayo*, in which he sets out to prove that the Huitotos and adjacent Indian groups are in reality descendant from the *orejones* of Cuzco in the interior of Peru—thus supposedly strengthening the Peruvian claims over the Putumayo rubber zone and its indigenous inhabitants.

69. Rocha, *Memorandum de un viaje*, 111.

dragged in front of your people? We are going to take vengeance of his death in you, you coward, that doesn't know how to die in battle like he did." Or else: "Remember when you and your people surprised my sister Jifisino bathing, captured her and while alive made a party of her flesh and tormented her until her last breath? Do you remember? Now you god-cursed man we are going to devour you alive and you won't die until all traces of your bloody flesh have disappeared from around our mouths."

Following this is the fourth and last act of the terrifying tragedy. One by one the dancers come forward and with his knife each one cuts a slice of meat off the prisoner, which they eat half roasted to the sound of his death rattle. When he eventually dies, they finish cutting him up and continue roasting and cooking his flesh, eating him to the last little bit.[70]

NARRATIVE MEDIATION:
EPISTEMIC MURK

It seems to me that stories like these were the groundwork indispensable to the formation and flowering of the colonial imagination during the Putumayo rubber boom. "Their imagination was diseased," wrote the Peruvian judge Rómulo Paredes in 1911, referring to the rubber-station managers, "and they saw everywhere attacks by Indians, conspiracies, uprisings, treachery etc.; and in order to save themselves from these fancied perils . . . they killed, and killed without compassion."[71] Far from being trivial daydreams indulged in after work was over, these stories and the imagination they sustained were a potent political force without which the work of conquest and of supervising rubber gathering could not have been accomplished. What is essential to understand is the way in which these stories functioned to create, through magical realism, a culture of terror dominating both whites and Indians.

The importance of this fabulous work extends beyond the epic and grotesque quality of its content. The truly crucial feature lies in creating an uncertain reality out of fiction, a nightmarish reality in which the unstable interplay of truth and illusion becomes a social

70. Ibid., 116–117.

71. Rómula Paredes, "Confidential Report to the Ministry of Foreign Relations, Peru," September 1911, translated in Eberhardt, *Slavery in Peru*, 146. Paredes's work is explained and put into context in a mass of testimony in the book of Carlos A. Valcarcel, *El proceso del Putumayo* (Lima: Imp. Comercial de Horacio La Rosa, 1915).

force of horrendous and phantasmic dimensions. To an important extent all societies live by fictions taken as reality. What distinguishes cultures of terror is that the epistemological, ontological, and otherwise purely philosophical problem of reality-and-illusion, certainty-and-doubt, becomes infinitely more than a "merely" philosophical problem. It becomes a high-powered tool for domination and a principal medium of political practice. And in the Putumayo rubber boom this medium of epistemic and ontological murk was most keenly figured and objectified as the space of death.

In his report, Paredes tells us that the rubber-station managers lived obsessed with death. They saw danger everywhere and thought solely of the fact that they were surrounded by vipers, tigers, and cannibals. It is these ideas of death, he writes, which constantly struck their imaginations, making them terrified and capable of any act. Like children who read the *Arabian Nights*, he goes on to say, they had nightmares of witches, evil spirits, death, treason, and blood. The only way they could live in such a terrifying world, he observes, was by themselves inspiring terror.[72]

SOCIOLOGICAL AND MYTHIC
MEDIATION: THE *MUCHACHOS*

If it was the telling of tales which mediated inspiration of the terror, then it behooves us to inquire a little into the sociological agency which mediated this mediation, namely, the corps of Indian guards trained by the company and known as the *muchachos*. For in Rómulo Paredes's words, they were "constantly devising executions and continually revealing meetings of Indians 'licking tobacco'—which meant an oath to kill white men—imaginary uprisings which never existed, and other similar crimes."[73]

Mediating as civilized or rational Indians between the savages of

---

72. Paredes, "Confidential Report," in Eberhardt, *Slavery in Peru,* 158.
73. Ibid., 147. I am grateful to Fred Chin and Judy Farquahar of the Department of Anthropology at the University of Chicago for impressing upon me the importance of the *muchachos* as a mediating force. Then of course one should not omit the role of the blacks recruited in Barbados, mediating between the whites and the Indians. In much the same way as the British army from the mid-nineteenth century on deployed

the forest and the whites of the rubber camps, the *muchachos* personi-
fied all the critical distinctions in the class and caste system of rubber
production. Cut off from their own kind, whom they persecuted and
betrayed and in whom they inspired envy and hatred, and now clas-
sified as civilized yet dependent on whites for food, arms, and goods,
the *muchachos* wrought to perfection all that was horrifying in the
colonial mythology of savagery—because they occupied the perfect
sociological and mythic space to do so. Not only did they create fictions stoking the fires of white paranoia, they embodied the brutality
which the whites feared, created, and tried to harness to their own
ends. In a very literal sense, the *muchachos* traded their identity as
savages for their new social status as civilized Indians and guards. As
Paredes notes, they placed at the disposal of the whites "their special
instincts, such as sense of direction, scent, their sobriety, and their
knowledge of the forest."[74] Just as they bought rubber from the wild
Indians of the forest, so the whites also bought the *auca*-like savage
instincts of the Indian *muchachos*.

Yet, unlike rubber, these savage instincts were manufactured
largely in the imaginations of the whites. All the *muchachos* had to do
in order to receive their rewards was to objectify and through words
reflect back to the whites the phantoms that populated colonist culture. Given the centuries of colonial mythology concerning the *auca*
and the Wild Man, and given the implosion of this mythology in the
contradictory social being of the *muchachos,* the task was an easy one.
The *muchachos'* stories were, in fact, stories within a much older
story encompassing the *muchachos* as objects of a colonialist discourse rather than as its authors.

The trading system of debt-peonage established by the Putumayo
rubber boom was thus more than a trade in white goods for rubber
gathered by the Indians. It was also a trade in terrifying mythologies
and fictional realities, pivoted on the mediation of the *muchachos,*
whose storytelling bartered betrayal of Indian realities for the confirmation of colonial fantasies.

---

different colonial and ethnic groups so as to maximize reputations for ferocity and
checking one against the other, the British and Peruvian rubber company used its
"ethnic soldiers" in the Putumayo.

74. Paredes, "Confidential Report," in Eberhardt, *Slavery in Peru,* 147.

THE COLONIAL MIRROR

I began this essay stating that my concern was with the mediation of the culture of terror through narration, and with the problems of writing against terror. In part my concern stemmed from my problems in evaluating and interpreting the "facts" constituted in the various accounts of the Putumayo atrocities. This problem of interpretation grew ever larger, eventually bursting into the realization that that problem is precisely what is central to the culture of terror—not only making effective talking and writing against terror extremely difficult, but, even more to the point, making the terrible reality of the death squads, disappearances, and torture all the more effectively crippling of people's capacity to resist.

While much attention is given to "ideology" in the social sciences, virtually none as far as I know is given to the fact that people delineate their world, including its large as well as its microscale politics, in stories and storylike creations and very rarely, if ever, in ideologies (as customarily defined). Surely it is in the coils of rumor, gossip, story, and chit-chat where ideology and ideas become emotionally powerful and enter into active social circulation and meaningful existence. So it was with the Putumayo terror, from the accounts of which it seems clear that the colonists and rubber company employees not only feared but also themselves created through narration fearful and confusing images of savagery—images which bound colonial society together through the epistemic murk of the space of death. The systems of torture they devised to secure rubber mirrored the horror of the savagery they so feared, condemned— and fictionalized. Moreover, when we consider the task of creating counterrepresentations and counterdiscourses, we must take stock of the way that most if not all the narratives reproduced by Hardenburg and Casement, referring to and critical of the atrocities, were similarly fictionalized, drawing upon the same historically molded source that men succumbed to when torturing Indians.

Torture and terror in the Putumayo were motivated by the need for cheap labor. But labor per se—labor as a commodity—did not exist in the jungles of the Caraparaná and Igaraparaná affluents of the Putumayo. What existed was not a market for labor but a society and culture of human beings whom the colonists called Indians, irrationals, and savages, with their very specific historical trajectory, form of life, and modes of exchange. In the blundering colonial attempt to dovetail forcibly the capitalist commodity structure to one or the other of the possibilities for rubber gathering offered by these modes of exchange, torture, as Casement alludes, took on a life of its own: "Just as the appetite comes in the eating so each crime led on to fresh crimes."[75] To this we should add that, step by step, terror and torture became *the* form of life for some fifteen years, an organized culture with its systematized rules, imagery, procedures, and meanings involved in spectacles and rituals that sustained the precarious solidarity of the rubber company employees as well as beating out through the bodies of the tortured some sort of canonical truth about Civilization and Business.

It was not commodity fetishism but debt fetishism drenched in the fictive reality of the debt-peonage institution, with its enforced "advances" and theaterlike farce of business exchanges, that exercised the decisive force in the creation of terror, transforming torture from the status of a means to that of the mode if not, finally, the very aim of production.

From the reports of both Timerman and Casement it is obvious that torture and institutionalized terror is like a ritual art form, and that far from being spontaneous, *sui generis,* and an abandonment of what are often called "the values of civilization," such rites have a deep history deriving power and meaning from those values. What demands further analysis here is the mimesis between the savagery attributed to the Indians by the colonists and the savagery perpetuated by the colonists in the name of what Julio César Arana called civilization.[76]

This reciprocating yet distorted mimesis has been and continues to be of great importance in the construction of colonial culture—the colonial mirror which reflects back onto the colonists the barbarity of their own social relations, but as imputed to the savage or evil figures they wish to colonize. It is highlighted in the Putumayo in the colonist lore as related, for instance, through Joaquin Rocha's lurid tale of Huitoto cannibalism. And what is put into discourse through the

---

75. Casement, *Putumayo Report,* 44.
76. See pages 259–60, above.

artful story telling of the colonists is the same as what they practiced on the bodies of Indians.[77]

Tenaciously embedded in this artful practice is a vast and mystifying Western history and iconography of evil in the imagery of the inferno and the savage—wedded to and inseparable from paradise, utopia, and the good. It is to the subversion of that apocalyptic dialectic that all of us would be advised to bend our counterdiscursive efforts, in a quite different poetics of good and evil whose cathartic force lies not with cataclysmic resolution of contradictions but with their disruption.

Post-Enlightenment European culture makes it difficult if not impossible to penetrate the hallucinatory veil of the heart of darkness without either succumbing to its hallucinatory quality or losing that quality. Fascist poetics succeed where liberal rationalism self-destructs. But what might point a way out of this impasse is precisely what is so painfully absent from all the Putumayo accounts, namely, the narrative and narrative mode of the Indians which does de-sensationalize terror so that the histrionic stress on the myste-

---

77. Illustrations of the way in which this following of the letter of the tale was enacted in the torture of Indians can be found in the rare instances of dialogue that Casement allows his witnesses in the section of his report given over to testimony by men recruited in Barbados, as, for example:

"And you say you saw the Indians burnt?" Consul-General Casement asked Augustus Walcott, born in the Caribbean island of Antigua but twenty-three years before.

"Yes."

"Burnt alive?"

"Alive."

"How do you mean? Describe this."

"Only one I see burnt alive."

"Well, tell me about that one?"

"He had not work 'caucho,' he ran away and he kill a 'muchacho,' a boy, and they cut off his two arms and legs by the knee and they burn his body. . . ."

"Are you sure he was still alive—not dead when they threw him on the fire?"

"Yes, he did alive. I'm sure of it—I see him move—open his eyes, he screamed out. . . ."

"Was Aurelio Rodriguez [the rubber-station manager] looking on—all the time?"

"Yes, all the time."

"Giving the directions?"

"Yes, Sir."

"He told them to cut off the legs and arms?"

"Yes."

There was something else the Consul-General could not understand and he called Walcott back to explain what he meant by saying, "because he told the Indians that we was Indians too, and eat those—." What he meant, Casement summarized, was that the station manager, Señor Normand, in order to "frighten the Indians told them that

rious side of the mysterious (to adopt Benjamin's formula) is indeed denied by an optic which perceives the everyday as impenetrable, the impenetrable as everyday. At least this is the poetics of the sorcery and shamanism I know about in the upper reaches of the Putumayo, but that is another history for another time, not only of terror but of healing as well.

---

the negroes were cannibals, and a fierce tribe of cannibals who eat people, and that if they did not bring in rubber these black men would be sent to kill and eat them" (Casement, *Putumayo Report,* 115, 118).

Another, more complicated, example follows:

"Have you ever seen Aguero kill Indians?" the Consul-General asked Evelyn Bateson, aged twenty-five, born in Barbados, and working in the rubber depôt of La Chorrera.

"No, Sir, I haven't seen him kill Indians—but I have seen him send 'muchachos' to eat, and they have a dance of it. . . ."

"You saw the man killed?"

"Yes, Sir. They tied him to a stake and they shot him, and they cut off his head after he was shot and his feet and hands, and they carried them about the section—in the yard and they carries them up and down and singing, and they carries them to their house and dances. . . ."

"How do you know they ate them?"

"I heard they eat them. I have not witnessed it, Sir, but I heard the manager Señor Aguero tell that they eat this man."

"The manager said all this?"

"Yes, Sir, He did." (Casement, *Putumayo Report,* 103)

This sort of stimulation if not creation of cannibalism by colonial pressure is also recorded in missionaries' letters concerning King Leopold's Congo Free State and the gathering of rubber there. See, for example, the account of Mr. John Harris in the work by Edmund Morel, *King Leopold's Rule in Africa* (New York: Funk and Wagnalls, 1905), 437–41.

MICHELLE Z. ROSALDO

8

Moral/Analytic Dilemmas Posed by the Intersection of Feminism and Social Science

Our questions are inevitably bound up with our politics. The character, constraint, and promise of our scholarship are informed as much by moral ends and choices as they are by the "objective" postures necessary to research. For feminists, especially, intellectual insight thrives in a complex relation with contemporary moral and political demands.[1]

Few social scientists writing today would deny the fact that feminists have changed our intellectual horizons. At a minimum, we have "discovered" women. More important, we have argued that certain categories and descriptions that at one time made good sense must be reformulated if we are to grasp the shape and meaning of *both* men's and women's lives.[2] That women have—at different times and in quite different ways—impressed their wills on not just "domestic" but also political and public life is something scholars formerly

Copyright © 1983 Columbia University Press. Reprinted by permission.
1. This paper is at once a commentary on contemporary feminist scholarship and a reflection on my own development as a feminist scholar. It develops certain aspects of the argument in Michelle Rosaldo, "The Use and Abuse of Anthropology: Reflections on Feminism and Cross-Cultural Understanding." *Signs* 5, no. 3 (1980), 389–417.
2. See, for example, Carol Gilligan's work.

found perplexing and anomalous. But as we come upon new data on the lives that women lead, it becomes clear that one must learn to understand the systematic impact of the strategies women use and to comprehend the forces that constrain the kinds of opportunities women are able to pursue and the symbols and beliefs that are used to define our actions. The desire of feminists to recover hidden facts about our past has led not merely to new information but to new questions about how one ought to understand human societies.

Or has it? Early feminist questions, born in a political context that made clear the injustices and silences that deserved to be addressed, had little need of either paradigm or doubt. Instead, a practical sense that all the data urgently needed to be revealed inspired a drive to hear our sisters speak, without reflection on the categories that would inform our understandings. Thus, feminist scholars over the past ten years provided challenges to certain biases in traditional accounts without supplying the conceptual frameworks necessary to undermine them. While recognizing enemies and blind men among teachers and peers, we failed to recognize *ourselves* as heirs to their traditions of political and social argument.[3] Simultaneously, we embraced and were at pains to redefine some of the gendered dualisms of past work. We found a source for questions in the most egregious errors of the past. But at the same time we stayed prisoners to a set of categories and preconceptions deeply rooted in traditional sociology.

My concern is essentially one of teasing out some of these categories and constraints. I want to deconstruct[4] conceptual frameworks that we use as though they were concrete reflections of the world "out there" in order both to free our moral thinking from assumptions bound to sex and to free feminism from the moralisms of our predominantly individualistic modes of sociological understanding.

---

3. The use of nineteenth-century accounts of "primitive matriarchy," discussed below, is perhaps the clearest case of feminists' following decidedly nonfeminist forms of social and historical reflection. I hope in subsequent work to show that our "return" is, as they say, no accident; nineteenth-century assumptions about men and women are, I believe, deeply embedded in the categories of contemporary social science, a fact which lends a certain circularity to recent attempts to use these categories to explain why we are as we are.

4. My allusion to Jacques Derrida, *Of Grammatology* (Baltimore: Johns Hopkins University Press, 1976), is intentional. I am concerned to "denaturalize" a set of categories; he is concerned to "denaturalize" the sign.

It never hurts to look at our assumptions or to probe the sources of our analytical ill-ease. Discomforts in which moral impulse and intellectual concern are joined may serve as both stimuli and resources if, as with the case at hand, we find ourselves at once excited and disturbed by trends within this clearly inspiring and troubling branch of scholarship.

THE SEARCH FOR ORIGINS

The significance of all these general remarks for an anthropologist like myself becomes clear when we consider the following observation.[5] Few historians, sociologists, or social philosophers writing today feel called on—as was common practice in the nineteenth century—to begin their tales "at the beginning" and probe the anthropological for, say, the origins of doctors in shamans or of Catholic ritual in the cannibalism of an imagined past. Whereas turn-of-the-century thinkers as diverse as Spencer, Maine, Durkheim, Engels, and Freud considered it necessary to look at evidence from "simple" cultures as a means of understanding both the origins and the significance of contemporary social forms, most modern social scientists have rejected both their methods and their biases. Rather than probe origins, contemporary theorists will use anthropology, if at all, for the comparative insight that it offers. Having decided, with good cause, to question evolutionary approaches, most would, unfortunately, go on to claim that data on premodern and traditional forms of social life have virtually no relevance to the understanding of contemporary society.

Yet quite the opposite is true of the vast majority of recent feminist writing. If anthropology has been too much ignored by most contemporary social thinkers, it has achieved a marked though problematic pride of place in classics like *Sexual Politics* and *The Second Sex*. Simone de Beauvoir, Kate Millett, Susan Brownmiller, Adrienne Rich, all introduce their texts with what appears to anthropologists an old-fashioned evocation of the human record. On the assumption

5. The discussion in this section draws extensively on Rosaldo, "Use and Abuse of Anthropology."

that preparing meals, enjoying talk with women friends, making demands of sons, or celebrating their fertility and sexual vitality will mean the same thing to women independent of their time and place, these writers catalogue the customs of the past in order to decide if womankind can claim through time to have acquired or lost such rightful "goods" as power, self-esteem, autonomy, and status. Though these writers differ in conclusions, methods, and particulars of theoretical approach, all move from some version of de Beauvoir's question "What is woman?" to a diagnosis of contemporary subordination and to the queries "Were things always as they are today?" and "When did it start?"

Much like the nineteenth-century writers who first argued about whether or not mother-right preceded patriarchal social forms or about whether or not women's difficult primeval lot has been significantly improved in civilized society, feminists differ in their diagnoses of our prehistoric lives, in their sense of suffering, conflict, and change. Some, like Rich, romanticize what they imagine was a better past, whereas others find in history an endless tale of female subjugation and male triumph. Most, however, find no cause to question a desire to ferret out our origins and roots. Nor would they challenge Shulamith Firestone, who, in her important book *The Dialectic of Sex,* quotes Engels to assert our need first to "examine the historic succession of events from which the antagonism has sprung in order to discover in the conditions thus created the means of ending the conflict."[6] Firestone suggests, in fact, that we seek out the roots of present suffering in a past which moves from history back to "primitive man" and thence to animal biology.

And most recently, Linda Gordon, in her splendid account of the relationship between birth control and developments in American political life, attempts in less than thirty pages to summarize the history of birth control throughout the premodern world, providing her readers with a catalogue of practices and beliefs that is unsatisfying both as history and as anthropology.[7] In a study demonstrating

6. Shulamith Firestone, *The Dialectic of Sex: The Case for Feminist Revolution* (New York: Bantam Books, 1970), 2.

7. Linda Gordon, *Women's Body, Women's Right* (New York: Penguin Books, 1975).

the place of birth control agitation in the history of leftist politics in the United States, changing as it did according to the nature and organization of our families and our economy, anthropology is, unfortunately, evoked primarily to universalize contemporary political demands and thus to undermine our present sense of singularity. Gordon turns to "primitives" to demonstrate the depth of what we think we need and to confirm her sense that even though Eve suffered as much as we do today, we can henceforth be optimistic in expecting female protests to be heard and social expectations, correspondingly, to be altered. To me, there is something wrong, indeed morally disturbing, in an argument that claims that the practitioners of infanticide in the past are ultimately our predecessors in an endless, although perhaps ascendant, fight to keep men from making claims to female bodies.

By using anthropology as precedent for modern arguments and claims, the "primitive" emerges in accounts like these as the bearer of primordial human need. Women elsewhere are, it seems, the image of ourselves undressed, and the historical specificity of their lives and of our own becomes obscured. *Their* strengths prove that we can be strong. But, ironically, at the same time that we fight to see ourselves as cultural beings who lead socially determined lives, the movement back in evolutionary time brings an inevitable appeal to biological givens and the determining impact of such "crude" facts as demography and technology. We infer that birth control is now available to human choice. But in the past—the story goes—women's abilities to shape their reproductive fates were either nonexistent or constrained by such logistical facts as a nomadic lifestyle, a need for helpers on the farm, or an imbalance between food supply and demography. We want to claim our sisters' triumphs as proof of our worth, but at the same time their oppression is artfully dissociated from our own because we live with choice, whereas they are seen as victims of biology.

My point is not to criticize these texts. Feminists (and I include myself) have with good reason probed the anthropological record for evidence that appears to tell us whether or not "human nature" is the sexist and constraining force that many of us were taught. Anthropology is, for most of us, a monument to human possibilities and constraints; it is a hall of mirrors wherein what Anthony Wallace called the "anecdotal exception" seems to challenge every would-be law; but at the same time, lurking in the oddest shapes and forms it promises familiar pictures of ourselves, so that by meditating on New Guinea menstrual huts and West African female traders, ritualists, or queens, we can begin to grasp just what, in universal terms, we "really" are.

But I would like to think that anthropology—and feminism—can offer more than that. I would rather claim that when anthropology is asked (by feminists or their enemies alike) to answer troubling ideologies and to give voice to universal human truths, anthropology becomes a discipline limited by the assumptions with which it first began and therefore unable to transcend the biases its questions presuppose. To look for origins is, in the end, to think that what we are today is something other than the product of our history and our present social world, and, more particularly, that our gender systems are primordial, transhistorical, and essentially unchanging in their roots. Quests for origins sustain, since they are predicated upon it, a discourse cast in universal terms; and universalism permits us all too quickly to assume—for everyone but ourselves perhaps—the sociological significance of what individual people do or, even worse, of what, in biological terms, they are.

Stated otherwise, our search for origins reveals a faith in ultimate and essential truths, a faith sustained in part by cross-cultural evidence of widespread sexual inequality. But any analysis that assumes that sexual asymmetry is the first subject we should attempt to question or explain fails in political terms to help us understand the choices we in fact pursue, just as it fails in analytical terms to undermine the sexist biases of much theorizing in contemporary social science.

These biases have their bases in two larger trends within traditional social science thought. First is the overwhelming and pervasive individualism that holds that social forms proceed from what particular persons need or do, activities (where gender is concerned) which seem to follow from presumed "givens" of our reproductive physiology. Second, more as complement than as concomitant of the first trend, is our tendency to think in dualistic terms, opposing individual to social, unconscious psyche to more conscious strategies and rules, biological to cultural law, domestic to political jural bonds, and woman to man. Taken together, these polarities lead both feminists and traditionalists alike to think of gender as, above all else, the creation of biologically based differences which oppose women and men instead of as the product of social relationships in distinct (and changeable) societies. Individualism, dualism, and biological determinism are thus linked in modern thought because they lead us to seek essential and presumably universal qualities in each sex instead of asking what in the relations of the sexes makes them appear the way they do and how the asymmetries that such relations typically entail are causally bound to socially specific forms of inequality and hierarchy.

QUESTIONING QUESTIONS

What are our options? For anthropologists in general, such difficulties begin with the embarrassment accompanying "cultural relativism" in our thought. Inevitably, we face the question of why and how distinctive cultures make a claim on our lives.[8] Can anthropologists describe the "other" without in some way commenting on the generalizations which emerge from observations of its similarities and differences from ourselves? Can students be taught the organization of power in some distant forest world without permitting them as well a glimpse of what they share with the inhabitants of that forest space, of perhaps an essential "human nature" lurking everywhere beneath diversity in cultural norms and rules? More specifically, can feminists be asked to dwell on anthropological details without inquiring if the "other" is, perhaps, an ancestress whose rise and fall describes our present state? Can we not see in women elsewhere our true "sisters," whose distinctive lots, for better or worse, reveal determinants that can tell us what we need and where we ought to go? Most anthropologists I respect remain uneasy with the search for origins and/or pan-human laws, but none has clarified how a discipline born of the contrast between "us" and "them" can

8. For a somewhat different explanation of this point, see Paul Rabinow's article "Humanism as Nihilism: The Bracketing of Truth and Seriousness in American Cultural Anthropology," in Norma Haan, Robert N. Bellah, Paul Rabinow, and William Sullivan, eds., *Social Science as Moral Inquiry* (New York: Columbia University Press, 1983), 52ff.

claim to learn from others in anything other than our culture's terms. None tells us how to reconcile a distrust of essences and a taste for local and historical detail with the suspicion/fear that women's lot is everywhere, in important ways, the same. How can one write a feminist ethnography without assuming, for example, that learning about women elsewhere must, in fact, provide a set of images that reflect immediately on ourselves?

These difficulties have sources more complex than can be addressed here. What is significant to my immediate concerns, however, is the relationship between dilemmas faced by feminists and those confronted by anthropologists. Wanting to speak and think of change, the feminist must distrust perspectives that stress "deep," essential commonalities in women's styles, relationships, and strengths. At the same time, a desire to discover previously hidden women's lives is rooted in a conviction about the "sisterhood" we share. Thus, on one level it appears that the anthropologists who talk of foreign peoples—so much like (the selfish, rational, existential, or just biologically viable "man") and yet so different from ourselves—are paralleled by those feminists who try to "rank" or otherwise describe our foreign sisters' goals and needs in terms at once related to and distant from our own. The interest in the "other" is, in every case, presented as a telling variant on our historically and politically shaped concerns.

Much more narrowly (although perhaps of more immediate relevance here), the anthropological arguments about whether or not family and kinship (both, of course, eminently social institutions built on what appears to be a biologically given base) are universal facts bear a close resemblance to contemporary arguments concerning both the pattern in and the determinants of such variable though universal terms as "woman" and "man"[9] In both instances, there is

9. The particular conundrums anthropologists confront when trying to think about apparently universal facts like kinship without prejudging the essence of particular cases or embedding causal (and naturalizing) presuppositions in descriptive terms are discussed from different points of view by David M. Schneider, "What Is Kinship All About?" in Priscilla Reining, ed., *Kinship Studies in the Morgen Centennial Year* (Washington, D.C.: Anthropological Society, 1972); Andrew Strathern, "Kinship, Descent, and Locality: Some New Guinea Examples," in J. Goody, ed., *The Character of Kinship* (London: Cambridge University Press, 1973); Steve Barnett and Martin Silverman, *Ideology and Everyday Life* (Ann Arbor: University of Michigan

the sense that variation is limited, that commonality is necessary and deep. Just as one would not fail, in the name of cultural relativism, to comment on the universal fact that heterosexuality and reproduction figure centrally in the organization of social bonds, so it seems necessary to acknowledge general patterns in our gendered hierarchies and roles, independent of particulars in cultural detail. Gender, much like kinship, seems to have an obvious transcultural core; but in both cases there is also cause to fear that such appearances are ideological and misleading. Precisely because our faith in "nature" is so readily evoked in these domains, we may well argue that our common sense must be surrendered lest a prior faith lead us to see what we expect to find and so obscure our grasp of what is really there.

For anthropology, of course, conundrums like these are the stuff of daily talk. When is difference really difference? What phenomena is it legitimate to compare? The rub—where feminists are concerned—is that something much more immediate than liberalism or relativism appears at issue when such questions as these are raised. If I decline to argue (when, let us assume, the natives disagree) that women elsewhere enjoy privileges more constrained than those of men, how can I claim that the American housewife who takes real pleasure in her role is—or at least ought to be—my ally in opposing women's secondary place today? If, instead, I find that certain African women, U.S. housewives, and professional women like myself can all agree on many of the pleasures and disabilities of women's lot, does the community so formed reflect real commonalities of concern or rather a political rhetoric that just happens to be available?

We may well want to claim that our community is real, that it is probably true that women everywhere (and for similar reasons) have social roles subordinate to men's, and that giving birth and caring for infants are core experiences that women everywhere share. But at the same time, and principally because the organization of gender *does* appear so universally bound up with biological capacities and

---

Press, 1979); and Sylvia Sunko Yanagisako, "Family and Household: The Analysis of Domestic Groups, *Annual Review of Anthropology* 8 (1979), 161–205. My point here is that discussions of gender—like those of kinship—are torn between appearances of naturalness and universality, on the one hand, and a fear that such appearances are blinding, on the other.

constraints, we have developed a distrust of observations such as these. A facile "sisterhood" appears too readily to cast biology as the immediate cause of women's lot, as though the now-discovered community were the product not of our political life but of our "deeper" and essentially presocial bodies. On the one hand, then, we are aware that our attention to commonalities appears not only reasonable but fundamental to both feminist scholarship and feminist political demands. On the other, it appears that feminists have a particular interest in challenging those unities most apparent to our sight and in questioning all claims that link the stereotypes and symbols that define a social group to a set of attributes bound up primarily with individual biology.

The argument over nature/nurture thus defines recurrent poles for feminist (as for much anthropological) thought. We seek and resist essences and yet, in doing so, appear recurrently to reproduce a set of arguments that remove us from the concrete forms that gender takes—and from its status, both as cause and as consequence, of the social bonds and needs produced in our historically quite various societies.

CATEGORIES AND FALSE CLARITY

My claim thus far has been that certain tensions within feminism, between essentialist universalism and a more relativist concern to understand what sorts of variants exist, have political consequences and roots that are in some ways paralleled by dilemmas concerning universalism and relativism in anthropology. Universalists stress commonalities in human bodies and in human lives but in so doing tend to focus on "inherent" properties of individuals independent of the social systems wherein individuals are formed, and then fail to probe the systematic ways that personal facts, like gender, are in all societies bound up with other forms of social inequality. The feminist use of anthropology—in particular, the search for an original state or cause—has thus tended to exacerbate some of the contradictions that emerge in any search for unity and/or difference across space and time.

But these difficulties are not feminism's or anthropology's alone.

Because feminist conundrums may well pave the way to positive critiques of modern social thought, I want now to dwell upon some ramifications of the tensions explicated above, suggesting how three common themes in the interpretation/explanation of gender roles are ultimately related to some of the morally and intellectually most troubling areas in contemporary social science. Overall, my claim is that recent feminist trends continue to reproduce a deep but analytically unexplicated faith that the idea of "women" (and/or gender) is related to all other statuses and roles in a way that parallels the opposition between our natural and our cultural selves, or, perhaps, between the individual and society. On the one hand, I acknowledge that this belief in many ways makes sense; certainly it corresponds to a persuasive and transcultural form of gender ideology.[10] At the same time, an overemphasis on commonalities and attendant biological forms of cause tends to inhibit systematic thought about those things that feminists can best help their fellow social scientists to learn: the very real cross-cultural variety in views of gender and, more broadly, in conceptions of the self; their roots in different forms of social life; and their implications for human action and relationship in diverse societies. Thus, at the same time that a sense of unity may help to ground our questions and our political demands, feminists who would avoid reproducing the past must first question that unity and, with it, some of the categories most current in contemporary social science.

THE NATURE/NURTURE ARGUMENT

First and foremost, then, is an emergent sense that feminists must criticize the nature/nurture argument in social thought. Without embracing relativisms that deny us a legitimate political voice, we must

---

10. For the generality of nature/culture formulations in gender ideologies, see, for example, Sherry Ortner, "Is Female to Male as Nature Is to Culture?" in M. Rosaldo and L. Lamphere, eds., *Woman, Culture, and Society* (Stanford: Stanford University Press, 1974); J. A. Barnes, "Genetrix:Genitor-Nature:Culture?" in Goody, *Character of Kinship;* and Edwin Ardener, "Belief and the Problem of Women," in J. LaFontaine, ed., *The Interpretation of Ritual* (London: Tavistock, 1972).

begin to clarify what has been called the "use and abuse of biology."[11] The reasonable claim that gender must "have something to do" with the biological characteristics associated with sex—and with this, the argument that we must or that we dare not tamper with our "natural" physiology—has, of course, recurred in feminist debates, the proponents ranging from technologists who think that test-tube fertilization and/or birth control will make us free to those who argue for new cults of motherhood, more midwives, or "essentially feminine" forms of relationship and sexuality.[12] The status of nature as an inevitable first cause is explicitly entertained by students of sex differences in the young; it is implicit in, for example, de Beauvoir's analysis of the experiences that constitute a "second sex"; and, of course, it figures heavily in the recent claims of sociobiologists. Clearly, arguments that link gender to some sort of natural source have been put to a variety of uses, each positing somewhat different links between apparently natural causes and their consequences in human society.

At the same time, however, all appeals to nature share certain assumptions. Biologically oriented explanations assume that differences are "really real." Not surprisingly, they tend to emphasize those presumably inborn traits (for example, lactation, ovulation, physical weakness, or propensities for nurturant care) that differentiate women from men, casting the average characteristics of two biologically opposed groups as cause for the things we presently believe that men and women are. Thus, if, overall, women "mother," this social fact reflects endowments in the average woman's genes; and if, overall, men engage in physical aggression more than women,

---

11. The reference goes ultimately to Friedrich Nietzsche, *The Use and Abuse of History* (New York: Liberal Arts Press, 1949), and, more immediately, to the recent polemic against sociobiology by Marshall Sahlins, *The Use and Abuse of Biology: An Anthropological Critique of Sociobiology* (Ann Arbor: University of Michigan Press, 1976). Both, of course, are relevant—although in different ways—to my discussion.

12. I am thinking here of a range of writers who have wanted to claim an immediate relationship between something like "control of reproduction" and "women's status." Such a correlation is implicit in Firestone, *Dialectic of Sex,* as it is in Adrienne Rich, *Of Woman Born: Motherhood as Experience and Institution* (New York: W. W. Norton, 1976); it is also central to Carl Degler's recent reinterpretation of the meanings of nineteenth-century American demography, *At Odds: Women and the Family in America from the Revolution to the Present* (Oxford: Oxford University Press, 1980).

this too reflects important facts about what all men, ultimately, are like.[13] Moreover, if male activities are celebrated more than female activities, such arguments suggest that this fact too reflects either the depth of individual male need or else the sheer superiority of men's biological endowments. Relationships, in such accounts, are contracts forged by individuals who are already fully formed. Natural differences are what make us unite, and from such instrumental unions grows society. The notion that most differences, where gender is concerned, are no more natural than the claim by Bushmen that women need male partners to light fires and shoot game[14] is something the biological determinists seem consistently to disregard.

What is it, then, that fuels this kind of argument? Although most of us would suspect appeals to biological fact in an attempt to understand phenomena like racism, elitism, or the privileges of social class, we readily forget the emperor's social clothes in talk of gender. We claim to know that social forms are not transparent products of individual desires, needs, or skills and argue at least minimally that social forms themselves determine much of our capacities and wants. But where gender is concerned, we find ourselves afraid to be skeptical of what appears brute natural truth. We rarely recognize that our need to give to nature its apparent due leads to a form of mechanistic, individualizing thought that stands immediately at odds with the most powerful approaches to inequality now available in social science. Of course, part of the problem is that the pervasive inclination to individualism and empiricism in our work means that all naturalizing claims will tend to have rhetorical appeal, a fact clearly illustrated by the contemporary success of sociobiology. What the feminist experience makes particularly clear, however, is that this rhetoric (like any other) promises much more than it can give. We fear complexity and diversity in our world, craving a "natural" moral

13. Alice Rossi, "A Biosocial Perspective on Parenting," *Daedalus* 106, no. 2 (1977), 1–31, has made one of the strongest statements of this point, although I think it is a feature generally associated with so-called sex difference research.

14. See Lorna Marshall, *The !Kung of Nyae Nyae* (Cambridge: Harvard University Press, 1976), for the Bushman reference. The point could be made equally well, however, for such bits of American folk ideology as the notion that women are good teachers because of "natural" nurturance or that men are good businessmen because of "natural" aggression.

law. Yet nature cannot bear the moral burden imposed on it: thus we think poorly and inconsistently about biology. Appeals to nature cannot justify, because they presuppose it, a moral stance, uniting "is" and "ought" or else confusing "being" of a physical sort with the identities and relationships forged within particular societies.

The point is not that our biology does not figure in the construction of our gendered lives but rather that descriptions of the physical self can never help us understand the things we want or the origins of desire in our relationships of conflict, trust, cooperation, and inequality. In other words, what the arguments surrounding gender reveal is that, for reasons we have yet to understand, there is a tendency in our social thought to feel distrustful of society and of sociological accounts and therefore to search for natural essences as often as we can in hopes of finding out the necessary and moral terms on which to base our social lives.

BIASED DICHOTOMIES

A second set of issues follows immediately from those discussed above. These issues emerge in the work of theorists who decline to think of gender in explicitly biological terms but try instead to argue that a grasp of men's and women's social place must be anchored in analyses of the functionally opposed domains in which they act. Thus, it is claimed (with more or less cogency, to be sure) that "woman" everywhere relates to "man" as reproduction to production, expressive to instrumental, domestic to jural-political, natural (maternal) to contingent (paternal) bonds, and family to society.[15] One characteris-

---

15. The gendered biases of jural-political/domestic are explicated in Yanagisako, "Family and Household," and Rosaldo, "Use and Abuse of Anthropology." For relatively ideological uses of related dichotomies, see Annette Kuhn and Ann Marie Wolpe, eds., *Feminism and Materialism* (London: Routledge & Kegan Paul, 1978), on production/reproduction; Talcott Parsons, *Social Structure and Personality* (New York: Free Press of Glencoe, 1964), on instrumental/expressive; Maurice Bloch, "The Long Term and Short Term: The Economic and Political Significance of the Morality of Kinship," in Goody, *Character of Kinship*, on interest/morality; Beverly L. Chinas, *The Isthmus Zapotecs: Women's Roles in Cultural Context* (New York: Holt, Rinehart & Winston, 1973), on formal/informal; and Barnes, "Genetrix:Genitor," on culture/nature.

tic of these pairs, of course, is that the first and, it usually emerges, implicitly feminine term appears more closely linked to nature than its mate, suggesting, for example, that mothering is apt to be more biologically constrained and less cross-culturally varying a role than fathering or "judging." Furthermore, it would appear at once across cultures and within any particular social group that the initial term will be less differentiated and far less institutionally complex than the more social term that follows. Not surprisingly, then, one finds a view of history embodied in these pairs wherein reading from left to right often supplies the guiding imagery of accounts of individual growth and of evolutionary progress. Nor, given my remarks above, is it surprising, since the nineteenth century, at least, that the second (instrumental, social, male) emerges either as the progressive or the competitive, morally suspect term, whereas the first tends to be linked to images of an altruism lacking interest or distrust, corresponding to notions that stress either unhealthy stasis or life-giving continuity and morality.[16]

Much as with the biological arguments discussed above, feminists have found a good deal that is attractive in these polarities. Because they speak at once about apparently biological (lactation, childbirth) and more clearly social (the seeming universality of, for example, the family and marriage) sorts of facts, such oppositions as, for instance, that between domestic and more public realms appear to offer a description that makes sense of social facts apparent in our world while giving equal weight to the activities and determinants of both men's and women's lives. Feminists concerned by the lack of female presence in conventional accounts have thus seen promise in the notion that one needs to explore how family and/or reproductive roles may interact with the activities described by persons interested in less gendered versions of political economy. In addition, all reminders of

16. My claim is that in nineteenth-century thought (and, less explicitly, in much social thought today) male and female were opposed in very similar terms, although with different valuations. Herbert Spencer, who was relatively optimistic about progress, feared female entry into the public world as something that would undermine progressive competition and the survival of the fittest, whereas John Ruskin hoped that women would be able to correct some of the excesses of modern capitalism by spreading their maternal influence, for example, through charity.

the place that biological reproduction must assume in any human social form have been particularly important for those analysts concerned with the discovery of first causes (we are constrained by child care or else oppressed by men who envy the capacities of our wombs) or mythic origins.

Unfortunately, however, domestic/public and similar analytic frames appear to replicate the difficulties they had sought to overcome.[17] Thinking of the home as women's and assuming women's place is naturally in the home, we fail to probe the possibility that our families are no more natural or universal than our religions or economies. We write of mothering and socialization in a single breath but rarely link these to the economics of the home or the pervasive familism of politics. Thus, an analysis in terms of opposed spheres—whatever its heuristic value or explanatory appeal—is suspect, first because it lets us think of women in terms less fully social than those we use to think of men and second because the opposites themselves derive from preconceptions that assume the nature and social implications of sex-linked endowments. We speak of spheres of women and of spheres of men as though such a separation were the product not of human action in a contradictory world but instead of (virtually) inevitable forms of natural logic.

The point is, ultimately, that a tendency to emphasize roles and contexts that oppose women and men leans heavily on the assumptions of a straightforward biological account. For dualists and biological determinists alike, significant social forms derive directly from a class of differentiating natural facts, with nature bound closely to the "feminine" pole, embracing family, trust, and mothers. Thus, dichotomous thinking tends to dull the analyst's eye to how our loves and interests interact. More disturbing still, it typically sustains a set of pieties about what our families—and our feminism—should be like, permitting use of questionable biofunctional accounts by persons who would universalize what is, in fact, a historically specific faith that families are the natural moral basis of human societies.

17. I have developed and criticized an essentially dichotomous account in a recent paper; see Michelle Rosaldo, "Woman, Culture, and Society: A Theoretical Overview," in Rosaldo and Lamphere, *Woman, Culture, and Society;* and Rosaldo, "Use and Abuse of Anthropology."

PSYCHOLOGY AND SOCIETY

The third area in which feminist arguments at once reflect and lead toward critiques of recent social thought again relates to the above, though here the issues have much less to do with recognition of the institutions in which women make important claims than do the conceptual categories appropriately evoked when we attempt to understand our sisters' lives. Is gender, in the broadest sense, a psychological fact? an ideological disguise? a name for roles, or statuses, or positions and relationships in production? More narrowly, feminists are concerned that neither Marxist nor conventional sociological accounts have properly addressed sex inequalities as social facts. Nor have these accounts theorized about the ways identities associated with such things as status, sex, and age must figure equally in subjective life and in the public ordering of society. Thus, feminists have suggested that we recognize sex-gender systems as complex psychocultural domains somewhat autonomous from such things as social organization and/or political economy.[18] And even though we learned from Weber about subjective features entering into economic realms, a theme emerging in much recent feminist work has been that understanding gender (more than, for example, understanding ethnicity or social class) requires a coupling of sociological accounts with depth psychology.

Unlike those theorists who claim a biological base for gendered roles or those who argue that female and male are necessarily defined by the opposition between domestic units and political society, the argument here has been that gender represents an aspect of identity in all social life. However, unlike the identities linked to the experience of ethnicity or class, gender figures early as an aspect of the developing infant self and so has deeper psychological roots than

18. See Gayle Rubin, "The Traffic in Women," in R. Reiter, ed., *Towards An Anthropology of Women* (New York: Monthly Review Press, 1975), for a classic statement of this position, and Nancy Chodorow, *The Reproduction of Mothering* (Berkeley and Los Angeles: University of California Press, 1978), and J. Mitchell, *Psychoanalysis and Feminism* (New York: Random House, 1974), for related arguments. Chodorow argues that the version of psychoanalytic theory that she uses is, explicitly and intentionally, sociological and sensitive to variants in configurations of social relations (in a way that might answer some of the reservations expressed here); but this "promise" is not developed in her text.

other categories of human action in adult society. Thus, it is claimed that attention to gender requires a renewed concern not for forgotten families or as yet uncovered facts about our genes but rather for subjective, often inarticulate aspects of identification, opposition, love, and fear, as these are shaped in early life and enter into an adult's experiences of the tension between unconscious impulse and conscious rule, between individual selfishness and social bond, and between desire and right.

Perhaps the most sophisticated transformation of the nature/ nurture opposition that pervades all feminist thought, recent appeals for psychological accounts still retain much of the rhetorical force and limitation of simpler theories that are based on biologically derived dichotomies. As noted earlier, questions of gender require attention to considerations many theorists have ignored—in this case, not the "hidden" facts of reproduction or the organization of the home but equally "hidden" issues linked to individual psychology. While rejecting sheer biology as the basis for a sociological account, theorists who emphasize subjective roots of gender roles tend toward a layered view wherein the unconscious psyche stands closer to the biological self than does the consciousness associated with society. In short, the psychological approach only partially transforms more mechanistic biological accounts because, while recognizing that gender is a feature of all social life, it argues for an explanation anchored largely in the *individual's* mind and body. Furthermore, a tendency to emphasize that gender (but not the motivations and styles associated, for example, with economic life and social class) is organized relatively early in the individual's life leads analysts to ignore the equally subjective bases of other social facts. Similarly, it makes it all too easy to forget that the determinants of gender roles go far beyond the infant's home, including contexts where adults make claims, explain their privileges to their peers, or argue about what is wrong and right.

Stated otherwise, much as with more biologically oriented accounts, talk of the psychological foundations of gendered roles attempts to link unconscious (and relatively presocial) drives to social rule while slighting questions of the public, relatively conscious, cultural forms in terms of which all human actors both interpret and attempt to shape the "outer" worlds and "inner" needs that they confront. No fact of nature in and of itself decides for human actors where that bit of nature leads; similarly, no aspect of unconscious life determines how in any given social form one's dispositions shape and are shaped by their social context. Society does not make our minds, nor does the unconscious make society. Rather, human beings, shaped by histories and relationships they only partially understand, interpret what they desire and see in terms provided by their social world and negotiated with the associates, friends, enemies, and kin with whom they share their lives.

The individual and society are thus joined in human consciousness throughout every human life, and gender probably figures constantly in the process. It is this fact that makes me wary of psychological accounts that see the gendered self take shape within familial cells that stand outside social wholes, without conceptualizing as well the ways that human beings, through their interactions, must forever reproduce and change the expectations that confer significance and direction to their projects. Thus, while it is obvious that gender is a central issue for developing infant selves and that it is bound up as well with the requirements of our reproductive physiology, we will never understand how gender operates in both our private lives and in society as a whole without examining the collectively forged symbolic terms that make gender both a resource and a constraint in conscious and political interactions among adults. That is, an understanding of the place of gender in unconscious realms will be inadequate until we come to understand how "male" and "female" work as cultural and social facts, whose significance for individuals cannot be analyzed apart from their significance in public life.

Feminists, of course, are not the only social thinkers presently attributing more centrality to conscious actors and their specific cultural milieu than they have previously enjoyed in social thought.[19] But by challenging the view that we are either victims of cruel social rule or the unconscious bearers of a set of natural traits that (most unfortunately) demeans us, feminists have highlighted our need for theories

19. See, for example, Anthony Giddens, *New Rules of Sociological Method* (London: Hutchinson, 1976), and Anthony Giddens, *Central Problems in Social Theory* (Berkeley and Los Angeles: University of California Press, 1979).

that attend to ways in which the actors shape their worlds, to interactions in which significance is conferred, and to the cultural and symbolic forms in terms of which expectations are organized, desires articulated, prizes conferred, and outcomes given meaning.

CONCLUSION

Analytical questions often have a practical source. Feminist scholarship—and more generally, the study of the sexes—has been motivated in large part by a desire to confront, refute, or otherwise rework the claim that gender is an individually anchored fact, the product not of social systems but of biology.[20] And yet our very interest in a "first," enduring, and essential cause reveals a lasting faith in biological accounts. Attempts to anchor gender in dynamics that are relatively independent of variety in social life all testify to the power of an assumption that takes gender as a natural fact shaped somehow outside of or prior to the historical ordering of particular societies.

Such contradictions are, of course, far from surprising. Were biologisms less compelling, they could not so have influenced our debates. Were our arguments more consistent and less ideologically constrained, we would not often find the claims of common sense, political impulse, and analytical regard so diversely ramified and so characteristically out of line. But nature does have a particular, morally potent sort of claim within our modern social world; it has the scientific status of permitting a reduction to the physically individuated self; and finally, it has the reasonableness of an insistence that however alienated our experience of social role, gender is one social fact associated not with an ideal self but with a concrete body. Surely,

20. Lest there be some confusion, my emphasis on the relatively asocial cast of much recent feminist thought—and its tendency to focus explanatory attention on the requirements and development of *individual* minds and bodies—is not intended as a rejection of all generalization in feminist social science. Generalities, like particulars, have their moral and analytical place; the issues ultimately concern the links between our general terms and the particulars illuminated by our categories. Given the present state of the art, I want to argue that what we need are general constructs that will help us grasp the particulars of gender systems as public, cultural, and political facts—of vital consequence for, but not determined by, individual biology or psychology.

no one can easily reject the hold of nature's claims. Yet there are particular and quite predictable ways in which they blind us.

The problem, in its most general form, is that the several oppositions here discussed—nature/nurture, stasis/change, domestic/ public, morality/competition, psychology/society—have a variety of longstanding ideological bonds, so that it is difficult to incorporate the insights they include without embracing as well some of the analytical difficulties they embody. All depend on more or less specified assumptions about sex. Therefore, although they may refer to different and nonisomorphic sets of facts, their gendered qualities tend to reproduce a relatively individualized and sexist picture of the working of our gender systems in human societies. None helps us think of power at the same time that we think of sex; none schools us in the contexts and relationships that connect women and men; none helps us understand the place of gender in the ways we think not just of sex but of such diverse things as youth and aging, competition, love and hate—in short, of almost every aspect of our social lives.

In other words, a set of prior understandings gave feminists a strategy and an object to attack. Yet these understandings have inhibited our grasp of just how tenuous our terms and oppositions are and of how adherence to the idioms of the past inhibits the development of a morally and intellectually satisfying feminist sociology. What gendered oppositions hide from view is the quite overwhelming fact that human beings live together in the world and that the seeming ease with which our roles and activities are differentiated and opposed reflects not natural law but human histories wherein our fellows have had cause at once to share and struggle, celebrate and cry.

Feminists are well aware, of course, that women are no more "natural" than men and, furthermore, that gender is no more natural than white racial dominance. We know that it is ludicrous to assume that women everywhere find their place within the home. We try, instead, to ask what forces limit female participation in political or economic realms and make it seem as though our separation from the world of men in this regard is born of natural logic. Finally, we know quite well that women's goals and needs are no more hidden and "psychological" than those of men who rule our governments and markets. In short, we recognize that gender is both a personal *and* a political fact, a feature not of individuals apart but of all interactions in human societies. But at the same time that our scholarly writings have revealed the limitations of a set of categories that political concerns have taught us to distrust, they have not yet created discourses that show consistently how we can begin to do without those categories or even radically to revise them. As critics, we feminists have remained, not surprisingly, the partial victims of the categories provided by our society.

My hope here has been less to challenge former work than to reflect on tensions within feminist thought that highlight the connections among ideology, moral impulse, intellectual difficulty, and intellectual promise. There is no question that we have both moral and analytical cause to undermine the individualism so prevalent in contemporary social thought. In doing so, we will in fact begin to think in less dichotomous terms, stressing ongoing action and interaction instead of static "natural" and "cultural" or "individual" and "collective" poles—and understanding meaning as something that happens in, as it yet underlies it, all interactive process. Furthermore, because issues of gender are so deeply intertwined with these enduring categories and dichotomies in our thought, I hope for new insight into our need both to exploit and to criticize the moral bases of our work within the ongoing quest for questions among feminist scholars.

DONALD A. SCHÖN

9

The Art of Managing
Reflection-in-Action within an Organizational Learning System

THE SPLIT IN THE FIELD
OF MANAGEMENT

The field of management has long been marked by a conflict between two competing views of professional knowledge. On the first view, the manager is a technician whose practice consists in applying to the everyday problems of his organization the principles and methods derived from management science. On the second, the manager is a craftsman, a practitioner of an art of managing that cannot be reduced to explicit rules and theories. The first view dates from the early decades of the twentieth century when the idea of professional management first came into good currency. The second has an even longer history, management having been understood as an art, a matter of skill and wisdom, long before it began to be understood as a body of techniques. But the first view has gained steadily in power.

The idea of management science, and the complementary idea of

From *The Reflective Practitioner: How Professionals Think in Action,* by Donald A. Schön. Copyright © 1983 by Basic Books, Inc., Publishers. Reprinted by permission of Basic Books, Inc.

the manager as a technician, has been carried by a social movement which has spread out from its center in the United States to encompass the whole of the industrialized world. The origins of this movement are difficult to identify, but a critically important milestone in its development was the work of Frederick Taylor who, in the 1920s, conceived of management as a form of human engineering based on a science of work.[1] While Taylor may not have invented these ideas, he was certainly the first to embody them in a practice of industrial management and consultation, and he popularized them in a way that has had enormous influence in industry, in business, and in the administration of public agencies.

Taylor treated work as a man/machine process which could be decomposed into measurable units of activity. Every industrial process, from the shovelling of coal to the processing of steel, could be subjected to experimental analysis. The design of tools, the bodily movements of the worker, and the sequencing of production steps, could be combined in an optimum configuration, a "one best way." Taylor saw the industrial manager as a designer of work, a controller and monitor of performance, and a distributor of rewards and punishments carefully selected and applied so as to yield optimally efficient production. Above all, he saw the manager as an on-line experimenter, a scientist in action, whose practice would consist in the trial and measurement of designs and methods aimed at the discovery and implementation of the one best way.

Taylor's views were by no means unique. Thorstein Veblen, to take one extraordinary example, also perceived that industry had taken on the characteristics of an organizational machine within which managers of the business enterprise must be increasingly concerned with standards, measures of performance, and the articulation of interlocking activities. But it was Taylor who embodied these ideas in practice, and it was Taylor's version of the practice of industrial engineering, efficiency expertise, and time and motion study which has evolved into the management science of the present day.

World War II gave an enormous impetus to the management science movement, first, because of the general rise in prestige of sci-

1. Frederick Taylor, *Principles of Scientific Management* (New York: Norton and Co., 1967, first published 1911).

ence and technology, and second, because of the birth of operations research and systems theory. These disciplines, which grew out of the use of applied mathematics to solve problems of submarine search and bomb tracking, were later exported to industry, commerce, and government. In the wake of World War II, management science grew to maturity. Teachers and researchers in the new schools of management, in partnership with managers in public and private sectors, have engendered a plethora of new techniques. There is no field of management which has been immune to the incursions of management science. What was once true only of industrial production has now become true of sales, personnel selection and training, budgeting and financial control, marketing, business policy, and strategic planning. Technical panaceas have appeared on the scene with clocklike regularity, old ones making way for new. Value analysis, management by objectives, planning programming and budgeting, and zero-based budgeting are only a few of the better-known examples. Even the human relations movement, which had originated as a reaction against Taylorism, has tended increasingly to present itself as a body of techniques.

Yet in spite of the increasingly powerful status of management science and technique, managers have remained persistently aware of important areas of practice which fall outside the bounds of technical rationality. This awareness has taken two forms.

Managers have become increasingly sensitive to the phenomena of uncertainty, change, and uniqueness. In the last twenty years, "decision under uncertainty" has become a term of art. It has become commonplace for managers to speak of the "turbulent" environments in which problems do not lend themselves to the techniques of benefit-cost analysis or to probabilistic reasoning. At least at the level of espoused theory, managers have become used to the instability of patterns of competition, economic context, consumer interests, sources of raw materials, attitudes of the labor force, and regulatory climate. And managers have become acutely aware that they are often confronted with unique situations to which they must respond under conditions of stress and limited time which leave no room for extended calculation or analysis. Here they tend to speak not of technique but of intuition.

Quite apart from these exceptions to the day-to-day routine of management practice, managers have remained aware of a dimension of ordinary professional work, crucially important to effective performance, which cannot be reduced to technique. Indeed, they are sometimes aware that even management technique rests on a foundation of nonrational, intuitive artistry.

Among theorists of management, the nonrational dimension of managing has had several notable exponents. In chapter 2, I have cited Chester Barnard's description of "nonlogical processes," Geoffrey Vickers's analysis of the art of judgment, and Michael Polanyi's reflections on tacit knowing. More recently, a Canadian professor of management, Henry Mintzberg, has caused a considerable stir with studies of the actual behavior of top managers that reveal a virtual absence of the methods that managers are "supposed to" use.[2] And in some of the most prestigious schools of management, where the curriculum depends on cases drawn from the actual experience of business firms, there is a widely held belief that managers learn to be effective not primarily through the study of theory and technique but through long and varied practice in the analysis of business problems, which builds up a generic, essentially unanalyzable capacity for problem solving.

It is no exaggeration, then, to say that the field of management is split into two camps, each of which holds a different view of the nature of professional knowledge. At the same time that management science and technique have grown increasingly in power and prestige, there has been a persistent and growing awareness of the importance of an art of managing which reveals itself both in crucially important situations of uncertainty, instability, and uniqueness, and in those dimensions of everyday practice which depend upon the spontaneous exercise of intuitive artistry. One sign of this split is that in some schools of management, representatives of the two tendencies—the professors of management science and the practitioners of case-method—no longer speak to one another. The representatives of each school of thought go about their business as though the other school of thought did not exist.

But a split of this kind, which is barely tolerable in a professional

2. Henry Mintzberg, *The Nature of Managerial Work* (New York: Harper and Row, 1973).

school, creates for thoughtful students and practitioners a particularly painful variant of the dilemma of "rigor or relevance." For if rigorous management means the application of management science and technique, then a "rigorous manager" must be selectively inattentive to the art which he brings to much of his day-to-day practice, and he must avoid situations—often the most important in organizational life—where he would find himself confronted with uncertainty, instability, or uniqueness.

But if the art of managing can be described, at least in part, and can be shown to be rigorous in a way peculiar to itself, then the dilemma of rigor or relevance need not be so painful. Indeed, it may be possible to bring the art of managing into dialogue with management science.

THE ART OF MANAGING

In management as in other fields, "art" has a two-fold meaning. It may mean intuitive judgment and skill, the feeling for phenomena and for action that I have called knowing-in-practice. But it may also designate a manager's reflection, in a context of action, on phenomena which he perceives as incongruent with his intuitive understandings.

Managers do reflect-in-action. Sometimes, when reflection is triggered by uncertainty, the manager says, in effect, "This is puzzling; how can I understand it?" Sometimes, when a sense of opportunity provokes reflection, the manager asks, "What can I make of this?" And sometimes, when a manager is surprised by the success of his own intuitive knowing, he asks himself, "What have I really been doing?"

Whatever the triggering condition, a manager's reflection-in-action is fundamentally similar to reflection-in-action in other professional fields. It consists in on-the-spot surfacing, criticizing, restructuring, and testing of intuitive understandings of experienced phenomena; often it takes the form of a reflective conversation with the situation. But a manager's reflection-in-action also has special features of its own. A manager's professional life is wholly concerned with an organization which is both the stage for his activity and the object of his inquiry. Hence, the phenomena on which he reflects-in-action are the phenomena of organizational life. Organizations, furthermore, are repositories of cumulatively built-up knowledge: principles and maxims of practice, images of mission and identity, facts about the task environment, techniques of operation, stories of past experience which serve as exemplars for future action. When a manager reflects-in-action, he draws on this stock of organizational knowledge, adapting it to some present instance. And he also functions as an agent of organizational learning, extending or restructuring, in his present inquiry, the stock of knowledge which will be available for future inquiry.

Finally, managers live in an organizational system which may promote or inhibit reflection-in-action. Organizational structures are more or less adaptable to new findings, more or less resistant to new tasks. The behavioral world of the organization, the characteristic pattern of interpersonal relations, is more or less open to reciprocal reflection-in-action—to the surfacing of negative information, the working out of conflicting views, and the public airing of organizational dilemmas. Insofar as organizational structure and behavioral world condition organizational inquiry, they make up what I will call the "learning system" of the organization. The scope and direction of a manager's reflection-in-action are strongly influenced, and may be severely limited, by the learning system of the organization in which he practices.

These distinctively organizational aspects of a manager's reflection-in-action must enter into any good description of the art of managing. In the examples that follow, I shall sample a range of organizational phenomena with which reflective managers concern themselves: the problem of interpreting the external environment's response to organizational action, the diagnosis of signs of trouble within an organization, the process by which an organization learns from its experience, and the effects of an organizational learning system on the way in which organizational problems are set and solved. I shall limit myself to the experience of business firms, not because business managers are more reflective than others but because they are the source of my freshest examples. In the business context, the kinds of organizational phenomena noted above may be illustrated by the behavior of a market, the problems of a production plant, the acquisition of knowledge about product development, and the learning system of a product development organization.

In all of these examples, I shall describe processes that managers often undertake but on which they seldom reflect. Managers do reflect-in-action, but they seldom reflect on their reflection-in-action. Hence this crucially important dimension of their art tends to remain private and inaccessible to others. Moreover, because awareness of one's intuitive thinking usually grows out of practice in articulating it to others, managers often have little access to their own reflection-in-action. The resulting mysteriousness of the art of managing has several harmful consequences. It tends to perpetuate the split in the field of management, creating a misleading impression that practitioners must choose between practice based on management science and an essentially mysterious artistry. And it prevents the manager from helping others in his organization to learn to do what he can do. Since he cannot describe his reflection-in-action, he cannot teach others to do it. If they acquire the capacity for it, they do so by contagion. Yet one of a manager's most important functions is the education of his subordinates.

For all of these reasons, it seems to me critically important to begin to describe how managers do reflect-in-action and how their reflection-in-action is limited.

Interpreting market phenomena. A business firm is continually in interaction with its markets, and markets are often in a state of flux—some of which is induced by the action of the business firm itself. In the contemporary business setting, inquiry into market phenomena has become a specialized function in its own right. Market researchers and strategists have developed principles of marketing, models of market behavior, and techniques of market exploration and analysis. Nevertheless, much of what managers encounter in the marketplace resists the application of ready-made theories and procedures.

Market research cannot say very much about consumer response to a radically new product. People cannot readily answer questions about their interest in something of which they have neither direct nor indirect experience. At best, if they are helped to carry out the imaginative feat of supposing themselves in possession of a nonexistent product, they may speculate on their future responses to it. But speculation of this sort is usually a very poor predictor of their behavior toward an actual product, more or less like the one described, which will appear one day, in a particular package and at a particular price, on supermarket shelves. If prototypes of the new product are produced (and it takes money to develop and produce them), then consumer panels may provide information from which managers can make inferences about actual market behavior. But the gap between panel response and market response is significant. Only with the introduction of large-scale market tests do manufacturers begin to get reliable information about market behavior, and regional market tests can also produce misleading results.

At each stage of the development of a radically new product, managers must make investment decisions in the absence of adequate information or rules for rational decision. Each such judgment is a unique case, and the market tests, which may reduce uncertainty, come only at the price of further investment.

The full-scale marketing of a product is also a test of sorts, and managers often find themselves confronted with surprising data that demand interpretation.

Shortly after World War II, to take one rather celebrated example, the 3M Corporation put on the market a clear cellulose acetate tape, coated on one side with pressure-sensitive adhesive, which they called Scotch Tape. They had intended it for use as a book-mending material, a way of preserving things that would otherwise have to be thrown away; hence the name Scotch. But in consumers' hands, the product came to be used in many different ways, most of which had nothing to do with mending books. It was used to wrap packages, to fasten pictures to the wall, to make labels, to decorate surfaces, even to curl hair. 3M's managers did not regard these surprising uses as a failure of their initial marketing plan, nor did they merely accept them as a happy accident. They *noticed* them and tried to make sense of them as a set of messages about potential markets. The company began to market types of Scotch Tape specially designed for use in such applications as packaging, decorating, and hair curling.

3M's marketing managers treated their product as a projective test for consumers. They reflected on unanticipated signals from the marketplace, interpreted them, and then tested their interpretations by adapting the product to the uses that consumers had already discovered. But their tests were also moves aimed at strengthening market position and probes which might yield additional surprises. Their marketing process was a reflective conversation with consumers.

Interpreting organizational troubles. When a manager first gets signals that something is going wrong in his organization, he usually has no clear, consensual account of the trouble. Various members of the organization, who occupy different positions and have different interests, tell different and often conflicting stories. If the manager is to take action, he must make some sense of the organizational *Rashomon;* but by inquiring into the situation, he also influences it. Hence he faces a two-fold problem: how to find out what (if anything) is wrong, and how to do so in a way that enhances rather than reduces his ability to fix what is wrong.

Consider a case drawn from the recent experience of a manufacturer of scientific instruments.

The company, based in a developing country, was founded some fifteen years ago by a nuclear physicist who, with a small group of former students and colleagues, built a very narrow product line into a $100 million dollar business. The company's main offices are in its home country, but it has sales and service facilities in thirteen foreign countries. It has captured about 15 percent of the market in its field.

The founder, now chairman of the board, attributes his success to two main principles: stay in close touch with the market, and deliver fast responses to changes in the field.

From these two principles, many organizational consequences have been made to follow. In order to get product improvements to the market quickly, the company often puts instruments in the field before all development problems have been resolved. They depend on highly skilled technical servicemen to complete the development task. In order to achieve fast response to market demand, customers' orders are frequently changed. About 30 percent of all manufacturing orders are subject to engineering changes. As a result, manufacturing has become a highly sophisticated job shop where speed and flexibility take precedence over efficiency, which depends on long production runs.

The company has deliberately refrained from establishing a fixed organizational structure. There are no organization charts. Roles are frequently overlapping and informal group problem solving is the norm. As the founder says, "This is no place for people who can't live with uncertainty."

Role flexibility is carried to an extreme. The present vice-president for finance is a former nuclear physicist who has learned finance as he might have learned a new branch of physics. And every member of the top-management team has filled virtually every major corporate function. The president of the company, G, who began with the company fifteen years ago, has worked in budgeting, finance, sales, and manufacturing. He is still regarded as "the best engineer in the company." Along with the founder and the vice-president for finance, he regards work as "fun," likes to put "impossible" demands on himself, and expects others to do likewise.

G is used to reaching down into the company to deal with whatever crisis presents itself. He has done this three or four times. Within the last year, for example, he spent three months at a computer console in order to resolve a critical software problem that threatened to stall a major new development.

The crisis presently facing G concerns a new production plant established a year ago to make metal parts for instruments manufactured in the two main production facilities. It is located in a development zone of the country, where it is eligible for generous government subsidies, although it lacks access to labor force and services which would have been available in one of the larger cities. The new manager of the plant, M, has been hired away from a large electronics firm. He has been in his position for a year, and during that time there have been increasingly troublesome production delays. Recently one of the managers of the two main instrument plants brought the problem to G, who discussed it with the manager of the other instrument plant, the vice-president for manufacturing, and the manager of the new plant, M.

The manager of the first plant describes the situation as follows:

> I want the parts on time and M wants efficiency! And I want 100 different kinds of parts. Opening the new plant caused a lot of crunches in our system. We worked night and day all last year to solve this problem. For a while, things were okay. Then, when the head of the metals section left because he couldn't get along with M, we had a big decline. M tried to manage the metals section by remote control. He should get in there and manage metals for himself. Or perhaps we should take the operation and bring it back to Central, in a metals shop of our own. M lacks the capacity to manage the problem. I see no light at the end of the tunnel.

Manager of the second plant:

> M's is a new plant built around new people. There are communications problems, because people there don't adapt to flexible demands. M is pressed between demands for efficiency and for fast response, and he's

not solving the problem. They need new staff functions. They have problems with orders because they don't know what's going on. They must see their raison d'etre as giving service to us, but they won't accept that definition. They are not equal. They feel second class.

M, manager of the new plant:

There's informal problem solving at Central, but between here and Central, it can't work. You have to have more rules, even with less flexibility, because as you grow, without new rules, you have a mess. G prefers that we use 50 percent of our capacity and hold people on standby to respond to orders when they come in, but that teaches people to be inefficient. And so I sell to outsiders, but I have to give preference to the company. It's an axiom that you should produce efficiently, but I have to be inefficient in order to get the parts in on time. Management attention is split.

Vice-president for manufacturing:

Right now, the new plant is G's crisis. First we must clean up the channels of communication, providing better, more sophisticated management tools. And we must resolve the conflict of priorities. Most of the problems grow out of the frequent engineering changes which are vital to the company. Two-thirds of the problem is to get the right man in the right place. One of our main problems is a shortage of upper-middle management.

The first plant manager, who brought the problem to G, says,

I know G is working on the problem, because he hasn't erased all the figures we put on the blackboard!

And he is right, G is working on the problem.

G has listened to the several stories about the production delays at M's plant, but he has chosen not to decide among them or even to try to put them all together to make a single coherent picture of the trouble. He has read the *Rashomon* as a sign of two main difficulties: a lack of effective communication among the several parties, and a split between the new plant and central operations. He has seen his problem as one of creating a process to deal with these two difficulties.

He has decided to treat the diagnosing of the problem as a central part of the resolution of the problem, and has assigned the task of diagnosis to those who are most centrally concerned. He has asked the vice-president for manufacturing, together with his staff of three, to spend two days a week at the new plant over the next three months.

They will work with their counterparts there to trace the sources of delays, to review and repair reporting systems, to fix whatever problems in operations they discover.

G has followed company traditions in turning the full force of management attention onto the crisis point. But this time he has not gone down to deal with the problem himself. He has seen his role as one of designing and putting in place a process to identify and fix the problem, leaving to others the task of working out their conflicting views of it. He has set up an organizational experiment, the essence of which is to bring into close interaction those who have been distant from one another.

M has reacted favorably to this move. He says, "For the first time, I think they are learning what it is really like here. New capacity won't solve our problem; it will barely let us keep up with growth. But as the atmosphere improves and we get a better handle on the problems, we'll gradually remove the delays. I'm optimistic."

And G says, "Perhaps as M comes to feel that people here understand his situation better, he will begin to feel more a part of the company, and then he may commit more fully to his frame of reference."

G has responded to the organizational crisis by designing a process which will involve the key participants in collective reflection-in-action.

Learning about product development. A large American consumer products firm has an extraordinary reputation as a developer of new products. Inside the firm, individual managers are very well aware of their corporate reputation, and attribute it to their success in learning about the process of conceiving, inventing, and commercializing new products.

What is remarkable about this firm is the consciousness that managers bring to this process, the sense they have of being members of a corporate culture which includes a great deal of knowledge about it, and the extent to which each manager sees himself both as a user of the store of corporate knowledge and a contributor to it. It is possible to dig down into the firm at least four layers deep without losing access to the corporate reservoir of knowledge about product development.

These are some examples of what product development managers believe they have learned.

1. "The target is a variable."

One of the heads of technology remarks, "Product development is a game you can win, so long as you keep it open—so long as you remember you can redefine the target." Typically, a product development project is worked out among representatives of marketing, technology, and general management. Once a target has been defined, general management commits the necessary resources. But as development proceeds, technical people learn more about the feasibility of the initial target and more about the properties of the materials with which they are working. They discover unexpected difficulties in achieving the target originally chosen, and they also discover technical possibilities they had not suspected at the outset. They can redefine targets to reflect these discoveries, so long as they also understand the marketing implications of their redefinition of the target.

Thus, in one project concerned with disposable paper products, the development director observes, "We found that the critical variable was not absorptive capacity but rate of absorption!" It was much more difficult to increase absorptive capacity than rate of absorption, but it was the latter that mattered most to the consumer. In the words of one researcher, "We knew we were on the right track when our panels no longer hated us!"

In order to treat the target as a variable, the development team must be able to see a technical property of materials in terms of its meaning to consumers, and they must be able to see a marketing target in terms of the technical demands that follow from it. Such a team cannot afford a "seesaw" between marketing and technology, in which marketing says to technology, "Make what we can sell!" or technology says to marketing, "Sell what we make!" Technical and marketing specialists must be able to share the uncertainty which they convert to risk by redefining the development target. And, like the marketing managers at 3M, they must be willing to give up the assumption that they *know* the target, once and for all, at the beginning of the development process. As they discover new properties in the phenomena and new meanings in the responses of consumer panels, they learn to restructure not only the means but the ends of development.

2. "The unit of development is not a new product but a game with the competition."

Members of the development team think of themselves as engaged in a game with the competition. For each major product line, there is a national market within which many companies struggle for position. Winning this game consists in establishing, maintaining, and extending market position at the expense of the competitors. Moves in the game consist in product improvements, advertising campaigns, and new product introductions. And for every move, competitors make counter moves. The game lasts for the duration of the life cycle of the product line.

Playing the game well means forming and implementing a development *strategy*. A given development (a paper product with a higher rate of absorption, for example) is likely to trigger competitive developments, and good strategy includes anticipation of the likely countermoves. The development team tries to have in the wings a set of long-term developments which they can activate in response to competitors' moves, when the time is right. Thus, the unit of development is not an individual product but a full cycle of the competitive game.

Within the game, however, there is always the question, "What is the situation now?" Depending on one's interpretation of the situation, construction of an appropriate strategy may vary significantly. In the case of the paper product described above, for example, there was a period in which the team believed that they had established the basic acceptability of their product and needed mainly to get the price down. But a competitor introduced a new product which came in at a higher price and achieved greater consumer acceptance than theirs. How should they interpret their situation in the game? A corporate vice-president made the suggestion, "Why don't you come up with a Cadillac?" This was surprising to the development team, because it ran counter to their strategy. They did not reject it out of hand, however. They waited to see what the market would do. Then, as they said, "When we discovered that our product was holding its own among the low-priced brands, we were freed to work on the Cadillac. Had we brought out a low-priced improvement, we would have cannibalized our own brand."

The new signals from the marketplace enabled the development team to construct a new picture of their situation, one which required them to revise their understanding of their position relative to other brands. And from the new description of the situation, they evolved a new strategy which they would test with the introduction of the "Cadillac" (a familiar metaphor which, like "cannibalizing," is a part of the repertoire they bring to their inquiry).

3. "The important thing is to keep the dialectic moving."

It is unusual to find the term "dialectic" in common usage within a corporate culture. But in this corporation, managers talk freely about dialectic, by which they mean the surfacing and working out of conflicting views among participants in the development process.

The vice-president of technology goes so far as to define his role in terms of the dialectic. He says, "I feel good when I see that engineering and development, advertising and manufacturing, are really surfacing and talking about their differences. It's my job to keep the dialectic alive."

And a general manager says, "You must keep the conflicts alive and on the surface. Once you have identified the conflicts, you see to it that *they* resolve them and that they let you know the results. If they agree ahead of time, too quickly, that can shield you from legitimate conflict. It breaks your heart when you see people have stopped talking about it."

The expectation is that "legitimate conflicts" will surface. The complexity of development situations is such that engineering and research, advertising and manufacturing, general management and finance, will have different and conflicting views of situation and strategy, all of which are important to the organization. A manager's task is to make sure that such conflicts are neither suppressed nor circumvented. Organizational learning about a present situation, and about product development more generally, depends on the "working out" of such conflicts. But no one can say ahead of time *how* they will be worked out, which will depend on the reciprocal reflection-in-action of the parties to the conflict.

LIMITS OF THE ORGANIZATIONAL LEARNING SYSTEM

The very same company that is so conscious of organizational learning about product development also provides a very good example of the ways in which an organizational learning system may constrain reflection-in-action.

As a consultant to this organization, I was asked to address the problem of the "burnout" of product development directors. These individuals, who work at the intersection of general management, advertising, and research, are hard to find, expensive to develop, and difficult to keep. They experience an unusually high incidence of alcoholism, health problems, divorce, and mental breakdown, and the vice-president for technology wanted to know why.

We agreed that my study would take the form of an analysis of a case of product development—Product X, as I will call it, a product for use in household appliances. The story of Product X was already famous in the company when I began my study. Nearly everyone described it in the same way: "A case in which we nearly failed because of problems we ought to have anticipated and dealt with better than we did. But we came through and bailed ourselves out."

Initially, there were three questions about the case:

- Why were we so late in detecting and admitting the problems?
- Why were we so unwilling to ask for help and to accept help once it was offered?
- How did we bail ourselves out?

The product had originated in a brainstorming session where development specialists had asked themselves, "What benefits can we deliver through products designed for use in household appliances?" When they had arrived at a basic product definition, they began to explore the technologies they would need, and they hit on a particular technology, owned by a private inventor, which they could turn to their purposes.

Their development process proceeded, as usual in this company, through a series of tests. They tested the product's effectiveness in delivering its intended benefit, and they tested it for possible harmful side effects. The testing process began in the laboratory where, for example, standard corrosion tests were performed by immersing steel plates in a bath made up of the product's components. And the process continued through blind tests with consumer panels (a standard element in all of their development processes), and finally to regional test markets. It is important to note that a successful passage through such a sequence of standard tests functioned, in this company, as an essential part of the dialogue between technical development specialists and general managers. The general managers, who controlled the commitment of resources, depended on the results of standard tests to make their decisions.

The product performed very well in panel tests, and was placed in its first regional test market. Two months into the test market, however, an appliance company which had been asked to test the product sent back word, "This product can get stuck in the machine, and if it does, you can get overheating. There is a risk of fire." Members of the development team at first said, "We don't think so." But the appliance company wrote a formal, threatening letter to general management: "If you market this product, we'll put stickers on our machines telling people not to use it."

With this exposure of the problem, everyone started to talk about it. General management, who had known nothing of the problem, were furious. Three different task groups were set up and they arrived at two different solutions. Both of these were subsequently accepted and incorporated in a new version of the product. But this created a new problem. What should be done with the existing test market? The old product had been successful in consumer panel blind tests, and general management said, "We'll keep the old test market going. It's the original product we invested in. It passed our tests." The technical group nearly mutinied. But general management took the position, "We can assume a liability if we want to; your job is to tell us the odds."

The sense of general management's position was, "The product is a black box. We make decisions about things that pass our tests. But we don't take the cover off the box because we get confused." And the sense of the technical group's position was, "We make decisions about particulars, not general probabilities. We understand what it is that makes a product pass tests. And we don't always trust the tests!"

A year later, the first test market was dropped and a new one, based on the revised product, was instituted. But technical people felt that the issue had "put them into short pants."

At this point, the development was some two years old, with $30 million invested.

A second major embarrassment occurred in the midst of the second test market. The product had been doing well, when a sprinkling of complaints came in from the field to the effect that the product caused rust in appliances. These complaints came in after the "sticking" problem, and after the laboratory immersion tests which had revealed no rusting. The technical team chose to ignore the complaints. The rusting detected by a few users of the product must have been produced by other causes.

Members of the corporate research laboratory who heard about the problem took a different view. One member of the research group lathered some of the product's ingredients on a tin can and left it overnight; in the morning the can had rusted. The researchers took the can to the vice-president for technology, who said, "There's no red light. Don't worry about it. We can handle it." But as letters from the field multiplied, the laboratory team became convinced that the rusting effect was real. They developed a model that would explain the rusting process, used X-ray spectroscopy to test the model, and brought in high-powered consultants from a university. The product development team reacted by asking, "Are you really sure of this? Why are you doing this to us? Why don't you do something constructive?"

The laboratory group was disillusioned. The head of the laboratory sent out a memo which forbade researchers to do more work on Product X. At this point, however, the vice-president for technology fired the head of the development team and appointed a researcher from the laboratory to become the new head. This man quickly satisfied himself, with the help of his former colleagues in the laboratory, that the rusting effect was real. This produced a new crisis.

The vice-president for technology then held a meeting with members of the two teams. At this meeting he said, "Are you guys men enough to keep this problem from general management and go ahead on faith, without knowing that you can really do it, to make an alternative work?" This set in motion a new process which led, eventually, to solution of the rusting problem. The laboratory group, who had been told not to work on the problem, continued to do so. They came up with a new ingredient which they believed not only solved the rusting problem but actually protected machines. The product development team criticized them for "shooting from the hip" and "overstepping their bounds." But the new head of the laboratory team proposed a technical-political compromise: the new ingredient was to be combined with 10 percent of the old. New tests showed that the rusting effect had been overcome and the product worked as well as ever. As one member of the laboratory group said, "It was all played out under the tent, for fear of tipping off general management and breaking their commitment to the product. But at each replay of the problem there was the same issue: Did the new element really work? What about negative side effects? It was a guerrilla war, and we used science as a weapon."

The interactions between product development team and research laboratory can be represented as a cycle of action and reaction, roughly as follows.

The product development team sought to protect themselves, to control the task and territory, and to win credit for their work and credibility with general management. To these ends, they

- resisted the problems pointed out by the laboratory,
- discredited laboratory findings,
- kept them in their place by confining them to narrow and unimportant problems,
- kept their own work quiet.

The laboratory team became angry and frustrated, distrusted the product development team, and felt a low sense of their own worth. They retaliated by

- taking an aggressive stance as they proved their points,
- seeking to win through science,
- continuing to work on the problem even when the boss told them not to,
- trying to capture the task,
- circumventing product development to get to management.

These strategies made the product development team angry, frustrated, fearful, and distrustful, and reinforced them in their efforts to win and protect themselves.

The consequences of the cycle were wasted effort, duplicated work, and delay in the recognition of problems. The product development team could not, under these circumstances, ask for help nor use it when it was offered. As the cycle amplified, researchers and developers were less and less able to work together. But management injected stopgap solutions. They shifted people around and they intervened directly at moments of crisis.

The pattern was one of "heroism under a tent." To quote some of the observations of the participants, "Three people told me not to work on Product X, but I wouldn't stop," "Don't tell management what you're doing," "Fix the problem first, then tell them about it."

What accounts for such a pattern? In order to answer this question, we must turn to the larger context in which the research/development cycle arose. For researchers and developers were involved in a more comprehensive process which I shall call "the product development game." The game has mainly to do with four variables: corporate commitment, credibility, confidence, and competence.

In order to set a new product in motion, general management must commit the necessary resources. But management commitment is deliberately made hard to win. This is partly a matter of thoroughness. As one of the managers said, "We're a very thorough company; we do our research well, and we don't accept just anything." But management commitment is also hard to win because managers tend to distrust research and development. As one manager said, "They are likely to flimflam and fool us if we're not careful." On the other hand, managers are aware of their dependence on research and development. They know that corporate growth depends on it.

Thus managers must commit to a process which they distrust. They respond by making the commitment of resources hard to win; and once resources are committed, they hold the product development director wholly accountable for performance, loading him with the full burden of uncertainty. And the maintenance of corporate commitment becomes touchier as investment in the product increases and the company becomes more exposed.

Under these circumstances, product development people try to win the game by gaining and retaining management commitment, while maintaining their own credibility within the company.

A participant's credibility behaves like a stock on the stock market, going up or down with the perception of his success or failure. There is a corporate market for credibility. Each person strives to maintain his credibility at all costs, because a loss of credibility can make it impossible for him to perform. As the former head of the product development team reported, "When the problems hit the fan, my credibility was shot and I was dead in the company."

Confidence and competence are closely tied together. An individual has a "confidence tank" whose level rises or falls, depending on his perception of his status in the company.

Credibility, commitment, confidence, and competence are interdependent, in this sense:

"The more credibility I have, the more confident I can be."

"The more confident I am, the more confident I appear."

"The more confident I appear, the more I am seen as credible and competent."

Conversely,

"If I lose credibility, I may lose confidence,"

"If I lose confidence, I appear to be incompetent and I lose more credibility."

As a result, the company is full of very confident-seeming people. It is seen as necessary to appear to be confident, no matter what the problems are, in order to maintain credibility. Indeed, old hands in technology management advise younger ones along the following lines:

> "Tell management enough of what you're doing to capture commitment, but not enough to make them uneasy. Commit yourself to do the things that are necessary, even if you're not sure you can do them. And do the work you see to be necessary, even if your boss says no."

Thus heroism and secrecy (mastery and mystery) are essential elements of the strategy for winning the product development game.

The game yields a double bind, even for winners. It puts the players into a situation in which they lose, eventually, whatever the consequences. A participant says to himself,

> "I must commit to what I'm not sure I can do, in order to secure corporate commitment. To this end, I lay my credibility on the line, without which I cannot function. So I must be heroic and secretive. If I fail, I lose big. But unless I play, I cannot win."

But old-time managers say,

> "If you're up, you can stay up, and it's a winnable game, because there's plenty of resource and time and room for the redefinition of targets, if you have the competence and the confidence. But you must keep it up."

So product-development is a high-wire act in which you eventually fall. Moreover, you don't whine or complain, because you would be seen to lack confidence. The effect is to put product development directors, those who occupy the pivotal position between general managers and the laboratory, under a great deal of strain. They strive to protect their own credibility, keeping problems "under a tent," with the result that in midstream, problems tend to be ignored. In order to retain corporate commitment, the product is changed as little as possible. Once a problem has been exposed, however, they "climb all over it." And they strive to retain ownership of the task, which makes them treat offers of help as though they were threats to security.

In the light of this product development game, most of the questions with which the case study began can be given plausible answers. It is clear why problems encountered in midstream tend to be ignored until they are unavoidable, and it is also clear why, upon unavoidable exposure, they are "oversolved." It is clear how the corporation bails itself out of its crises, through stopgap "patching" solutions which resolve the crisis at hand without affecting the underlying processes that produce crises. It is also clear how product development directors are placed under extraordinary stress, which might well cause them to "burn out."

Considered more broadly as an organizational learning system, the product development game determines the directions and the limits of reflection-in-action. When crises present themselves, managers subject them to inquiry—often with successful results—but they do not reflect publicly on the processes which lead to such crises, for this would surface the games of deception by which product development deals with general management. While these games are open secrets within the organization, they are not publicly discussable.

Managers reflect on the strategies by which product development can be made into a winnable game. But neither general managers nor product development directors reflect on the Model I theories-in-use which create the conditions for the game. All participants try to achieve their objectives as they see them: general managers, to keep the burden of uncertainty on the shoulders of product development; product development directors, to retain corporate commitment while maintaining their own credibility. Each participant tries to protect himself unilaterally from being tagged with failure and from the resulting loss of credibility. Each seeks to gain unilateral control over the situation, to win and avoid losing in a situation he perceives as irretrievably win/lose. And each one withholds negative information from the other, as long as he believes it is a winning strategy to do so. Participants may be aware of these strategies, particularly as they are evinced by other players in the game, but they do not subject them to public reflection-in-action. To do so would be to make oneself vulnerable in an intensely win/lose world and, in the context of the product development game, might look like a failure of confidence.

This is not to say, however, that members of the organization are not able to recognize the game when it is described for them. When the results of the study of Product X were presented to those who had been involved in the story, there was a generally favorable reaction. Although most participants had never put the whole picture together for themselves, they recognized its validity. Some were highly amused. They seemed to feel that the study elaborated the open secret with which they were all familiar. But with very few exceptions, they did not believe that the system was susceptible to change. The risks seemed too great, the stakes too high, and the chances of success too low.

THE ART OF MANAGING AND ITS LIMITS

Returning now to the questions with which we began this chapter, let us consider the lessons that may be drawn from the several examples of managerial practice which have occupied our attention.

It is clear that managers do sometimes reflect-in-action. Beginning with questions like, What do consumers really see in our product? What's really going on underneath the signs of trouble in our organization? or What can we learn from our encounters with the competition? managers sometimes try to make sense of the unique phenomena before them. They surface and question their intuitive understandings; and in order to test their new interpretations, they undertake on-the-spot experiments. Not infrequently, their experiments yield surprising results that cause them to reformulate their questions. They engage in reflective conversations with their situation.

The reflection-in-action of managers is distinctive, in that they operate in an organizational context and deal with organizational phenomena. They draw on repertoires of cumulatively developed organizational knowledge, which they transform in the context of some unique situation. And as they function as agents of organizational learning, they contribute to the store of organizational knowledge. G's inquiry into production delays becomes a corporate exemplar for diagnosis of the troubles of the internal environment. In the consumer products firm, managers build up a corporate repertoire of cases, maxims, and methods which becomes accessible to new generations of managers.

But managers function as agents of organizational learning within an organizational learning system, within a system of games and norms which both guide and limit the directions of organizational inquiry. The case of Product X reveals a learning system that creates a pattern of corporate crises and at the same time prohibits public reflection-in-action on their causes.

As a consequence, the organizational learning system becomes immune to reflection-in-action. It is not publicly discussable; and because managers do not discuss it, they are often unable to describe it—although they may recognize the descriptions constructed by an outsider to the organization. Public discussion of the product development game would reveal the strategies by which general managers distance themselves from the uncertainties inherent in product development and the complementary strategies by which technical personnel protect themselves against the loss of corporate commitment. To reveal these strategies publicly, in an actual present instance where some action might be taken, would violate the norms of the product development game and would carry a perceived risk of vulnerability and loss of control.

Thus organizational learning systems, of the sort revealed by the case of Product X, become diseases that prevent their own cure. Managers could not extend the scope of reflection-in-action to their own learning systems without transforming the theories of action which they bring to their lives within the organization. And these, under the normal conditions of corporate life, are also immune to reflection-in-action.

We might begin to heal the split in the field of management if we were to recognize that the art of management includes something like science in action. When practicing managers display artistry, they reveal their capacity to construct models of unique and changing situations, to design and execute on-the-spot experiments. They also reveal a capacity to reflect on the meanings of situations and the goals of action. A more comprehensive, useful, and reflective management science could be built by extending and elaborating on what skillful managers actually do. Practitioners might then become not only the users but the developers of management science.

But extending and elaborating on artistry means reflecting on artistry and its limits, that is, on the ways in which managers do reflect-in-action and on the theories-in-use and organizational learning systems that constrain them.

HUBERT L. DREYFUS
STUART E. DREYFUS

10

From Socrates to Expert Systems

The Limits of Calculative Rationality

For the past quarter of a century researchers in artificial intelligence
(AI) have been trying without success to write programs which will
enable computers to exhibit general intelligence like Hal in *2001*.
Now out of this work has recently emerged a new field called knowledge engineering, that, by limiting its goals, has applied this research
in ways that actually work in the real world. The result is the so-
called "expert system," which has been the subject of recent cover
stories in *Business Week* and *Newsweek,* and Edward Feigenbaum's
book, *The Fifth Generation: Artificial Intelligence and Japan's Computer
Challenge to the World.*[1]

The occasion for this new interest in machine intelligence is no
specific new accomplishment, but rather a much publicized competition with Japan to build a new generation of computers with built-in
expertise. This is the so-called "fifth generation." (The first four generations were computers whose components were vacuum tubes,
transistors, chips, and large-scale integrated chips.)

According to a *Newsweek* headline, "Japan and the United States

From "From Socrates to Expert Systems: The Limits of Calculative Rationality,"
in *Philosophy and Technology II,* edited by C. Mitcham and Alois Huning, pp. 111–30.
Copyright © 1986 by D. Reidel Publishing Company, Dordrecht, Holland.
1. Edward Feigenbaum and Pamela McCorduck, *The Fifth Generation: Artificial Intelligence and Japan's Computer Challenge* (Reading, Mass.: Addison-Wesley, 1983).

are rushing to produce a new generation of machines that can very nearly think." Feigenbaum, one of the original developers of expert systems, who stands to profit greatly from this competition, spells out the goal.

> In the kind of intelligent system envisioned by the designers of the Fifth Generation, speed and processing power will be increased dramatically, but more important, the machines will have reasoning power: they will automatically engineer vast amounts of knowledge to serve whatever purpose humans propose, from medical diagnosis to product design, from management decisions to education.[2]

HEURISTIC KNOWLEDGE

What the knowledge engineers claim to have discovered is that in areas which are cut off from everyday common sense and social intercourse, all a machine needs in order to behave like an expert are some general rules and lots of very specific knowledge. As Feigenbaum puts it:

> The first group of artificial intelligence researchers . . . was persuaded that certain great, underlying principles characterized all intelligent behavior . . .
> In part, they were correct . . . [Such strategies] include searching for a solution (and using "rules of good guessing" to cut down on the search space); generating and testing (does this work? no; try something else); reasoning backward from a desired goal, and the like.
> These strategies are necessary, but not sufficient, for intelligent behavior. The other ingredient is knowledge—specialized knowledge, and lots of it . . . No matter how natively bright you are, you cannot be a credible medical diagnostician without a great deal of specific knowledge about diseases, their manifestations, and the human body.[3]

This specialized knowledge is of two types:

> The first type is the *facts* of the domain—the widely shared knowledge . . . that is written in textbooks and journals of the field, or that forms the basis of a professor's lectures in a classroom. Equally important to the practice of the field is the second type of knowledge called *heuristic knowl-*

2. Ibid., 56.
3. Ibid., 38.

edge, which is the knowledge of good practice and good judgment in a field. It is experiential knowledge, the "art of good guessing," that a human expert acquires over years of work.[4]

Using all three kinds of knowledge, Feigenbaum developed a program called DENDRAL, which is an expert in the isolated domain of spectrograph analysis. It takes the data generated by a mass spectrograph, and deduces from this data the molecular structure of the compound being analyzed. Another program, MYCIN, takes the results of blood tests, such as the number of red cells, white cells, sugar in the blood, etc., and comes up with a diagnosis of which blood disease is responsible for this condition. It even gives an estimate of the reliability of its own diagnosis. In their narrow areas, such programs are almost as good as the experts.

PROGRAMMED EXPERTISE

And is not this success just what one would expect? If one agrees with Feigenbaum that: "almost all the thinking that professionals do is done by reasoning . . . ,"[5] we can see that once computers are used for reasoning and not just computation, they should be as good or better than we are at following rules for deducing conclusions from a host of facts. So we would expect that if the rules which an expert has acquired from years of experience could be extracted and programmed, the resulting program would exhibit expertise. Again Feigenbaum puts the point very clearly:

> [T]he matters that set experts apart from beginners are symbolic, inferential and rooted in experiential knowledge. Human experts have acquired their expertise not only from explicit knowledge found in text books and lectures, but also from experience by doing things again and again, failing, succeeding . . . getting a feel for a problem, learning when to go by the book and when to break the rules. They therefore build up a repertory of working rules of thumb, or "heuristics," that, combined with book knowledge, make them expert practitioners.[6]

4. Ibid., 76–77.
5. Ibid., 18.
6. Ibid., 64.

Since each expert already has a repertory of rules in his mind, all the expert system builder need do is get the rules out and program them into a computer.

This view is not new. In fact, it goes back to the beginning of Western culture, when the first philosopher, Socrates, stalked around Athens looking for experts in order to draw out and test their rules. In one of his earliest dialogues, the *Euthyphro,* Plato tells us of such an encounter between Socrates and Euthyphro, a religious prophet and so an expert on pious behavior. Socrates asks Euthyphro to tell him how to recognize piety: "I want to know what is characteristic of piety . . . to use as a standard whereby to judge your actions and those of other men." But, instead of revealing his piety-recognizing heuristic, Euthyphro does just what every expert does when cornered by Socrates. He gives him examples from his field of expertise; in this case, situations in the past in which men and gods have done things which everyone considers pious. Socrates persists throughout the dialogue in demanding that Euthyphro tell him his rules, but, although Euthyphro claims he knows how to tell pious acts from impious ones, he will not state the rules which generate his judgments.

FORGOTTEN RULES

Plato admired Socrates and sympathized with his problem. So he developed an account of what caused the difficulty. Experts once had known the rules they use, Plato said, but they had forgotten them. The role of the philosopher was to help people remember the principles on which they act. Knowledge engineers would now say that the rules the experts use have been put in a part of their mental computers where they work automatically. "When we learned how to tie our shoes, we had to think very hard about the steps involved. . . . Now that we've tied many shoes over our lifetime, that knowledge is 'compiled,' to use the computing term for it; it no longer needs our conscious attention."[7] On this Platonic view the rules are there, functioning in the expert's mind, whether he is conscious of them or not. How else could we account for the fact that he can perform the task?

7. Ibid., 55.

Now 2000 years later, thanks to Feigenbaum and his colleagues, there is a new name for what Socrates and Plato were doing: "We are able to be more precise . . . and with this increased precision has come a new term, *knowledge acquisition research.*"[8] But, although philosophers and even the man in the street have become convinced that expertise consists in applying sophisticated heuristics to masses of facts, there are few available rules. As Feigenbaum explains: "An expert's knowledge is often ill-specified or incomplete because the expert himself doesn't always know exactly what it is he knows about his domain."[9] So the knowledge engineer has to help him recollect what he once knew.

> [An expert's] knowledge is currently acquired in a very painstaking way; individual computer scientists work with individual experts to explicate the expert's heuristics—to mine those jewels of knowledge out of their heads one by one . . . the problem of knowledge acquisition is the critical bottleneck in artificial intelligence.[10]

When Feigenbaum suggests to an expert the rules the expert seems to be using, he gets a Euthyphro-like response. "That's true, but if you see enough patients/rocks/chip designs/instrument readings, you see that it isn't true after all,"[11] and Feigenbaum comments with Socratic annoyance: "At this point, knowledge threatens to become ten thousand special cases."[12]

THE CHECKERS CHAMPION MYTH

There are also other hints of trouble. Ever since the inception of artificial intelligence, researchers have been trying to produce artificial experts by programming the computer to follow the rules used by masters in various domains. Yet, although computers are faster and more accurate than people in applying rules, master-level performance has remained out of reach. Arthur Samuel's work is typical.

8. Ibid., 79.
9. Ibid., 85.
10. Ibid., 79–80.
11. Ibid., 82.
12. Ibid.

In 1947 when electronic computers were just being developed, Samuel, then at IBM, decided to write a checker-playing program. Samuel did not try to make a machine play checkers by brute force calculation of all the chains of moves clear to the end. He calculated that, if you tried to look to the end of the game with the fastest computer you could possibly build, subject to the speed of light, it would take ten followed by 21 zeros centuries to make the first move. So he tried to elicit heuristic rules from checkers masters, and program a computer to follow these rules. When the rules the experts came up with did not produce master play, Samuel became the first and almost only AI researcher to make a learning program. He programmed a computer to vary the weights used in the rules, such as the trade-off between center control and loss of a piece, and to retain the weights that worked best. After playing a great many games with itself, the computer could beat Samuel, which shows that in some sense computers can do more than they are programmed to do. But the program still could not beat the sort of experts whose heuristic rules were the heart of the program.

The checkers program is not only the first and one of the best experts ever built, but it is also a perfect example of the way fact turns into fiction in AI. The checkers program once beat a state checkers champion. From then on, AI literature cites the checkers program as a noteworthy success. One often reads that it plays at such a high level that only the world champion can beat it. Feigenbaum, for example, reports that "by 1961 [Samuel's program] played championship checkers, and it learned and improved with each game."[13] Even the usually reliable *The Handbook of Artificial Intelligence* states as a fact that "today's programs play championship-level checkers."[14]

In fact, Samuel said in a recent interview at Stanford University, where he is a retired professor, that the program did once defeat a state champion, but the champion "turned around and defeated the program in six mail games." According to Samuel, after thirty-five years of effort, "the program is quite capable of beating any amateur

13. Ibid., 179.
14. Avron Barr and Edward A. Feigenbaum, *The Handbook of Artificial Intelligence,* vol. 1 (Los Altos, Calif.: William Kaufmann, 1981), 7.

player and can give better players a good contest." It is clearly no champion. Samuel is still bringing in expert players for help but he "fears he may be reaching the point of diminishing returns." This does not lead him to question the view that the masters the program cannot beat are using heuristic rules; rather, like Socrates and Feigenbaum, Samuel thinks that the experts are poor at recollecting their compiled heuristics: "the experts do not know enough about the mental processes involved in playing the game."[15]

The same story is repeated in every area of expertise, even in areas unlike checkers where expertise requires the storage of large numbers of facts, which should give an advantage to the computer. In each area where there are experts with years of experience the computer can do better than the beginner, and can even exhibit useful competence, but it cannot rival the very experts whose facts and supposed heuristics it is processing with incredible speed and unerring accuracy.

WHAT A SKILL IS

In the face of this impasse, it is necessary, in spite of the authority and influence of Plato and two thousand years of philosophy, to take a fresh look at what a skill is, and what an expert acquires when he achieves expertise. One must be prepared to abandon the traditional view that a beginner starts with specific cases and, as he becomes more proficient, abstracts and interiorizes more and more sophisticated rules. It might turn out that skill acquisition moves in just the opposite direction: from abstract rules to particular cases. Since everyone has many areas in which he is an expert, the necessary data is available, so let us look at how adults learn new skills.

Stage 1: Novice

Normally, the instruction process begins with the instructor decomposing the task environment into context-free features which the be-

---

15. These quotations are taken from an interview with Arthur Samuel, released by the Stanford University News Office, April 28, 1983.

ginner can recognize without benefit of experience. The beginner is then given rules for determining actions on the basis of these features, like a computer following a program. The beginning student wants to do a good job, but lacking any coherent sense of the overall task, he judges his performance mainly by how well he follows his learned rules. After he has acquired more than just a few rules, so much concentration is required that his capacity to talk or listen to advice is severely limited.

For purposes of illustration, two variations will be considered: a bodily or motor skill, and an intellectual skill. The reader wishing to see real-life examples of the process to be outlined should consult Patricia Benner's *From Novice to Expert: Excellence and Power in Clinical Nursing Practice.*[16] The student automobile driver learns to recognize such interpretation-free features as speed (indicated by his speedometer) and distance (as estimated by a previously acquired skill). Safe following distances are defined in terms of speed; conditions that allow safe entry into traffic are defined in terms of speed and distance of oncoming traffic; timing of shifts of gear is specified in terms of speed, etc. These rules ignore context. They do not refer to traffic density or anticipated stops.

The novice chess player learns a numerical value for each type of piece, regardless of its position, and the rule: "always exchange if the total value of the pieces captured exceeds the value of pieces lost." He also learns that, when no advantageous exchanges can be found, center control should be sought, and he is given a rule defining center squares and one for calculating extent of control. Most beginners are notoriously slow players, as they attempt to remember all these rules and their priorities.

Stage 2: Advanced Beginner

As the novice gains experience actually coping with real situations, he begins to note—or an instructor points out—perspicuous examples of meaningful additional components of the situation. After seeing a sufficient number of examples, the student learns to recognize them. Instructional maxims now can refer to these new *situa-*

16. Patricia Benner, *From Novice to Expert: Excellence and Power in Clinical Nursing Practice* (Reading, Mass.: Addison-Wesley, 1984).

tional aspects recognized on the basis of experience, as well as to the objectively defined *nonsituational features* recognizable by the novice. The advanced beginner confronts his environment, seeks out features and aspects, and determines his actions by applying rules. He shares the novice's minimal concern with quality of performance, instead focusing on quality of rule following. The advanced beginner's performance, while improved, remains slow, uncoordinated, and laborious.

The advanced beginner driver uses (situational) engine sounds as well as (nonsituational) speed in his gear-shifting rules, and observes demeanor as well as position and velocity to anticipate behavior of pedestrians or other drivers. He learns to distinguish the behavior of the distracted or drunken driver from that of the impatient but alert one. No number of words can serve the function of a few choice examples in learning this distinction. Engine sounds cannot adequately be captured by words, and no list of objective facts about a particular pedestrian enables one to predict his behavior in a crosswalk as well as can the driver who has observed many pedestrians crossing streets under a variety of conditions. Already at this level one leaves features and rules and turns to learning by prototype, now being explored by researchers such as Eleanor Rosch at Berkeley and Susan Block at MIT.

With experience, the chess beginner learns to recognize overextended positions and how to avoid them. Similarly he begins to recognize such situational aspects as a weakened king's side or a strong pawn structure, despite the lack of precise and universally valid definitional rules.

Stage 3: Competence

With increasing experience, the number of features and aspects to be taken account of becomes overwhelming. To cope with this information explosion, the performer learns, or is taught, to adopt a hierarchical view of decision-making. By first choosing a plan, goal or perspective which organizes the situation and by then examining only the small set of features and aspects that he has learned are the most important, given that plan, the performer can simplify and improve his performance.

Choosing a plan, a goal or perspective is no simple matter for the competent performer. It is not an objective procedure, like the feature recognition of the novice. Nor is the choice avoidable. While the advanced beginner can get along without recognizing and using a particular situational aspect until a sufficient number of examples makes identification easy and sure, to perform competently *requires* choosing an organizing goal or perspective. Furthermore, the choice of perspective crucially affects behavior in a way that one particular aspect rarely does.

This combination of necessity and uncertainty introduces an important new type of relationship between the performer and his environment. The novice and the advanced beginner applying rules and maxims feel little or no responsibility for the outcome of their acts. If they have made no mistakes, an unfortunate outcome is viewed as the result of inadequately specified elements or rules. The competent performer, on the other hand, after wrestling with the question of a choice of perspective or goal, feels responsible for, and thus emotionally involved in, the result of his choice. An outcome that is clearly successful is deeply satisfying and leaves a vivid memory of the situation encountered as seen from the goal or perspective finally chosen. Disasters, likewise, are not easily forgotten.

Remembered whole situations differ in one important respect from remembered aspects. The mental image of an aspect is flat in the sense that no parts stand out as salient. A whole situation, on the other hand, since it is the result of a chosen plan or perspective, has a "three-dimensional" quality. Certain elements stand out as more or less important with respect to the plan, while other irrelevant elements are forgotten. Moreover, the competent performer, gripped by the situation that his decision produced, experiences and therefore remembers the situation not only in terms of foreground and background, but also in terms of senses of opportunity, risk, expectation, threat, etc. These gripping holistic memories cannot guide the behavior of the competent performer, since he fails to make contact with them when he reflects on problematic situations as a detached observer, and holds to a view of himself as a computer following better and better rules. As we shall soon see, however, if he does let them take over, these memories become the basis of the competent performer's next advance in skill.

A competent driver beginning a trip decides, perhaps, that he is in a hurry. He then selects a route with attention to distance and time, ignores scenic beauty, and, as he drives, he chooses his maneuvers with little concern for passenger comfort or for courtesy. He follows more closely than normal, enters traffic more daringly, occasionally violates a law. He feels elated when decisions work out and no police car appears, and shaken by near accidents and traffic tickets. (Beginners, on the other hand, can perpetrate chaos around them with total unconcern.)

The class A chess player, here classed as competent, may decide after studying a position that his opponent has weakened his king's defenses so that an attack against the king is a viable goal. If the attack is chosen, features involving weaknesses in his own position, created by his attack, are ignored as are losses of pieces inessential to the attack. Removal of pieces defending the enemy king becomes salient. Successful plans induce euphoria and mistakes are felt in the pit of the stomach.

In both of these cases, there is a common pattern: detached planning, conscious assessment of elements that are salient with respect to the plan, and analytical, rule-guided choice of action, followed by an emotionally involved experience of the outcome.

Stage 4: Proficiency

Considerable experience at the level of competency sets the stage for yet further skill enhancement. Having experienced many situations, chosen plans in each, and having obtained vivid, involved demonstrations of the adequacy or inadequacy of the plan, the performer sees his current situation as similar to a previous one, and so spontaneously sees an appropriate plan. Involved in the world of the skill, the performer "notices," or is "struck by," a certain plan, goal or perspective. No longer is the spell of involvement broken by detached conscious planning.

There will, of course, be breakdowns of this "seeing," when, due perhaps to insufficient experience in a certain type of situation or to more than one possible plan presenting itself, the performer will need to take a detached look at his situation. But between these breakdowns, the proficient performer will experience longer and longer intervals of continuous, intuitive, understanding.

Since there are generally far fewer "ways of seeing" than "ways of acting," after understanding without conscious effort what is going on, the proficient performer will still have to think about what to do. During this thinking, elements that present themselves as salient are assessed and combined by rule to produce decisions about how best to manipulate the environment. The spell of involvement in the world of the activity will thus be temporarily broken.

On the basis of prior experience, a proficient driver approaching a curve on a rainy day may sense that he is traveling too fast. He then consciously decides whether to apply the brakes, remove his foot from the accelerator, or merely to reduce pressure on the accelerator.

The proficient chess player, who is classed a master, can recognize a large repertoire of types of positions. Recognizing almost immediately and without conscious effort the sense of a position, he sets about calculating the move that best achieves his goal. He may, for example, know that he should attack, but he must deliberate about how best to do so.

Stage 5: Expertise

The proficient performer, immersed in the world of his skillful activity, sees what needs to be done, but *decides* how to do it. For the expert, not only situational understandings spring to mind, but also associated appropriate actions. The expert performer—except, of course, during moments of breakdown—understands, acts, and learns from results without any conscious awareness of the process. What transparently *must* be done *is* done. People do not usually make conscious deliberative decisions when they walk, talk, ride a bicycle, drive, or carry on most social activities. An expert's skill has become so much a part of him that he need be no more aware of it than he is of his own body.

We have seen that experience-based similarity recognition produces the deep situational understanding of the proficient performer. No new insight is needed to explain the mental processes of the expert. With enough experience with a variety of situations, all seen from the same perspective or with the same goal in mind, but requiring different tactical decisions, the mind of the proficient performer seems gradually to decompose this class of situation into subclasses, each member of which shares not only the same goal or perspective, but also the same decision, action or tactic. At this point, a situation, when seen as similar to members of this class, is not only thereby understood but simultaneously the associated decision, action or tactic presents itself.

The number of classes of recognizable situations, built upon the basis of experience, must be immense. It has been estimated that a master chess player can distinguish roughly 50,000 types of positions. Automobile driving probably involves a similar number of typical situations. Human beings doubtless store far more typical situations in their memories than words in their vocabularies. Consequently, these reference situations, unlike the situational elements learned by the advanced beginner, bear no names and, in fact, defy complete verbal description.

The expert chess player, classed as an international master or grandmaster, in most situations experiences a compelling sense of the issue and the best move. Excellent chess players can play at the rate of 5–10 seconds a move and even faster without any serious degradation in performance. At this speed they must depend almost entirely on intuition, and hardly at all on analysis and comparison of alternatives. The authors recently performed an experiment in which an international master, Julio Kaplan, was required to add numbers presented to him audibly at the rate of about one number per second, while at the same time playing five-second-a-move-chess against a slightly weaker, but master level, player. Even with his analytical mind completely occupied by adding numbers, Kaplan more than held his own against the master in a series of games. Deprived of the time necessary to see problems and discuss plans, Kaplan still produced fluid and coordinated play.

The expert driver, generally without any awareness, not only knows by feel and familiarity when an action such as slowing is required, but he knows how to perform the act without evaluating and comparing alternatives. He shifts gears when appropriate with no conscious awareness of his acts. Most drivers have experienced the disconcerting breakdown that occurs when suddenly one reflects on the gear-shifting process and tries to decide what to do. Suddenly the smooth, almost automatic sequence of actions that results from the performer's involved immersion in the world of his skill is disrupted,

and the performer sees himself, just as does the competent performer, as the manipulator of a complex mechanism. He detachedly
calculates his actions even more poorly than does the competent performer, since he has forgotten many of the guiding rules that he
knew and used when competent, and his performance suddenly becomes halting, uncertain, and even inappropriate.

It seems that a beginner makes inferences using rules and facts
just like a heuristically programmed computer, but that with talent
and a great deal of involved experience, the beginner develops into
an expert who intuitively sees what to do without applying rules. Of
course, a description of skilled behavior can never be taken as con-
clusive evidence as to what is going on in the mind or in the brain. It
is always possible that what is going on is some unconscious process
using more and more sophisticated rules. But our description of skill
acquisition counters the traditional prejudice that expertise necessarily involves inference.

NO RULES AT ALL

Given this account of the five stages of skill acquisition, we can
understand why knowledge engineers from Socrates, to Samuel, to
Feigenbaum, have had such trouble getting the expert to articulate
the rules he is using. The expert is simply not following any rules!
He is doing just what Feigenbaum feared he might be doing—recognizing thousands of special cases. This, in turn, explains why expert systems are never as good as experts. If one asks the experts for
rules, one will, in effect, force the expert to regress to the level of
beginner and state the rules he still remembers, but no longer uses. If
one programs these rules into a computer, one can use the speed and
accuracy of the computer and its ability to store and access millions
of facts to outdo a human beginner using the same rules. But no
amount of rules and facts can capture the understanding an expert
has when he has stored his experience of the actual outcomes of tens
of thousands of situations.

The knowledge engineer might still say that, in spite of appearances, the mind and brain *must* be reasoning—making millions of
rapid and accurate inferences like a computer. After all the brain is

not "wonder tissue," and how else could it work? But there *are* other models for what might be going on in the hardware. The capacity of experts to store in memory tens of thousands of typical situations and rapidly and effortlessly to see the present situation as similar to one of these, suggests that the brain does not work like a heuristically programmed digital computer applying rules to bits of information. Rather it suggests, as some neuropsychologists already believe, that the brain—at times, at least—works holographically, superimposing the records of whole situations and measuring their similarity. Dr. Karl Pribram, a Stanford neurophysiologist, who has spent the past decade studying holographic memory, explicitly notes the implication of this sort of process for expertise. When asked in an interview whether holograms would allow a person to make decisions spontaneously in very complex environments, he replied, "Decisions fall out as the holographic correlations are performed. One doesn't have to think things through . . . a step at a time. One takes the whole constellation of a situation, correlates it, and out of that correlation emerges the correct response."[17]

We can now understand why, in a recent article in *Science*, two expert system builders, Richard Duda and Edward Shortliffe, who assume rather cautiously, but without evidence, that "experts seem to employ rule-like associations to solve routine problems quickly"[18] are, nonetheless, finally forced by the phenomenon to conclude:

> The identification and encoding of knowledge is one of the most complex and arduous tasks encountered in the construction of an expert system . . . Even when an adequate knowledge representation formalism has been developed, experts often have difficulty expressing their knowledge in that form.[19]

One should not be surprised that—in the area of medicine, for example—one finds doctors concluding that:

> The optimistic expectation of 20 years ago that computer technology would also come to play an important part in clinical decisions has not

17. Daniel Coleman, "Holographic Memory: An Interview with Karl Pribram," *Psychology Today* 12, no. 9 (February 1979), 80.
18. Richard O. Duda and Edward H. Shortliffe, "Expert Systems Research," *Science* 220, no. 4594 (April 15, 1983).
19. Ibid., 265.

been realized, and there are few if any situations in which computers are being routinely used to assist in either medical diagnosis or the choice of therapy.[20]

In general, based on the above model, the authors' prediction is that in any domain in which people exhibit holistic understanding, no system based upon heuristics will consistently do as well as experienced experts, even if they were the informants who provided the heuristic rules. Since there already seem to be many exceptions to our prediction, we will now deal with each alleged exception in turn.

THE EXCEPTIONS
THAT PROVE THE RULE

To begin with, there is a system developed at MIT, called MACSYMA, for doing certain manipulations required in calculus. MACSYMA began as a *heuristic* system. It has evolved, however, into an *algorithmic* system, using procedures guaranteed to work which involve so much calculation people would never use them, so the fact that, as far as can be determined, MACSYMA now outperforms all the experts in its field, does not constitute an exception to our hypothesis.

Next there are expert systems that are, indeed, heuristic, and which perform as well as anyone in the field. This happens when the domain is so combinatorial that even experienced specialists fail to develop holistic understanding. This is the case with the very impressive R1 developed at Digital Equipment Corporation to decide how to combine components of VAX computers to meet customers' needs. Even the experienced "technical editors" who perform the job at DEC depend on heuristic-based problem solving and take about ten minutes to work out even simple cases. Spectrograph analysis is also quite probably a domain in which there are no experts. Duda notes that: "For the molecular families covered by [its] empirical rules, [DENDRAL] is said to surpass even expert chemists in speed and accuracy."[21] But expert chemists need not be expert spectro-

20. G. Otto Barnett, M.D., "The Computer and Clinical Judgment," *New England Journal of Medicine,* 307 no. 8 (August 19, 1982), 493.

21. Ibid., 255.

graph interpreters. Before DENDRAL, chemists did their own spectrograph analysis, but it was not their main work, so no one chemist need have dealt with sufficient cases to become an expert. Thus it would be no surprise if DENDRAL outperforms all comers.

CHESS

Chess seems an obvious exception to our prediction, since chess programs have already achieved master ratings. The chess story is complicated and stimulating. Programs that play chess are among the earliest examples of expert systems. The first such program was written in the 1950s and by the early '60s fairly sophisticated programs had been developed. The programs naturally included the facts of the chess world (i.e., the rules of the game), and also heuristics elicited from strong players.

Master players, in checking out each plausible move that springs to mind, generally consider one to three plausible opponent responses, followed by one to three moves of their own, etc. Quite frequently, only one move looks plausible at each step. After looking ahead a varying number of moves, depending on the situation, the terminal position of each sequence is assessed, based on its similarity to positions previously encountered. In positions where the best initial move is not obvious, about 100 terminal positions will typically be examined. This thinking ahead generally confirms that the initial move intuitively seen as the most plausible is, indeed, best, although there are occasional exceptions.

To imitate players, the program designers attempted to elicit from the masters heuristic rules that could be used to generate a limited number of plausible moves at each step, and evaluation rules that could be used to assess the worth of the roughly 100 terminal positions. Since masters are not aware of following any rules, the rules they suggested did not work well and the programs played at a marginally competent level.

As computers grew faster in the 1970s, chess programming strategy changed. In 1973, a program was developed at Northwestern University by David Slate and Larry Atkin which rapidly searched *every* legal initial move, every legal response, etc., to a depth determined by the position and the computer's speed, generally about three moves for each player. The roughly one million terminal positions in the look-ahead were still evaluated by rules. Plausible-move generation heuristics were discarded, the program looked less like an expert system, and quality of play greatly improved. By 1983, using these largely brute-force procedures and the latest, most powerful computer (the Cray X-MP, capable of examining about ten million terminal positions in choosing each move), a program called Cray-Blitz became world computer chess champion and achieved a master rating based on a tournament against other computers which already had chess ratings.

Such programs, however, have Achilles' heels. While they are perfect tacticians when there are many captures and checks and a decisive outcome can be found within the computer's foreseeable future (now about four moves ahead for each player), computers lack any sense of chess strategy. Fairly good players who understand this fact can direct the game into long-range strategic channels, and can thereby defeat the computer, even though these players have a somewhat lower chess rating than the machine has achieved based on play against other machines and humans who do not know and exploit this strategic blindness. The ratings held by computers and reported in the press accurately reflect their performance against other computers and human players who do not know or exploit the computer's weakness, but greatly overstate their skill level when play is strategic.

A Scottish International Master chess player, David Levy, who is a computer enthusiast (he is chairman of a company called Intelligent Software in London), and who is ranked as roughly the thousandth best player in the world, bet about $4000 in 1968 that no computer could defeat him by 1978. He collected by beating the best computer program at that time 3.5 games to 1.5 games in a five-game match. He was, however, impressed by the machine's performance and the bet was increased and extended until 1984, with Levy quite uncertain about the outcome. When the 1984 match approached and the Cray-Blitz program had just achieved a master-level score in winning the world computer championship, Levy decided to modify his usual style of play so as maximally to exploit the computer's strategic blindness. Not only did he defeat the computer decisively, four games to zero, but, more importantly, he lost his long-held opinion about computer play. As he confessed to the *Los Angeles Times* on May 12, 1984,

> During the last few years I had come to believe more and more that it was possible for programs, within a decade, to play very strong grandmaster chess. But having played the thing now, my feeling is that a human world chess champion losing to a computer program in a serious match is a lot further away than I thought. Most people working on computer chess are working on the wrong lines. If more chess programmers studied the way human chess masters think and tried to emulate that to some extent, then I think they might get further.

Levy summed up his recent match by saying, "The nature of the struggle was such that the program didn't understand what was going on."[22] Clearly, when confronting a player who knows its weakness, Cray-Blitz is not a master-level chess player.

The authors could not agree more strongly with Levy's suggestion that researchers give up current methods and attempt to imitate what people do. But since strong, experienced chess players use the holistic similarity recognition described in the highest of our five levels of skill, imitating people would mean duplicating that pattern recognition process, rather than returning to the typical expert system approach. Since similarity for a strong chess player means similar "fields of force," such as interrelated threats, hopes, fears, and strengths, not similarity of the location of pieces on the board, and since no one can describe such fields, there is little prospect of duplicating human performance in the foreseeable future.

BACKGAMMON

The only remaining game program that appears to challenge our prediction is Hans Berliner's backgammon program, BKG 9.8. There is no doubt that the program used heuristic rules obtained from masters to beat the world champion in a seven-game series. But backgammon is a game involving a large element of chance, and Berliner himself is quite frank in saying that his program "did get the better

22. *Los Angeles Times,* May 12, 1984.

of the dice rolls," and could not consistently perform at championship level. He concludes:

> The program did not make the best play in eight out of 73 non-forced
> situations . . . An expert would not have made most of the errors the pro-
> gram made, but they could be exploited only a small percent of the
> time. . . . My program plays at the Class A, or advanced intermediate
> level.[23]

PROSPECTOR

The above cases are clearly not counter examples to our claim. Neither is a recent SRI contender named PROSPECTOR, a program
which uses rules derived from expert geologists to locate mineral deposits. Millions of viewers heard about PROSPECTOR on the CBS
Evening News in September 1983. A special Dan Rather report
called "The Computers Are Coming" showed first a computer and
then a mountain (Mount Tolman) as Rather authoritatively intoned,
"This computer digested facts and figures on mineral deposits, then
predicted that the metal molybdenum would be found at this mountain in the Pacific Northwest. It was." Such a feat, if true, would indeed be impressive. Viewers must have felt that the authors were
foolish when, later on the same program, we were shown asserting
that, using current AI methods, computers would never become intelligent. (While we explained and defended this claim during an
hour-long taped interview with CBS, all of this was necessarily
omitted during the five-minute segment on computers that was
aired.)

In reality, the PROSPECTOR program was given information
concerning prior drilling on Mount Tolman where a field of molybdenum *had already been found.* The expert system then mapped out
undrilled portions of that field, and subsequent drilling showed it to
be basically correct about where molybdenum did and did not exist.[24]

---

23. Hans Berliner, "Computer Backgammon," *Scientific American* 242 (June 1980),
64–72.

24. See *BYTE* 6 (September 1981), 262, caption under figure. The CBS news report is not the only sensationalized and inaccurate report on PROSPECTOR spread

Unfortunately, economic-grade molybdenum was not found in the previously unmapped area; drilling disclosed the ore to be too deep to be worth mining. These facts do not justify the conclusion that the program can outperform experts. So far there is no further data comparing experts' predictions with those of the system.

MYCIN

This leaves MYCIN, mentioned earlier; INTERNIST-1, a program for diagnosis in internal medicine; and PUFF, an expert system for the diagnosis of lung disorders, as the only programs that we know of which meet all the requirements for a test of our hypothesis. They are each based exclusively on heuristic rules extracted from experts, and their performance has been compared with that of experts in the field.

Let us take MYCIN first. A systematic evaluation of MYCIN was reported in *The Journal of the American Medical Association*. MYCIN was given data concerning ten actual meningitis cases and asked to prescribe drug therapy. Its prescriptions were evaluated by a panel of eight infectious disease specialists, who had published clinical reports dealing with the management of meningitis. These experts rated as acceptable 70% of MYCIN's recommended therapies.[25]

The evidence concerning INTERNIST-1 is even more detailed. In fact, according to *The New England Journal of Medicine,* which published an evaluation of the program, "the systematic evaluation of the model's performance is virtually unique in the field of medi-

---

by the mass media. The July 9, 1984, issue of *Business Week* reports in its cover story, "Artificial Intelligence: It's Here": "Geologists were convinced as far back as World War I that a rich deposit of molybdenum ore was buried deep under Mount Tolman in eastern Washington. But after digging dozens of small mines and drilling hundreds of test borings, they were still hunting for the elusive metal 60 years later. Then, just a couple of years ago, miners hit pay dirt. They finally found the ore because they were guided not by a geologist wielding his rock hammer, but by a computer located hundreds of miles to the south in Menlo Park, California."

25. Victor L. Yu et al., "Antimicrobial Selection by a Computer," *Journal of the American Medical Association* 242, no. 12 (September 21, 1979), 1270–1282.

cal applications of artificial intelligence."[26] INTERNIST-1 is described as follows:

> From its inception, INTERNIST-1 has addressed the problem of diagnosis within the broad context of general internal medicine. Given a patient's initial history, results of a physical examination, or laboratory findings, INTERNIST-1 was designed to aid the physician with the patient's work-up in order to make multiple and complex diagnoses. The capabilities of the system derive from its extensive knowledge base and from heuristic computer programs that can construct and resolve differential diagnoses.[27]

The program was run on 19 cases, each with several diseases, so that there were 43 correct diagnoses in all, and its diagnoses were compared with those of clinicians at Massachusetts General Hospital and with case discussants. Diagnoses were counted as correct when confirmed by pathologists. The result was "of 43 anatomically verified diagnoses, INTERNIST-1 failed to make a total of 18, whereas the clinicians failed to make 15 such diagnoses and the discussants missed only eight."[28] The evaluators found that: "The experienced clinician is vastly superior to INTERNIST-1 in the ability to consider the relative severity and independence of the different manifestations of disease and to understand the temporal evolution of the disease process."[29]

Dr. G. Otto Barnett, in his editorial comment on the evaluation, wisely concludes:

> Perhaps the most exciting experimental evaluation of INTERNIST-1 would be the demonstration that a productive collaboration is possible between man and computer—that clinical diagnosis in real situations can be improved by combining the medical judgment of the clinician with the statistical and computational power of a computer model and a large base of stored medical information.[30]

26. Randolph A. Miller, M.D., Harry E. Pople, Jr., Ph.D., and Jack D. Myers, M.D. "INTERNIST-1, an Experimental Computer-Based Diagnostic Consultant for General Internal Medicine," *New England Journal of Medicine* 307, no. 8 (August 19, 1982), 494.
27. Ibid., 468.
28. Ibid., 475.
29. Ibid., 494.
30. Ibid.

PUFF is an excellent example of an expert system doing a useful job without being an expert. PUFF was written to perform pulmonary function test interpretations. One sample measurement is the patient's *Total Lung Capacity* (TLC), that is, the volume of air in the lungs at maximum inspiration. If the TLC for a patient is high, this indicates the presence of obstructive airway disease. The interpretation and final diagnosis is a summary of this kind of reasoning about the combinations of measurements taken in the lung test. PUFF's principal task is to interpret such a set of pulmonary function test results, producing a set of interpretation statements and a diagnosis for each patient.

Using 30 heuristic rules extracted from an expert, Dr. Robert Fallat, PUFF agrees with Dr. Fallat in 75–85% of the cases. Why it does as well as the expert it models in only 75–85% of the cases is a mystery if one believes, as Robert MacNeil put it on the MacNeil-Lehrer television news, that researchers "discovered that Dr. Fallat used some 30 rules based on his clinical expertise to diagnose whether patients have obstructive airway disease." Of course, the machine's limited ability makes perfect sense if Dr. Fallat does not in fact follow these 30 rules or any others. But in any case, PUFF does well enough to be a valuable aid. As Dr. Fallat put it:

> There's a lot of what we do, including our thinking and our expertise, which is routine, and which doesn't require any special human effort to do. And that kind of stuff should be taken over by computers. And to the extent that 75% of what I do is routine and which all of us would agree on, why not let the computer do it and then I can have fun working with the other 25%.[31]

Feigenbaum himself admits in one surprisingly honest passage that expert systems are very different from experts:

> Part of learning to be an expert is to understand not merely the letter of the rule but its spirit . . . he knows when to break the rules, he understands what is relevant to his task and what isn't . . . Expert systems do not yet understand these things.[32]

---

31. The MacNeil-Lehrer Report on Artificial Intelligence, April 22, 1983.
32. E. Feigenbaum and P. McCorduck, *The Fifth Generation*, 184–85.

But because of his philosophical commitment to the rationality of expertise and thus to underlying unconscious heuristic rules, Feigenbaum does not see how devastating this admission is.

Once one gives up the assumption that experts must be making inferences and admits the role of involvement and intuition in the acquisition and application of skills, one will have no reason to cling to the heuristic program as a model of human intellectual operations. Feigenbaum's claim that "we have the opportunity at this moment to do a new version of Diderot's *Encyclopedia,* a gathering up of all knowledge—not just the academic kind, but the informal, experiential, heuristic kind"[33]; as well as his boast that thanks to Knowledge Information Processing Systems (KIPS), we will soon have "access to machine intelligence—faster, deeper, better than human intelligence"[34] can both be seen as a late stage of Socratic thinking with no rational or empirical basis. In this light those who claim we must begin a crash program to compete with the Japanese Fifth Generation Intelligent Computers can be seen to be false prophets blinded by Socratic assumptions and personal ambition—while Euthyphro, the expert on piety, who kept giving Socrates examples instead of rules, turns out to have been a true prophet after all.

33. Ibid., 229.
34. Ibid., 236.

FREDRIC JAMESON

11

The Politics of Theory
Ideological Positions in the Postmodernism Debate

The problem of postmodernism—how its fundamental characteristics are to be described, whether it even exists in the first place, whether the very *concept* is of any use, or is, on the contrary, a mystification—this problem is at one and the same time an aesthetic and a political one. The various positions which can logically be taken on it, whatever terms they are couched in, can always be shown to articulate visions of history, in which the evaluation of the social moment in which we live today is the object of an essentially political affirmation or repudiation. Indeed, the very enabling premise of the debate turns on an initial, strategic presupposition about our social system: to grant some historic originality to a postmodernist culture is also implicitly to affirm some radical structural difference between what is sometimes called consumer society and earlier moments of the capitalism from which it emerged.

The various logical possibilities, however, are necessarily linked with the taking of a position on that other issue inscribed in the very designation "postmodernism" itself, namely, the evaluation of what must now be called high or classical modernism itself. Indeed, when

Originally published in *New German Critique* 33 (Fall 1984). Reprinted by permission.

we make some initial inventory of the varied cultural artifacts that might plausibly be characterized as postmodern, the temptation is strong to seek the "family resemblance" of such heterogeneous styles and products, not in themselves but in some common high modernist impulse and aesthetic against which they all, in one way or another, stand in reaction.

The seemingly irreducible variety of the postmodern can be observed fully as problematically within the individual media (of arts) as between them: what affinities, besides some overall generational reaction, to establish between the elaborate false sentences and syntactic mimesis of John Ashbery and the much simpler talk poetry that began to emerge in the early 1960s in protest against the New Critical aesthetic of complex, ironic style? Both register, no doubt, but in very different ways indeed, the institutionalization of high modernism in this same period, the shift from an oppositional to a hegemonic position of the classics of modernism, the latter's conquest of the university, the museum, the art gallery network and the foundations, the assimilation, in other words, of the various high modernisms, into the "canon" and the subsequent attenuation of everything in them felt by our grandparents to be shocking, scandalous, ugly, dissonant, immoral and antisocial.

The same heterogeneity can be detected in the visual arts, between the inaugural reaction against the last high modernist school in painting—Abstract Expressionism—in the work of Andy Warhol and so-called pop art, and such quite distinct aesthetics as those of conceptual art, photorealism and the current New Figuration or neo-Expressionism. It can be witnessed in film, not merely between experimental and commercial production, but also within the former itself, where Godard's "break" with the classical filmic modernism of the great "auteurs" (Hitchcock, Bergman, Fellini, Kurosawa) generates a series of stylistic reactions against itself in the 1970s, and is also accompanied by a rich new development of experimental video (a new medium inspired by, but significantly and structurally distinct from, experimental film). In music also, the inaugural moment of John Cage now seems far enough from such later syntheses of classical and popular styles in composers like Phil Glass and Terry Riley, as well as from punk and New Wave rock of the type of The Clash, The Talking Heads and The Gang of Four, themselves significantly distinct from disco or glitter rock. (In film or in rock, however, a certain historical logic can be reintroduced by the hypothesis that such newer media recapitulate the evolutionary stages or breaks between realism, modernism and postmodernism, in a compressed time span, such that the Beatles and the Stones occupy the high modernist moment embodied by the "auteurs" of 1950s and 1960s art films.)

In narrative proper, the dominant conception of a dissolution of linear narrative, a repudiation of representation, and a "revolutionary" break with the (repressive) ideology of storytelling generally, does not seem adequate to encapsulate such very different work as that of Burroughs, but also of Pynchon and Ishmael Reed; of Beckett, but also of the French *nouveau roman* and its own sequels, and of the "nonfiction novel" as well, and the New Narrative. Meanwhile, a significantly distinct aesthetic has seemed to emerge both in commercial film and in the novel with the production of what may be called nostalgia art (or *la mode rétro*).

But it is evidently architecture which is the privileged terrain of struggle of postmodernism and the most strategic field in which this concept has been debated and its consequences explored. Nowhere else has the "death of modernism" been felt so intensely, or pronounced more stridently; nowhere else have the theoretical and practical stakes in the debate been articulated more programmatically. Of a burgeoning literature on the subject, Robert Venturi's *Learning from Las Vegas* (1971), a series of discussions by Christopher Jencks, and Pier Paolo Portoghesi's Biennale presentation, *After Modern Architecture,* may be cited as usefully illuminating the central issues in the attack on the architectural high modernism of the International Style (Le Corbusier, Wright, Mies): namely, the bankruptcy of the monumental (buildings which, as Venturi puts it, are really *sculptures*), the failure of its protopolitical or Utopian program (the transformation of all social life by way of the transformation of space), its elitism including the authoritarianism of the charismatic leader, and finally its virtual destruction of the older city fabric by a proliferation of glass boxes and of high rises that, disjoining themselves from their immediate contexts, turn these last into the degraded public space of an urban no-man's-land.

Still, architectural postmodernism is itself no unified or monolithic period style, but spans a whole gamut of allusions to styles of the past, such that within it can be distinguished a baroque postmodernism (say, Michael Graves), a rococo postmodernism (Charles Moore or Venturi), a classical and a neoclassical postmodernism (Rossi and De Porzemparc respectively), and perhaps even a Mannerist and a Romantic variety, not to speak of a High Modernist postmodernism itself. This complacent play of historical allusion and stylistic pastiche (termed "historicism" in the architectural literature) is a central feature of postmodernism more generally.

Yet the architectural debates have the merit of making the political resonance of these seemingly aesthetic issues inescapable, and allowing it to be detectable in the sometimes more coded or veiled discussions in the other arts. On the whole, four general positions on postmodernism may be disengaged from the variety of recent pronouncements on the subject; yet even this relatively neat scheme or *combinatoire* is further complicated by one's impression that each of these possibilities is susceptible of either a politically progressive or a politically reactionary expression (speaking now from a Marxist or more generally left perspective).

One can, for example, salute the arrival of postmodernism from an essentially anti-modernist standpoint.[1] A somewhat earlier generation of theorists (most notably Ihab Hassan) seems already to have done something like this when they dealt with the postmodernist aesthetic in terms of a more properly post-structuralist thematics (the *Tel quel* attack on the ideology of representation, the Heideggerian or Derridean "end of Western metaphysics"): here what is often not yet called postmodernism (see the Utopian prophecy at the end of Foucault's *The Order of Things*) is saluted as the coming of a whole new way of thinking and being in the world. But since Hassan's celebration also includes a number of the more extreme monuments of high modernism (Joyce, Mallarmé), this would be a relatively more ambiguous stance, were it not for the accompanying celebration of a new information high technology which marks the affinity between such evocations and the political thesis of a properly *post-industrial society*.

All of which is largely disambiguated in Tom Wolfe's *From Bau-*

---

1. The following analysis does not seem to me applicable to the work of the *boundary two* group, who early on appropriated the term "postmodernism" in the rather different sense of a critique of establishment "modernist" thought.

haus to Our House, an otherwise undistinguished book report on the recent architectural debates by a writer whose own New Journalism itself constitutes one of the varieties of postmodernism. What is interesting and symptomatic about this book is, however, the absence of any Utopian celebration of the postmodern and—far more strikingly—the passionate hatred of the Modern that breathes through the otherwise obligatory camp sarcasm of the rhetoric; and this is not a new, but a dated and archaic passion. It is as though the original horror of the first middle-class spectators of the very emergence of the Modern itself—the first Corbusiers, as white as the first freshly built cathedrals of the 12th century, the first scandalous Picasso heads, with two eyes on one profile like a flounder, the stunning "obscurity" of the first editions of *Ulysses* or *The Waste Land:* as though this disgust of the original philistines, Spiessbürger, bourgeois or Main Street Babbittry had suddenly come back to life, infusing the newer critiques of modernism with an ideologically very different spirit, whose effect is on the whole to reawaken in the reader an equally archaic sympathy with the protopolitical, Utopian, anti-middle-class impulses of a now extinct high modernism itself. Wolfe's diatribe thus offers a stunning example of the way in which a reasoned and contemporary theoretical repudiation of the modern— much of whose progressive force springs from a new sense of the urban and a now considerable experience of the destruction of older forms of communal and urban life in the name of a high modernist orthodoxy—can be handily reappropriated and pressed into the service of an explicitly reactionary cultural politics.

These positions—anti-modern, pro-postmodern—then find their opposite number and structural inversion in a group of counterstatements whose aim is to discredit the shoddiness and irresponsibility of the postmodern in general by way of a reaffirmation of the authentic impulse of a high modernist tradition still considered to be alive and vital. Hilton Kramer's twin manifestoes in the inaugural issue of his new journal, *The New Criterion,* articulate these views with force, contrasting the moral responsibility of the "masterpieces" and monuments of classical modernism with the fundamental irresponsibility and superficiality of a postmodernism associated with camp and with the "facetiousness" of which the Wolfe style is a ripe and obvious example.

What is more paradoxical is that politically Wolfe and Kramer

have much in common; and there would seem to be a certain inconsistency in the way in which Kramer must seek to eradicate from the
"high seriousness" of the classics of the modern their fundamentally
anti-middle-class stance and the protopolitical passion which informs the repudiation, by the great modernists, of Victorian taboos
and family life, of commodification, and of the increasing asphyxia-
tion of a desacralizing capitalism, from Ibsen to Lawrence, from Van
Gogh to Jackson Pollock. Kramer's ingenious attempt to assimilate
this ostensibly anti-bourgeois stance of the great modernists to a
"loyal opposition" secretly nourished, by way of foundations and
grants, by the bourgeoisie itself—while most unconvincing indeed—is surely itself enabled by the contradictions of the cultural
politics of modernism proper, whose negations depend on the persistence of what they repudiate and entertain—when they do not,
very rarely indeed (as in Brecht), attain some genuine political self-
consciousness—a symbiotic relationship with capital.

It is, however, easier to understand Kramer's move here when the
political project of *The New Criterion* is clarified: for the mission of the
journal is clearly to eradicate the 1960s and what remains of that legacy, to consign that whole period to the kind of oblivion which the
1950s was able to devise for the 1930s, or the 1920s for the rich political culture of the pre–World War I era. *The New Criterion* therefore
inscribes itself in the effort, on-going and at work everywhere today,
to construct some new conservative cultural counter-revolution,
whose terms range from the aesthetic to the ultimate defense of the
family and of religion. It is therefore paradoxical that this essentially
political project should explicitly deplore the omnipresence of politics in contemporary culture—an infection largely spread during the
1960s, but which Kramer holds responsible for the moral imbecility
of the postmodernism of our own period.

The problem with the operation—an obviously indispensable one
from the conservative viewpoint—is that for whatever reason its
paper-money rhetoric does not seem to have been backed by the
solid gold of state power, as was the case with McCarthyism or in
the period of the Palmer raids. The failure of the Vietnam War seems,
at least for the moment, to have made the naked exercise of repressive power impossible,[2] and endowed the 1960s with a per-

2. Written in spring 1982.

sistence in collective memory and experience which it was not given to the traditions of the 1930s or the pre–World War I period to know. Kramer's "cultural revolution" therefore tends most often to lapse into a feebler and sentimental nostalgia for the 1950s and the Eisenhower era.

It will not be surprising, in the light of what has been shown for an earlier set of positions on modernism and postmodernism, that in spite of the openly conservative ideology of this second evaluation of the contemporary cultural scene, the latter can also be appropriated for what is surely a far more progressive line on the subject. We are indebted to Jürgen Habermas [3] for this dramatic reversal and rearticulation of what remains the affirmation of the supreme value of the Modern and the repudiation of the theory, as well as the practice, of postmodernism. For Habermas, however, the vice of postmodernism consists very centrally in its politically reactionary function, as the attempt everywhere to discredit a modernist impulse Habermas himself associates with the bourgeois Enlightenment and with the latter's still universalizing and Utopian spirit. With Adorno himself, Habermas seeks to rescue and to recommemorate what both see as the essentially negative, critical and Utopian power of the great high modernisms. On the other hand, his attempt to associate these last with the spirit of the 18th-century Enlightenment marks a decisive break indeed with Adorno and Horkheimer's somber *Dialectic of Enlightenment,* in which the scientific ethos of the *philosophes* is dramatized as a misguided will to power and domination over nature, and their own desacralizing program as the first stage in the development of a sheerly instrumentalizing world view which will lead straight to Auschwitz. This very striking divergence can be accounted for by Habermas's own vision of history, which seeks to maintain the promise of "liberalism" and the essentially Utopian content of the first, universalizing bourgeois ideology (equality, civil rights, humanitarianism, free speech and open media) over against the failure of those ideals to be realized in the development of capital itself.

As for the aesthetic terms of the debate, however, it will not be

---

3. See his "Modernity—An Incomplete Project," in Hal Foster, ed., *The Anti-Aesthetic* (Port Townsend, Wash.: Bay Press, 1983), pp. 3–15. The essay was first published in *New German Critique* 22 (Winter 1981): 3–14, under the different title "Modernity versus Postmodernity." Reprinted in this volume.

adequate to respond to Habermas's resuscitation of the Modern by some mere empirical certification of the latter's extinction. We need to take into account the possibility that the national situation in which Habermas thinks and writes is rather different from our own: McCarthyism and repression are, for one thing, realities in the Federal Republic today, and the intellectual intimidation of the Left and the silencing of a left culture (largely associated, by the West German right, with "terrorism") has been on the whole a far more successful operation than elsewhere in the West.[4] The triumph of a new McCarthyism and of the culture of the Spiessbürger and the philistine suggests the possibility that in this particular national situation Habermas may well be right, and the older forms of high modernism may still retain something of the subversive power which they have lost elsewhere. In that case, a postmodernism which seeks to enfeeble and to undermine that power may well also merit his ideological diagnosis in a local way, even though the assessment remains ungeneralizable.

Both of the previous positions—anti-modern/pro-postmodern, and pro-modern/anti-postmodern—are characterized by an acceptance of the new term which is tantamount to an agreement on the fundamental nature of some decisive "break" between the modern and the postmodern moments, however these last are evaluated. There remain, however, two final logical possibilities both of which depend on the repudiation of any conception of such a historical break and which therefore, implicitly or explicitly, call into question the usefulness of the very category of postmodernism. As for the works associated with the latter, they will then be assimilated back into classical modernism proper, so that the "postmodern" becomes little more than the form taken by the authentically modern in our own period, and a mere dialectical intensification of the old modernist impulse toward innovation. (I must here omit yet another series of debates, largely academic, in which the very continuity of modernism as it is here reaffirmed is itself called into question by some vaster sense of the profound continuity of Romanticism itself, from the late 18th century on, of which both the modern and the postmodern will be seen as mere organic stages.)

---

4. The specific politics associated with the "Greens" would seem to constitute a reaction to this situation rather than an exception from it.

The two final positions on the subject thus logically prove to be a positive and negative assessment respectively of a postmodernism now assimilated back into the high modernist tradition. Jean-Francois Lyotard[5] thus proposes that his own vital commitment to the new and the emergent, to a contemporary or postcontemporary cultural production now widely characterized as "postmodern," be grasped as part and parcel of a reaffirmation of the authentic older high modernisms very much in Adorno's spirit. The ingenious twist or swerve in his own proposal involves the proposition that something called "postmodernism" does not *follow* high modernism proper, as the latter's waste product, but rather very precisely *precedes* and prepares it, so that the contemporary postmodernisms all around us may be seen as the promise of the return and the reinvention, the triumphant reappearance, of some new high modernism endowed with all its older power and with fresh life. This is a prophetic stance, whose analyses turn on the anti-representational thrust of modernism and postmodernism; Lyotard's aesthetic positions, however, cannot be adequately evaluated in aesthetic terms, since what informs them is an essentially social and political conception of a new social system beyond classical capitalism (our old friend, "postindustrial society"): the vision of a regenerated modernism is in that sense inseparable from a certain prophetic faith in the possibilities and the promise of the new society itself in full emergence.

The negative inversion of this position will then clearly involve an ideological repudiation of modernism of a type which might conceivably range from Lukács's older analysis of modernist forms as the replication of the reification of capitalist social life all the way to some of the more articulated critiques of high modernism of the present day. What distinguishes this final position from the anti-modernisms already outlined above is, however, that it does not speak from the security of an affirmation of some new postmodernist culture, but rather sees even the latter itself as a mere degeneration of the already stigmatized impulses of high modernism proper. This particular position, perhaps the bleakest of all and the most implaca-

---

5. See "Answering the Questions: What Is Postmodernism?" in J. F. Lyotard, *The Postmodern Condition* (Minneapolis: University of Minnesota Press, 1984), pp. 71–82; the book itself focuses primarily on science and epistemology rather than on culture.

bly negative, can be vividly confronted in the works of the Venetian architecture historian Manfredo Tafuri, whose extensive analyses[6] constitute a powerful indictment of what we have termed the "protopolitical" impulses in high modernism (the "Utopian" substitution of cultural politics for politics proper, the vocation to transform the world by transforming its forms, space or language). Tafuri is however no less harsh in his anatomy of the negative, demystifying, "critical" vocation of the various modernisms, whose function he reads as a kind of Hegelian "ruse of History," whereby the instrumentalizing and desacralizing tendencies of capital itself are ultimately realized through just such demolition work by the thinkers and artists of the modern movement. Their "anticapitalism" therefore ends up laying the basis for the "total" bureaucratic organization and control of late capitalism, and it is only logical that Tafuri should conclude by positing the impossibility of any radical transformation of culture before a radical transformation of social relations themselves.

The political ambivalence demonstrated in the earlier two positions seems to me to be maintained here, but *within* the positions of both of these very complex thinkers. Unlike many of the previously mentioned theorists, Tafuri and Lyotard are both explicitly political figures, with an overt commitment to the values of an older revolutionary tradition. It is clear, for example, that Lyotard's embattled endorsement of the supreme value of aesthetic innovation is to be understood as the figure for a certain kind of revolutionary stance; while Tafuri's whole conceptual framework is largely consistent with the classical Marxist tradition. Yet both are also, implicitly, and more openly at certain strategic moments, rewritable in terms of a post-Marxism which at length becomes indistinguishable from anti-Marxism proper. Lyotard has for example very frequently sought to distinguish his "revolutionary" aesthetic from the older ideals of political revolution, which he sees as either being Stalinist, or as archaic and incompatible with the conditions of the new postindustrial social order; while Tafuri's apocalyptic notion of the total social revolution

6. See in particular *Architecture and Utopia* (Cambridge: MIT Press, 1976) and *Modern Architecture,* with Francesco Dal Co (New York: Abrams, 1979); and also my "Architecture and the Critique of Ideology," in *ReVisions: Papers in Architectural Theory and Criticism* 1, no. 1 (Winter 1984).

	ANTI-MODERNIST	PRO-MODERNIST
PRO-POSTMODERNIST	Wolfe − Jencks +	Lyotard $\left\{ \begin{matrix} + \\ - \end{matrix} \right.$
ANTI-POSTMODERNIST	Tafuri $\left\{ \begin{matrix} - \\ + \end{matrix} \right.$	Kramer − Habermas +

FIGURE A

implies a conception of the "total system" of capitalism which, in a period of depolitization and reaction, is only too fatally destined for the kind of discouragement which has so often led Marxists to a renunciation of the political altogether (Adorno and Merleau-Ponty come to mind, along with many of the ex-Trotskyists of the 1930s and 1940s and the ex-Maoists of the 1960s and 1970s).

The combination scheme outlined above can now be schematically represented as shown in Figure A; the plus and minus signs designating the politically progressive or reactionary functions of the positions in question.

With these remarks we come full circle and may now return to the more positive potential political content of the first position in question, and in particular to the question of a certain *populist* impulse in postmodernism which it has been the merit of Charles Jencks (but also of Venturi and others) to have underscored—a question which will also allow us to deal a little more adequately with the absolute pessimism of Tafuri's Marxism itself. What must first be observed, however, is that most of the political positions which we have found to inform what is most often conducted as an aesthetic debate are in reality moralizing ones, which seek to develop final judgments on the phenomenon of postmodernism, whether the latter is stigmatized as corrupt or on the other hand saluted as a culturally and aesthetically healthy and positive form of innovation. But a genuinely historical and dialectical analysis of such phenomena—particularly when it is a matter of a present of time and of history in which we ourselves exist and struggle—cannot afford the impoverished luxury of such absolute moralizing judgments: the dialectic is "beyond good and evil" in the sense of some easy taking of sides, whence the glacial and inhuman spirit of its historical vision (something that already disturbed contemporaries about Hegel's original system). The point is that we are *within* the culture of postmodernism to the point where its facile repudiation is as impossible as any equally facile celebration of it is complacent and corrupt. Ideological judgment on postmodernism today necessarily implies, one would think, a judgment on ourselves as well as on the artifacts in question; nor can an entire historical period, such as our own, be grasped in any adequate way by means of global moral judgments or their somewhat degraded equivalent, pop-psychological diagnosis (such as those of Lasch's *Culture of Narcissism*). In the classical Marxian view, the seeds of the future already exist within the present and must be conceptually disengaged from it, both through analysis and through political praxis (the workers of the Paris Commune, Marx once remarked in a striking phrase, "*have no ideals to realize*"; they merely sought to disengage emergent forms of new social relations from the older capitalist social relations in which the former had already begun to stir). In place of the temptation either to denounce the complacencies of postmodernism as some final symptom of decadence, or to salute the new forms as the harbingers of a new technological and technocratic Utopia, it seems more appropriate to assess the new cultural production within the working hypothesis of a general modification of culture itself within the social restructuration of late capitalism as a system.[7]

As for emergence, however, Jencks's assertion that postmodern architecture distinguishes itself from that of high modernism through its populist priorities,[8] may serve as the starting point for some more general discussion. What is meant, in the specifically architectural context, is that where the now more classical high modernist space of a Corbusier or a Wright sought to differentiate itself radically from the fallen city fabric in which it appears—its forms thus dependent on an act of radical disjunction from its spatial context (the great *pilotis* dramatizing separation from the ground and safeguarding the

---

7. I have tried to do this in "Postmodernism, Or, The Cultural Logic of Late Capitalism," *New Left Review* 146 (July–August 1984): 53–92; my contribution to *The Anti-Aesthetic*, op. cit., is a fragment of this definitive version.

8. See, for example, Charles Jencks, *Late-Modern Architecture* (New York: Rizzoli, 1980); Jencks here however shifts his usage of the term from the designation for a cultural dominant or period style to the name for one aesthetic movement among others.

Novum of the new space)—postmodernist buildings on the contrary celebrate their insertion into the heterogeneous fabric of the commercial strip and the motel and fast-food landscape of the post-superhighway American city. Meanwhile a play of allusion and formal echoes ("historicism") secures the kinship of these new art buildings with the surrounding commercial icons and spaces, thereby renouncing the high modernist claim to radical difference and innovation.

Whether this undoubtedly significant feature of the newer architecture is to be characterized as *populist* must remain an open question: since it would seem essential to distinguish the emergent forms of a new commercial culture—beginning with advertisements and spreading on to formal *packaging* of all kinds, from products to buildings and not excluding artistic commodities such as television shows (the "logo") and bestsellers and films—from the older kinds of folk and genuinely "popular" culture which flourished when the older social classes of a peasantry and an urban *artisanat* still existed and which, from the mid–19th century on, have gradually been colonized and extinguished by commodification and the market system.

What can at least be admitted is the more universal presence of this particular feature, which appears more unambiguously in the other arts as an effacement of the older distinction between high and so-called mass culture, a distinction on which modernism depended for its specificity, its Utopian function consisting at least in part in the securing of a realm of authentic experience over against the surrounding environment of philistinism, of schlock and kitsch, of commodification and of Reader's Digest culture. Indeed, it can be argued that the emergence of high modernism is itself contemporaneous with the first great expansion of a recognizable mass culture (Zola may be taken as the marker for the last coexistence of the art novel and the bestseller to be within a single text).

It is now this constitutive differentiation which seems on the point of disappearing: we have already mentioned the way in which, in music, after Schönberg and even after Cage, the two antithetical traditions of the "classical" and the "popular" once again begin to merge. In a more general way, it seems clear that the artists of the "postmodern" period have been fascinated precisely by the whole new object world, not merely of the Las Vegas strip, but also of the late show and the grade-B Hollywood film, of so-called paraliterature with its airport paperback categories of the gothic and the romance, the popular biography, the murder mystery and the science-fiction or fantasy novel (in such a way that the older generic categories discredited by modernism seem on the point of living an unexpected reappearance). In the visual arts, the renewal of photography as a significant medium in its own right and also as the "plane of substance" in pop art or photorealism is a crucial symptom of the same process. At any rate, it becomes minimally obvious that the newer artists no longer "quote" the materials, the fragments and motifs, of a mass or popular culture, as Joyce (and Flaubert) began to do, or Mahler; they somehow incorporate them to the point where many of our older critical and evaluative categories (founded precisely on the radical differentiation of modernist and mass culture) no longer seem functional.

But if this is the case, then it seems at least possible that what wears the mask and makes the gestures of "populism" in the various postmodernist apologias and manifestoes is in reality a mere reflex and symptom of a (to be sure momentous) cultural mutation, in which what used to be stigmatized as mass or commercial culture is now received into the precincts of a new and enlarged cultural realm. In any case, one would expect a term drawn from the typology of political ideologies to undergo basic semantic readjustments when its initial referent (that Popular-front class coalition of workers, peasants and petty bourgeois generally called "the people") has disappeared.

Perhaps, however, this is not so new a story after all: one remembers, indeed, Freud's delight at discovering an obscure tribal culture, which alone among the multitudinous traditions of dream-analysis on the earth had managed to hit on the notion that all dreams had hidden sexual meanings—except for sexual dreams, which meant something else! So also it would seem in the postmodernist debate, and the depoliticized bureaucratic society to which it corresponds, where all seemingly cultural positions turn out to be symbolic forms of political moralizing, except for the single overtly political note, which suggests a slippage from politics back into culture again. I have the feeling that the only adequate way out of this vicious circle, besides praxis itself, is a historical and dialectical view which seeks to grasp the present as History.

ROBERT N. BELLAH

12

The Quest for the Self

Individualism, Morality, Politics

It was the belief of the authors of *Habits of the Heart*[1] that the discussion of individualism in Tocqueville's *Democracy in America* is illuminating with respect to contemporary American social life. Our research was in many ways a continuing conversation with Tocqueville as well as with our fellow citizens. In this paper I would like to bring Emerson into the conversation and suggest how close attention to these nineteenth-century texts is helpful in illuminating current social reality.

TOCQUEVILLE AND EMERSON ON INDIVIDUALISM

In a famous chapter entitled "Of Individualism in Democracies," Tocqueville points out that "'Individualism' is a word recently coined to express a new idea. Our fathers only knew about egoism." Individualism is more moderate and orderly than egoism, but in the end its results are much the same: "Individualism is a calm and consid-

---

1. Robert N. Bellah, Richard Madsen, William M. Sullivan, Ann Swidler and Steven M. Tipton, *Habits of the Heart: Individualism and Commitment in American Life* (Berkeley and Los Angeles: University of California Press, 1985). Much of this paper derives from our joint authorship.

ered feeling which disposes each citizen to isolate himself from the mass of his fellows and withdraw into the circle of family and friends; with this little society formed to his taste, he gladly leaves the greater society to look out after itself."[2] As this tendency grows, he wrote, "there are more and more people who, though neither rich nor powerful enough to have much hold over others, have gained or kept enough wealth and enough understanding to look after their own needs. Such folk owe no man anything and hardly expect anything from anybody. They form the habit of thinking of themselves in isolation and imagine that their whole destiny is in their hands." Finally such persons come to "forget their ancestors," but also their contemporaries. "Each man is forever thrown back on himself alone, and there is danger that he may be shut up in the solitude of his own heart."[3]

Tocqueville saw the isolation to which Americans are prone as ominous for the future of our freedom. It is just such isolation which is always encouraged by despotism. And so Tocqueville is particularly interested in all those countervailing tendencies which pulled people back from their isolation into social communion. Immersion in private economic pursuits undermines the person as citizen. On the other hand involvement in public affairs is the best antidote for the pernicious effects of individualistic isolation: "Citizens who are bound to take part in public affairs must turn from the private interests and occasionally take a look at something other than themselves."[4] It is precisely in these respects that the mores become important. The habits and practices of religion and democratic participation educate the citizen to a larger view than his purely private world would allow. These habits and practices rely to some extent on self-interest in their educational work, but it is only when self-interest has been to some degree transcended that they will have succeeded. Tocqueville even saw the family as playing an important role in tempering individualism, particularly through the role of women who, under the influence of religion, counter the economic self-interest of their

2. Alexis de Tocqueville, *Democracy in America,* trans. George Lawrence (Garden City, N.Y.: Doubleday-Anchor, 1969), 506.
3. Ibid., 508.
4. Ibid., 510.

husbands and communicate to children a morality transcending the interests of the self.[5]

Tocqueville is at his most brilliant in his analysis of the social consequences of American individualism. He is, however, not without interest in his observations about its personal consequences. He comments on the competitiveness of Americans and their "restlessness in the midst of prosperity." "In America," he says, "I have seen the freest and best educated of men in circumstances the happiest to be found in the world; yet it seemed to me that a cloud habitually hung on their brow, and they seemed serious and almost sad even in their pleasures," because they "never stop thinking of the good things they have not got." This restlessness and sadness in pursuit of the good life makes it difficult to form "strong attachments between man and man." The efforts and enjoyments of Americans are livelier than in traditional societies, but the disappointments of their hopes and desires are keener, and their "minds are more anxious and on edge." Of such restless, competitive, and anxious people Tocqueville says, "they clutch everything and hold nothing fast."[6]

Ralph Waldo Emerson, writing at much the same time, gives a remarkably similar picture of American individualism except for his more positive, even celebratory tone. But that more positive tone is perhaps related to an effort to give individualism a moral meaning that for Tocqueville it did not have. Toward the end of his Phi Beta Kappa address of 1837, "The American Scholar," Emerson also describes something that he sees as new in his time:

> Another sign of our times, also marked by an analogous political movement, is the new importance given to the single person. Everything that tends to insulate the individual,—to surround him with barriers of natural respect, so that each man shall feel the world is his, and man shall treat with man as a sovereign state with a sovereign state;—tends to true union as well as greatness. "I learned," said the melancholy Pestalozzi, "that no man in God's wide earth is either willing or able to help any other man." Help must come from the bosom alone.[7]

5. Ibid., 291.
6. Ibid., 535–538, 565.
7. Ralph Waldo Emerson, *Essays and Lectures* (New York: The Library of America, 1983), 70.

At moments Emerson tends to inflate the self until it is identical with Universal Being, with unfortunate consequences for any mere earthly attachments:

> Crossing a bare common, in snow puddles, at twilight, under a clouded sky, without having in my thoughts any occurrence of special good fortune, I have enjoyed a perfect exhilaration. I am glad to the brink of fear . . . I become a transparent eye-ball; I am nothing; I see all; the currents of Universal Being circulate through me; I am part or particle of God. The name of the nearest friend sounds then foreign and accidental: to be brothers, to be acquaintances,—master or servant, is then a trifle and a disturbance.[8]

Emerson's devotion to what he calls "the capital virtue of self-trust" makes him leery of the dependence of the self on others but also of others on the self: "A sympathetic person is placed in the dilemma of a swimmer among drowning men, who all catch at him, and if he give so much as a leg or a finger, they will drown him."[9] The conclusion of these views for social ethics is clear enough, confirming Tocqueville's analysis. In the famous essay on "Self-Reliance" Emerson wrote: "Then, again, do not tell me, as a good man did to-day, of my obligation to put all poor men in good situations. Are they *my* poor? I tell thee, thou foolish philanthropist, that I grudge the dollar, the dime, the cent, I give to such men as do not belong to me and to whom I do not belong."[10] Here we see tangible evidence of Emerson's rejection of the normative authority of the New Testament and his intention to deliver a comparable revelation for his own day.

Finally Emerson confirms Tocqueville's observation that individualism cuts us off from the past. He advises us to "desert the tradition" because, "The perpetual admonition of nature to us, is, 'The world is new, untried. Do not believe the past. I give you the universe a virgin to-day.'"[11]

What is surprising about this quick look at the teachings of Tocqueville and Emerson on individualism is how accurately they describe our condition today, whether we like it or not. The contemporaneity of Emerson as well as the sharply conflicting views about

8. From the introduction to "Nature" in ibid., 10.
9. From "Experience" in ibid., 490.
10. Ibid., 262.
11. From "Literary Ethics" in ibid., 100, 101.

his significance are evidenced in two recent essays, one by John Updike and the other by Harold Bloom.[12] Updike, in a long appreciative essay, finds Emerson finally too optimistic about the self and too coldly absorbed in it to be much help to Americans today. Bloom in an essay that is clearly a rejoinder to Updike, significantly entitled "Mr. America," glories in just those aspects of Emerson's teachings that Updike deplores. Brushing aside Updike's objections as "church-wardenly mewings," Bloom praises Emerson for proclaiming the only God in which Americans can any longer believe, "the god in the self."[13]

Ordinary Americans may be less conscious of their link to an earlier America than the literary intellectuals but in the interviews we gathered for *Habits of the Heart*[14] we found that the individualism that Tocqueville described and Emerson exemplified is more vigorous than ever among middle-class Americans. We will consider briefly toward the end of this paper whether the mores that Tocqueville found holding that individualism in check are still vigorous today.

THE QUEST FOR THE SELF

Middle-class Americans share Emerson's emphasis on self-reliance and his belief that help comes only from our own bosom. As one of the therapists we interviewed put it, "In the end you're really alone and you really have to answer to yourself." They also tend to share Emerson's view that society is inimical to the individual and that the quest for the self involves freeing ourselves from society. As Emerson put it, "Society is everywhere in conspiracy against the manhood of every one of its members."[15] Thus the quest for the self is a quest for autonomy, for leaving the past and the social structures that have previously enveloped us, for stripping off the obligations

---

12. John Updike, "Emersonianism," *The New Yorker,* June 4, 1984, pp. 112–132; Harold Bloom, "Mr. America," *The New York Review of Books,* November 22, 1984, pp. 19–24.

13. Bloom, "Mr. America," p. 24.

14. "Habits of the heart" is a phrase Tocqueville uses to describe the mores. Op. cit., 287.

15. From "Self-Reliance," in op. cit., 261.

370 Robert N. Bellah

and constraints imposed by others, until at last we find our true self which is unique and individual.

One of the strongest imperatives of our culture is that we must leave home. Unlike many peasant societies where it is common to live with parents until their death and where one worships parents and ancestors all one's life, for us leaving home is the normal expectation and childhood is in many ways a preparation for it. For some the process is quite smooth; for others there is considerable conflict. The presence of conflict does not mean that the cultural pattern of leaving home is in doubt. Indeed, a degree of conflict over this issue is to some extent expected. However painful the process of leaving home, for parents or for children, the really frightening thing would be the prospect of the child never leaving home.

For the middle-class child the process of leaving home, though associated with becoming gainfully employed and starting a family of one's own, often occurs earlier, when one goes away to college. Leaving home involves not only leaving the family but often leaving one's local community, going to a "good college," where one's chances of getting a really good job and perhaps attaining higher status than one's parents will be enhanced. Part of the "self-reliance" involved in leaving home involves taking care of oneself without immediate dependence on parents, perhaps working to contribute toward paying for one's education. But an equally important aspect of self-reliance is taking responsibility for one's own views. Very often this means not only leaving home but leaving church as well.

One may not literally have to leave one's church. One may continue to belong to the church of one's parents. But the expectation is that at some point one will decide on one's own that that is the church to belong to. One cannot defend one's views by saying that they are simply those of one's parents or of the church in which one was raised. On the contrary they must be particularly and peculiarly one's own. Traditionally Protestant piety demanded that a young person experience a unique conversion experience of his own, even while specifying more or less clearly the content of that experience. More recently we expect even greater autonomy. On the basis of our interviews we were not surprised to learn that a 1978 Gallup poll found that 80 percent of Americans agreed with the statement, "An individual should arrive at his or her own religious beliefs independent of any churches or synagogues."[16]

Finding the right occupation is certainly an important part of the quest for the true self. But for middle-class Americans today work is less of a calling and more of a career; less something one deeply identifies with and more a means toward self-fulfillment. Getting locked into a particular slot or organization is often seen as constricting to the autonomy of the self and midlife job changes or even career changes are widely advocated.

Where work is frustrating and confining and contains few intrinsic satisfactions, as it is for many Americans at all status levels, the quest for the true self may be pursued most urgently in the sphere of leisure and private life. In urban middle-class America the choice of private "lifestyle" is probably freer than ever before in our history. Most of the constraints of traditional marriage have been called into question. (The expectation that it is normal to get married at all has dropped sharply over the past thirty years.[17]) One young mother of two whom we interviewed decided that it was immoral to go on living with her husband when sex had lost its excitement, so the couple separated, each had therapy, and only after a year and the resolution of the problem did they resume living together. Many of those to whom we talked, involved in long and apparently satisfying marriages, indicated that their commitment to the marriage was contingent on the continued satisfactions that it offered. We need not believe they will actually act on their ideology to notice how powerfully the ideology of self-fulfillment undercuts all sustained commitments in our society.

The quest for the self, then, pursued under the predominant ideology of individualism, involves separating out from family, religion, and calling as sources of authority, duty, and moral example. It means autonomously pursuing happiness, and satisfying one's own wants. But what are the wants the self satisfies, and by what measure

---

16. Reported in Dean R. Hoge, *Converts, Dropouts, Returnees: Religious Change Among Catholics* (New York: Pilgrim Press, 1981), 167.

17. Joseph Veroff, Elizabeth Douvan and Richard A. Kulka, *The Inner American: A Self-Portrait from 1957 to 1976* (New York: Basic Books, 1981), 147.

does it identify its happiness? In the face of such insistent questions the predominant *ethos* of American individualism seems determined more than ever to press ahead with the task of letting go of all criteria other than a radically private validation. And it is very frequently to psychology that Americans turn. As Robert Coles says, "Psychology, in this instance, means a concentration, persistent, if not feverish, upon one's thoughts, feelings, wishes, worries—bordering on, if not embracing, solipsism: the self as the only or main form of (existential) reality."[18]

Frequently when we sought to discover the criteria that Americans use to measure the success of their quest for the true self we found them using the term "values." "Values" turn out to be the incomprehensible, rationally indefensible thing that the individual chooses when he or she has thrown off the last vestige of external influence and reached pure contentless freedom. The ideal self in its absolute freedom is completely "unencumbered," to borrow a term from Michael Sandel.[19] The improvisational self chooses values to express itself; but it is not constituted by them as from a preexisting source. The language of "values" as commonly used is self-contradictory precisely because it is not a language of value, of moral choice. It presumes the existence of an absolutely empty, unencumbered, and provisional self.

I want to make it clear that we do not believe that the people to whom we talked have empty selves. Most of them are serious, engaged people, deeply involved in the world. But insofar as they are limited to a language of radical individual autonomy, as many of them are, they cannot think about themselves or others except as arbitrary centers of volition. They cannot express the fullness of being that is actually theirs.

18. Robert Coles, "Civility and Psychology," *Daedalus* 180 (Summer 1980), 136–37.
19. Michael Sandel, *Liberalism and the Limits of Justice* (New York: Cambridge University Press, 1982).

REACHING OUT

However much Americans extol the autonomy and self-reliance of the individual, they do not imagine that a good life can be lived alone. Those we interviewed would almost all agree that connectedness to others in work, love, and community is essential to happiness, self-esteem, and moral worth. We must now consider how they, as autonomous individuals, reach out to others and how they conceive of the community that results.

Radical American individualism seems to contain two conceptions of human relatedness that at first glance may appear incompatible, but that were firmly asserted by Emerson and many Americans today. Looking at individuals as "sovereign states," one might imagine the only relations possible between them to be by treaty, that is by contract. The contractarian model has long been popular in America and takes new, psychologically nuanced, forms today. But Emerson also noted that "sovereign" individuals, when they have freed themselves from convention and tradition, are identical to "nature" which is the same for all. The idea that deep within our unique and individual selves there is an expressive identity with all other selves is an idea that we found widespread among the Americans with whom we talked. But these two notions of relatedness apply to radically different spheres. Expressive identity applies most of all to situations of love and intimacy, usually intense but of short duration. Contractual bargaining is the norm of everyday relationships, even the everyday aspects of marriage and friendship. What links the two seemingly disparate types together is the fact that both depend on the absolutely autonomous wills of the individuals involved. What both types avoid is the notion that there is any objective normative order governing the relationship, any transcendent loyalty above the wishes of the individuals involved, any community that is really there independent of the wills of the individuals who compose it. Naturally relationships that are dependent entirely on spontaneous feeling or contractual bargaining alone are fragile, frustrating, and difficult to sustain.

Since "conventional roles" no longer have authority for many middle-class Americans and spontaneous feeling, though highly valued, is often untrustworthy and transient, the contractual model, long familiar in our economic life, has more and more entered the sphere of private relationships, often under the aegis of popular psychology. It is, however, not always an easy model to live with and exacts a high price in terms of the stability of relationships. "Commitments take work, and we're tired of working," sighs Alec, a young therapist, "and we come home from work, the last thing I want to do, you know, is for people to sit down and say, 'Well, let's sit and work on our relationship. Let's talk about it.' Yes, but I worked eight and a half hours today, you know. Let's just sit down and watch the boob tube." His protest ends in a confession: "It's like you periodically ask yourself, like, 'Is this worth my effort? Is this worth that?'" Faced with ongoing demands to work on their relationships as well as their jobs, separate and equal selves are led to question the contractual terms of their commitments to each other: Are they getting what they want? Are they getting as much as they are giving? As much as they could get elsewhere? If not, they are tempted to withdraw and look elsewhere for fulfillment. Therapeutic experts may counsel them that lasting commitments are necessary for self-fulfillment. But within this "giving-getting" model each person must test such claims against his experience, case by case, and judge them in the light of his own "values." Because each person's feelings and values are subjective, the difficulties in figuring out the bottom line and interacting appropriately with others are daunting enough to make "long-term relationships" almost as unstable in their actual prospects as they are formidable in their therapeutic demands.

Yet many of those with whom we talked who seem to be committed to a radically individualistic ideology do not really seem to live in accordance with their belief, or better, they find their usual individualistic language inadequate to explain how they actually live. A successful California lawyer who has sustained a long marriage and who is accustomed to explain all his actions in cost/benefit terms, was finally pressed in our interview to see that no interest-maximizing calculus could really account for what was in those terms an irrational commitment. At last he affirms that his happiness with his wife comes from "proceeding through all these stages together. It makes life meaningful and gives me the opportunity to share with somebody, have an anchor, if you will, and understand where I am. That for me is a real relationship." Here he is groping for words that would express his marriage as a community of memory and hope, a context that actually defines who he is, not a forum in which an empty self maximizes satisfactions.

In another case a woman who had renewed her commitment to Judaism at first explained her action in individualistic terms. Judaism provides "structure" in a chaotic world. In the religious community she has found help with daycare as well as a place where the joys and sufferings of everyday life can be shared. In her highly educated mentality it was as though communal ties and religious commitments can be recommended only for the benefits they yield to the individual, for the social, emotional, and cultural functions they perform. But there was a moment in our conversation with her when she transcended these presuppositions. She told us, "the woman who took care of my daughter when she was little was a Greek Jew. She was very young, nine, ten, eleven, when the war broke out, and was lying at the crematorium door when the American troops came through. So that she has a number tattooed on her arm. And it was always like being hit in the stomach with a brick when she would take my baby and sit and circle her with her arm, and there was the number." In that moment she was no longer in the "giving-getting" mode. She knew herself as a member of a people, which includes the living and the dead, parents and children, inheritors of a history and a culture that tells her who she is and that she must nurture through memory and hope.

Many of those to whom we talked seemed caught in the tensions created by radical American individualism. We strongly assert the value of our self-reliance and autonomy. We deeply feel the emptiness of a life without sustaining social commitments. Yet we are afraid to articulate our sense that we need each other as much as we need to stand alone, for fear that if we did we would lose our independence altogether. The tensions of our lives would be even greater if we did not in fact engage in practices that constantly limit the effects of an isolating individualism, even though we cannot articulate these practices nearly as well as we can the quest for autonomy.

POLITICS AND THE PUBLIC SPHERE

If the ideology of American individualism creates problems in sustaining intimate relationships it causes even greater difficulty for involvement in the public sphere. Just as, in spite of our individualism, Americans do sustain long-term relationships so do they also frequently become publicly involved. But our individualism skews and limits the kind of public undertaking we are likely to engage in as well as our understanding of them.

Middle-class Americans view success in the occupational sphere as an essential prerequisite for a fulfilled life. But many of them do not think that personal success is enough. Only if one makes a personal, voluntary effort to "get involved" in helping others will one's life be complete. And Americans in larger numbers than in many societies do join voluntary associations, service clubs and church societies whose main purpose is to help the unfortunate or better the community. Such activities bring great personal satisfaction. The happiness and joy of giving are earned by making a free individual decision to join such an organization, to accept its discipline, and to participate in its charitable work. For these Americans the self-interest demanded by the individualistic pursuit of success needs to be balanced by the sympathy of the voluntary act of concern for others. Without the joyful experience of support from such a community, an individual would find it difficult to make the effort to be a success, and success achieved would likely turn to ashes in his mouth. Without some individually deserved success, an individual would have little voluntarily to contribute to his chosen community.

It is of course no easy task to strike a balance between the kind of self-interest implicit in the individualistic search for success and the kind of concern required to gain the joys of community and public involvement. A fundamental problem is that the ideas which Americans have traditionally used to give shape and direction to their most generous impulses no longer suffice to give guidance in controlling the destructive consequences caused by the pursuit of economic success. It is not, as many recent social critics have claimed, that Americans have today become less generous than in the past. Practically all of those we talked with are convinced, at least in theory, that a selfish seeker after purely individual success could not live a good, happy, joyful life. But when they think of the kind of generosity which could redeem the individualistic pursuit of economic success, they often imagine voluntary involvements in local, small-scale activities resembling a family, club, or idealized community in which individuals' initiatives interrelate to improve the life of all. They have difficulty relating this ideal image to the large-scale forces and institutions shaping their lives. This is what provides the pathos underlying many of our conversations about work, family, community, and politics. Many of those we talked with convey the feeling that sometimes their very best efforts to pursue their finest ideals seem senseless.

It is rarely "getting involved" as a moral act that is thought senseless. Instead the difficulty has to do with the realm of politics. For a good number of those we talked to the very notion of politics connotes something morally unsavory, as though voluntary involvement is commendable and even fulfilling up to the point at which it enters the realm of office-holding, campaigning, and organized negotiating. Thus their judgments about the goodness of citizenship in the wide sense of public involvement and responsibility turn negative in peculiar ways when they extend beyond the bounds of their local concerns and into the activities and institutions Americans term "politics."

In one sense, politics is making operative the moral consensus of the community, where that consensus is thought to flow from agreement among individuals reached through free face-to-face discussion. The process of reaching such a consensus is one of the central meanings of the word "democratic" in America. It idealizes an individualism without rancor. For this understanding, citizenship is virtually coextensive with "getting involved" with one's neighbors for the good of the community. Many times Americans do not think of this process as "politics" at all. But where this understanding is seen as a form of politics it is the New England township of legend, the self-governing small town singled out by Tocqueville, that remains as the ideal exemplar.

In sharp contrast to the image of consensual community stands another understanding, for which politics means the pursuit of differing interests according to agreed-upon, neutral rules. This is the realm of coalitions among groups with similar interests, of conflicts between groups with opposing interests, and of mediators and brokers of interests, the professional politicians. The "politics of interest," which is what we call this second type, is what Americans frequently mean by the term "politics." It is sometimes celebrated by political scientists as "pluralism," but for ordinary Americans the connotation is often negative. The politics of interest is frequently seen as a kind of necessary evil in a large diverse society, as a reluctantly agreed-to second best to consensual democracy.

Instead of a realm of spontaneous involvement with others to whom one feels akin, one enters the politics of interest for reasons of utility, to get what one or one's group needs or wants. To the extent that many of those we talked to see "politics" as meaning the politics of interest, they regard it as not entirely legitimate morally. Hence the generally low opinion of "the politician" as a figure in American life. Politics suffers in comparison with the market. The legitimacy of the market rests in large part on the belief that it rewards individuals impartially on the basis of fair competition, a legitimacy helped by the fact that economic transactions are widely dispersed and often invisible. By contrast, the politics of negotiation at local, state, and federal levels, though it shares the utilitarian attitudes of the market, often exposes a competition among groups in which inequalities of power, influence and moral probity become highly visible as determinants of the outcome. At the same time the politics of interest provides no framework for the discussion of issues other than the conflict and compromises of interests themselves. Thus the routine activities of interest politics, visibly conducted by professionals and apparently rewarding all kinds of inside connections while favoring the strong at the expense of the weak, must appear as an affront to true individualism and fairness alike.

Citizenship in this second understanding of politics is more difficult and discordant for the individual than in the ideal of community consensus. It means entering the complicated, professional, yet highly personal business of adversarial struggles, alliance building, and interest bargaining. It requires dealing with others from quite different consensual communities. For most people it lacks the immediacy of everyday involvement unless urgent interests are at stake. Thus supporting candidates by voting is the typical expression of this understanding of politics for most people, as a way of keeping politics at arm's length.

Thus the culture of individualism does not prevent Americans from entering the public sphere but it does limit and distort their understanding of it. If human action is always either the spontaneous expression of sympathy or the rational calculation of self-interest then when the former fails only the latter is left. The public realm is not considered exclusively as a realm of Hobbesian conflict because most Americans see the national community, at moments at least, as a local community writ large. Thus millions of Americans could identify with the individual American athletes competing in the Los Angeles Olympic Games and root for "U.S.A., U.S.A." as they would for the local high school football team. But where it is a question not of our similarities but of our differences then most Americans see only conflict and power. Objective political norms that speak not only of individual rights and fair procedures, but of substantive justice, are hard to comprehend within an individualist vocabulary. Thus national politics, when the veneer of local rhetoric, of "family, neighborhood, and work," is removed, makes little sense to most Americans. It is not narcissism or hedonism that prevents Americans, who continue in many ways to be a generous and compassionate people, from understanding those different from themselves. It is the limitations of their cultural resources.

INDIVIDUALISM AND AMERICAN MORES

We have described American individualism from Emerson to the present and have considered some of its consequences for private and public life, for morality and politics. It is time to return to Tocqueville to consider whether the restraints he saw the American mores of his day placing on individualism are still operative, or whether the destructive consequences he feared an unchecked individualism would have are beginning to materialize.

By way of summary of what has been said so far we may reformulate Tocqueville's argument in a way somewhat more explicit than he ever does himself. We have characterized individualism, following Tocqueville and with the help of Emerson, as a way of thinking about human action which can conceive of human relatedness only as the result of spontaneous feeling or calculated interest. Tocqueville is fully aware of both of these aspects of an individualistic culture. He stresses repeatedly the "natural compassion" or "sympathy" which citizens in a democracy feel for one another:

> It often happens in the most civilized countries of the world that a man in misfortune is almost as isolated in the crowd as a savage in the woods. That is hardly ever seen in the United States. The Americans, always cold in manner and often coarse, are hardly ever insensitive, and though they may be in no hurry to volunteer services, yet they do not refuse them.[20]

Tocqueville, who is fully aware of the importance of self-interest in the motivation of Americans, often sees sympathy and interest working together to promote public-spirited actions. At times Tocqueville even seems to feel that a combination of sympathy and an educated self-interest, a "self-interest properly understood," would be enough to sustain free institutions in America.

There is an ambiguity in the way Tocqueville uses the term "mores." On the one hand it is a purely descriptive term. American mores are simply the way Americans do things, the pattern of American life, close to what we would mean when we speak of "American culture." On the other hand "mores" has a normative meaning. It includes the notion of duty, obligation, or moral rightness, and refers particularly to social obligations. Here "mores" is close to the German *Sittlichkeit,* the institutionalized pattern of social obligations. From this understanding of mores individualism is ambiguous. It is certainly part of a cultural pattern. It even has a normative component, one we can understand better perhaps with the help of Emerson than Tocqueville: the obligation to remain true to the self regardless of all other considerations. Yet from individualism a *social* ethic does not flow. Social relatedness depends entirely on the spontaneous feeling or rational calculation of individual wills. The social order has no normative validity in itself. It is merely the instrument or the expression of individual selves. From this point of view individualism cannot be part of the mores but is antithetical to them.

I think it is clear that however subtly Tocqueville analyzes the possibility that individualism in America can be turned to the service

---

20. Op. cit., 571.

of the common good and the preservation of free institutions, in the end he does believe that only an objective moral order, with obligations that transcend individual feelings and interests, will be equal to that task. In the narrower sense, therefore, the term "mores" refers to that objective moral order. As we have said, there are two spheres where Tocqueville finds mores in this second sense significant: political participation and religion.

In both of these spheres in America an objective moral order is problematic because both of them are so heavily invaded by self-interest. In the important chapter "How the Americans Combat the Effects of Individualism by Free Institutions," Tocqueville points out how it is self-interest, often quite petty self-interest, that often motivates Americans to participate in the public sphere. But in the end, he says, "The free institutions of the United States and the political rights enjoyed there provide a thousand continual reminders to every citizen that he lives in society. At every moment they bring his mind back to this idea, that it is the duty as well as the interest of men to be useful to their fellow."[21] It is precisely the element of duty that cannot be derived from interests and feelings of individuals alone.

In the chapter "How the Americans Apply the Doctrine of Self-Interest Properly Understood to Religion," Tocqueville comments on the American tendency to propagate religion on the basis of its earthly or at least heavenly rewards. "Nevertheless," he says, "I refuse to believe that all who practice virtue from religious motives do so only in hope of reward."[22] And a few pages later on, in one of the most earnestly admonitory chapters in the whole book, Tocqueville says, "By their practice Americans show that they feel the urgent necessity to instill morality into democracy by means of religion. What they think of themselves in this respect enshrines a truth which should penetrate deep into the consciousness of every democratic nation."[23] Tocqueville had already pointed out that religion provided for Americans a morality that was objective, certain and stable, which the unimpeded pursuit of interest in the economic and political spheres could never do.[24]

21. Op. cit., 512.
22. Op. cit., 528.
23. Op. cit., 542.
24. Op. cit., 292.

And so we may ask whether today there exist in America, in the midst of our triumphant individualism, mores in the sense of *Sittlich-keit* that would resist our proclivity to become a collection of atomized individuals who would be easy prey to administrative despotism.

We have already indicated that the ideology of individualism does not describe adequately the lives even of those who espouse it. A completely empty self that operates out of purely arbitrary choice is theoretically imaginable but performatively impossible. The family, the church, the local community, which the middle-class person seeks to shuffle off in the effort to rise in the social hierarchy free of encumbrances, cannot be wholly denied, for we are indelibly consti-tuted by them. On the other hand for those many Americans for whom objective moral communities still exist, most frequently in the form of churches or other religious associations, but often also in po-litical associations, the insistent language of individualism constantly threatens to make commitment contingent on psychological or mate-rial reward.

This is not the place to review our findings on the present state of American mores. At best what we found are signs of the times, which are far from allowing a prediction of future trends. We did find many Americans for whom an objective moral order embodied in living communities clearly does exist. Indeed in *Habits of the Heart* we describe a number of people that one could call genuine heroes and heroines of everyday life, dedicated to the common good and joyful in their dedication. We also found a great deal of nostalgia for a more coherent America, for "traditional values" and stable communities. The image of the small town we found to be deeply attractive to Americans regardless of their political or ethical views. Yet it would be hard to deny that the individualism that Tocqueville described and Emerson embodied is stronger than ever today. For many Americans the world is indeed divided into the two realms of rational calculation and spontaneous feeling, even though the emptiness of a life that alternates between those realms alone is increasingly recognized.

Perhaps not surprisingly, the alternatives to radical individualism that we discovered among present-day Americans are not different from those pointed out by Tocqueville: republican politics and bibli-cal religion. Reappropriating those traditions and reviving the com-munities that carry them seem to be our best hope. Only they can overcome the chasm between person and society that individualism creates. Only they show us that we can be true to our selves, individualists in the best sense, only when we are true to our ethical commitments and collective loyalties in private and public life. Indeed it is only such commitments and loyalties that constitute a real self, that tell us who we are. Biblical religion and republican politics involve us in communities of memory and hope within which we can sustain the moral ecology that makes a good life possible. The fact that in the research for *Habits of the Heart* we found so many serious, dedicated citizens for whom these communities are still alive and effective gives grounds, if not for optimism, at least for hope.

Index

Designer: Mark Ong
Compositor: G&S Typesetters
Text: 10/12 Fournier
Display: Palatino
Printer: Maple-Vail Book Mfg. Group
Binder: Maple-Vail Book Mfg. Group